Criminal Justice in Scotland

Criminal Justice in Scotland

Edited by

Hazel Croall, Gerry Mooney and Mary Munro

LONDON AND NEW YORK

First published by Willan Publishing 2010
This edition published by Routledge 2013
2 Park Square, Milton Park, Abingdon, Oxon OX14 4RN
711 Third Avenue, New York, NY 10017 (8th Floor)

Routledge is an imprint of the Taylor & Francis Group, an informa business

First published 2010

ISBN 978-1-84392-785-3 paperback
978-1-84392-786-0 hardback

British Library Cataloguing-in-Publication Data

A catalogue record for this book is available from the British Library

Project managed by Deer Park Productions, Tavistock, Devon
Typeset by GCS, Leighton Buzzard, Bedfordshire

Contents

Foreword and acknowledgements *vii*
List of abbreviations *ix*
Notes on contributors *xiii*

Part 1 Thinking about crime and criminal justice in Scotland: introduction and social context

1 Criminal justice in contemporary Scotland: themes, issues and questions 3
Hazel Croall, Gerry Mooney and Mary Munro

2 Social inequalities, criminal justice and discourses of social control in contemporary Scotland 21
Gerry Mooney, Hazel Croall and Mary Munro

3 Urban 'disorders', 'problem places' and criminal justice in Scotland 43
Alex Law, Gerry Mooney and Gesa Helms

Part 2 Issues in criminal and social justice

4 Youth crime and justice in Scotland 67
Lesley McAra and Susan McVie

5 Gender, crime and criminal justice in Scotland 90
Lesley McMillan

6 Race, ethnicity, crime and justice in Scotland 111
Hazel Croall and Liz Frondigoun

7 Corporate crime in Scotland 132
Jenifer Ross and Hazel Croall

8 Environmental crime in Scotland 152
Reece Walters

Part 3 Aspects of criminal justice process and practice

9 Policing, surveillance and security in contemporary Scotland 175
Nicholas R. Fyfe

10 Sentencing and penal decision-making: is Scotland losing its distinctive character? 195
Cyrus Tata

11 Fines, community sanctions and measures in Scotland 216
Mary Munro and Fergus McNeill

12 Prisons and imprisonment in Scotland 238
Jacqueline Tombs and Laura Piacentini

Part 4 Looking ahead

13 Criminal justice in Scotland: overview and prospects 261
Mary Munro, Gerry Mooney and Hazel Croall

Index *279*

Foreword and acknowledgements

This book has been some time in gestation. It emerges from a shared concern that there is no collection of essays that offer a critical account and interrogation of key issues relating to criminal justice in contemporary Scotland.

As editors we would like to thank the contributors for their willingness to respond to our comments, feedback and sometimes additional demands. We would also like to thank Brian and Jules Willan for their encouragement, patience and perseverance with this project. We would also like to thank the referees of our initial proposal for their helpful comments and to Pat Carlen, David Garland and Richard Sparks for their willingness to offer testimonials for the book. Thanks also to Jenny Robertson at the Open University in Scotland for her invaluable help in preparing the final manuscript.

We hope that this book will make a contribution to the important debate that is urgently needed about the state of criminal justice in contemporary Scotland. However, a key theme of the book is that criminal justice is not something that sits in isolation from wider Scottish (and UK) society; it reflects in important ways and is entangled with structural inequalities, social divisions and social differentiation, with diverse and competing political projects and with the changing position that Scotland and the UK occupy in the global world today. *Criminal Justice in Scotland* is concerned to promote a critical account of criminal justice in Scotland – an account which sees criminal justice policy-making as part and parcel of the wider social relations of power and inequality.

Hazel Croall, Gerry Mooney and Mary Munro
Glasgow

List of abbreviations

ACPOS	Association of Chief Police Officers in Scotland
ACT	Australian Capital Territories
ADSW	Association of Directors of Social Work
ASB	Antisocial Behaviour
ASBO	Anti-Social Behaviour Order
BEMIS	Black and Ethnic Minorities Infrastructure in Scotland
BME	Black and Minority Ethnic
CCR	City Centre Representative
CCTV	Closed-Circuit Television
CEMVO	Council of Ethnic Minority Voluntary Sector Organisations
CITES	Convention on the International Trade in Endangered Species of Fauna and Flora
CJA	Community Justice Authority
CJSW	Criminal Justice Social Work(er)
CMCHA	Corporate Manslaughter and Corporate Homicide Act 2007
COMARE	Committee on Medical Aspects of Radiation in the Environment
COMEAP	Committee on the Medical Effects of Air Pollutants
COPFS	Crown Office and Procurator Fiscal Service
CPAG	Child Poverty Action Group
CPP	Community Planning Partnership
CSJ	Centre for Social Justice
Defra	Department for Environment, Food and Rural Affairs
DWP	Department for Work and Pensions

ELREC	Edinburgh and Lothians Racial Equality Council
EM	Electronic Monitoring
ESYTC	Edinburgh Study of Youth Transitions and Crime
ETA	Environmental Transport Association
FACK	Families Against Corporate Killers
FIP	Family Intervention Project
FoES	Friends of the Earth Scotland
FPN	Fixed Penalty Notice
GARA	Glasgow Anti-Racist Alliance
GROS	General Register Office for Scotland
HDC	Home Detention Curfew
HMICS	HM Inspectorate of Constabulary for Scotland
HMIP	HM Inspectorate of Prisons
HSE	Health and Safety Executive
HSWA	Health and Safety at Work etc. Act 1974
IPCC	Intergovernmental Panel on Climate Change
IPP	Imprisonment for Public Protection
IUU	Illegal, Unregulated and Unreported
KPI	Key Performance Indicator
LPG	Liquid Petroleum Gas
MAPPA	Multi-Agency Public Protection Arrangements
MSP	Member of the Scottish Parliament
NCC	National Consumer Council
NIEPA	Northern Ireland Environmental Protection Agency
NOS	National Objectives and Standards
NPM	New Public Management
ODS	Ozone-Depleting Substance
OFT	Office of Fair Trading
OLR	Order for Lifelong Restriction
PAW	Partnership for Action Against Wildlife Crime
PF	Procurator Fiscal
RMA	Risk Management Authority
SA	Scotland Act 1998
SAO	Supervised Attendance Order
SAP	Sentencing Advisory Panel
SCCCJ	Scottish Consortium on Crime and Criminal Justice
SCCJR	Scottish Centre for Crime and Justice Research
SCJS	Scottish Crime and Justice Survey
SCP	Signal Crimes Perspective
SCRA	Scottish Children's Reporter Administration
SCS	Scottish Court Service
SCVS	Scottish Crime and Victimisation Survey

SEMSA	Scottish Ethnic Minority Sports Association
SEPA	Scottish Environmental Protection Agency
SER	Social Enquiry Report
SGC	Sentencing Guidelines Council
SIMD	Scottish Index of Multiple Deprivation
SIPR	Scottish Institute for Policing Research
SIS	Sentencing Information System
SLAB	Scottish Legal Aid Board
SNP	Scottish National Party
SOA	Single Outcome Agreement
SPS	Scottish Prison Service
SPSA	Scottish Police Services Authority
STUC	Scottish Trades Union Congress
SWIA	Social Work Inspection Agency
UNEP	United Nations Environment Programme
UNESCO	United Nations Educational, Scientific and Cultural Organisation
UNICRI	United Nations Interregional Crime and Justice Institute

Notes on contributors

Hazel Croall is Emerita Professor at Glasgow Caledonian University where she set up the BA programme in Criminology. She has taught on a wide range of criminology courses and has published extensively in the areas of white-collar and corporate crime, crime and inequality and Scottish Criminal Justice. She is the co-author of *Criminal Justice in England and Wales* (Pearson 2010), now in its fourth edition, is currently working on the second, enlarged edition of *Crime and Society in Britain* (Longman 1998), and is contributing an article on Scottish criminal justice to Gerry Mooney and Gill Scott, *Social Justice and Social Welfare in Contemporary Scotland* (Policy Press forthcoming 2011).

Gerry Mooney is Senior Lecturer in Social Policy and Criminology and Staff Tutor, Department of Social Policy and Criminology, Faculty of Social Sciences at the Open University. He is also visiting Professor in the Humanities and Social Sciences Faculty, University of Strathclyde. He has written widely on social class, social policy, Scottish devolution and urban studies. Among other publications he is co-author with Jason Annetts, Alex Law and Wallace McNeish of *Understanding Social Welfare Movements* (Policy Press 2009); co-editor with Sarah Neal of *Community: Welfare, Crime and Society* (Open University Press 2009); co-editor with Alex Law of *New Labour/Hard Labour?* (Policy Press 2007) and co-editor with Gill Scott of *Social Justice and Social Welfare in Contemporary Scotland* (Policy Press forthcoming 2011).

Mary Munro has practised as both a solicitor and probation officer in the north of England. Since migrating to Scotland nearly 20 years ago she has been fascinated by its distinct legal and criminal justice practice traditions. She has taught criminology peripatetically at Stirling, Glasgow, Glasgow Caledonian, Strathclyde and the Open Universities and also runs the CjScotland website (www.cjscotland.org.uk).

Liz Frondigoun is a Lecturer in Sociology/Criminology in the School of Law and Social Science at Glasgow Caledonian University. She contributes to under- and post-graduate teaching on the BA Social Sciences, BA Criminology, MSc Degree Programmes and PhD Supervision. Liz has considerable research experience in policing, with marginalised, socially excluded and hard-to-reach populations, including minority ethnic groups, in youth crime – violence and gangs, in violence in institutional settings, in gender and in poverty. Her teaching research interests are in blended learning and flexible innovative pedagogy to encourage active student engagement in their learning to enhance communication and collaboration within the academy and the wider community. She also has a responsibility for Community Engagement within the School in the Social Science Division. She is a member of the Scottish Institute for Policing Research, the Scottish Network Coordinator of the British Society of Criminology, and a member of the Steering Group for developing a National Teaching award in Criminology.

Nicholas R. Fyfe is Director of the Scottish Institute for Policing Research, Professor of Human Geography at the University of Dundee and a Fellow of the Scottish Police College. He has been engaged in policing research for over 20 years, having undertaken pioneering work on witness protection arrangements, and has written widely on the nature and impact of witness intimidation. Among his current research interests are the role of policing in missing persons investigations, the policing of the night-time economy, and the nature and implications of the pluralisation of policing in Scotland. In addition to contributing to academic debates, he works closely with police practitioners and the policy community and has held several public appointments, including being a Special Advisor to the Scottish Parliament's Justice Committee for its inquiries into the use of police resources and community policing.

Gesa Helms lives and works as a geographer in Glasgow and Berlin. Her research explores social practice and discipline in the context of policing and labour process. She is the author of *Towards Safe City Centres? Remaking the Spaces of an Old-Industrial City* (Ashgate 2008).

Alex Law is Senior Lecturer in Sociology at the University of Abertay Dundee. He is co-author of *Understanding Social Welfare Movements* (Policy Press 2009) and is currently finishing a textbook *Key Concepts in Classical Social Theory* (Sage 2010).

Lesley McAra is Professor of Penology at Edinburgh University and is Co-Director (with Susan McVie and David Smith) of the Edinburgh Study of Youth Transitions and Crime, a longitudinal study of pathways into and out of offending. She is a member of the Editorial Boards of the *British Journal of Criminology* and *Youth Justice* and is also a member of the Advisory Board of the *European Journal of Criminology*.

Lesley McMillan is Senior Lecturer in Sociology at Glasgow Caledonian University. Her research interests mainly surround violence and gendered violence with a particular emphasis on community and statutory responses to rape and sexual assault including the problem of attrition. She is interested in all aspects of policing and also has research interests in missing persons. She is currently Principal Investigator on a large ESRC-funded study examining the problem of attrition in rape case and is author of *Feminists Organising Against Gendered Violence* (Palgrave 2007), a comparative study of alternative welfare provision for women survivors of violence.

Fergus McNeill is Professor of Criminology and Social Work at the University of Glasgow, where he is based in the Scottish Centre for Crime and Justice Research (http://www.sccjr.ac.uk). Prior to becoming an academic in 1998, Fergus worked for a number of years in residential drug rehabilitation and as a criminal justice social worker. His research interests and publications have addressed a range of criminal justice issues including sentencing, community penalties, ex-offender reintegration and youth justice. Latterly his work has focused on the policy and practice implications of research evidence about the process of desistance from offending. His books include *Reducing Reoffending: Social Work and Community Justice in Scotland* (with Bill Whyte Willan 2007) and *Youth Offending and Youth Justice* (co-edited with Monica Barry, Jessica Kingsley 2009). He is currently editing (with Peter Raynor and Chris Trotter) a major new collection on *Offender Supervision: New Directions in Theory, Research, Practice* (Willan 2010).

Susan McVie is a Senior Research Fellow within the School of Law at the University of Edinburgh and currently holds three major roles within the School. She is Co-Director of the Edinburgh Study of Youth Transitions and Crime, a prospective longitudinal study of youth offending based at the University of Edinburgh since 1998, and Leader of the CJ-Quest network for the Scottish Centre for Crime and Justice Research, which has responsibility for conducting and facilitating high-quality quantitative criminological research in Scotland. Susan is also Director of the newly established Applied Quantitative Methods Network (AQMeN) in Scotland, a collaborative network of social scientists which provides training in quantitative methods. Susan has published work on a variety of topics, although mainly in the areas of youth crime and justice, criminal careers, and crime trends and patterns. Her current research includes studies on racism and marginalisation among young people and gangs and knife crime.

Laura Piacentini is Reader in Criminology at Strathclyde Law School, University of Strathclyde. She has been actively researching and publishing in the area of contemporary Russian imprisonment for over ten years having been the first westerner to conduct empirical and theoretical prison research in Russia. With the universities of Oxford and Birmingham, she is currently a co-grant holder on a major three-year ESRC project on the penological and spatial exclusion of women in Russian prisons with a specific emphasis on the gendered nature of exile and isolation. Her work also seeks to animate debates on how political shifts or extreme events have given way to trends towards 'liberalisation' in penal environments. Her first book, *Surviving Russian Prisons*, won the British Society of Criminology Book of the Year award in 2005 and was nominated for the Distinguished Book of the Year of the International Division of the American Society of Criminology.

Jenifer Ross is a legal academic and solicitor. She teaches, researches and writes on both criminal law and employment law, with particular interest in discrimination law. She also has a particular interest in corporate criminal liability which she views as a bridge between the two major areas. She has had a long association with the Ethnic Minorities Law Centre in Glasgow and is on its Board of Directors.

Cyrus Tata is Co-Director of the Centre for Sentencing Research and Senior Lecturer in Law at Strathclyde University Law School. He has conducted research into sentencing consistency in Scotland, social enquiry reports, summary justice, public defence lawyers, legal aid spending and performance, and the Sentencing Information System for the High Court of Justiciary of Scotland. He is co-editor of *Sentencing and Society: International Perspectives* (Ashgate), and is co-editor of a special issue of *Punishment and Society: The International Journal of Penology* (2010) on 'pre-sentence reports in the sentencing process'. He has been a visiting fellow of the New South Wales Judicial Commission, Rutgers University and the USA National Center for State Courts, and an adviser to the Irish Court Service. He teaches courses in criminal justice discretion, penology, and law and society.

Jacqueline Tombs is Professor of Criminology and Social Justice and Director of the Institute for Society and Social Justice Research at Glasgow Caledonian University. She has published widely in the areas of criminal justice and penal policy. Her publications include *Reducing the Prison Population: Penal Policy and Social Choices, A Unique Punishment: Sentencing and the Prison Population in Scotland, Making Sense of Drugs and Crime, The Chance for Change: A Study of the Throughcare Centre Edinburgh Prison, Rethinking Criminal Justice in Scotland, Social Work and Criminal Justice: The Impact of Policy* (with F. Paterson), *The British Crime Survey: Scotland* (with G. Chambers) and *Prosecution in the Public Interest* (with S. Moody). She is a committee member of the Howard League for Penal Reform in Scotland and an associate member of the Scottish Consortium on Crime and Criminal Justice.

Reece Walters is Professor of Criminology in the Department of Social Policy and Criminology at the Open University. His research focuses on crimes of the powerful, notably the ways in which corporate and government officials abuse their authority for personal or political gain. He has published widely on the politics and governance of criminological knowledge and on environmental harm and justice. In doing so, his research examines the political economy of water, air and food and how these essential ingredients for human and non-human life are constantly threatened and exploited by the harmful acts of governments and corporations.

Part I

Thinking about crime and criminal justice in Scotland: introduction and social context

Chapter 1

Criminal justice in contemporary Scotland: themes, issues and questions

Hazel Croall, Gerry Mooney and Mary Munro

Introduction

Let us begin with a short anecdote. The three of us were meeting one day in mid-March 2010 to reflect on the progress of this book. Passing the time looking at the magazines and newspapers at the newsagents on the main concourse of Glasgow Central Station, we were struck by the number of books devoted to gangs, gangsters and 'hard men', and to serious crime in Glasgow and across Scotland more generally. An entire display unit was devoted to this genre, some of the books focusing more on (in)famous Glasgow criminals or other notable episodes in the city's criminal past, others considering different gangs, gang activity and more contemporary criminal escapades and episodes.

This is not of course unique to Glasgow, or to other Scottish cities, or perhaps even to Scotland, though the large number of book titles arguably reflects Glasgow's unenviable reputation for much of the past century and more as a hard and violent place. In many respects Glasgow stands out from the rest of Scotland, never mind the UK, in relation to a diverse range of social 'problems', from concentrated poverty and ill-health through a long history of slum and unfit housing to unemployment and what is often now referred to by politicians and policy-makers as 'worklessness', and of course to violence and criminal activities.

We explore some aspects of this particular Glasgow narrative in Chapter 2 in relation to notions of a 'gangs, booze and blades' culture in the city and in the urban west of Scotland more generally and go on in Chapter 3 to look at how Glasgow and some of the towns that surround it and other cities, for instance Dundee, have frequently been 'othered' in media reporting, political narratives, policy-making and some academic commentary – both from within Scotland as much as from other parts of the UK. Glasgow has since the 1960s been ever present in Scottish criminology, and in particular those branches that emerged from sociological research. And as we have observed above, it features prominently in the sensationalised, journalistic accounts of crimes and criminals to be found in railway-station bookshops (in passing we note perhaps less so in airport bookshops, possibly as such stories and images do not fit the Glasgow reborn narrative which is central to the attraction of tourists). However, the existence across Scotland of a book industry, and surely a considerable proportion of journalistic and media activity in addition, devoted to different aspects of crime, criminality and criminal justice tells us that while there is a fear of crime, this is accompanied by a public fascination with different forms of transgression.

Crime, in Scotland as elsewhere, features strongly in popular media, forming a major staple of newspapers, television series, documentaries and films (Reiner 2007). This is evident not only in the 'true crime' genre but also in television series such as the major Scottish export *Taggart* (which one of the authors has seen dubbed into Dutch), films such as *Trainspotting* and the flourishing 'tartan noir' (see McCracken 2009) writings of Edinburgh's Ian Rankin, Glasgow's Alex Gray and Denise Mina and Aberdeen's Stuart McBride. Preceding *Taggart* was the fictional Glasgow detective, Inspector Laidlaw, made famous in a series of novels by William McIlvanney. These of course differ from the image presented by more folksy series such as *Hamish McBeth* or *Sutherland's Law*, and humorous accounts of the 'polis' such as Rikki Fulton's apocryphal Police Officer in *Scotch and Wry*.

Beyond these popular and often fictional or mythical accounts what we do know is that, first of all, recorded crime overall in Scotland has been falling; secondly, the imprisonment rate is at record levels in common with England and Wales, and deviantly so in comparison with most other European jurisdictions; and that third, there is a gross over-representation of men and women from disadvantaged backgrounds in the criminal justice system. However, this book attempts to go behind the raw data and ask questions such as what have been the dominant trends in criminal justice policy and the key influences and ideologies that have shaped it? Is policy now changing and, if so, in what direction(s)? Are these directions which are widely supported – or criticised? Has devolution in 1998 and the re-establishment of a Scottish Parliament at Holyrood in 1999 made a difference to criminal justice policy and practice, and if so what are the key elements of this?

This book aims to fill the need for a collection of writings that offer a critically informed analysis and understanding of criminal justice in Scotland, especially since devolution in 1999. There is also a concern to consider the extent to which criminal justice in Scotland is, or is becoming, more divergent from other UK jurisdictions as well as pressures that may lead to convergences in particular areas, for instance in relation to youth justice. However, while this book has a Scottish focus, it also seeks to follow and engage with some of the newer ways of thinking about criminal justice. In particular it is concerned to relate criminal justice to wider social divisions, inequalities and questions of power in contemporary Scottish and UK society (see Grover 2008). This also takes us to some of the recent attempts to extend the criminological 'gaze' (see, for example, Muncie *et al.* 2009; Drake *et al.* 2010) to explore issues such as environmental crime and urban disorders as well as crimes of the rich and powerful and corporate crime.

In this respect, then, we do not see this project as an inward-looking or narrowly focused 'Scottish' book – though with the growth in criminology as an undergraduate and postgraduate area of study in Scottish universities and the changing governance of research around criminal justice in Scotland, with the emergence of the Scottish Institute for Policing Research (SIPR), the Scottish Centre for Crime and Justice Research (SCCJR) and the Criminal Justice Social Work Development Centre, there is a growing need for an up-to-date jurisdiction-specific and critical text for a range of audiences and we hope that this book goes some way to meeting that need. It is also our hope that this book will have a relevance and resonance beyond Scotland.

Criminal justice in Scotland: addressing a neglect?

In this collection we have brought together a number of leading academics and researchers who are actively engaged in developing an understanding of a disparate range of crime and criminal justice issues from a 'Scottish perspective'. However, although the chapters introduce a range of topics, all address the central concern of this book: to enhance our knowledge of the state of criminal justice in Scotland today, perhaps pointing to possible future directions and to address what we think are a number of myths and misunderstandings about criminal justice in Scotland.

In part these myths and misunderstandings may be due to what can only be described as a general neglect of 'Scotland' in many key criminology and criminal justice texts, other than the occasional ritual nod to the 'unique' children's hearing system (see, for example, Cavadino and Dignan 2006). Scotland and Scottish criminal justice is either overlooked completely or marginalised, at best 'tacked on' to a discussion that otherwise is England and Wales centred and driven by the concerns of policy-making in that jurisdiction – as Garland, in his preface to a previous collection of articles on Scottish criminal justice, pointed out, 'the UK' all too often 'really means England and Wales' (Garland 1999: xiv). A relatively recent *Student Handbook of Criminal Justice and Criminology* (Muncie and Wilson 2004), for example, contains one chapter devoted to 'Scotland' (Reuss 2004) for which there is no other index reference in the preceding 18 chapters covering key criminological and criminal justice areas. What is regarded as the major British criminology text, the *Oxford Handbook of Criminology* (Maguire *et al.* 2007), contains 32 chapters. Without singling out individual chapters it is fair to say that the vast majority focus almost entirely on England and Wales, even where there are significant divergences not only with Scotland but also Northern Ireland, and indeed between England and Wales. It is notable that the index for 'comparative criminal justice' refers specifically to France, Germany, Holland, Italy, Japan and the United States (Maguire *et al.* 2007: 1144) but not to Scotland or Northern Ireland. Similarly, a 2004 collection on *Criminal Justice and Political Cultures: National and International Dimensions of Crime Control* (Newburn and Sparks 2004), which includes chapters on policy transfer, divergence and convergence, includes only four index references to Scotland, all in relation to youth justice (Muncie 2004). A chapter on US and UK crime control policy takes English and Welsh policies and Criminal Justice Acts as examples of UK policy and there is only one mention of Scotland in relation to the Strathclyde Police 'Spotlight' initiative as an example of changes in policing (Jones and Newburn 2004). In this, as in so many British texts, it is (without acknowledgement) typically the English system which is used as an example of general points. We suggest that this is an unjustifiable and curious omission and propose that a wider consciousness of what is both shared and diverse within and across all the UK jurisdictions (including Northern Ireland) would contribute to a richer, more complex and more challenging British criminology.

In part some of these omissions are a product of the nomenclature that is applied to key knowledge sources. As Ian Jack (2009) has recently commented:

> Readers of London newspapers are used to blank spaces north of the border. Maps illustrating variations in house prices, healthcare provision, obesity rates, knife crime, tourist numbers – they show white beyond the diagonal that links a point north of Berwick to another point north of Carlisle. These maps and charts might describe their statistics as 'national' or 'British' but in fact they reflect the society of England and Wales (and sometimes just England alone).

The 'British' Crime Survey, for example, is concerned only with the patterns of crimes in England and Wales, as are most Home Office criminal justice statistics. Not only that, but the governance and administration of institutions and agencies of Scottish criminal justice, from prosecution to social work to prisons, are distinct from those south of the border. However, this all helps to promote a general confusion among students and not a few academics (and of course among journalists and the wider public) about the existence of different jurisdictions and the relations between them.

Other confusions arise from the misconception that devolution created a new set of arrangements for Scottish criminal justice and that prior to 1999 criminal justice policies, institutions and law, while distinctive in important respects, largely followed a Britain-wide model. On the contrary, Scotland's legal system was one of the three 'pillars' of Scottish 'civil society', along with the education system and Presbyterian Church Government, that were protected by the 1707 Act of Union of the Scottish and English Parliaments The evolution of Scottish justice has, in many senses, been uninterrupted by the existence of the Union.

To help us address such confusions, and to develop a more informed understanding of the current state of criminal justice in Scotland, several interrelated themes underpin this collection. Contributors were asked to address first, and where appropriate and feasible, the distinctiveness of crime and criminal justice in Scotland in both UK and wider international contexts and, secondly, the extent to which devolution has made any significant difference to this. A key concern is whether devolution has led to a deepening and widening of such distinctiveness – or alternatively to a lessening of it and arguably to a convergence between Scottish criminal justice and other jurisdictions.

A third important analytical theme is to locate questions of criminal justice within the wider realm of social policy and social welfare. Issues of social justice and injustice, inequalities, social divisions and power recur across the chapters. This critical voice departs from the tone of other texts which have been concerned with aspects of criminal justice in Scotland.

Duff and Hutton's (1999) edited collection on *Criminal Justice in Scotland* represented what was at the time an extremely valuable collection of work on a wide range of aspects of crime and criminal justice in Scotland. While it did address some of the most distinctive aspects of Scottish criminal justice, and many articles explored the influence of global trends, it could only look forward to devolution and, unlike this volume, it did not seek to move beyond more conventional criminological concerns to address issues of inequalities or social justice. It remains nonetheless an invaluable source of information about the state of key areas of Scottish criminal justice immediately prior to devolution. Other books relating to Scotland, or containing substantial amounts of work on Scotland such as McIvor's (2004) collection on *Women Who Offend*, which contains a number of Scottish articles, Donnelly and Scott's (2005) *Policing Scotland* and McNeill and White's (2007) book on *Social Work and Community Justice in Scotland* have focused on specific areas of Scottish criminal justice policy. This collection is distinct therefore in addressing the major themes identified below from the vantage point of over ten years of devolution.

Criminal justice in Scotland: themes

Criminal justice in Scotland: towards 'detartanisation'?

The aim here is not to provide a comprehensive discussion of the devolution process as it relates to Scotland (cf. Adams and Robinson 2002; Adams and Schmeuker 2005; McGarvey and Cairney 2008), but to consider what this has meant for criminal justice policy-making at the macro level. In particular we are concerned with the overall shape and direction of criminal justice in Scotland – and how this might have changed as a result of devolution, or more correctly as a result of a combination and coming together of other developments, of which devolution has been a key aspect.

One of the recurring debates around devolution concerns the extent to which this provided the context for significant divergence in policy-making in relation to social policy (see Critical Social Policy 2006; Mooney and Scott 2005; Social Policy and Society 2009). Free personal care for the elderly and the abolition of up-front student fees are two of the early key policy changes in Scotland which have been heralded as marking a growing degree of policy divergence (Stewart 2004). However, these aside, there is a general view that thus far, devolution has not produced radically different forms of government across the UK, nor has policy-making across the devolved countries and England/UK been as significantly divergent as was anticipated. A number of limiting factors have been suggested from issues as broad as neoliberalism and globalisation through to continuing Treasury control over the Scottish budget. The dominance of New Labour at the UK level and in the Scottish and Welsh Parliaments, prior to the formation of a minority Scottish National Party government in May 2007, at least until May 2010, is also seen as acting as a brake on innovatory policy-making.

What does this mean for our understanding of criminal justice policy in Scotland today and its likely shape and direction in the near future? One of the recurring stories told of criminal justice in Scotland is that is has been characterised by a distinctively welfarist approach (see Croall 2006; Duff and Hutton 1999; McAra 1999, 2007, 2008), particularly in relation to the Children's Hearing System (see Chapter 4), sentencing policies that have been supposedly insulated from popular punitivism (see Chapters 10 and 11) and the continuing central role of criminal justice social work in community sanctions, with its strong emphasis on rehabilitation and welfare values (see Chapter 11). In relation to children and youth justice, offenders were seen primarily as being in need of care and protection – thereby avoiding the worst aspects of criminalisation and stigmatisation evident in other jurisdictions, not least in England and Wales but also in many other European, Western and other English-speaking jurisdictions.

The impression of criminal justice in Scotland in the period prior to devolution was that it was 'relatively immune from the populist tendencies that were rapidly infecting its southern neighbour' (Cavadino and Dignan 2006: 231). Lesley McAra claims that this commitment to welfarism resulted from the 'distinctive nature of Scottish civic and political culture – with its greater emphasis on the public provision of welfare and mutual support' (McAra 2008: 493), aided by 'progressive' civil servants. It was this culture, supposedly based on a more general commitment to communitarian, collectivist and egalitarian values in Scotland than elsewhere, that worked to moderate the worst effects of Conservative social and criminal justice policies during the 1980s and 1990s.

That Scotland, as a small country, was in some sense 'protected' by a progressive civil society committed to a strongly social democratic tradition is contentious (cf. Keating 2007; Law and Mooney 2006; McCrone 2001; Mooney and Poole 2004; Paterson 1994; Paterson *et al.* 2004). Nonetheless such claims have been central to important recent narratives about the direction of Scottish criminal justice over recent decades – and in particular since devolution. Notable here have been arguments advanced by McAra that there has been a 'detartanisation' of Scottish adult and youth justice (McAra 2008: 494; see also McAra 2007). The welfarist basis and trajectory of Scottish criminal justice, it is claimed, has been eroded by a shift towards a more punitive policy ethos, reflected in, for example, cornerstone policy measures such as the Antisocial Behaviour (Scotland) Act 2004, closely mirroring in important respects similar legislation for England and Wales.

What is being claimed is that there is growing policy convergence between Scotland and other UK jurisdictions, typified by an increasing emphasis on managerialism, efficiency, target setting, monitoring and evaluation (see also Croall 2006: chapter 4). That much of this has been implemented by a New Labour UK government and a New Labour dominated Scottish government between 1999 and 2007 is also seen as an important factor in contributing to declining Scottish distinctiveness, that is 'detartanisation'. The importance of these arguments for us is that they allow us to raise wider questions about the nature of criminal justice – and indeed of social justice – in the devolved Scotland.

Criminal justice, social justice and inequalities

Claims of a detartanisation are premised on claims that Scotland is being subjected to the same neoliberalising pressures that are evident elsewhere in the UK and globally (see Cumbers and Whittam 2007; Davidson *et al.* 2010; Law and Mooney 2006; Newlands *et al.* 2004). This is reflected in a widespread assault on welfarism, enabled by successive UK governments, both Conservative and New Labour, an increasing emphasis on managerialism and privatisation and the wholesale restructuring of social welfare more generally. One of the key aspects of neoliberalism and the neoliberalisation of Scottish society has been a significant increase in inequalities, again mirroring sharp increases in economic and social inequality and social polarisation at a transnational and global level. There is significant and growing evidence that devolution has had little impact on rising levels of inequality in Scotland – as in other parts of the UK – and indeed on some measures inequality is greater in Scotland compared with other parts of the UK (see Mooney *et al.* 2009; Morelli and Seaman 2007a, 2007b, 2009). In addition poverty remains a significant feature of contemporary Scottish society (see Kenway *et al.* 2008; McKendrick *et al.* 2007; Scott and Mooney 2009). More recently, and with the election of an SNP government in Edinburgh in 2007, poverty and inequality have been highlighted as central issues to be addressed (Scottish Government 2007, 2008a, 2008b).

There is growing evidence that societies which are more unequal also have more social problems and rising rates of, for example, youth and property crime have been associated with a widening gap between the most and least affluent (Box 1987; Hale 2009), which increases relative as opposed to absolute deprivation (Lea and Young 1993). Richard Wilkinson argues that the inequitable distribution of wealth in a society is the key factor that explains a diverse range of social problems, from obesity and mental illness through to crime, teenage pregnancy and rates of imprisonment. More unequal societies are socially dysfunctional in a diverse range of ways: levels of trust, respect and community are markedly lower than in societies which are more equal. As a result people tend to feel inferior, less respected and valued, and excluded (Wilkinson 2005; see also Wilkinson and Pickett 2009). In a comparison of perceptions of insecurity in Iceland and Scotland, Kristjánsson (2007) argues that it is the much higher levels of income inequality, more pronounced spatial polarisation between different localities and the greater class differences in Scotland which are the key explanatory factors in accounting for the much higher levels of insecurity and more acute fear of crime across Scottish society as a whole.

We return to consider some of the consequences of this for our understanding of criminal justice in Scotland in Chapter 2. Important here is the extent to which neoliberalism and the shift to a more conditional form of social welfare, together with a drift towards responsibilisation and a harsher welfare regime, have resulted in an erosion of welfarism across all areas of Scottish criminal justice. In this respect a central theme is that criminal justice can only be understood as part of a wider realm of social policy-making (see Cook 2006; Newman and Yeates 2008; Young 2007).

This question is related to ongoing debates about the criminalisation of social policy and the socialisation of crime. For example, 'antisocial behaviour' has become a concern in policy areas that have traditionally been outside criminal justice, narrowly defined, such as urban social policy where it is central to debates around safer and sustainable communities (see Chapter 3, this volume; see also Atkinson and Helms 2007; Cochrane 2007; Mooney and Neal 2009).

Criminology has traditionally been concerned with the behaviours and activities of particular 'problem' groups, usually the less powerful and more disadvantaged sections of society. A key argument we wish to advance here is that the complex relationship between inequalities and crimes, transgression, criminalisation and criminal justice cannot be fully understood solely by a focus on the less powerful. We therefore exemplify a wider concern with social harm by including chapters on corporate and environmental crime (see Chapters 7 and 8, this volume; see also Croall 2001; Drake *et al.* 2010; Muncie *et al.* 2009).

The structure of *Criminal Justice in Scotland*

The criminological gaze of Criminal Justice in Scotland

This book has not been conceived as a 'traditional' criminal justice or criminology text but one that, while seeking to offer a detailed exploration of many – though certainly not all – aspects of criminal justice in contemporary Scotland, also seeks to extend and deepen the understanding of the nature of crime and justice in Scottish society today. It can be used along with more general criminology texts such as Newburn (2007), Hale *et al.* (2009), the *Oxford Handbook of Criminology* (Maguire *et al.* 2007) and more explicitly sociological approaches such as Carrabine *et al.* (2004) or Croall (2011). It aims to offer a critically informed analysis and understanding of different aspects of criminal justice in contemporary Scotland. It seeks, therefore, to go beyond conventional or traditional accounts of criminal justice by understanding this in its social, historical and – importantly – political contexts. It seeks to advance a critical exploration of the criminal justice politics and policy-making embedded within a wider appreciation of the structures, politics and dominant social trends that characterise recent Scottish (and of course UK and global) society.

Here, it is also important to understand that globalisation, Europeanisation and transnational trends and developments also work in different, unequal and uneven ways to shape policy-making in the Scottish context. The SNP government has sought to locate its policies and vision for an independent Scotland in a global context, and in particular in relation to Europeanisation. The positioning of Scotland in relation to Nordic and (at least prior to the global financial and economic crisis which was unleashed in 2008) so-called 'arc of prosperity' countries, Ireland, Iceland, Norway, Finland and Denmark) points to some possible routes of policy transfer – and we should not neglect the possibilities of policy transfer from other parts of the world (see Adams 2008). And devolution has also thrown up the possibilities of policy transfer across the different constituent countries of the UK. Transnationalism, in this respect, works within the UK as it does on a global level.

Introducing the chapters

The chapters in various ways raise issues related to these central themes. Chapter 2 on 'Social inequalities and criminal justice in Scotland' is concerned to situate questions of criminal justice in Scotland in the context of wider social divisions and inequalities. It critically explores how crime in Scotland has, both historically and contemporarily, been popularly and academically related to socio-economic inequalities, social deprivation, the underclass and the socially excluded, most recently through discussions of the 'booze and blade' culture associated with parts of Glasgow. It also points to the different involvement of different social groups in crime by looking at the crimes of the professional middle classes, who are less likely to people Scotland's courts and prisons. In so doing it demonstrates that criminal justice cannot be adequately understood apart from a consideration of larger questions of social control.

The thematic concerns of Chapters 1 and 2 are also reflected in Chapter 3 which is concerned with the issue of 'urban "disorders", "problem places" and criminal justice'. In particular Alex Law, Gerry Mooney and Gesa Helms are primarily concerned with the extent to which the regulation of particular urban spaces is a crucial component of criminal justice in modern Scotland. This connects with the reconstruction of urban space which is central to area-based and regeneration policies in the devolved Scotland. Alongside gentrification and the privatisation of urban space, claims that urban disorders have to be tackled to make Scotland a safer and more secure place will also be explored.

Taking as examples 'city centre representatives' and the policing of public spaces, Chapter 3 also explores some of the ways in which notions of 'problem places' containing 'problem populations' inform policy-making in Scotland, albeit implicitly. The chapter also considers the extent to which the 'problem council estate' is a focus of policy-making and there will also be a consideration of new forms of gentrification as part of 'new urbanist' efforts to manage and regulate urban space. In conclusion the chapter will consider some of the ways in which a spatial imagination (reflected in the historical and diverse constructions of particular locales as deviant or problematic) is crucial to criminal justice policy and practice.

There then follows a collection of chapters highlighting issues in criminal and social justice. Scotland's famously distinctive youth justice system has featured strongly in the 'detartanisation' argument and this is reflected in Chapter 4 by Lesley McAra and Susan McVie. The chapter begins with a review of the history of juvenile justice and then moves on to an outline of current arrangements. Some key findings of the major longitudinal research project Edinburgh Study of Youth Transitions and Crime (the Edinburgh Study), together with official data, illuminate young people's experiences of both offending and victimisation in Scotland. The chapter concludes by offering an assessment of the effectiveness of the system, including discussion of three critical issues: controversies over early intervention; the impact of youth justice interventions on subsequent offending; and youth to adult criminal justice transitions. The authors argue that the evidence points to the importance of maintaining and strengthening welfarist practices in order to deal with juvenile offending.

In Chapter 5 on the themes of gender, crime and criminal justice in Scotland, Lesley McMillan focuses on women as both perpetrators and victims of crime, exploring sentencing and imprisonment, the characteristics and experiences of women offenders and community sanctions for women offenders. The chapter also considers young women's relationship with crime and then moves to examine prostitution, domestic abuse and sexual victimisation, considering the distinctive feature of these in the Scottish context.

Chapter 6 by Hazel Croall and Liz Frondigoun tackles the often contested issues of race, ethnicity, crime and justice in respect of which the 'Scotland blindness' of British criminology is particularly evident with its preoccupation with issues of urban unrest and institutional racism on the part of largely the English police. Scotland has a distinctive pattern of ethnic settlement and issues of ethnicity, crime and criminal justice have been played out in a very different political, social and economic context where immigration has been encouraged and there has been a perception, however mythical, of greater tolerance. Nonetheless, as this chapter illustrates, Scotland has not been immune from terrorism and globalised fears of the terrorist threat associated with 'other' groups. Scotland's minority ethnic communities experience racism on an everyday basis and, while in some respects policing has not attracted the criticisms characteristic of England, it has nonetheless been experienced by some groups as insensitive.

In keeping with our theme of inequalities and concern to ensure that our criminological gaze considers the activities of the powerful, Chapter 7 from Jenifer Ross and Hazel Croall explores corporate crime. With the high toll of deaths associated with headline cases such as Piper Alpha, Transco and the Stockline explosion, the issue of the extent to which companies, whose sometimes blatant and persistent neglect of routine safety regulations is explored, can be made criminally liable and quite literally pay for their crimes has been considered by Scottish legislators, as has been the case not only in England and Wales but in many other jurisdictions. While there were strong arguments for a distinctively Scottish approach, particularly in view of the different nature of Scottish criminal law, it was decided, for largely political reasons, to have one law for the entire United Kingdom although some leeway remains in respect of sentencing.

Environmental crime also involves powerful corporate and indeed state actors and the environment is of great significance to Scotland, whose governments have sought 'green credentials'. In Chapter 8 Reece Walters explores some of the many different harms associated with environmental crime in Scotland and looks at aspects of its control, arguing that in some respects a Scottish approach can be discerned and that the creation of specialist prosecutors could herald a stronger approach to this form of crime.

We then consider aspects of criminal justice process and practice. The issue of policing is covered more fully by Nick Fyfe in Chapter 9. Among the themes explored here are the increasing involvement of the public in tackling disorders and the increasing pluralisation of policing in Scotland, that is the development of diverse policing strategies. Here the contrast between those approaches that focus on law enforcement and order maintenance and approaches which prioritise community engagement is highlighted. A further theme that Fyfe considers is the issue of police governance and accountability. While of course this issue has a wider UK and global relevance, Fyfe addresses the question of the uniqueness of such matters as they relate to the Scottish context.

In Chapter 10 on sentencing and penal practices, Cyrus Tata foregrounds the question of Scottish distinctiveness in these areas and asks if this is being eroded as a consequence of global shifts in sentencing policies and practices. The idea that we live in a new penal world wherein traditional penal values have been diminished in the context of growing fears and insecurities provides an important backdrop to considering shifts in the Scottish context. In particular the extent to which the welfarist basis of Scottish sentencing policy is being challenged is considered. Tata provides a case study approach based on recent research in order to test the suggestion that the basic values of Scottish discretionary sentencing are shifting in the direction of a convergence with the actuarial and efficiency approaches advocated in other jurisdictions. He concludes that while there is some confirmation of convergence in terms of rhetoric, actual practices on the ground are less convincing in this respect.

In Chapter 11, which considers the issues of fines, community sanctions and measures, Mary Munro and Fergus McNeill consider how together monetary penalties and social work orders remain the penalties most frequently imposed for crimes and offences in Scotland, and that the post-release supervision of prisoners, especially those convicted of sexual and violent offending, is an area that equally repays both academic and policy attention. Integrated across the discussion is a critical questioning of the claim that a welfarist ethos, resistant to elements of managerialism especially in criminal justice social work practices, survives to a greater degree here than elsewhere in the UK. The impact and significance of inequalities in the imposition and experience of such sanctions are also explored. The significance of recent attempts to repackage community sanctions as 'payback' and promote these as an alternative to short custodial sentences is distinguished from similar rhetoric in England and Wales as being more consistent with desistence and philosophically defensible.

A key element of criminal justice concerns incarceration and in Chapter 12 on prisons and imprisonment in Scotland, Jackie Tombs and Laura Piacentini provide a review and critique of how incarceration features in contemporary penal policy and practices in Scotland. In particular it shows how incarceration reflects wider social divisions and inequalities in Scottish society and comments on questions of penal distinctiveness. In doing so, it aims to address three main questions. First, how did prisons and imprisonment emerge and develop in Scotland? Second, what are the key contemporary features of imprisonment and the prison population? Third, what are the future prospects for prisons and imprisonment in Scotland?

The concern of the final 'review' chapter, Chapter 13, is to highlight and reflect on the main themes emerging from the different chapters and consider these in light of our main concerns with convergences and divergences in Scottish criminal justice. Here we also return to our initial concern with claims of 'detartanisation', and also consider the key influences which are working to shape the direction of criminal justice in Scotland today.

References

Adams, L. (2008) 'Chicago gangs expert in Glasgow to advise on youth crime', *The Herald*, 13 October.

Adams, J. and Robinson, P. (eds) (2002) *Devolution in Practice*. London: Institute of Public Policy Research.

Adams, J. and Schmeuker, K. (eds) (2005) *Devolution in Practice 2006*. Newcastle: Institute of Public Policy Research North.

Atkinson, R. and Helms, G. (eds) (2007) *Securing an Urban Renaissance: Crime, Community and British Urban Policy*. Bristol: Policy Press.

Box, S. (1987) *Recession, Crime and Punishment*. London: Macmillan.

Carrabine, E., Iganski, P., Lee, M., Plummer, K. and South, N. (2004) *Criminology: A Sociological Introduction*. London: Routledge.

Cavadino, M. and Dignan, J. (2006) *Penal Systems: A Comparative Approach*. London: Sage.

Cochrane, A. (2007) *Understanding Urban Policy*. London: Sage.

Cook, D. (2006) *Criminal and Social Justice*. London: Sage.

Critical Social Policy (2006) Special Issue on Devolution and Social Policy, *Critical Social Policy*, 26 (3).

Croall, H. (2001) *Understanding White Collar Crime*. Buckingham: Open University Press.

Croall, H. (2006) 'Criminal justice in post-devolutionary Scotland', *Critical Social Policy*, 26 (3): 587–607.

Croall, H. (Forthcoming 2011) *Crime and Society in Britain*, 2nd edn. London: Pearson.

Cumbers, A. and Whittam, G. (eds) (2007) *Reclaiming the Economy*. Biggar: Scottish Left Review Press.

Davidson, N., Miller, D. and McCafferty, T. (eds) (2010) *Neoliberal Scotland*. Newcastle: Cambridge Scholars Press.

Donnelly, D. and Scott, K. (2005) *Policing Scotland*. Cullompton: Willan Publishing.

Drake, D., Muncie, J. and Westmarland, L. (eds) (2010) *Criminal Justice: Local and Global*. Cullompton: Willan Publishing.

Duff, P. and Hutton, N. (eds) (1999) *Criminal Justice in Scotland*. Aldershot: Ashgate.

Garland, D. (1999) 'Preface', in P. Duff and N. Hutton (eds) *Criminal Justice in Scotland*. Aldershot: Ashgate, pp. xiii–xvi.

Greer, S. L. (ed.) (2009) *Devolution and Social Citizenship in the UK*. Bristol: Policy Press.

Grover, C. (2008) *Crime and Inequality*. Cullompton: Willan Publishing.

Hale, C. (2009) 'Economic marginalization, social exclusion and crime', in C. Hale, K. Hayward, A. Wahidin and E. Wincup (eds), *Criminology*, 2nd edn. Oxford: Oxford University Press.

Hale, C., Hayward, K., Wahidin, A. and Wincup, E. (eds) (2009) *Criminology*, 2nd edn. Oxford: Oxford University Press.

Jack, I. (2009) 'Powered by patriotic flim-flam', *The Guardian*, 14 November.

Johnstone, C. and Mooney, G. (2007) '"Problem" people, "problem" spaces? New Labour and council estates', in R. Atkinson and G. Helms (eds), *Securing an Urban Renaissance: Crime, Community and British Urban Policy*. Bristol: Policy Press, pp. 125–39.

Jones, T. and Newburn, T. (2004) 'The convergence of US and UK crime control policy: exploring substance and process', in T. Newburn and T. Jones (eds), *Criminal Justice and Political Cultures: National and International Dimensions of Crime Control*. Cullompton: Willan Publishing, pp. 123–51.

Keating, M. (2002) 'Devolution and public policy in the United Kingdom: convergence or divergence?', in J. Adams and P. Robinson (eds), *Devolution in Practice*. London: Institute for Public Policy Research, pp. 3–21.

Keating, M. (ed.) (2007) *Scottish Social Democracy: Progressive Ideas for Public Policy*. Brussels: Peter Lang.

Kenway, P., MacInnes, T. and Palmer, G. (2008) *Monitoring Poverty and Social Exclusion in Scotland 2008*. York: Joseph Rowntree Foundation/New Policy Institute.

Kristjánsson, A. L. (2007) 'On social equality and perceptions of insecurity', *European Journal of Criminology*, 4 (1): 59–86.

Law, A. (2005) 'Welfare nationalism: social justice and/or entrepreneurial Scotland', in G. Mooney and G. Scott (eds), *Exploring Social Policy in the 'New' Scotland*. Bristol: Policy Press, pp. 53–83.

Law, A. and Mooney, G. (2006) '"We've never had it so good": the problem of the working class in the devolved Scotland', *Critical Social Policy*, 26 (3): 523–42.

Lea, J. and Young, J. (1993) *What Is to Be Done about Law and Order?*, 2nd edn. London: Pluto Press.

McAra, L. (1999) 'The politics of penality: an overview of the development of penal policy in Scotland', in P. Duff and N. Hutton (eds), *Criminal Justice in Scotland*. Aldershot: Ashgate, pp. 355–80.

McAra, L. (2007) 'Welfarism in crisis: crime control and penal practice in post-devolution Scotland', in M. Keating (ed.), *Scottish Social Democracy: Progressive Ideas for Public Policy*. Brussels: Peter Lang, pp. 107–39.

McAra, L. (2008) 'Crime, criminology and criminal justice in Scotland', *European Journal of Criminology*, 5 (4): 481–504.

McCracken, E. (2009) 'When crime pays', *Sunday Herald*, 13 September.

McCrone, D. (2001) *Understanding Scotland: The Sociology of a Nation*, 2nd edn. London: Routledge.

McEwen, N. (2002) 'State welfare nationalism: the territorial impact of welfare state development in Scotland', *Regional and Federal Studies*, 12: 66–90.

McEwen, N. (2006) *Nationalism and the State: Welfare and Identity in Scotland and Quebec*. Brussels: PIE/Peter Lang.

McGarvey, N. and Cairney, P. (2008) *Scottish Politics: An Introduction*. London: Palgrave.

McIvor, G. (ed.) (2004) *Women Who Offend*. London: Jessica Kingsley.

McKendrick, J. H., Mooney, G., Dickie, J. and Kelly, P. (eds) (2007) *Poverty in Scotland 2007*. London: Child Poverty Action Group.

McNeill, F. and White, B., (2007) *Reducing Re-offending: Social Work and Community Justice in Scotland*. Cullompton: Willan Publishing.

Maguire, M., Morgan, R. and Reiner, R. (eds) (2007) *The Oxford Handbook of Criminology*, 4th edn. Oxford: Clarendon Press.

Mooney, G. (2008) '"Problem" populations, "problem" places', in J. Newman and N. Yeates (eds) *Social Justice: Welfare Crime and Society*. Maidenhead: Open University Press, pp. 97–128.

Mooney, G. and Neal, S. (eds) (2009) *Community: Welfare, Crime and Society*. Maidenhead: Open University Press.

Mooney, G. and Poole, L. (2004) '"A land of milk and honey"? Social policy in Scotland after devolution', *Critical Social Policy*, 24 (4): 458–83.

Mooney, G. and Scott, G. (eds) (2005) *Exploring Social Policy in the 'New' Scotland*. Bristol: Policy Press.

Mooney, G., Morelli, C. and Seaman, P. (2009) 'The question of economic growth and inequality in contemporary Scotland', *Scottish Affairs*, 67 (Spring): 72–89.

Mooney, G., Sweeney, T. and Law, A. (eds) (2006) *Social Care, Health and Welfare in Contemporary Scotland*. Paisley: Kynoch & Blaney.

Morelli, C. and Seaman, P. (2007a) 'Devolution and inequality: a failure to create a community of equals?', *Transactions of the Institute of British Geographers*, 32: 523–38.

Morelli, C. and Seaman, P. (2007b) 'Regional diversity and child poverty: the case of Child Benefit in the United Kingdom and the need for joined up thinking', *The International Journal of Interdisciplinary Social Sciences*, 2 (7): 1833–82.

Morelli, C. and Seaman, P. (2009) 'Devolution and entrenched household poverty: is Scotland less mobile?', *Social Policy and Society*, 8 (3): 367–77.

Muncie, J. (2004) 'Youth justice: globalisation and multi-modal governance', in T. Newburn and T. Jones (eds) *Criminal Justice and Political Cultures: National and International Dimensions of Crime Control*. Cullompton: Willan Publishing, pp. 152–83.

Muncie, J. and Wilson, D. (eds) (2004) *Student Handbook of Criminal Justice and Criminology*. London: Cavendish.

Muncie, J., Talbot, D. and Walters, R. (eds) (2009) *Crime: Local and Global*. Cullompton: Willan Publishing.

Newburn, T. (2007) *Criminology*. Cullompton: Willan Publishing.

Newburn, T. and Sparks, R. (eds) (2004) *Criminal Justice and Political Cultures: National and International Dimensions of Crime Control*. Cullompton: Willan Publishing.

Newlands, D., Danson, M. and McCarthy, J. (eds) (2004) *Divided Scotland?* Aldershot: Ashgate.

Newman, J. and Yeates, N. (eds) (2008) *Social Justice: Welfare, Crime and Society*. Maidenhead: Open University Press.

Paterson, L. (1994) *The Autonomy of Modern Scotland*. Edinburgh: Edinburgh University Press.

Paterson, L., Bechhofer, F. and McCrone, D. (2004) *Living in Scotland: Social and Economic Change since 1980*. Edinburgh: Edinburgh University Press.

Reiner, R. (2007) '"Media made criminality": the representation of crime in the mass media', in M. Maguire, R. Morgan and R. Reiner (eds), *The Oxford Handbook of Criminology*, 4th edn. Oxford: Clarendon Press, pp. 302–40.

Reuss, A. (2004) 'Criminal justice in Scotland', in J. Muncie and D. Wilson (eds) *Student Handbook of Criminal Justice and Criminology*. London: Cavendish, pp. 279–94.

Scott, G. and Mooney, G. (2009) 'Poverty and social justice in the devolved Scotland: neoliberalism meets social democracy?', *Social Policy and Society*, 3 (4): 379–89.

Scottish Government (2007) *The Government Economic Strategy*. Edinburgh: Scottish Government.

Scottish Government (2008a) *Achieving Our Potential: A Framework to Tackle Poverty and Income Inequality in Scotland*. Edinburgh: Scottish Government.

Scottish Government (2008b) *Taking Forward the Government Economic Strategy: Discussion Paper on Tackling Poverty, Inequality and Deprivation in Scotland*. Edinburgh: Scottish Government.

Social Policy and Society (2009) Special Themed Section on Social Policy and Devolution in Scotland, *Social Policy and Society*, 8 (3).

Stewart, J. (2004) *Taking Stock: Scottish Social Welfare after Devolution*. Bristol: Policy Press.

Sutherland, E. H. (1949) *White Collar Crime*. New York: Holt Rinehart & Winston.

Wilkinson, R. G. (2005) *The Impact of Inequality*. London: Routledge.

Wilkinson, R. G. and Pickett, K. (2009) *The Spirit Level*. London: Allen Lane.

Wincott, D. (2006) 'Social policy and social citizenship: Britain's welfare states', *Publius: The Journal of Federalism*, 36 (1): 169–88.

Young, J. (2007) *The Vertigo of Late Modernity*. London: Sage.

Chapter 2

Social inequalities, criminal justice and discourses of social control in contemporary Scotland

Gerry Mooney, Hazel Croall and Mary Munro

Introduction

The typical offender is popularly represented as young, male and working-class, from a 'dangerous' area and often from an 'outsider' group. This pervasive assumption, reinforced in the media, is reflected in political and policy priorities in Scotland as elsewhere. It must, however, be subjected to critical scrutiny. While, for example, the criminal justice process is indeed dominated by people from working-class backgrounds, this can partly be accounted for by the focus of policing and criminal justice on crimes which are perceived to be policy priorities, perceptions which tend to neglect middle-class or white-collar crimes (an issue which is also picked up in Chapter 7, this volume). This is further related to a focus on class and offending rather than victimisation. This chapter will focus on inequalities of social class and socio-economic status, while later chapters focus on other dimensions of inequality and stratification, in particular gender and ethnicity. It will explore the complex relationships between crime, victimisation and social inequalities, with a specific focus on Scotland, and contrast images of crime and deprivation with the less high-profile crimes of the middle classes. It will then turn to the criminal justice process and to issues of criminalisation.

Perceptions of crime and social inequality

From depictions of the 'underworld' of Dickensian London to the drugs and violence of the Baltimore 'projects' so vividly portrayed in the American television drama, *The Wire*, popular culture has long reflected the relationship between crime and social disadvantage. Associations with crime involve largely 'lower'-class life and culture with the distinction, underlying nineteenth-century social policy, between the 'undeserving poor' of the 'submerged class' depicted as 'idle' or 'workshy' and the deserving poor, poor through no fault of their own, affecting policy discussions (Mooney 1998, 2008; Morris 1994). More recent perceptions echo earlier themes, with the widely used term the 'underclass' having been used to depict a geographically excluded class whose members 'choose' not to work, to be dependent on welfare and are characterised by high rates of illegitimacy and violent crime (Bagguley and Mann 1992; Grover 2008; Muncie *et al.* 2010; Murray 1996; Wacquant 2008, 2009). These notions gave way to discourses of social exclusion which will be explored below.

In Scotland's major towns and cities, repeated and continuing connections are drawn in many different ways between places of disadvantage/impoverished communities and issues of crime and disorder (Damer 1989a). From the slums of nineteenth-century Dundee, Edinburgh and Glasgow to the recurring focus on the 'problems' of Scotland's public housing schemes in the late twentieth century and early 2000s, we do not have to look far to uncover such associations, even if many are problematic in multiple ways.

Mainstream criminological theories and research echoed these perceptions by accepting the assumption that the 'lower' classes were more prone to crime and investigating their assumed 'problems' such as physical or psychological pathologies, 'dysfunctional' families, social *dis*organisation and delinquent *sub*cultures. To structural theorists crime was dysfunctional and indicated a problem with the social structure, often related to a 'strain' between the notion that all could achieve wealth and high status and the impossibility for many of achieving these cultural goals by legitimate means (Merton 1938). While this did highlight the significance of social disadvantage and unequal opportunities, it reflected a tendency to 'blame the poor' and indeed to 'over-predict' lower-class crime (Matza 1964). It is important to recognise that not all lower-class individuals resort to crime, nor is all crime committed by lower-class individuals. Indeed the very existence of 'middle-class' and corporate crime, explored in later chapters in this book, challenges these assumptions.

Crime in Scotland, with its high levels of socio-economic inequality (outlined in the following section), has long been attributed to aspects of social deprivation. While much attention has been focused on the former heavy industrial areas of Glasgow and Clydeside, with their reputation for gang violence and organised crime, other cities have also been depicted as places where crime and disorder are factors of everyday life. This is exemplified in the Edinburgh-set film *Trainspotting* (1996) while Dundee's gang culture from the 1960s and 1970s, a period in which the city was being badly affected by long-term economic change and decline, featured in BBC Scotland's Radio Programme *Street Gangs of Dundee* (2007) and Gary Robertson's *Gangs of Dundee* (2007). Scotland's cities, or particular districts within them, together with other towns across the country also feature in the growing number of websites devoted to detailing youth gang activities, gang cultures and the 'hardness' of one locale compared with others.

Many politicians have stressed the significance and negative consequences of Scotland's 'booze and blade' culture, often linked to issues of poverty and deprivation. Responding to widely publicised indications in the Scottish Crime and Victimisation survey that victims attributed around 45 per cent of minor assaults to perpetrators under the influence of alcohol, Kenny MacAskill, then SNP spokesperson, stated that the 'social factors that contribute to crime' were 'chiefly drink, drugs and deprivation'.[1] Here MacAskill is echoing the commonplace analysis of criminality prevalent a century ago:

> Drunkenness has long been a social evil [in Scotland] of very grave magnitude. The poverty, squalor, vice, and crime of the slum districts of the large towns are largely traceable to this evil. But the drink demon lurks in every corner of the land and among all classes, and its shadow is a blot on the fair name of Scotland. (MacKinnon 1921: 262)

Crime and income inequality in Scotland

In order to explore these popular perceptions more critically, it is important to look at the extent and nature of socio-economic inequality in relation to crime in Scotland. In Chapter 1 we argue that social inequalities and social divisions must be central to any comprehensive understanding of crime (see also Grover 2008; Wilkinson 2005; Wilkinson and Pickett 2009). There is a growing body of evidence that points to the extent of persistent class inequalities in Scottish society (see Hanlon, *et al.* 2006; Kenway *et al.* 2008; Law and Mooney 2006 2010; McKendrick *et al.* 2007; Mooney *et al.* 2009; Morelli and Seaman

2007, 2009), and inequality, albeit in a somewhat vague way, has been highlighted by the Scottish National Party minority government as a key area for policy intervention (see Scottish Government 2007a, 2008; Scott and Mooney 2009; Scottish Affairs 2009).

Relating social and economic inequalities to both victimisation and offending is far from straightforward, and the largely quantitative data which constitute the main sources of information are limited and difficult to interpret. Scottish crime and justice statistics[2] include annual statistical returns of crimes recorded by the police, proceedings in criminal courts and the now annual Scottish Crime and Justice Survey (SCJS). Information about social inequality can be found in the Scottish Index of Multiple Deprivation (SIMD) which includes a crime domain, and there is also useful data in the 'Scotland's People Annual Report' (or Scottish Household Survey). Other sources of information include reports compiled by groups such as the Scottish Consortium for Crime and Criminal Justice (SCCCJ), voluntary organisations and government and academic research.[3]

Most of the relevant statistics are collected separately from the rest of the UK and plentiful though this data may appear, they have many limitations. The problems of police recorded criminal statistics are widely acknowledged (Maguire 2007): for example, they exclude the many offences which victims choose not to report, and offences which are not the responsibility of the police but of other specialist reporting agencies, such as SEPA and trading standards. As will be seen below, these omissions include many offences committed by more affluent groups of the population. Moreover, most of these sources contain no information about the socio-economic status of offenders and while statistical sources indicate broad relationships they tell us little about what some have called the 'lived reality' of crime (Goodey 2005; Lea and Young 1993). In some areas for example, victimisation may be so commonplace that it cannot accurately be 'counted' in victim surveys.

Despite the limitations of information, few dispute that the criminal justice process deals mainly with lower-class offenders, and that much offending takes place within areas of deprivation. SIMD figures, while limited to crimes of violence, domestic house breaking, vandalism, drug offences and minor assault, give some idea of these relationships, indicating an association between areas characterised by high rates of social deprivation defined by indices of unemployment, income, housing, health and police recorded crime (see McKendrick *et al.* 2007). Thus in 2008–9:

- Nearly 26 per cent of data zones[4] in Glasgow City were in the 15 per cent most deprived areas in terms of SIMD crime and Glasgow City had the largest (but falling) proportion of the 15 per cent most deprived national data zones (at 18 per cent of all Scottish deprived data zones for crime) (Scottish Government 2009d).
- In the 15 per cent most deprived data zones, there was roughly one SIMD crime per 10 people reported in 2007–8 compared with one SIMD crime per 25 people in the rest of Scotland (Scottish Government 2009e).
- In Inverclyde, for example, 24 per cent of the total population are 'income deprived' (14 per cent for Scotland overall) and a similar skew is reflected in a range of indices including health, education and employment. To take one, the rate of admission to hospital for alcohol abuse in Inverclyde over 2001–4 was 1,106 per 100,000 population compared with 723 across Scotland (Scottish Government 2009c). Local police crime statistics show high rates of violent crime related to alcohol abuse, murder and attempted murder, serious and indecent assaults along with vandalism and fire-raising (Frondigoun and Addidle 2009).

There has been considerable investigation of the relationship between economic conditions, unemployment and income differentials and crime. While few studies have covered Scotland specifically, in general terms evidence suggests a complex relationship. Indeed economic theories suggest two conflicting hypotheses (Hale 2009). *Opportunity theory* suggests that crime will rise along with rising income levels as there are more goods in circulation and more opportunities for crime, whereas *motivational theory* suggests that crime increases during a recession with the unemployed turning to crime as their legitimate income decreases.

In general terms, crime in England and Wales rose during the recession of 1989–92 (Hale 2009) although not during the depression of the 1930s (Lea and Young 1993). While some forms of property crime rise during recession, some forms of violent crime fall. Many minor violent incidents take place in public and are alcohol-related – in a recession people spend less and go out less often. The more people have to spend, the lower the crime rate, whereas crime rises as personal consumption falls (Field 1990, 1996). The role of unemployment is also complex as its effects vary by age and local employment patterns (Grover 2008). Young people, for example, commit more crime – thus youth unemployment rates are more significant than general rates. Changes in the nature of employment are also crucial. For Hale (1999, 2009), the shift from more permanent to casual employment is significant as for those facing poorly paid, unrewarding and casual work, crime may be an attractive option.

The growing gap between high and low incomes rather than low income in itself is also important (Machin and Meghir 2003), and has been associated with a growth in burglary which to Hale reflects the growing polarisation between the 'work rich' and the 'work poor'. This is echoed by Wilkinson and Pickett, who argue that what matters in understanding the extent of social problems, including crimes, is the 'scale of material differences between people within each society being too big' (2009: 25). Other research indicates that areas benefiting most from the introduction of the minimum wage saw the greatest decreases in crime (Hansen and Machin 2003), whereas the later job seekers allowance, which reduced incomes, was associated with rising crime (Machin and Marie 2004). Like other statistical correlations, however, these tell us little about the motivational processes underlying these relationships although they do suggest the role of relative as opposed to absolute deprivation.

Victimisation

The relationship between victimisation and social inequality is also complex. Whereas the more affluent, with higher levels of conspicuous consumption, present attractive targets to economically motivated offenders, both in terms of physical and identity crime, they are able to protect themselves, for example by purchasing security devices and insurance. Incidence levels of victimisation for England and Wales have consistently indicated higher rates of victimisation from property crime among those living in the most affluent *and* the most deprived urban areas (Bangs *et al.* 2008). Where repeat victimisation (reports of three or more victimisations) is concerned a different picture emerges, with those in more deprived, high-crime areas suffering disproportionately (Croall 2007; Hope 2001). While similar breakdowns are not available for Scotland, the 2006 survey (Brown and Bolling 2007) reported higher rates of repeat victimisation in areas characterised by 'struggling singles' and 'developing families'. The most recent figures comparing the 15 per cent most deprived SIMD data zones with the rest of Scotland in 2008/9 indicate that adults in these areas have a greater risk of being a victim of crime (26 per cent : 19 per cent); property crime (23 per cent : 17 per cent); violent crime (6 per cent : 4 per cent) and were more likely to be injured as a result (62 per cent : 58 per cent). They were also more likely to say that they felt unsafe walking alone (46 per cent : 30 per cent) and in their own homes after dark (12 per cent : 6 per cent) (Scottish Government 2009a). The Scottish Household Survey also suggests that neighbourhood deprivation (15 per cent most deprived data zones) is linked to perceptions of the local area. People living in such areas are:

- less likely to agree that their area is 'pleasant, safe or has a sense of community and friendly people';
- more likely to say that there is no sense of community and identify problems with substance abuse (45 per cent : 20 per cent)
- more likely to report perceptions of prevalence and experience of antisocial behaviour, for example vandalism/graffiti/damage to property (22 per cent : 10 per cent).

(Scottish Household Survey 2009f).

It is also important to recognise that victimisation is likely to have a more severe effect on poorer families – goods cannot readily be replaced and once victimised, insurance is less easy to obtain (Croall 2007). In this regard, then, the unequal risk and impact of victimisation are laid bare.

Dimensions of crime and inequality

This section focuses on the contrasting crimes of different socio-economic groups and the way in which these are socially constructed, analysed and subjected to different levels of criminalisation. As indicated above, the focus on the 'booze and blade' culture reflects a long history, particularly in Glasgow and in some other ex-industrial towns, of violent gang crime in areas of social deprivation. In contrast the crimes of 'respectable' middle classes receive very little attention yet, as the following section illustrates, these are associated with multiple harms although they are dealt with very differently.

'Gangs, booze and blades'! Glasgow: from 'Europe's Chicago' to Europe's 'murder capital'?

Gang violence in Glasgow, from the 1930s, through the youth gangs of the 1960s, to the 170 gangs identified in a recent report (Centre for Social Justice 2008), has led to the city's reputation as Scotland's or Europe's 'Chicago', characterised dramatically in the 1935 novel *No Mean City* (McArthur and Long 1984; see also Damer 1989b). Glasgow's so called 'hard men' have provided autobiographical accounts such as Jimmy Boyle's (1977) *A Sense of Freedom* and Paul Ferris' *The Ferris Conspiracy* (Ferris with McKay 2002) and have been subject to journalistic accounts by writers such as Reg McKay (2006) and Robert Jeffrey (2002a, 2002b, 2006). Research includes Davies' (1998, 2007a, 2007b) historical work and Patrick's (1973) controversial and heavily criticised book *A Glasgow Gang Observed* (see Damer 1989a, 1989b). Much publicised have been revelations of stabbings and a 'knife pandemic' – according to the head of Glasgow's violence reduction unit, the worst offenders are poorly educated young men aged between 15 and 25 brought up in council housing (*Times*, 19 July 2005) – all contributing to the city's reputation as the 'murder capital' of Britain and/or of Europe (see Kelbie 2003; MacDonald 2008; McKay 2006; Martin 2004). Indeed, while Scotland as a whole has a homicide rate higher than both England and Wales and Northern Ireland, the Glasgow rate of 6.64 per 100,000 in the period 2003–5, was seen as particularly high among European cities, exceeding London's rate of 2.64. A substantial proportion of homicides (45 per cent) were committed with a 'sharp instrument' (Scottish Government 2007b) and Glasgow's high rate has been associated with more use of lethal weapons, whereby more violent incidents result in death (Brookman 2005). Numbers have since dropped with later figures indicating a fall from the 39 murders recorded in 2003–4 to 24 in 2008–9 (BBC 2010). Inequalities of age and gender (murders are more likely to involve young male confrontational homicides) combine with clear spatial and economic inequalities to link deprivation with violence (Dorling 2006).[5]

How much of this reputation is true? Davies' historical research on the Glasgow gangs of the 1920s and 1930s suggests that gang activity and particularly the volume of economic crime was small in comparison with Chicago – although gangs were far from the 'men of honour' they presented themselves as. They were involved in protection rackets which victimised the poor although profits were relatively modest. They consisted of a mixture of sectarian gangs based on religion (such as the Catholic Norman Conks and the Protestant Billy Boys) and those based on territorialism – a picture also found across some parts of the city today. Davies also recounts a tendency, on the part of the police, to 'talk up' the problem and exaggerate police successes. Nonetheless, he and others argue that Glasgow is unique in Britain in relation to gang activity, especially with regard to territorially based youth gangs (see Peev 2008; Sweeney 2009).

Accounts of these gangs stress a combination of social deprivation and cultural factors. During the 1930s, argues Davies, unemployment provided an economic motivation for older men to remain involved. Autobiographical and journalistic accounts of the kind highlighted at the very start of Chapter 1 (cf. Ferris and McKay 2002; Jeffrey 2002) highlight, as does the infamous and controversial novel *No Mean City*, life in the 'slums' and later in the 'schemes'. Crime is portrayed as a valuable source of income and an alternative career. The notorious 'ice cream wars' of the 1980s illustrate how competition over something as seemingly mundane as pitching ice cream vans can become subject to intense competition and violence (Campbell and McKay 2001). To Ferris, a criminal career provided an opportunity to make money more speedily and with more excitement than the legitimate alternatives and some of the gangs' economic activities provide examples of the skilled criminal entrepreneurs utilising a variety of legitimate and illegitimate opportunities described in other cities (Hobbs 2002).

Cultural influences are global as well as local. In the 1930s for example, gang leaders modelled themselves on the methods and style of Chicago mobsters popularised through Hollywood films (Davies 1998; Jeffrey 2002b, 2006). Later the 'crime lord' Arthur Thomson was said to be fixated with the *Godfather* movies and Ferris is said to have revelled in his celebrity status and 'Mafia Don' image (Jeffrey 2002b). Gang culture has its own local vocabulary. Campbell (2001: 59) describes the notorious 'Glesca kiss' as a 'heider to the nose' and the 'Glesca kiss-off' as 'a bullet up the arse', also known as a 'Glasgow goodbye' (Jeffrey 2002a: 164). Ferris describes a culture in which knife violence is acceptable, a sign of 'manhood', a means of settling grievances, a form of economic control and meting out rough justice, and a source of excitement and pride (Croall 2003; Quinn 2003). Scars are, in these narratives but also in gang cultures, seen as a mark of respect, masculinity is a major theme, and violence against 'civilians' and non-combatants, including women, was disapproved of, as was sexual violence.

In Glasgow, participation in violence and membership in gangs can be inter-generational as illustrated in a recent study of the East End (Frondigoun *et al.* 2008). Respondents reported that 'grandparents, parents, brothers have all been in the gang' and 'they pass on a lot of stuff'. There were reports of parents shouting encouragement – when a gang fight broke out:

> it is not unusual for a mother and father to agree with what their sons and daughters are doing in being out gang fighting.

This strongly suggests that economic and cultural factors combine to make involvement in violence and crime an attractive and exciting option, though in other ways it can work to exacerbate feelings of social exclusion and limit ambitions and horizons (Deuchar 2009; Deuchar and Holligan 2010). At the same time, however, it is important to recognise the strong elements of demonisation inherent in many accounts of Glasgow's violence and its relationship to social deprivation. The report of the Centre for Social Justice (2008), used by the Conservative politician Ian Duncan Smith to highlight 'Broken Britain', emphasises the role played by families and individuals and the 'disease of worklessness', thus contributing to the 'poor blaming' tendencies of many media, popular and academic approaches (Mooney 2009; see also Wacquant 2009). In passing we should note, however, that such commentary is not applied to Glasgow alone, but is also a recurring feature of representations of other disadvantaged localities and populations across the UK. The death of 'Baby P' in August 2007 (see Ferguson and Lavalette 2009a, 2009b) and the kidnapping of Shannon Matthews in 2008 also fuelled media stories of a welfare-dependent and disorderly 'underclass' (for example, *Daily Telegraph*, 6 December 2008; Mooney and Neal 2010).

Crimes of the middle classes

In contrast to the lurid headlines attracted by the 'hard men', the crimes of the 'middle classes' are virtually invisible and subject to less popular or academic attention (Croall 2009). Nonetheless, a few examples, many from Scotland, illustrate their pervasive impact. To these could also be added the crimes of the powerful, which are discussed in Chapters 7 and 8 (this volume):

- Major financial losses are occasioned by fraud, said to cost every person in Scotland £330 each year (Scottish Government Press Release, 12 May 2008), *excluding* the cost of tax evasion. These figures are inevitably 'guesstimates' as it is not systematically counted – indeed a report by HM Inspectorate of Constabulary for Scotland in 2008 concludes that the real extent of fraud is impossible to assess. Many forms of fraud are widely practised. Karstedt and Farrell's (2006) research, for example, describes crimes such as not paying TV licence fees, evading taxes and making false insurance claims as 'everyday crimes of the middle classes'.

- Fraud on the part of doctors, dentists and pharmacists has prompted the Scottish government to declare a policy of 'zero tolerance' of fraud in the NHS. Examples reported included dentists claiming to have used precious instead of non-precious metals in fillings and falsifying claims for NHS work, opticians claiming for more expensive lenses than have been either needed or supplied, pharmacists claiming for expensive brand name drugs when cheaper alternatives have actually been dispensed, and GPs, responsible for prescribing these drugs, having been found to have had 'inappropriate' relationships with representatives of pharmaceutical companies (Scottish Government Press Release, 28 January 2008; *Sunday Herald*, 26 January 2008; http://www.cfs.scot.nhs.uk/).
- Businesses have also been associated with a variety of environmental, consumer and health and safety offences, often associated with 'corporate' crime but also with small, local 'respectable' businesses (Croall 2010). These include, for example, the sale of out-of-date or underweight food or bread, breaches of environmental health laws which seek to protect against food poisoning or the sale of falsely described second-hand cars. One of the most notorious Scottish cases involved the conviction of the butcher, John Barr, for breaches of food safety laws following the death of 21 old age pensioners in Wishaw in 1997. Farmers can also be involved in fraud, from subsidies frauds on the European Union to participation in illegal trades involving 'diversification'. Smith (2004, 2009) recounts, in the North East of Scotland among other areas in Britain, the involvement of 'gentlemen farmers' and the 'petit bourgeoisie', along with 'likeable' and 'dislikeable' rogues in activities such as the theft of cattle, the use and sale of so called 'red diesel', the sale of out-of-date animal medicines and illegal businesses in pedigree dogs.

Many of these offences are not widely perceived as or reported as 'crimes' and their treatment contrasts sharply with the crimes described in the previous section. Victims are often unaware of being harmed, they do not see themselves as victims of 'crime' nor can they attribute their offences directly to offenders. They receive relatively little publicity unless mass deaths have been involved and do not appear in standard crime statistics or victim surveys. Many are not the province of the police today,[6] but of enforcement agencies such as the Health and Safety Executive or Environmental or Trading Standards Officers, long associated with a 'compliance' form of enforcement consisting of warnings and advice rather than prosecution – which is relatively rare (Croall 2004). Enforcement is logistically difficult and indeed the recording of fraud in Scotland has been recognised as 'one of the weaker areas of police data capture' (Scottish Government Press Release, 12 May 2008). Moreover there has been widespread cultural tolerance of many of these activities which, like tax evasion, are not seen as morally wrong (Cook 1989; Karstedt and Farrell 2006), though in the light of the scandal of MPs' expenses in 2009 and the 'bonus culture' which has contributed to the global financial world crisis in recent years, this may change. Phrases such as 'misselling' or 'wrongdoing' are often used to describe what are, in effect, fraudulent or corrupt practices (Croall 2001).

Social exclusion, social inequality and crime

Previous sections have indicated that the social construction of crime around 'lower'-class crime has strongly influenced academic theories and criminal justice policy-making. Contemporary approaches reflect this tendency, particularly versions of the influential notion of 'social exclusion', which, in contrast to the notion of the 'underclass', do appear to recognise structural, economic, spatial and political dimensions of exclusion (Grover 2008; Young 1999, 2007). This came, particularly from the late 1990s, to dominate discussions of social inequality to the extent that the term virtually replaced 'poverty'. It is, however, a difficult concept to define and many refer to it as a 'discourse' reflecting the way in which it, and government policies based on inclusion, contain a number of different assumptions about its nature, causes and links with crime. These are illustrated in a Cabinet Office statement of 2008 (cited in Clarke 2008: 52):

> Social exclusion is about more than income poverty. It is a short-hand term for what can happen when people or areas have a combination of linked problems such as unemployment, discrimination, poor skills, low incomes, poor housing, high crime and family breakdown. These problems are linked and mutually reinforcing.

It is generally accepted that there are 'strong' and 'weak' versions of this discourse, with the 'weak version', associated with many New Labour policies, stressing individual and family circumstances and the role of work as a way out of exclusion through policies such as 'welfare to work' (Byrne 2005; Grover 2008; Levitas 2005; Veit-Wilson 1998; Young 2007). This downplays the structural and systemic causes of exclusion stressed in the 'strong' version, such as the labour market changes referred to above which cannot be overcome by such policies. The strong version also incorporates issues of power, social justice and human rights.

There is, argues Young, continuity between the neoliberal assumptions inherent in the underclass thesis and the weaker version from New Labour which incorporates a nostalgic vision of the role of work and family. Moreover, these assumptions tend to reflect simplistic, binary divisions between the excluded and the included. Young (1999, 2007) argues that, far from being spatially and culturally excluded, the inhabitants of the poorest areas live in close proximity to and are well aware of the greater prosperity and material circumstances of the included – for whom they work and provide services. A key point in his critique is that there is strong cultural inclusion – the media disseminates global cultural and materialistic goals and political rhetoric stresses their availability to all. This produces relative deprivation and a 'bulimic society' in which this inclusion is accompanied by exclusion brought about by structural barriers to success. In turn this is related to a 'culture of vindictiveness' in which the 'included', themselves occupying a precarious position, stigmatise the excluded and to a growing tide of punitivism, reflected in higher rates of imprisonment – in itself a contributory factor to exclusion.

The assumptions of the exclusion discourse also depict the excluded as offenders and neglect the role of victimisation, which, along with high rates of crime, can themselves lead to exclusion. For many of the most excluded, the homeless or immigrants, for example, victimisation is both a cause and a consequence of exclusion, producing a vicious circle – particularly as they are likely to be perceived, if reporting crime, as offenders rather than victims (Goodey 2005; Croall 2007).

These kinds of analysis also underplay the role of the neoliberal economy and its underlying values of, for example, consumerism. The stress on work as a solution neglects the massive changes in the nature of work and its rewards referred to above which render such a solution inadequate. Work may not provide sufficient income to bring up a family, leading to some families needing two or more jobs. For Elliot Currie (1996, 2007) a 'market society' with its Darwinian culture of competition has a corrosive effect on family stability rendering parents less capable of raising children. For those unable to obtain jobs with a secure income and job satisfaction, crime may provide an attractive solution as we have seen above.

Inequalities and criminal justice

Previous sections have illustrated the very different way in which the crimes of different groups are dealt with. While data about the socio-economic status of offenders is not routinely collected, research suggests that many young offenders have few educational qualifications, are unemployed and have experienced abuse in the home (SCCCJ 2000; Waterhouse *et al.* 2004; see also Chapter 4, this volume). Persistent young offenders have been found to come disproportionately from homes experiencing family, housing and educational problems (Tombs 2000). A report by Houchin (2005) related Scottish prisoners' postcodes to the socio-economic classification of areas, and found that:

- 28 per cent of prisoners, compared with 10 per cent of the general population, came from the 'poorest council estates'. For Glasgow the figure was 60 per cent;
- half of the prisoner population came from 155 of 1,222 local government wards in Scotland, many of them socially deprived;
- the male imprisonment rate from the 27 most deprived wards amounted to 953 per 100,000 of the population compared with the national average of 237;
- the imprisonment rate for 23-year-old men from the 27 most deprived wards amounted to 3,427 per 100,000;
- one in nine young men from the most deprived communities will spend time in prison when they are 23.

These figures should not be taken to indicate higher levels of criminality in these areas – as demonstrated above, middle-class crime is processed very differently. They do, however, illustrate the extent to which the 'hard end' of the system is dominated by lower-class offenders. This is the end of a long process characterised by a series of discretionary decisions raising questions about the extent to which lower-class individuals may be more likely to proceed through the system, from policing to imprisonment.

Policing and prosecution

The police are described as the gatekeepers of the criminal justice process, being responsible for investigating crime, street policing and passing cases forward. While there has been less research in Scotland on operational policing (Donnelly 2005; see also Chapter 9, this volume) than other jurisdictions, that which exists suggests that policing focuses on the 'usual suspects' (see Chapter 4, this volume). As resource constraints mean that they cannot police all areas equally, they will concentrate their resources on areas identified as posing problems – decisions affected by local and governmental policy priorities and targets in relation to, for example, knife crime, violence and anti-social behaviour. Popular and political demands for more police 'on the streets' also leads to what some describe as the 'over-policing' of youths who spend more time on the streets, making, as suggested in an Edinburgh study, youth a more visible and easy target for policing (Anderson *et al.* 1994). As seen above, the focus on the 'booze and blade' culture has also led to the resourcing of innovative policing policies in areas such as Inverclyde or the East End of Glasgow (Frondigoun *et al.* 2008; Frondigoun and Addidle 2009). In contrast, as indicated above (and this is returned to in Chapters 7 and 8, this volume) the policing of fraud, environmental, consumer or health and safety offences is less likely to lead to prosecution. While the guidance issued to Procurator Fiscals, responsible in Scotland for prosecution, is not available to the public, it could be argued that lower-class crimes and offenders stand a higher chance of being prosecuted. The Fiscal is able to 'divert' cases from formal prosecution, and has extensive powers to impose 'direct measures' in summary cases including the imposition of 'Fiscal Fines' to a maximum of £300. This could well benefit defendants with the resources to pay and who are considered to be at less risk of committing further crimes – assumptions less likely to apply to persistent offenders from high-crime areas. It will also be seen in Chapter 4 (this volume) that young people from the most deprived backgrounds are 'up-tariffed' more speedily.

Conviction, sentencing and imprisonment

As is the case for earlier stages in the process, social inequalities may well affect subsequent decisions, and, as seen above, the population of prisons and young offender institutions is overwhelmingly working class. Research in other jurisdictions strongly suggests that lower-class defendants can be severely disadvantaged throughout trial, conviction and sentencing. While more affluent offenders can employ legal and other expertise, can generally speak the 'language' of the court and present themselves well, lower-class defendants lack this ability (Carlen 1976). Unemployed and particularly homeless defendants may be disadvantaged in relation to remand and custody decisions as, quite simply, they have less to lose and may be seen to pose a greater threat of recidivism. In contrast, more affluent defendants regularly claim that the 'process is the punishment' (Levi 1989), claiming that their offences were one-off mistakes and that severe punishment would unfairly disadvantage their families and employment.

Concluding comments: criminalisation, criminal justice and social control

A key thread running through this chapter, and reflected across a number of the chapters which follow, points to the ideological significance of the way in which crime is constructed around poor and disadvantaged sections of society (see Lister 2004; Mooney 2008). In highlighting processes of criminalisation, as opposed to a focus solely on crime, we point to the fact that living in an unequal and socially divided society matters immensely for our understanding of crime and criminal justice. In the chapters that follow, the concerns with inequalities and social injustices in Scotland today are underlined. All the contributors to this collection recognise, however, that the relationships between crime and social inequality are complex. The predominance of working-class individuals in the criminal justice process and the construction of the 'problems' of crime around lower-class crime does not in any way imply a commensurate propensity towards crime among any particular group. Rather, different kinds of crime are associated with specific social groups and, in turn, related to a variety of economic conditions and inequalities and to different opportunities. The Commissioner of the California Department of Savings and Loans is reported as commenting in 1987 for example that the 'best way to rob a bank is to own one' (cited in Calavita et al. 1997). Braithwaite (1992) argues that unequal societies produce *both* crimes of poverty (often motivated by 'need') and crimes of wealth and power (motivated by greed and power). Nor is it the case that the crimes of the disadvantaged are more serious – while undoubtedly knife crime, homicides and stabbings are serious, they are mercifully rare in comparison with many other crimes and, as will be seen in Chapters 7 and 8 (this volume), with the crimes of the powerful also extract a large toll of social harm (see Muncie *et al.* 2010).

Notes

1 http://www.scotland.gov.uk/News/Releases/2007/09/26155318
2 These can be accessed at http://www.scotland.gov.uk/Topics/Statistics/Browse/Crime-Justice
3 A very good link to access this information by topic is http://www.cjscotland.org
4 Data zones have a median population of 767 in SIMD 2009 (http://www.scotland.gov.uk/Topics/Statistics/SIMD/) (accessed 11 November 2009).
5 These associations also apply to suicide: Scotland has significantly higher rates of suicide than other parts of the UK and most other countries in Europe. Suicide is, like homicide, especially linked to younger men living in deprived areas (see http://www.chooselife.net/home/Home.asp (accessed 12 November 2009).
6 Though interestingly many of these were police matters when the police were first founded and for much of the nineteenth century (Barrie 2008).

References

Anderson, S., Kinsey, R., Loader, I. and Smith, C. (1994) *Cautionary Tales: Young People, Crime and Policing in Edinburgh*. Aldershot: Avebury.

Bagguley, P. and Mann, K. (1992) 'Idle thieving bastards? Scholarly representations of the "underclass"', *Work, Employment and Society*, 6 (1): 113–26.

Bangs, M., Roe, S. and Higgins, N. (2008) 'Geographic patterns of crime', in N. Kershaw, S. Nicholas and A. Walker (eds), *Crime in England and Wales 2007/8*. London: Home Office, pp. 143–64.

Barrie, D. G. (2008) *Police in the Age of Improvement: Police Development and the Civic Tradition in Scotland, 1775–1865*. Cullompton: Willan Publishing.

BBC News (2010) 'Drop in Homicides for second year', 23/02/10. http://news.bbc.co.uk/1/hi/scotland/8529971.stm

Boyle, J. (1977) *A Sense of Freedom*. London: Pan.

Braithwaite, J. (1992) 'Poverty, power and white-collar crime: Sutherland and the paradoxes of criminological theory', in K. Schlegel and D. Weisburd (eds), *White Collar Crime Reconsidered*. Boston, MA: Northeastern University Press, pp. 78–107.

Brookman, F. (2005) *Understanding Homicide*. London: Sage.

Brown, M. and Bolling, K. (2007) *2006 Scottish Crime and Victimisation Survey: Main Findings*. Edinburgh: BMRB Social Research/Scottish Government Social Research.

Byrne, D. (2005) *Social Exclusion*, 2nd edn. Maidenhead: Open University Press.

Calavita, K., Tillman, R. and Pontell, H. (1997) 'The savings and loan debacle, financial crime, and the state', *Annual Review of Sociology*, 23: 19–38.

Campbell, T. C. and McKay, R. (2001) *Indictment: Trial by Fire*. Edinburgh: Canongate.

Carlen, P. (1976) *Magistrates' Justice*. London: Martin Robertson.

Centre for Social Justice (2008) *Breakthrough Glasgow: Ending the Cost of Social Breakdown*. London: Centre for Social Justice.

Clarke, J. (2008) 'Looking for social justice: welfare states and beyond', in J. Newman and N. Yeates (eds), *Social Justice: Welfare, Crime and Society*. Maidenhead: Open University Press, pp. 29–62.

Cook, D. (1989) *Rich Law, Poor Law: Different Responses to Tax and Supplementary Benefit Fraud*. Milton Keynes: Open University Press.

Croall, H. (2001) *Understanding White Collar Crime*. Buckingham: Open University Press.

Croall, H. (2003) 'Review of indictment: trial by fire, the Ferris conspiracy, deadly divisions and Glasgow's hard men', *Scottish Journal of Criminal Justice Studies*, 9: 104–12.

Croall, H. (2004) 'Combatting financial crime: regulatory versus crime control approaches', *Journal of Financial Crime*, 11: 45–55.

Croall, H. (2007) 'Victims of white collar and corporate crime', in P. Davies, P. Francis and C. Greer (eds), *Victims, Crime and Society*. London: Sage, pp. 78–108.

Croall, H. (2010) 'Middle range business crime: rogue and respectable businesses, family firms and entrepreneurs', in M. Maguire and F. Brookman (eds), *Handbook of Crime*. Cullompton: Willan Publishing, pp. 678–97.

Currie, E. (1996) 'Social crime prevention strategies in a market society', in J. Muncie, E. McLaughlin and M. Langan (eds), *Criminological Perspectives*. London: Sage.

Currie, E. (2007) 'Social action', in M. E. Vogel (ed.), *Crime, Inequality and the State*. London: Routledge, pp. 326–37.

Daily Telegraph, The (2008) 'Karen Matthews and the underclass thrive on Labour's welfare state', *The Daily Telegraph*, 6 December.

Damer, S. (1989a) *From Moorepark to 'Wine Alley': The Rise and Fall of a Glasgow Housing Scheme*. Edinburgh: Edinburgh University Press.

Damer, S. (1989b) *Glasgow: Going for a Song*. London: Lawrence & Wishart.

Davies, A. (1998) 'Street gangs, crime and policing in Glasgow during the 1930s: the case of the beehive boys', *Social History*, 23 (3): 251–67.

Davies, A. (2007a) 'The Scottish Chicago: from "hooligans" to "gangsters" in inter-war Glasgow', *Cultural and Social History*, 4 (4): 511–27.

Davies, A. (2007b) 'Glasgow's "reign of terror": street gangs, racketeering and intimidation in the 1920s and 1930s', *Contemporary British History*, 21 (4): 405–27.

Deuchar, R. (2009) *Gangs, Marginalised Youth and Social Capital*. Oakhill: Trentham.

Deuchar, R. and Holligan, C. (2010) 'Gangs, sectarianism and social capital: a qualitative study of young people in Scotland', *Sociology*, 44 (1): 13–30.

Donnelly, D. (2005) 'Policing the Scottish community', in D. Donnelly and K. Scott (eds), *Policing Scotland*. Cullompton: Willan Publishing.

Dorling, D. (2006) 'Prime suspect: murder in Britain', *Prison Service Journal*, 166: 3–10.

Ferguson, I. and Lavalette, M. (2009a) 'Social work after "Baby P"', *International Socialism*, 122: 115–32.

Ferguson, I. and Lavalette, M. (2009b) *Social Work After Baby P: Issues, Debates and Alternative Perspectives*. Liverpool: Liverpool Hope University.

Ferris, P. with McKay, R. (2002) *The Ferris Conspiracy*. Edinburgh: Mainstream Publishing.

Field, S. (1990) *Trends in Crime and their Interpretation: A Study of Recorded Crime in Post War England and Wales*, Home Office Research Study No. 119. London: HMSO.

Field, S. (1996) 'Crime and consumption', in J. Muncie, E. McLaughlin and M. Langan (eds), *Criminological Perspectives*. London: Sage.

Frondigoun, L. and Addidle, G. (2009) *An Evaluation of the Inverclyde Initiative*. Strathclyde Police and Glasgow Caledonian University.

Frondigoun, L., Nicholson, J., Robertson, A. and Monigatti, S. (2008) *Building Safer Communities: An Evaluation of the Enhanced Policing Plan in the Shettleston, Baillieston and Greater Easterhouse Areas of Glasgow*. Glasgow: Glasgow Caledonian University.

Goodey, J. (2005) *Victims and Victimology: Research, Policy and Practice*. London: Pearson, Longman.

Grover, C. (2008) *Crime and Inequality*. Cullompton: Willan Publishing.

Hale, C. (1999) 'The labour market and post-war crime trends in England and Wales', in P. Carlen and R. Morgan (eds), *Crime Unlimited: Questions for the 21st Century*. London: Macmillan.

Hale, C. (2009) 'Economic marginalization, social exclusion and crime', in C. Hale, K. Hayward, A. Wahidin and E. Wincup (eds), *Criminology*, 2nd edn. Oxford: Oxford University Press.

Hanlon, P., Walsh, D. and Whyte, B. (2006) *Let Glasgow Flourish: A Comprehensive Report on Health and its Determinants in Glasgow and West Central Scotland*. Glasgow: Glasgow Centre for Population Health.

Hansen, K. and Machin, S. (2003) 'Spatial crime patterns and the introduction of the UK minimum wage', *Oxford Bulletin of Economics and Statistics*, 64: 677–97.

Hobbs, D. (2002) 'The firm: organizational logic and criminal culture on a shifting terrain', *British Journal of Criminology*, 42 (1): 549–60.

Hope, T. (2001) 'Crime victimisation and inequality in risk society', in R. Matthews and J. Pitts (eds), *Crime, Disorder and Community Safety: A New Agenda?* London: Routledge, pp. 193–218.

Houchin, R. (2005) *Social Exclusion and Imprisonment in Scotland*. Glasgow: Glasgow Caledonian University.

Jeffrey, R. (2002a) *Glasgow's Hard Men*. Edinburgh: Black & White Publishing.

Jeffrey, R. (2002b) *Gangs of Glasgow*. Edinburgh: Black & White Publishing.

Jeffrey, R. (2006) *Crimes Past: Glasgow's Crimes of the Century*. Edinburgh: Black & White Publishing.

Karstedt, S. and Farrall, S. (2006) 'The moral economy of everyday crime: markets, consumers and citizens', *British Journal of Criminology*, 46 (6): 1011–36.

Kelbie, P. (2003) 'Glasgow is Britain's murder capital as knife crime spirals', *The Independent*, 29 November.

Kenway, P., MacInnes, T. and Palmer, G. (2008) *Monitoring Poverty and Social Exclusion in Scotland 2008*. York: Joseph Rowntree Foundation/New Policy Institute.

Law, A. and Mooney, G. (2006) '"We've never had it so good": the problem of the working class in the devolved Scotland', *Critical Social Policy*, 26 (3): 523–42.

Law, A. and Mooney, G. (2010) 'Financialisation and proletarianisation: changing landscapes of neoliberal Scotland', in N. Davidson, P. McCafferty and D. Miller (eds), *Neoliberal Scotland*. Newcastle: Cambridge Scholars Publishing, pp. 137–59.

Lea, J. and Young, J. (1993) *What Is to Be Done about Law and Order?*, 2nd edn. London: Pluto Press.

Levi, M. (1989) 'Suite justice: sentencing for fraud', *Criminal Law Review*, 420–34.

Levitas, R. (2005) *The Inclusive Society*, 2nd edn. London: Palgrave.

Lister, R. (2004) *Poverty*. Cambridge: Polity Press.

McArthur, A. and Long, H. K. (1984) *No Mean City*. London: Corgi.

MacDonald, S. (2008) 'Glasgow is youth murder capital', *Sunday Times*, 26 October.

Machin, S. and Marie, O. (2004) *Crime and Benefit Cuts*. Paper presented to the Annual Conference of the Royal Economic Society, Swansea, April (cited in Hale, 2009, op. cit.).

Machin, S. and Meghir, C. (2003) 'Crime and economic incentives', *Journal of Human Resources*, 39: 958–79.

McKay, R. (2006) *Murder Capital: Life and Death on the Streets of Glasgow*. Edinburgh: Black & White Publishing.

McKendrick, J., Mooney, G., Kelly, P. and Dickie, J. (eds) (2007) *Poverty in Scotland 2007*. London: CPAG.

MacKinnon, J. (1921) *The Social and Industrial History of Scotland*. London: Longmans, Green & Co.

Maguire, M. (1997) 'Crime data and statistics', in M. Maguire, R. Morgan and R. Reiner (eds), *The Oxford Handbook of Criminology*, 4th edn. Oxford: Clarendon Press.

Martin, L. (2004) 'Murder capital paints itself the wrong shade of black', *The Observer*, 11 April.

Matza, D. (1964) *Delinquency and Drift*. New York: Wiley.

Merton, R. K. (1938) 'Social structure and anomie', *American Sociological Review*, 3: 672–82.

Mooney, G. (1998) 'Remoralising the poor? Gender, class and philanthropy in Victoria Britain', in G. Lewis (ed.), *Constructing Nation: Framing Welfare*. Routledge, pp. 49–91.

Mooney, G. (2008) '"Problem" populations, "problem" places', in J. Newman and N. Yeates (eds), *Social Justice: Welfare Crime and Society*. Open University Press, pp. 97–128.

Mooney, G. (2009) 'The "Broken Society" election: class hatred and the politics of poverty and place in Glasgow East', *Social Policy and Society*, 3 (4): 1–14.

Mooney, G., Morelli, C. and Seaman, P. (2009) 'The question of economic growth and inequality in contemporary Scotland', *Scottish Affairs*, 67: 92–109.

Mooney, G. and Neal, S. (2010) '"Welfare worries": mapping the directions of welfare futures in the contemporary UK', *Research, Policy and Planning*, 27 (3): 141–50.

Morelli, C. and Seaman, P. (2007) 'Devolution and inequality: a failure to create a community of equals?', *Transactions of the Institute of British Geographers*, 32: 523–38.

Morelli, C. and Seaman, P. (2009) 'Devolution and entrenched household poverty: Is Scotland less mobile?', *Social Policy and Society*, 3 (4): 367–77.

Morris, L. (1994) *Dangerous Classes*. London: Routledge.

Muncie, J., Talbot, D. and Walters, R. (eds) (2010) *Crime: Local and Global*. Cullompton: Willan Publishing.

Murray, C. (1996) 'The underclass', in J. Muncie, E. McLaughlin and M. Langan (eds), *Criminological Perspectives*. London: Sage.

Patrick, J. (1973) *A Glasgow Gang Observed*. London: Eyre Methuen.

Peev, G. (2008) 'Teenage gang plague "six times worse in Glasgow than London"', *The Scotsman*, 5 February.

Quinn, P. (2003) 'Review of the Ferris Conspiracy', *Scottish Journal of Criminal Justice Studies*, 9: 100–3.

Robertson, G. (2007) *Gangs of Dundee*. Edinburgh: Luath Press.

Scott, G. and Mooney, G. (2009) 'Poverty and social justice in the devolved Scotland: neoliberalism meets social democracy?', *Social Policy and Society*, 3 (4) 379–89.

Scottish Affairs (2009) Special Themed Section on Poverty in Scotland, *Scottish Affairs*, 67, Spring.

Scottish Consortium on Crime and Criminal Justice (SCCCJ) (2000) *Rethinking Criminal Justice in Scotland*. Edinburgh: SCCCJ.

Scottish Government (2007a) *Government Economic Strategy*. Edinburgh: Scottish Government.

Scottish Government (2007b) *Homicide in Scotland, 2006-07*. Edinburgh: Scottish Government.

Scottish Government (2008) *Taking Forward the Government Economic Strategy: Discussion Paper on Tackling Poverty, Inequality and Deprivation in Scotland*. Edinburgh: Scottish Government.

Scottish Government (2009a) *2008/09 Scottish Crime and Justice Survey: First Findings*. (web publication only).

Scottish Government (2009b) *Scotland's People Annual Report: Results from 2007/2008 Scottish Household Survey*. (web publication only).

Scottish Government (2009c) *Scottish Neighbourhood Statistics*. Database at http://www.sns.gov.uk/Reports/ReportHome.aspx) (accessed 11November 2009).

Scottish Government (2009d) *SIMD Local Authority Text Summaries Glasgow City*. http://www.scotland.gov.uk/Topics/Statistics/SIMD/LATextGlaCit (accessed 11 November 2009).

Scottish Government (2009e) *Analysis of SIMD Against Other Indicators*. http://www.scotland.gov.uk/Topics/Statistics/SIMD/IndicatorsPaper (accessed 11 November 2009).

Scottish Government (2009f) *Scottish Household Survey*. Available online at: http://www.scotland.gov.uk.

Scottish Neighbourhood Statistics (2008) *Area Profile Report for Local Authority: Inverclyde*. Edinburgh: Scottish Government, at http://www.sns.gov.uk (accessed 16 March 2009).

Smith, R. (2004) 'Rural rogues: a case story on the "smokies" trade", *International Journal of Entrepreneurial Behaviour and Research*, 10 (4) 277–94.

Smith, R. (2009) 'A Case Study on "Illegal Pluriactivity" in the Farming Community'. Unpublished paper.

Sweeney, C. (2009) 'Glasgow's gang rule imprisons young on their own streets', *The Times*, 3 August.

Tombs, J. (2000) *Youth, Crime and Justice*. Edinburgh: Scottish Consortium for Crime and Criminal Justice.

Veit-Wilson, J. (1998) *Setting Adequacy Standards*. Bristol: Policy Press.

Wacquant, L. (2008) *Urban Outcasts*. Cambridge: Polity Press.

Wacquant, L. (2009) *Punishing the Poor*. Durham, NC: Duke University Press.

Waterhouse, L., McGhee, J. and Loucks, N. (2004) 'Disentangling offenders and non-offenders in the Scottish Children's Hearings: a clear divide?', *Howard Journal of Criminal Justice*, May, pp. 164–79.

Wilkinson, R. G. (2005) *The Impact of Inequality*. London: Routledge.

Wilkinson, R. G. and Pickett, K. (2009) *The Spirit Level*. London: Allen Lane.

Young, J. (1999) *The Exclusive Society: Social Exclusion, Crime and Difference in Late Modernity*. London: Sage.

Young, J. (2007) *The Vertigo of Late Modernity*. London: Sage.

Chapter 3

Urban 'disorders', 'problem places' and criminal justice in Scotland

Alex Law, Gerry Mooney and Gesa Helms

Introduction

As Chapter 1 highlights, the city has become something of a geographical cliché in narratives of crime and disorder in Scotland. Books, articles, films, TV documentaries, dramas, soap operas (together with a vast array of websites), present urban life as the staple location for tales of criminality, disorder and danger, even if these are sometimes too long-standing a staple source for many a comic. Typically these are the streets, pubs and public spaces – the 'problem places' – of urban Scotland. Here gangs, violence and disorderly behaviour lie in wait round every corner. This is the familiar fare from Rankin or Welsh's Edinburgh, MacBride's Aberdeen, Denise Mina or Taggart's Glasgow, to Chris Longmuir's debut crime novel *Dead Wood* set against 'grim Dundee', as well as the 'true crime' genre, insider accounts of street gangs and football hooligans, and biographies of police officers or urban Scotland's most notorious criminals. Dangerous neighbourhoods are also prominently represented by a burgeoning website culture dedicated to condemning or celebrating certain neighbourhoods as pathologically gang-ridden and disorderly. While some non- or semi-urban areas feature, 'problem places' are overwhelmingly pictured as distinctively urban, typically council or social housing estates, and inner urban areas, such as the East End of Glasgow.

Urban conditions form the often implicit backdrop for more substantive areas of criminal justice covered by other chapters in the present volume. It is precisely this 'taken for granted' aspect of the city in routine assumptions about a supposedly criminogenic urban (dis)order that this chapter seeks to challenge through a closer understanding of the relationship between the Scottish city and narratives about criminality. The reverse side of a criminogenic urban ecology is the relative absence of narratives of 'rural crime and disorder' (see Walters, this volume). A spatial binary operates to reinforce the idea of urban criminality and disorder in opposition to rural lawfulness and tranquillity. Crime seems to inhere in the very ecology of 'the urban' in contrast to rural areas, as if produced by something lurking deep in the nature of the dense built environment and concentrated populations. A similarly ideological approach to urban ecology has underscored decades of town planning in Scotland. Not a few politicians and planners anticipated that crime, deviance and delinquency of Scotland's old inner-city slums could be controlled through 'thinning out' and dispersing urban populations through slum clearance and the building of peripheral sub-urban housing schemes though such concerns also coexisted alongside more welfarist sentiments to provide better housing. That such planning policies displaced rather than resolved social phenomena such as gang culture, violence, vandalism and substance misuse quickly became apparent. This rather mixed planning legacy in Scotland should be a cause for pause in the constant chase after environmental remedies for social problems resulting from long-term economic upheaval and social dislocation.

An ecological explanation of delinquency shifts the focus of analysis away from the crimes of the powerful such as financial crimes, tax evasion, high-level corruption, criminal warfare and corporate crime (see Croall and Ross, this volume). The relationship between crime or antisocial behaviour and the city takes on a rather different hue if the focus is on the role of 'the City', rather than 'the city', as evident in the antisocial consequences of financial scandals and economic crises. In this context disadvantaged neighbourhoods are further impoverished by the diffuse impacts of tax evasion and corruption and through government support for those who are already privileged (Croall 2009). Urban elites are able to shape the discourse of community safety in city regeneration strategies through the prism of commercial priorities (Coleman 2004; Coleman *et al.* 2005). Also neatly glossed over in much of the commentary is the relationship between leisure and consumer-driven city centre regeneration, especially the spatial concentration of pubs and clubs servicing the nightlife economy, and alcohol-related social problems in public spaces (Crawford and Flint 2009; Talbot 2007). Alcohol retail in Glasgow correlates weakly with areas of deprivation, suggesting societal-wide use (and misuse) of alcohol consumption (Ellaway *et al.* 2010). An alcohol-crime paradox emerges here: as one part of urban governance promotes consumer-led economic regeneration, another part manages its socially destructive consequences. For example, Dundee City Council's Antisocial Behaviour Team is collaborating with NHS Tayside to protect health workers in the Accident and Emergency department at Ninewells Hospital from being abused, assaulted or disrupted by alcohol-fuelled patients and visitors, some of whom have been drinking heavily elsewhere in the city as participants in the 'night-time economy' (Kerr 2009).

Because of the relative neglect of socio-spatial dynamics, criminology in Scotland often seems 'space-less'. Its almost constant and generally taken-for-granted urban referent to the Central Belt appears inexplicable. In this chapter we attempt to redress this omission by resituating Scotland's cities in ideological narratives of crime and disorder, in policy responses, and in the governance of crime more generally. More than two out of three people in Scotland live in an 'urban' environment, with another 12 per cent in small towns (Scottish Government 2003). We should not be surprised, then, that recorded crime is strongly correlated with where most people live. However, ideological representations of urban disorder, crime and violence do not apply uniformly across urban Scotland. Particular places are singled out as symbolic locales of disorder. Historically, Glasgow has been labelled as particularly dangerous and brutal, notwithstanding three decades of public relations exercises to lose its 'no mean city' image. A range of smaller, ex-industrial towns also figure prominently in popular and media narratives of crime and disorder. On 13 September 2009, for example, a full-page article 'Crime Scene' in *The Sunday Times* (Scotland) pinpointed the 'hot spots' of crime in Scotland between April 2007 and March 2009 (Macaskill and Belgutay 2009). As might be expected, Scotland's larger cities figure prominently, as do ex-manufacturing towns such as Paisley, Kilmarnock and Hamilton and the main towns of Inverclyde (see this volume, Chapter 2). However, smaller towns in otherwise rural areas also feature, including Dumfries, Elgin, Stranraer and Peterhead. Similarly, when BBC's *Panorama* website invited viewers to identify 'no go' areas across Britain by answering the fully loaded question: 'Do you feel terrorised by yobs, abandoned by the authorities and trapped in your home?' (BBC 2006), the areas identified by respondents as dangerous included towns such as Aberfeldy, Inverkeithing, Largs, Linlithgow and Musselburgh, as well as smaller towns and villages across Scotland. While such journalistic coverage can hardly be described as objective, nonetheless it does highlight that fear of crime and disorder extends well beyond urban areas, and contributes to popular concerns that disorders are now the staple of everyday life across the country.

Statistics show that the geography of crime and victimisation mirrors the geography of multiple deprivation (see discussion in Chapter 2, this volume). Conversely a 'near absolute correlation' exists between local rates of imprisonment in Scotland and urban deprivation (Houchin 2005; see also Chapter 12, this volume). Every year, around one in nine 23-year-old men from Scotland's most deprived communities will spend time in jail. A grotesquely disproportionate rate of imprisonment is simply one of the lifecycle risks for men living in deprived urban areas, alongside poverty, unemployment, low educational attainment and reduced life expectancy through ill health, accident and suicide. While prisoners come from impoverished areas across Scotland, Glasgow has the most pronounced relationship between deprivation and imprisonment. Half of all Scottish prisoners in 2003 had home addresses in Glasgow, typically concentrated in the most deprived postcodes (see Table 3.1).

More recent data shows that in June 2008 Glasgow's imprisonment rate (both men and women (see also Chapter 5, this volume)) was by far the highest in Scotland at 337 (per 100,000), followed by other former industrial west of Scotland areas such as Inverclyde (246) and contrasting with more affluent cities such as Edinburgh (156) and rural areas such as the Highlands (109) (Scottish Government 2009b).

Table 3.1 Urban deprivation and prisoners

Cities/districts	% of prisoners from most deprived areas
Glasgow	59
West Dumbartonshire	44
Renfrewshire	38
Edinburgh	34
Dundee	32
Inverclyde	30
Aberdeen	20

Adapted from Houchin (2005: 37).

Given the multiple connections between crime and the city, this chapter is necessarily restricted to a few key aspects. First, we situate more recent concerns within a much longer ideological tradition of treating urban poverty and criminality as virtually synonymous. This has been given a fresh impetus with neoliberal urban governance and city 'regeneration' strategies. Alongside processes of gentrification and the growing privatisation of urban space, insistent claims are made that urban disorders have to be tackled to make Scotland a safer place, especially to attract highly mobile inward investment (see Glaeser 2005). There is a strong emphasis in this chapter, therefore, on the linkages between crime and space/place in neoliberal urban governance. Second, we highlight informal strategies for securing potentially 'problem places', exemplified by the semi-official policing of public spaces by 'city centre representatives'. Third, we then examine media and policy representations of the 'problem council scheme', supposedly populated by disorderly and unruly people, above all the Scottish folk devil figure of 'the ned'. Ideological discourses about 'neds', we argue, are merely the other side of neoliberal gentrification and controlled consumption, that is regulated and standardised consumption. In sum, the chapter points towards a wider neoliberal punitivism in Scotland in a thorny entanglement of criminal justice, welfare reform and urban policy.

An ecology of urban 'disorder'?

Criminological interest in the relationship between crime and the city is hardly new (see Macek 2006; Mooney and Talbot 2010; Pile *et al.* 1999). The idea that morally suspect and politically dangerous lower classes festered in the bowels of the nineteenth-century city was a particular source of anxiety for the Victorian middle and upper classes (Wilson 2007). A long line of social scientists regarded the Scottish city as a social, political and moral problem of the first order. Such concerns stretch back to Frederick Engels, who reported the findings of Poor Law research in the 1840s on the foetid state of working-class districts in Glasgow and Edinburgh (Engels 2009). These represented some of the very worst slums in urban Europe, making it impossible to maintain 'health, morals and common decency' according to an 1842 Parliamentary Report. Sixty years later, Patrick Geddes tried to redress urban squalor and its effect on morality in Scotland by the use of civic surveys and practical conservation projects in Edinburgh's old town (see Law 2005). In the 1920s and 1930s, Geddes's urban ecology was given a scientific gloss by the Chicago School of Sociology, which was to profoundly influence both twentieth-century town planning movements and thinking about the causes of crime. Particular areas of the city – what Burgess (1967) called 'zones in transition' – were so fast-changing and transient that crime and deviancy readily took hold and became dominant social norms.

While we can identify important shifts in the assumed relationship between crime and the city, there are also important continuities in the identification of particular places, populations and behaviours as contributing to a generalised feeling of urban disorder. Since the mid-1990s the punitive regulation of urban space in the UK has been made a major policy priority, echoing in some respects nineteenth-century concerns about urban disorders (see Imrie and Raco 2003). However, this has taken on a new potency in the early twenty-first century:

> The interlinking of 'crime' and the 'city' is not a new concern, yet a renewed emphasis on the connections between these fields of public administration and governance has developed to the point where commonsense understandings of how to deal with the renewal of deprived areas, the security of iconic spaces, and broader city economies have become almost synonymous with an agenda of law and order, anti-social behaviour, and incivility. (Atkinson and Helms 2007: 2)

These concerns often revolve around ideas of community safety, involving official efforts to reverse a perceived decline in urban civility, promote respect and, where required, impose order (Cummings 1999). The target of community safety became identified under the catch-all expression 'antisocial behaviour' (ASB). Tackling ASB was elevated by the Blair government as a policy priority alongside countering terrorism, impacting not only on criminal justice but also on urban policy, housing policies and related areas of social welfare policy. Here again the city has a special role to play as the principal locale which nurtures and induces ASB. Addressing fears of crime and ASB is now regarded as essential in order to remake the city by securing new developments in housing, retail and leisure. Relatedly, middle-class colonisation of former working-class areas has become an established feature of the urban landscape in Scotland. Gentrification of an area through mixed-tenancy social engineering is seen by local elites as an effective way to regulate and civilise populations defined as particularly problematic (Uitermark *et al.* 2007). In this sense, then, urban policy not only gentrifies space, but also attempts to gentrify 'problem' subjects. Crime is to be 'designed out' and 'undesirables' forced out or tightly regulated in public spaces like shopping centres and pedestrianised streets. In this way, inward investment and consumers may be enticed to occupy ordered spaces as preferred subjects. Public space becomes de facto privatised space for city retail, leisure and business centres, a process further enabled by new techniques of surveillance, including the proliferation of CCTV, new forms of policing and a wider securitisation of urban spaces.

While the notion of urban 'disorder' is itself highly ambiguous and contested (see Cochrane 2007; Mooney 1999), definitions of urban 'disorder' have moved from physical signs of neglect to include a variety of 'problem populations' (Mooney 2008). Discourses surrounding ASB are replete with ecological narratives that equate physical decay with 'problem' behaviour. But the limits to physical solutions to endemic urban alienation were illustrated graphically by the demolition of the Avonspark Street development in Springburn, Glasgow only eight years after an award-winning £1 million renovation (Cummings 1999: 14). Degraded urban environments reinforce the criminalisation of welfare recipients. An austere and invasive regulation of unemployment and sickness/disability-related benefits deepens neoliberal policy practices, reinforces social inequalities and entrenches disciplinary mechanisms. Social welfare and criminal justice are increasingly mixed up together in a stale brew of mutually reinforcing practices that construct the urban poor as suspect subjects. Suspect populations are required to actively demonstrate compliance with a new array of responsibilities. A wide range of training and welfare-to-work disciplines take on precisely those kinds of tasks deemed essential to creating 'greener, safer, cleaner' urban spaces: notably, environmental maintenance, cleansing, recycling and wardening initiatives.

A further instance of the regulation of the urban suspect subject is in the governance of social housing. The residualisation of council housing during much of the past three decades has led to the spatial concentration of some of the most disadvantaged and economically marginalised sections of Scotland's population. As part of multi-agency intervention, social housing management has become an instrument for tackling ASB, what has been termed 'policing through social housing' (see Flint and Pawson 2009). Since the early 2000s, much of Scotland's council housing has been transferred to a range of other 'social landlords' (Daly *et al.* 2005; Kintrea 2006). As a key element of a set of broader political changes, there is increasing concern with ASB and other problematic behaviours in a revival of the loaded terminology popular in the 1960s and 1970s that spoke of problem tenants, families and communities (Damer 1989; Flint 2006a). But while housing agency officers perceive that ASB has improved or stabilised in Scotland, this was not a view widely shared by residents (Casey and Flint 2008). While it is the case that some behaviours do pose problems for neighbour relations, crime consciousness is amplified by highly visible police interventions to deal with low-level disputes and nuisance youth who crowd together in full view of the street.

As city spaces are restructured to enable neoliberal forms of production and consumption in the service of competitive capital accumulation, such social punitivism pervades contemporary urban policy. Growing processes and patterns of segmentation, fragmentation, polarisation and heightened inequalities increase fears about 'other' people and 'other' places regarded as a threat to urban prosperity (Young 2007). 'Pro-social' behaviour, modelled after the productive consuming subject, therefore, needs to be enforced and reinforced against a seemingly constant threat of antisocial behaviour from suspect subjects.

Welfare reform meets policing in the Scottish city

In a number of Scottish cities, tackling ASB is increasingly part of 'the extended policing family' (Crawford 2003; see also Fyfe, Chapter 9, this volume). A wide range of agencies regulate city centres and other spaces of consumption (see Hayward 2004; Minton 2009). Security-conscious street and neighbourhood wardens, private security guards and city centre and shopping centre 'representatives' are supported by surveillance technologies such as CCTV. More than a decade ago, research commissioned by the Scottish Office established that CCTV not only does not reduce the fear of crime but that it counter-productively heightens crime consciousness and helps empty streets and public spaces (Waiton 2008: 151). Different kinds of suspect subjects are targeted: young people dressed in 'hoodies', 'aggressive beggars', homeless people, sex workers, drug takers and alcoholics. Efforts to promote city centres as safe places for consumers and passers-by are constantly placed in danger by 'undesirables'. This extends to youth cults such as Goths, whose highly visible presence in city centres came to be regarded as a particular 'nuisance' (see Horne 2007) and other 'odd' looking people whose presence is deemed a threat to economic prosperity. As city centres become increasingly 'managed' by a variety of public and private agencies, tackling retail crime and securing the 'night-time economy', 'problem' groups are monitored and moved. Under Orwellian labels such as 'Shopwatch', 'Pubwatch' or 'CarPark Watch' everyone is invited to 'watch' for suspect subjects (Cummings 1997).

In a general context of employment insecurity and work intensification, promoting city centres as private islands of economic growth and vitality is a potent symbol of urban regeneration. For example, as an older industrial city that has undergone profound post-industrial change, re-branded as a modernised centre of consumption and leisure, Glasgow markets itself as the UK's second largest shopping 'destination' and with a thriving night-time economy. Public safety in highly visible spaces of the city centre is therefore an important tool in the fragile business of place marketing. Glasgow pioneered the presence of highly visible – thanks to their bright red uniforms – 'city centre representatives' (CCRs). Other Scottish cities and not a few towns have followed suit with similar CCR schemes. Of course such wardens play a role in helping those who become ill, disoriented or are just plain 'lost', and they deal with litter and other issues that surface on busy streets – so we should not ignore their 'welfare' and helpfulness role. However, through work by one of us (see Helms 2007), it is evident that wardens act as informal street managers to enforce 'civilised behaviours'. They are supported by local by-laws and other criminal justice legislation, ranging from the controls on drinking alcohol in unregulated public spaces to moving on vagrants and illegal vendors and dispersing groups of young people. While a distinction between CCRs and other kinds of wardens is not always straightforward, they do differ in important respects from Police Community Support Officers in England and Wales in that community wardens in Scotland have no police powers (Donnelly 2008).

Helms further notes that such schemes are often part of an intermediate labour market training programme. Unskilled, long-term unemployed are helped into paid employment through job opportunities and training offered by wardens' programmes alongside other low-paid work in the security industries as car park attendants, bouncers and security guards. Street-level security helps support other social policy goals such as welfare to work and labour market activation strategies. A zero tolerance approach to suspect subjects allows some to escape from its gaze to become its street-level enforcers.

'Broken' places and 'problem populations' in the Scottish city

Large-scale post-industrial economic restructuring and the impact of changes to the built environment have led to competing claims about the nature of such shifts. In Dundee, Glasgow, Greenock and elsewhere, such changes are heralded by local planners and politicians to proclaim the 'success' of urban renewal. We do not wish to get involved in the very long and ongoing debate around the validity of such claims. The important point here is a wider neoliberalisation of the urban landscape. By this we mean that the city is secured for entrepreneurial activities, leisure, retail and other forms of consumption, and also supplies a stream of well-adapted labour power. Punitive workfare schemes pave the way for low-paid, flexible employment. Degraded work conditions are closely related to processes of territorial stigmatisation in what Löic Wacquant has termed 'advanced marginality' (Wacquant 2008, 2009). The advanced marginality of particular locales and populations is constructed as impeding economic growth and prosperity. Such marginalised localities are found across urban Scotland in narratives that speak primarily of disorder, delinquency, deprivation and decline (see Allen 2008; Wacquant 2008).

Of course, people in marginalised localities actually experience severe personal, economic and social hardships. It is, however, but a short step from understanding problems in an area to presenting them as problems of an area or its population. Throughout Scotland, areas of multiple deprivation are firmly in the sights of an increasingly punitive welfarism. The overwhelming emphasis of recent welfare reforms is on increasing conditionality and on the responsibilities of individuals to take up any work offered (DWP 2008a, 2008b). With a disproportionate incidence of unemployment and sickness benefit, Glasgow has been selected as one of five UK cities for a three year pilot plan starting in March 2011 to force those on sickness benefits into work (Peev 2008).

'Shettleston man' and the 'broken society' of Glasgow East!

Advanced marginality is reiteratively asserted as somehow inhering in the suspect subjects themselves. This trope resurfaced with particular venom in hyperbolic representations of poverty during the UK media frenzy over the Glasgow East by-election in July 2008 (Mooney 2009). Glasgow East was portrayed by the national media as symptomatic of a 'broken society' and served as a convenient backdrop for UK-wide narratives about poverty and welfare reform. In no small part this was prompted by the publication of the 'Breakthrough Glasgow' report by the Conservative's Centre for Social Justice (CSJ) policy unit in 2008. In this report Glasgow East is where a 'dependency culture' has spawned a wide range of social problems, including disorder and family and community dysfunction:

> You only need to look at the social housing system that successive governments have pursued to realise why, on so many of these estates, lone parenting, worklessness, failed education and addiction are an acceptable way of life. Over the years we have put all the most broken families, with myriad problems, on the same estates. Too few of the children ever see a good role model: for the dysfunctional family life is the norm. (Smith 2008a; see also Smith 2008b; Centre for Social Justice 2007: 21; 2008: 7)

The key message here is the familiar right-wing refrain that state welfare is the problem because it creates 'perverse incentives' to languish in welfare dependency rather than pursue individual autonomy. Ill-health, unemployment and poverty are conceived as failures of individual responsibility. 'Worklessness' and welfare 'dependency' are pinpointed as the principal reasons for the multitude of social problems being experienced by the population of Glasgow East (Smith 2008a).

Simon Heffer (2008b) in the *Daily Telegraph* similarly comments that, 'In Glasgow, the weapon of mass destruction has been welfarism'. He describes Glasgow East as a 'hell-hole' serviced by 'epic amounts of public money'. Elsewhere *The Times* headlined an article 'Glasgow's Guantanamo':

> Shettleston, Barlanark, Garthamlock, Easterhouse, Parkhead ... communities that figure with monotonous regularity both on the charge sheet at Glasgow Sheriff Court and at the top of the lists of the most socially deprived wards in Britain. They might as well be called Guantanamo. For many thousands of welfare prisoners on sink estates, marooned by bad housing, violence, addiction, unemployment, ill health and shattered relationships, there is little chance of escape. (Reid 2008)

A new problematic welfare subject was identified, 'Shettleston Man', the personification of the urban deprivation–crime nexus. With the discovery of Shettleston Man, the discredited 'underclass' narrative took on a renewed salience to once again pathologise structural deprivation as amoral 'self-exclusion'. Inferior social housing in Glasgow East became a synonym for individual failure (see Johnstone and Mooney 2007; Watt 2008). Stigmatised as 'welfare ghettoes' (Nelson 2009) or 'a ghetto ringed by some of the saddest statistics in Britain' (Macintyre 2008), Glasgow East is overwhelmingly constructed as a homogenised site of misery, apathy and despair, a place redolent of the dangers of welfare 'failure', where the 'meta-humiliation' of poverty is physically inscribed (Young 2007: 76–7).

Council schemes as Scotland's internal-exotic other

Historically Glasgow has played the part of UK 'problem city', rivalled only perhaps in recent decades by Liverpool. Constituencies like Glasgow East epitomise an unreconstructed Glasgow, a national internal-exotic that needs to be forced to embrace successful urban regeneration and economic prosperity for Scotland as a whole. Large postwar housing schemes are envisaged as both a problematic form of housing tenure and a breeding ground of social problems (see Card 2006; Flint 2006b; Flint and Pawson 2009; Hanley 2007; Johnstone and Mooney 2007). Council housing had a long history of negative associations. It became a residualised form of tenure of last resort due to the combined effects of right to buy policies, credit excess and an over-inflated property bubble. Urban renaissance narratives see in social housing the survival of an archaic, maladjusted internal-exotic 'other' in Scottish society today.

Council and social housing cater for the most vulnerable social groups, often defined in some way as 'problematic', characterised by difficult behaviours, assorted forms of social disorganisation and, of course, 'worklessness'. Recently, sweeping claims about people who live in social housing accompanied episodes such as the murder of Baby P in a council flat in London in 2007 and the Shannon Matthews kidnapping in 2008 (see also Chapter 2, this volume). In Dundee the death of 23-month-old Brandon Muir in 2008 led to severe criticism of the city's child protection services amid media preoccupations with drug addiction, single parenting and social housing. More routinely, reports of families or neighbours 'from hell' and ASB are the staple of many national and local media reporting. As Scott and Parkey (1998) observe, ASB is principally underscored as a social housing issue. However, there is no evidence that social housing functions as a one-way causal mechanism in the production of ASB.

Together with other forms of intervention, social housing, long a tightly regulated space but arguably more so now, is becoming the strategic nub of ASB policies (Cummings 1999). Under New Labour social housing providers and even their tenants are increasingly expected to manage ASBs. As Flint and Pawson (2009: 430) note, 'social rented housing has always been a key vehicle for the imagining and delivery of government rationales'. Social landlords in Scotland now play a greater role than hitherto in regulating urban spaces, with a range of powers to obtain and use Anti-Social Behaviour Orders (ASBOs) and other means at their disposal to discipline troublesome tenants, and especially those 'neighbours from hell' who regularly feature in the popular press. A range of behaviours is considered problematic, from alcohol and drug misuse and violence within domestic premises through to disorders involving young people and noisy neighbours. In the 1990s Glasgow's Good Neighbour Charter led to legal writs being issued to 'families from hell' who didn't take turns to clean the close stairs (Cummings 1999). Many social landlords are proactive in the design of urban spaces, using CCTV and other forms of surveillance to ensure and enforce community safety. However, the activities of social landlords are not the only forms of regulation in deprived housing schemes.

As further action against ASB following a visit to the Dundee Family Intervention Project (FIP), in October 2009 then Prime Minister Gordon Brown promised to introduce FIPs across the UK to retrain 50,000 'chaotic families' at behaviour training centres: 'Family Intervention projects work,' he claimed. 'They change lives, they make our communities safer and they crack down on those who're going off the rails' (see Gentleman 2009). This followed a speech at the 2009 Labour Party Conference in which he drew a distinction between the 'hard working' majority and others:

> The decent hard-working majority feel the odds are stacked in favour of a minority, who will talk about their rights, but never accept their responsibilities … I stand with the people who are sick and tired of others playing by different rules or no rules at all. Most mums and dads do a great job – but there are those who let their kids run riot and I'm not prepared to accept it as simply part of life. Because there is also a way of intervening earlier to stop anti-social behaviour, slash welfare dependency and cut crime. Family intervention projects are a tough love, no nonsense approach with help for those who want to change and proper penalties for those who don't or won't.

Devised in 1996 by Dundee City Council's Social Work and Housing departments and NCH Action for Children, the FIP originally represented a multi-agency support programme for vulnerable families alongside a concern to address dysfunctional and problem behaviour (Parr and Nixon 2008). Unlike the Dundee model, however, UK-wide FIPs foreground the use of sanctions, regulation and surveillance by means such as Parenting Orders (though research has shown a reluctance on the part of many local authorities across Scotland to use such orders – see Walters and Woodward 2007), ASBOs or tenancy repossession, accompanied by pejorative media rhetoric about 'scum', 'neighbours from hell', 'troublemakers', 'yobs', 'nightmare neighbours' and so on, to be locked down in 'sin bins' (managed residential accommodation) (Garrett 2007; Nixon 2007; Parr and Nixon 2008: 168).

Material dilapidation and employment decline has led to the socio-spatial pathologisation of supposedly distinctive housing scheme cultures around criminality, transgression and welfare dependency (see Cook 2006: 43–6; Haylett 2003: 61–3). Now, after decades of neglect, 'remaking' social housing is a key focus for Scottish government intervention, from housing stock transfer to non-local authority housing landlords, community regeneration, community safety initiatives and local economic development schemes. Importantly, however, remaking council schemes is also about remaking council scheme subjects, above all through combating ASB, crime and 'dependency cultures'.

The place of 'neds' in the scheme of things

Problematic working-class youth cultures are seen as virtually indistinguishable from 'problem places' in Scottish cities. As such the 'problem youth/problem places' couplet resonates with many of the key organising principles of the 'New Urbanism' (see Smith 2002) with its focus on regulated spaces of economic growth, consumption and leisure. In the context of urban Scotland, disorderly youth are epitomised by 'ned culture' (see also Chapter 4, this volume). Although the figure of 'the ned' (a contested term with ambiguous meanings – see Law and Mooney 2006) has been around a long time in Scottish popular culture, policy-making and policing, in recent decades it has been placed at the epicentre of ASB policy formation in Scotland, as well as contributing to a mini-publishing industry of books and websites devoted to 'neds', 'nedworld' and youth gangs.

Concern about neds is almost synonymous with recurring disquiet about 'masculinity out of control', gangs and 'knife culture' in Scotland's towns and cities. In January 2008, for example, the Channel 4's Dispatches documentary *Why Kids Kill* compared public fears over youth gangs in London to Glasgow, a city with a long history of territorially based youth gangs (see also Chapter 2, this volume). In 2006 it was claimed that there were 170 teenage gangs in Glasgow, the same number as in London, a city six times the size (Kelbie 2006). Ned subcultures are discursively constructed as inherently antisocial and a threat to new urban spaces of consumption and leisure. Symbolic of social housing scheme culture – the presumed location of 'ned behaviour/culture' – neds and social housing neighbourhoods excite and disgust in equal measure as the exotic other to Scotland's new urban consumerism.

At the second Scottish Parliament Elections in May 2003, the Labour Party signalled its desire to combat crime and 'disorder' in urban Scotland. In signing the subsequent Partnership Agreement, the government coalition partners, Scottish New Labour and the Scottish Liberal Democrats, wanted to be seen to be responding to 'the problem of crime', especially 'antisocial behaviour' among urban and semi-urban youth. As the then Communities Minister, and ex-community worker, Margaret Curran put it:

> We've been shaken by the scale of what we've seen in our own constituencies. I didn't think it was as severe and persistent as it is. We've changed the debate into saying that this is an issue, it's happening in certain communities and we've ignored it for 20 to 30 years. (Margaret Curran, quoted in Fraser 2004)

Such sentiments heralded a much tougher approach to problematic urban youth. In 1993 Operation Blade involved a nightclub curfew in Glasgow city centre and the stop and search of thousands of young people. Although branded a failure and opposed by the city licensing board and nightclub operators association, it paved the way for CityWatch, now with support from city centre businesses (Cummings 1997). Under media reports that one in three young men carried knives, in March 2000 Strathclyde police carried out 20,500 weapons searches only to uncover one knife for every 40 searches (Waiton 2008: 86). Pilot Fast Track hearings for youth offenders and a Pilot Youth Court scheme were launched at Hamilton and Airdrie Sheriff Courts (Piacentini and Walters 2006). In 2004 the Anti-Social Behaviour etc. (Scotland) Act included the extension of ASBOs to include 12–16 year olds, police powers to disperse groups, the provision of electronic tagging to under 16s, Community Reparation Orders (for those aged 12+) and Parenting Orders. Arguably the ASB Scotland Act was the 'flagship' policy of the Scottish Parliament's second term. Promising 'safer communities and safer streets' then First Minister Jack McConnell talked of the need to 'stop the rot', of 'gangs of youth running riot', of 'neighbours from hell' (http://www.scottishlabour.org.uk/manfestolaunch, accessed 10 May 2006). Attacking critics of the 2004 ASB Act and the Executive's general approach to criminal and youth justice, McConnell commented that:

> I remember the arguments that said that poverty, deprivation and unemployment caused crime. But today, in a Scotland of low unemployment and even lower youth unemployment, in a country where significant steps have been taken to reduce poverty and increase opportunity, I am increasingly convinced that the person who offends, and then offends repeatedly, chooses to do so. (McConnell 2003)

In a speech in 2006 Minister for Justice Cathy Jamieson reinforced this attack on 'woolly liberal intellectuals':

> We need to challenge anyone who tells us that antisocial behaviour is not a big concern in communities. And to those who still don't believe we need to go further, or want to only continue a woolly liberal intellectual debate on this, let me start with a very clear message. Look through the eyes of the people who see the graffiti and vandalism on their streets and in their closes. (Jamieson 2006)

Amid the political rhetoric about 'plagues of group disorder', to quote Minister Curran in *The Scotsman* (18 June 2004), we can clearly identify links with Wilson and Kelling's 'broken windows' thesis (Wilson and Kelling 1982). In this argument controlling minor crime and tackling antisocial behaviour are seen as pivotal elements in area regeneration strategies and 'social inclusion' policies – policies which are overwhelmingly constructed around paid employment. With the arrival of a minority SNP government in 2007, there are some, albeit limited and partial, signs of a shift in thinking with a new emphasis on diversionary activities for young people as part of a 'Cashback for Communities' programme, funded through cash seized from organised criminals. There remains, however, a concern to tackle antisocial behaviour though this represents some departure from the rhetoric deployed by the New Labour coalition governments prior to 2007.

While not exclusively an 'urban phenomenon', dominant representation of ned subcultures calls upon images of a disorderedly urban landscape. Ned culture is associated with the practices of disaffected and alienated working-class youth in 'the schemes'. Indeed, in Dundee dispossessed youth are fashioned as 'schemies'. This imaging of ned culture feeds the symbolic, cultural and policy construction of council schemes as criminogenic environments, inscribed with worklessness, confidence and aspirational deficits and other difficult socio-behavioural traits. Curfews and searches are much less to do with serious criminal activity than responses to hyperbolic discourses about children out of control, especially at night (Waiton 2007). This pathologisation of youth is only the sharpest expression of urban cultures of dependency. It assumes a moralising view of 'normality' in which suspect subjects have no place and exist only as an 'abnormal' problem to be controlled or 'fixed'. In this regard ned culture is made to bear the trauma (and fascination) of middle-class revanchism in the new entrepreneurial, professional and creative classes in 'renaissance cities' such as Glasgow and Dundee.

Concluding comments

In this chapter we highlighted some of the overlapping ways in which criminal control, urban and welfare policies combine to promote punitive urban renewal. These are further entwined with narratives that portray certain practices, places and groups as 'other' to the story of successful urban prosperity and modernisation. In turn, this is linked with wider processes of economic restructuring and welfare reform. The regulation and containment of 'problematic' lifestyles and people are made central to a range of spatial policies, from housing management through to urban renewal programmes. Under such regulation, discipline and geography come to be interlinked. The impoverished working class is counterposed to an otherwise modern and prosperous Scottish city as suspect. Ideologies of irresponsibility, dysfunctionality and worklessness depict the poor as culturally impoverished, aspirationally deficient and individually defective: a pathological, amoral urbanism in contrast to the 'normal', moral urbanism of regulated consumption and production. Further, these manifestations of urban pathology are only extreme versions of a supposedly generalised crisis of confidence in Scotland (see Craig 2003).

'Risky' working-class lifestyles are frequently identified not only with particular people, but also through criminogenic thinking with particular places (Hancock 2007). Long a fixation of urban governance, a degraded urban ecology instructs criminal justice and policing in the contemporary Scottish city. Such thinking is thoroughly imbued with a moral geography of stigmatisation produced through elite ambitions to remoralise and reorder populations and places. Key here is to fix and identify those internal others in the city who are the problem, entrenching the binary division between 'us' and 'them'. This othering of suspect subjects, their symbolic misrecognition, is the axis upon which the regulation of urban space turns in Scotland today.

References

Allen, C. (2008) *Housing Market Renewal and Social Class*. London: Routledge.

Atkinson, R. and Helms, G. (eds) (2007) *Securing an Urban Renaissance: Crime, Community and British Urban Policy*. Bristol: Policy Press.

BBC (2006) *Panorama: No Go Britain*, 10 November. http://news.bbc.co.uk/1/hi/programmes/panorama/6058212.stm (accessed 20 September 2009).

Burgess, E. W. (1967 [1925]) 'The growth of the city: an introduction to a research project', in R.E. Park, E.W. Burgess and R.D. McKenzie (eds), *The City*. Chicago: University of Chicago Press, pp. 47–62.

Card, P. (2006) 'Governing tenants: from dreadful enclosures to dangerous places', in J. Flint (ed.), *Housing, Urban Governance and Anti-Social Behaviour: Perspectives, Policy and Practice*. Bristol: Policy Press, pp. 37–56.

Casey, R. and Flint, J. (2008) 'Governing through localism, contract and community: evidence from anti-social behaviour strategies in Scotland', in P. Squires (ed.), *ASBO Nation: The Criminalisation of Nuisance*. Bristol: Policy Press, pp. 103–16.

Centre for Social Justice (2007) *Breakthrough Britain Volume 2: Economic Dependency and Worklessness*. London: Centre for Social Justice.

Centre for Social Justice (2008) *Breakthrough Glasgow: Ending the Costs of Social Breakdown*. London: Centre for Social Justice.

Cochrane, A. (2007) *Understanding Urban Policy*. London: Sage.

Coleman, R. (2004) *Reclaiming the Streets: Surveillance, Social Control and the City*. Cullompton: Willan Publishing.

Coleman, R., Tombs, S. and Whyte, D. (2005) 'Capital, crime control and statecraft in the entrepreneurial city', *Urban Studies*, 42 (13): 2511–30.

Cook, D. (2006) *Criminal and Social Justice*. London: Sage.

Craig, C. (2003) *The Scots' Crisis of Confidence*. Edinburgh: Big Thinking.

Crawford, A. (2003) 'The pattern of policing in the UK: policing beyond the police', in T. Newburn (ed.), *The Handbook of Policing*. Cullompton: Willan Publishing, pp. 136–68.

Crawford, A. and Flint, J. (2009) 'Urban safety, anti-social behaviour and the night-time economy', *Criminology and Criminal Justice*, 9 (4): 403–13.

Croall, H. (2009) 'Community safety and economic crime', *Criminology and Criminal Justice*, 9 (2): 165–85.

Cummings, D. (1997) *Surveillance and the City*. Glasgow: Urban Research Group.

Cummings, D. (1999) *In Search of Sesame Street: Policing Civility for the Twenty-First Century*. Sheffield: Sheffield Hallam University Press.

Daly, G., Mooney, G., Poole, L. and Davis, H. (2005) 'Housing stock transfer in the UK: the contrasting experiences of two UK cities', *European Journal of Housing Policy*, 5 (3): 327–41.

Damer, S. (1989) *From Moorepark to 'Wine Alley': The Rise and Fall of a Glasgow Housing Scheme*. Edinburgh: Edinburgh University Press.

Department for Work and Pensions (2008a) *No One Written Off: Reforming Welfare to Reward Responsibility*. London: DWP.

Department for Work and Pensions (2008b) *Raising Expectations and Increasing Support: Reforming Welfare for the Future*. London: DWP.

Donnelly, D. (2008) 'Community wardens in Scotland: practitioners' views', *Howard Journal of Criminal Justice*, 47 (4): September: 371–82.

Ellaway, A., Macdonald, L., Forsyth, A. and Macintyre, S. (2010) 'The socio-spatial distribution of alcohol outlets in Glasgow city', *Health & Place*, 16 (1): 167–72.

Engels, F. (2009) *The Condition of the Working Class in England*. London: Penguin.

Flint, J. (2006a) *Housing, Urban Governance and Anti-Social Behaviour*. Bristol: Policy Press.

Flint, J. (2006b) 'Maintaining an arm's length? Housing, community governance and the management of "problematic" populations', *Housing Studies*, 21 (2): 171–86.

Flint, J. and Pawson, H. (2009) 'Social landlords and the regulation of conduct in urban spaces in the United Kingdom', *Criminology and Criminal Justice*, 9 (4): 415–35.

Fraser, D. (2004) 'Street fighting woman' (Profile of Communities Minister Margaret Curran), *Sunday Herald*, 22 February.

Garrett, P. (2007) '"Sinbin" solutions: the pioneer projects for "problem families" and the forgetfulness of social policy research', *Critical Social Policy*, 27 (2): 203–30.

Gentleman, A. (2009) 'How Gordon Brown plans to tackle Britain's anti-social behaviour problem', *The Observer*, 1 November.

Glaeser, R. (2005) 'Four challenges for Scotland's cities', in D. Coyle, W. Alexander and B. Ashcroft (eds), *New Wealth for Old Nations: Scotland's Economic Prospects*. Princeton, NJ: Princeton University Press, pp. 27–50.

Grover, C. (2008) *Crime and Inequality*, Cullompton: Willan Publishing.

Hancock, L. (2007) 'Is regeneration criminogenic?', in R. Atkinson and G. Helms (eds), *Securing an Urban Renaissance: Crime, Community and British Urban Policy*. Bristol: Policy Press, pp. 57–70.

Hanley, J. (2007) *Estates: An Intimate History*. London: Granta.

Harvey, D. (1997) 'The new urbanism and the communitarian trap', *Harvard Design Magazine*, Winter/Spring, pp. 1-3.

Haylett, C. (2003) 'Culture, class and urban policy: reconsidering equality', *Antipode*, 35 (1): 55–73.

Hayward, K. (2004) *City Limits: Crime, Consumer Culture and the Urban Experience*. London: Routledge.

Helms, G. (2007) 'Municipal policing meets the New Deal: the politics of a city centre warden project', *European Urban and Regional Studies*, 14 (4): 291–305.

Horne, M. (2007) 'Goma Goths banned – heaven knows they're miserable now', *Scotland on Sunday*, 9 December.

Houchin, R. (2005) *Social Exclusion and Imprisonment: A Report*. Glasgow: Glasgow Caledonian University.

Imrie, R. and Raco, M. (eds) (2003) *Urban Renaissance?* Bristol: Policy Press.

Jamieson, C. (2006) Speech to the Scottish Labour Party Conference, Aviemore, 25 February.

Johnstone, C. and Mooney, G. (2007) '"Problem" people, "problem" spaces? New Labour and council estates', in R. Atkinson and G. Helms (eds) *Securing an Urban Renaissance: Crime, Community and British Urban Policy*. Bristol: Policy Press, pp. 125–39.

Kelbie, P. (2006) 'The streets of Scotland: Britain's knife capital', *Independent on Sunday*, 4 June.

Kerr, D. (2009) 'A&E antisocial behaviour scheme', *Evening Telegraph*, 18 November.

Kintrea, K. (2006) 'Having it all? Housing reform under devolution', *Housing Studies*, 21 (2): 187–207.

Law, A. (2005) 'The ghost of Patrick Geddes', *Sociological Research Online*, 10 (2).

Law, A. and Mooney, G. (2006) *From the 'Underclass' to 'Neds': Continuity and Change in Class-Based Representations of Working-Class Youth*. British Society of Criminology 2006 Annual Conference, Glasgow, 5–7 July.

Macaskill, M. and Belgutay, J. (2009) 'Crime scene', *Sunday Times*, 13 September.

McConnell, J. (2003) *Respect, Responsibility and Rehabilitation in Modern Scotland*. Apex Lecture, Edinburgh, 16 September.

Macek, S. (2006) *Urban Nightmares: The Media, the right, and the Moral Panic Over the City*. Minneapolis, MN: University of Minnesota Press.

Macintyre, B. (2008) 'Inside Glasgow East, where Gordon Brown's a cursed name', *The Times*, 12 July.

Minton, A. (2009) *Ground Control*. London: Penguin.

Mooney, G. (1999) 'Urban "disorders"', in S. Pile, C. Brook and G. Mooney (eds), *Unruly Cities?* London: Routledge, pp. 53–102.

Mooney, G. (2008) '"Problem" populations, "problem" places', in J. Newman and N. Yeates (eds), *Social Justice: Welfare Crime and Society*. Maidenhead: Open University Press, pp. 97–128.

Mooney, G. (2009) 'The "broken society" election: class hatred and the politics of poverty and place in Glasgow East', *Social Policy and Society*, 3 (4): 1–14.

Mooney, G. and Neal, S. (eds) (2009) *Community: Welfare, Crime and Society*. Maidenhead: Open University Press.

Mooney, G. and Talbot, D. (2010) 'Global cities, segregation and transgression', in J. Muncie, D. Talbot and R. Walters (eds), *Crime: Local and Global*. Cullompton: Willan Publishing, pp. 37–70.

Muncie, J., Talbot, D. and Walters, R. (eds) (2010) *Crime: Local and Global*. Cullompton: Willan Publishing.

Nelson, F. (2009) 'The tragedy of welfare ghettoes', *The Spectator*, 6 February.

Newman, J. and Yeates, N. (eds) (2008) *Social Justice: Welfare, Crime and Society*. Maidenhead: Open University Press.

Nixon, J. (2007) 'Deconstructing "problem researchers" and "problem families": a rejoinder to Garrett', *Critical Social Policy*, 27 (4): 546–64.

Parr, S. and Nixon, J. (2008) 'Rationalising Family Intervention Projects', in P. Squires (ed.), *ASBO Nation: The Criminalisation of Nuisance*. Bristol: Policy Press, pp. 161–78.

Peev, G. (2008) 'Glasgow tests benefits "revolution" in drive to get thousands back to work', *The Scotsman*, 22 December.

Piacentini, L. and Walters, R. (2006) 'The politicization of youth crime in Scotland and the rise of the "Burberry Court"', *Youth Justice*, 6 (1): 43–59.

Pile, S., Brook, C. and Mooney, G. (eds) (1999) *Unruly Cities*. London: Routledge.

Reid, M. (2008) 'A political timebomb in Glasgow's Guantanamo', *The Times*, 3 July.

Scott, S. and Parkey, H. (1998) 'Myths and reality: anti-social behaviour in Scotland', *Housing Studies*, 13 (3): 325–45.

Scottish Government (2003) *Social Focus on Urban Rural Scotland*. Edinburgh: Scottish Government.

Scottish Government (2009a) *Scottish Indicators of Multiple Deprivation, General Report*. Edinburgh: Scottish Government.

Scottish Government (2009b) *Prison Statistics Scotland 2008–9*. Edinburgh: Scottish Government.

Smith, I. D. (2008a) 'Living and dying, on welfare in Glasgow East', *Daily Telegraph*, 13 July.

Smith, I. D. (2008b), 'Why talk alone will never end the misery I saw in Glasgow East', *Mail on Sunday*, 13 July.

Smith, N. (2002) 'New globalism, new urbanism: gentrification as a global urban strategy', *Antipode*, 34, 427–51.

Talbot, D. (2007) *Regulating the Night: Race, Culture and Exclusion in the Making of the Night-Time Economy*. Aldershot: Ashgate.

Uitermark, J., Duyvendak, J. and Kleinhans, R. (2007) 'Gentrification as a governmental strategy: social control and social cohesion in Hoogvliet, Rotterdam', *Environment and Planning A*, 39 (1): 125–41.

Wacquant, L. (2008) *Urban Outcasts*. Cambridge: Polity Press.

Wacquant, L. (2009) *Punishing the Poor*. Durham, NC: Duke University Press.

Waiton, S. (2007) *The Politics of Antisocial Behaviour: Amoral Panics*. London: Routledge.

Waiton, S. (2008) *Scared of the Kids? Curfews, Crime and the Regulation of Young People*. Dundee: Abertay University Press.

Walters, R. and Woodward, R. (2007) Punishing "poor parents": "respect", "responsibility" and Parenting Orders in Scotland', *Youth Justice*, 7 (1), 5–20.

Watt, P. (2008) '"Underclass" and "ordinary people" discourses: representing/re-presenting council tenants in a housing campaign', *Critical Discourse Studies*, 5 (4): 345–57.

Wilson, B. (2007) *Decency and Disorder: The Age of Cant 1789–1837*. London: Faber & Faber.

Wilson, J. Q. and Kelling, G. (1982) 'Broken windows', *Atlantic Monthly*, March, pp. 29–37.

Young, J. (2007) *The Vertigo of Late Modernity*. London: Sage.

Part 2

Issues in criminal and social justice

Chapter 4

Youth crime and justice in Scotland

Lesley McAra and Susan McVie

> Society is, we believe, seriously concerned to secure a more effective and discriminatory machinery for interventions for the avoidance and reduction of juvenile delinquency. (Kilbrandon Committee 1964)

Introduction

This quotation from the report of the Kilbrandon Committee which set up the existing system of juvenile justice in Scotland gives a flavour of the Scottish civic culture which has shaped Scotland's unique institutions and processes for dealing with young offenders (McAra 2008). It highlights a sense of common ownership of the problems posed by young offenders and a commitment to the development of effective practice. It also reflects a recurrent preoccupation of policy elites that extant structures of juvenile justice are inadequate for the task of reducing offending among children and young people and require to be reformed.

This chapter on youth crime and justice in Scotland has four parts. The first part provides an overview of the historical development of Scottish juvenile justice. The second part describes the operation of the current system while the third part presents empirical data relating to the nature and pattern of youth crime in Scotland, including data from the Edinburgh Study of Youth Transitions and Crime (the Edinburgh Study). The fourth part assesses the effectiveness of the system.

The history and development of juvenile justice

Punishment, deterrence and reform

Early institutions for child offenders in Scotland first emerged in the nineteenth century in a somewhat piecemeal fashion (McAra 2002). As with England and Wales, these included reformatories and industrial schools. However, institutions specific to Scotland also developed, including Dr Guthrie's Ragged Schools for the poor and destitute in 1847, William Quarrier's children's homes for children with special educational/behavioural needs in 1878 and Canon Jupp's children's homes at Aberlour in 1875.

The formal separation of the adult and juvenile justice systems in Scotland occurred in 1908, after which Sheriff, Burgh and Justice of the Peace courts in Scotland were required to act as juvenile courts on certain days of the week. Although court procedures were modified to facilitate children's understanding, no fundamental changes were made to the principles of criminal procedure. It was not until the 1930s that specially constituted juvenile courts appeared in Scotland, enabled by the Children and Young Persons (Scotland) Act 1932, which imposed a duty on the courts to have regard for the welfare of the child. Only four juvenile courts were ever established and most cases of juvenile offenders continued to be dealt with in Sheriff and Burgh courts (McAra 2002). The age of criminal responsibility was set at age 8 by the Children and Young Persons (Scotland) Act 1937.

Early developments were characterised by an ambiguity in penal aims between concerns to 'rescue' and reform children and also to punish and deter them (Gelsthorpe and Morris 1994). Both industrial schools and reformatories, for example, were described, in the 1908 Children Act, as places in which children could be 'lodged, taught and fed'. However, conditions were often extremely harsh (Radzinowicz and Hood 1986). While Borstals were introduced in 1908 to provide treatment and training for 16–21 year olds and the 1908 Children Act did institute some restrictions on the use of imprisonment for young offenders, periods of penal servitude were retained as an incapacitative measure for the 'truly depraved and unruly', as was corporal punishment (Gelsthorpe and Morris 1994).

Such ambiguity was a direct reflection of the competing interests which underpinned the emergent institutional infrastructure. This included balancing philanthropic concerns about child welfare with the requirement to maintain a disciplined and orderly workforce to service the needs of industrial capital, and with social imperialist concerns about the physical and moral degeneracy of the children of the so-called 'dangerous classes' (Radzinowicz and Hood 1986). Such interests themselves have to be understood against a backdrop of broader social, political and economic change brought about by the full flowering of industrial capitalism and the concomitant process of urbanisation. Such processes had a major impact on the nature and function of family life and on conceptions of childhood as a separate phase requiring special protection (Aries 1973; McAra 2002).

As the twentieth century progressed, welfarist impulsions increasingly came to dominate reforms. School psychological services and child guidance clinics for children with behavioural difficulties were established in the 1930s along with police liaison schemes in some areas. The Children Act 1948 created local authority children's departments with an obligation to consider the needs and abilities of children in their care. Legislation was also passed to enable the probation service to supervise juvenile offenders in need of care and control.

As with England and Wales, these changes stemmed partly from the massive social, economic and political fallout from the Second World War, and the increased dominance of core expert groups including child psychiatry and social work. However, unlike England and Wales, they also stemmed from an emergent and distinctively Scottish civic culture, grounded in more localised institutions, as discussed in more detail below.

The triumph of welfarism

The period between 1968 and 1995 can be seen as the high point of welfarism in juvenile justice in Scotland. This was set in train by the Social Work (Scotland) Act 1968, which abolished the existing juvenile courts and established a new institutional framework for juvenile justice, the Children's Hearings system. These changes were driven by the 'Kilbrandon philosophy'. According to this philosophy, juvenile offending and other troublesome behaviours should be regarded as manifestations of deeper social and psychological malaise and/or failures in the normal upbringing process (Kilbrandon Committee 1964). The overall aim of the new juvenile justice system (implemented in 1971) was to deal with the child's needs (whether referred on offence or care and protection grounds), with the best interests of the child to be paramount in decision-making.

At the outset, the Crown reserved the right to prosecute children who had committed the most serious offences (such as rape, serious assault or homicide) in the criminal courts. A number of commentators have argued that although this undermined important aspects of the Kilbrandon ethos, it was a necessary compromise in order to ensure the support of the Crown Office, the judiciary and the police for the new hearings system (Morris and McIsaac 1978).

The drive towards welfarism set the Scottish juvenile justice system on a different trajectory from that in England and Wales. A review of juvenile justice in England and Wales had recommended a similar commitment to welfare principles which were enshrined in the Children and Young Persons Act 1969. This Act, however, was never fully implemented and the 1970s saw a major increase in youth custody with a concomitant retreat from welfare concerns (Gelsthorpe and Morris 1994).

The divergence of the systems in the 1970s must be understood against the backdrop of political, social and penal change. The retreat from welfarism in England and Wales was precipitated by the election of a Conservative government committed to law and order principles, the resistance of magistrates and the police to the main precepts of the Act and a growing moral panic about youth crime in the context of a broader penal crisis linked to prison overcrowding and declining faith in rehabilitation (Cavadino and Dignan 1997).

By contrast, in Scotland the new institutions of juvenile justice had the support of key elites within the Scottish Office and the criminal justice system itself. In addition there was a concerted media campaign extolling the uniqueness of the new institutions of juvenile justice which helped garner public support (Morris and McIsaac 1978). However, as noted above, one of the principal factors marking out Scotland from England and Wales was the distinctive nature of Scottish civic culture which had emerged by the 1960s. This culture stemmed from a strong democratic tradition in key civic institutions such as the education system and the church, accompanied by a growing dominance of socialist and communitarian principles at local government level (McAra 2005). This civic culture enabled the Scottish justice system to resist the voices proclaiming the decline of the rehabilitative ideal in other western jurisdictions and it provided anchorage for the predominantly welfare-based penal culture which framed both the adult and juvenile justice systems in Scotland during the 1970s and 1980s (McAra 2005, 2008).

The period of 'detartanisation'

The dominance of welfarism lasted until around the mid-1990s. In the following decade, however, core elements of the Kilbrandon philosophy were abandoned and a more punitive and actuarial set of rhetorics was grafted onto the system. In the context of this more conflicted policy framework, juvenile justice was restyled by policy-makers as youth justice and issues relating to youth crime became increasingly politicised. While the roots of these changes can be found pre-devolution,[1] the pace of change gained momentum in the post-devolutionary era as ministers in the Scottish Parliament gradually embraced the new labour crime agenda. Indeed it is somewhat ironic that the full-flowering of devolution (which might have been thought to nurture all things Scottish) led to a degree of policy convergence with the system south of the border in England and Wales (McAra 2006, 2008).

Early signs of change were evident as far back as the arrangements for secure accommodation introduced by Health and Social Services and Social Security Adjudications Act 1983. As a result of this Act, the hearings were enabled to require a child to reside in secure accommodation where he or she was likely 'to injure other persons'. The penetration of public interest discourse into the hearings system was, however, more explicitly marked by a number of the changes introduced by the Children (Scotland) Act 1995. This Act enabled the hearings system to place the principle of public protection above that of the child's best interests in cases where the child presented a significant risk to the public. It also empowered Sheriffs to substitute their own decision for that of the panel in disputed (and appealed) cases.

Turning in more detail to post-devolutionary convergent trends, these were set in train by a series of published reviews and action plans, such as *Safer Communities in Scotland* (Scottish Executive 1999), *It's a Criminal Waste: Stop Youth Crime Now* (Scottish Executive 2000) and *Scotland's Action Programme to Reduce Youth Crime* (Scottish Executive 2002). A key point of commonality between the Scottish and English and Welsh systems was the increased level of managerialism evident within each jurisdiction. For example, within Scotland, national standards for youth justice were published for the first time in 2002 setting out key performance indicators in respect of service provision and timescales. A new bureaucratic infrastructure was also created within Scotland to take forward the youth justice agenda, which included multi-agency youth justice teams (involving representatives from the police, social work, the local community, health services, the voluntary sector and the Children's Reporter – see below).

Convergent trends were also evident in the ways in which the public protection, risk management and effective evidence-based practice began to frame youth justice interventions. Within Scotland, a key element of the Action Plan to Reduce Youth Crime was that 'what works' principles should be incorporated into an expanded range of social work programmes for persistent offenders. Such principles arguably undermine the holistic Kilbrandon ethos as they involve careful calibration of programme intensity to level of risk posed by the child (rather than focusing on the welfare needs of the child) and are predicated on cognitive behavioural methods (rather than more traditional casework) (McGuire 1995).

In the early post-devolutionary years there was also a gradual elision between the social exclusion, crime prevention and youth justice policy frameworks in both jurisdictions. Within Scotland, the Action Plan to Reduce Youth Crime reiterated a need for more developed neighbourhood and community safety programmes, and Community Safety Partnerships were given additional funding in 2003 to improve access to sports and leisure facilities for young people, with the aim of diverting them into meaningful structured activity (McAra 2006).

A further convergent trend was the embracing of restorative principles in both Scotland and England and Wales (exemplified by the expanding number of victim–offender mediation schemes, conferencing and police restorative cautioning initiatives). Other similarities were the focus on reducing persistent offending and tackling anti-social behaviour. Both jurisdictions legislated to enable the use of civil orders to tackle low-level crime and disorder (Anti-Social Behaviour and Parenting Orders).[2] Finally a youth court model was piloted in Scotland (discussed in more detail below). At the launch of the pilot courts the then Justice Minister, Cathy Jamieson, stated that 'punishment is a key part of the youth justice process' (Scottish Executive 2003).

These convergent themes led to increased tension within Scottish youth justice policy. Some elements of the policy frame were underpinned by a desire to promote social inclusion, to reintegrate and to enhance citizenship; other elements by contrast were aimed at exclusion, dispersal and punishment. These tensions were indicative of the ways in which juvenile and adult criminal justice institutions lost cultural anchorage in the post-devolutionary era (McAra 2008).

Indeed, civic culture in Scotland went into a period of drift post-devolution. Politics became less polarised and there was greater ideological congruence between the Scottish labour/liberal democratic coalition government and the new labour government at Westminster. This served initially to weaken a sense of political identity in Scotland with a concomitant weakening of the purchase of welfarism as a principal framework around which debates on criminal justice took place.

The era of prevention and early intervention

From this conflicted and punitive third phase, there is evidence that juvenile justice in Scotland may be moving into a fourth phase characterised by a renewed emphasis on prevention and early intervention based on a risk factor paradigm.

Changes were heralded during the final term of the labour/liberal democratic coalition government with the publication of *Getting it Right for Every Child: Proposals for Action* (Scottish Executive 2005). This document set out a vision for high-quality children's services (including those for child offenders), somewhat at odds with the more populist political rhetoric on youth crime described above.

A change of government in 2007 produced a successor document: *Preventing Offending by Young People: A Framework for Action* (Scottish Government 2008a), which was underpinned by an uneasy mixture of welfarist, actuarialist and retributive impulsions. On the one hand, the document was committed to universal, holistic services aimed at promoting child well-being and explicitly situated the youth crime agenda within the framework of education and health (part of the new SNP administration's aim to construct a joined-up approach to governance and a core legacy of *Getting it Right for Every Child*). At the same time, however, the document highlighted the need to develop targeted programmes and services for at-risk children and their families, favouring early but intensive intervention for those who were most risky. A core assumption was that such children and families would be readily identifiable and that risk assessment was generally a watertight process.

Finally, the document also contained shades of a just deserts/retributive perspective, particularly with its emphasis on the notion of responsibilisation – that children and families should take responsibility for their behaviour and, indeed, responsibility for change, with interventions requiring to be proportionate, timely and fair.

These tensions notwithstanding, there is some anecdotal evidence that the SNP administration, thus far, has evolved stronger and less confrontational relationships with policy and practitioner elites. Indeed, a distinctive feature of its early months in office was the lack of political pronouncements on youth crime. Ministers quietly withdrew key targets set by the previous administration for reducing the numbers of persistent offenders and abandoned core elements of the antisocial behaviour agenda (including ASBOs for 12–15 year olds). However, other more progressive sounding features of its current legislative programme are rather less so when the fine detail is considered. Of particular note are the provisions relating to the prosecution of children in the Criminal Justice and Licensing Bill (introduced into the Scottish Parliament in March 2009) which have been flagged by ministers as raising the age of criminal responsibility. Importantly, the new Bill prohibits prosecution of a child under the age of 12 in the courts, but it does not explicitly raise the age of criminal responsibility. Thus a child will continue to be held criminally responsible from the age of 8 but all such cases will be dealt with by the Children's Hearings system.

The current SNP Government is a minority administration and legislative success is dependent on its capacity to make compromises and negotiate with other political parties. It will be interesting to observe whether the new administration can continue to refrain from the temptation of populist rhetoric in a context where it has limited political power to push through its own agenda. That it has failed to raise the age of criminal responsibility (by decriminalising the under-12s) is indicative of a cautious rather than revolutionary modus operandi.

The structure and operation of the juvenile justice system

Under the Children's Hearings system, children who have offended or are in need of care or protection are referred to the Children's Reporter. While anyone can refer a case to the Reporter, in practice most referrals come from the police, with a smaller number of cases being referred by the social work department, the Procurator Fiscal Service or schools.

The task of the Reporter is to investigate referrals and on the basis of the evidence decide whether there is a prima facie case that at least one of the grounds for referral to a hearing has been met and that the child is in need of compulsory measures of care. The overwhelming majority of referrals result in no further action by the Reporter or are diverted away from the Children's Hearings system for more informal measures of support.

There are currently twelve grounds on which a case may be referred to a hearing as set out in the Children (Scotland) Act 1995 (see http://www.childrens-hearings.co.uk). These grounds are principally concerned with (a) the child being at risk of harm from others (through, for example, lack of parental care or living in the same household as a victim or perpetrator of child sexual abuse) and (b) with the child's behaviour (through, for example, offending, truanting from school, being beyond control of any relevant person, the misuse of drugs, alcohol or volatile substances). In order for a hearing to proceed the child and the parents must accept the grounds for referral. For children referred on offence grounds this means admitting guilt. Where the grounds are disputed, the case will be referred to the Sheriff court for a proof hearing.

The hearing itself is a tribunal consisting of three members (to include at least one woman and one man) drawn from the Children's Panel for the particular local government area.[3] Members of the Children's Panel are volunteers and should be selected from a wide range of occupations, social backgrounds and neighbourhoods. The representativeness of panels has been a matter of concern over many years, the evidence until recently suggesting that women, older people and the middle class were over-represented (Hallet *et al.* 1998).

The Reporter attends the hearing to advise on legal and procedural matters and to record the reason for the decision. Children and their parents or guardian are normally expected to attend and participate in the hearing. They can be accompanied by a representative who may be a lawyer. The overall task of the hearing is to decide whether compulsory measures of care are necessary. The Children (Scotland) Act 1995 has identified three main principles on which such decisions should be based:

1 The welfare of the child should be the paramount consideration.

2 Taking account of the age and maturity of the child, the hearing should give the child the opportunity to express his views and have regard to these views.

3 No order should be made unless the hearing considers that it would be better for the child that their requirement or order be made than none should be made at all.

The Act also enabled the hearing to make a decision which is not consistent with the welfare principle where this is necessary to protect the public from serious harm.

Where compulsory measures of care are considered necessary, the hearing can impose a supervision requirement which ensures statutory social work involvement. The most common outcome of a hearing is the imposition of a non-residential supervision requirement. Supervision requirements normally last up to one year but are subject to review and can be extended. The decision of a hearing can be appealed to the Sheriff court.

The majority of children dealt with by the hearings system are under the age of 16. However, children can be kept in the system until the age of 18 through the extension of supervision requirements. In practice most offenders between the ages of 16 and 18 are dealt with in the adult criminal justice system, although courts do have the power to remit such cases to the hearings system for advice and/or disposal. As noted earlier, the courts also deal with children aged between 8 and 15 who are accused of serious crimes such as rape or homicide or (in the case of children aged 15) for certain driving offences.

In 2003, two pilot youth court projects were instigated in Scotland to deal with persistent offenders (charged with summary offences) aged 16–17 and children aged 15 who would otherwise have been dealt with in the Sheriff summary court. The criterion for referral to the youth court was three or more police referrals to the Procurator Fiscal in a six-month period. The youth courts did not have an easy gestational period. While the government-sponsored evaluation of the pilots (McIvor *et al.* 2006) was largely positive, a controversial 'minority report' was published in the journal *Youth Justice* (Piacentini and Walters 2006) which claimed that the fast-track proceedings undermined human rights. Plans to roll out the courts were put on ice. At the time of writing, the results of an internal government review are still pending.

The extent and pattern of youth offending

The availability of national data on youth crime in Scotland is limited. Trend data can only be obtained from official sources, such as the routine data collated by the eight police forces, the Scottish Children's Reporter Administration (SCRA), the Scottish courts and the Scottish Prison Service. These data vary enormously in terms of their focus, structure and content. Nevertheless, a consistent picture emerges which suggests that youth crime in Scotland has remained stable or fallen over the last decade or so. The only major fluctuations in these figures appear to coincide with the punitive third phase of youth justice, described earlier in this chapter.

The total number of young people who were referred to the Reporter on offence grounds between 1995/6 and 2002/3 remained steady at around 14,500 per year, as shown in Figure 4.1. Between 2002/3 and 2005/6, however, there was an 18 per cent increase in the number of children referred on offence grounds. This represented a major failure on the part of the labour/liberal democratic administration which had set a target of reducing the number of 'persistent young offenders' in Scotland by 10 per cent over that time period.

The trend since 1996/7 in the number of 16- and 17-year-olds who were convicted of a criminal offence in the Scottish courts is presented in Figure 4.2, shown as a rate per 1,000 of the population to adjust for changes in population size. This chart shows that the rate of conviction among 17-year-olds fell steeply between the mid- 1990s and the early 2000s, while rates for 16-year-olds also showed a steady decline over this period. Since 2000/1, rates have been relatively stable, although there was a slight rise in 2006/7, again coinciding with the more punitive phase in Scottish youth justice policy.

Statistics relating to the imprisonment of young people in Scotland have also shown a declining trend, at least until very recently. Figure 4.3 shows that the average daily prison population for those aged under 21 declined at a steady rate between 1996/7 and 2004/5, before starting to rise again during the period when the labour/liberal democratic coalition's focus on youth offending was at its peak.

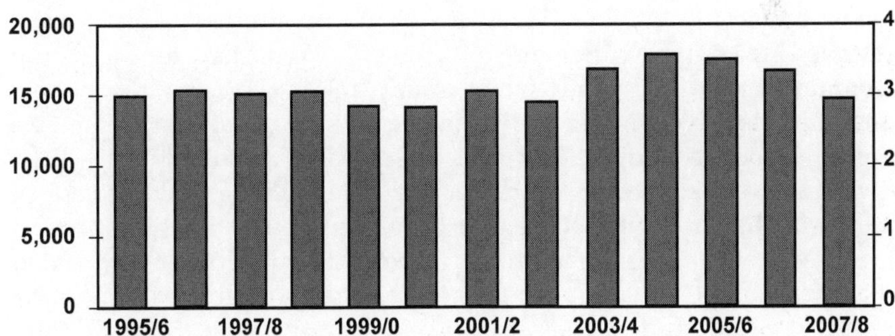

Figure 4.1 Number of people aged under 18 referred to the Reporter on offence grounds
Source: SCRA (2008).

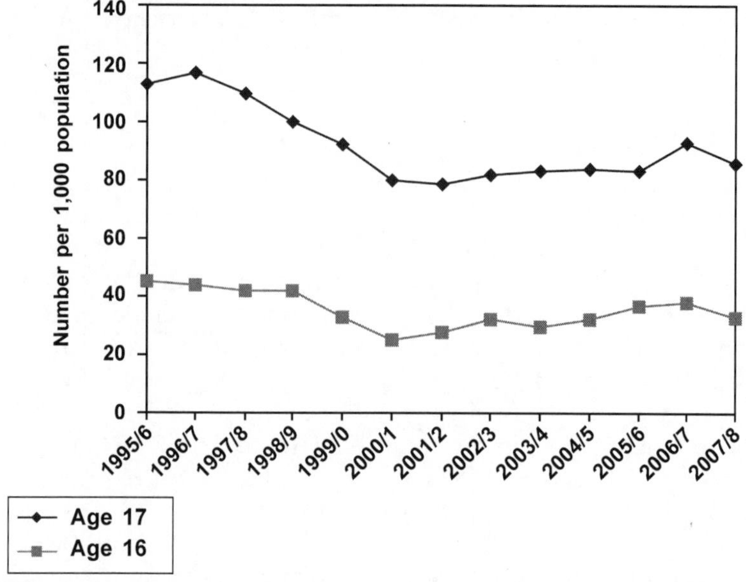

Figure 4.2 Criminal convictions in the Scottish courts per 1,000 population of 16 and 17 year olds
Source: Scottish Government (2009); Scottish Executive (2006).

These data do not give any indication that youth crime is, or has been, a persistently rising problem over the last 15 years or so. However, a high political profile and consistently negative media coverage, including that about so-called 'neds', might suggest otherwise. Evidence of a 'moral panic' at the height of this political posturing was evident in the results of the Scottish Social Attitudes Survey, which revealed that 69 per cent of the Scottish population believed that youth crime was higher in 2004 than it had been ten years previously (Anderson *et al.* 2005). In addition, this survey revealed that the four biggest 'problems' reported to be facing communities in Scotland were issues relating to young people and their involvement in antisocial behaviour. Ambiguity emerges, however, between adult perceptions of these problems and their own direct experience of them. For example, although 69 per cent of adults in the survey reported that groups of youths hanging around the streets were either very or fairly common, only 15 per cent stated that they had personally been affected by the problem and only 4 per cent had been affected a great deal.

Turning to the Edinburgh Study, this large-scale prospective longitudinal study of youth offending started in 1998 and surveyed more than 4,000 young people over six annual sweeps of data

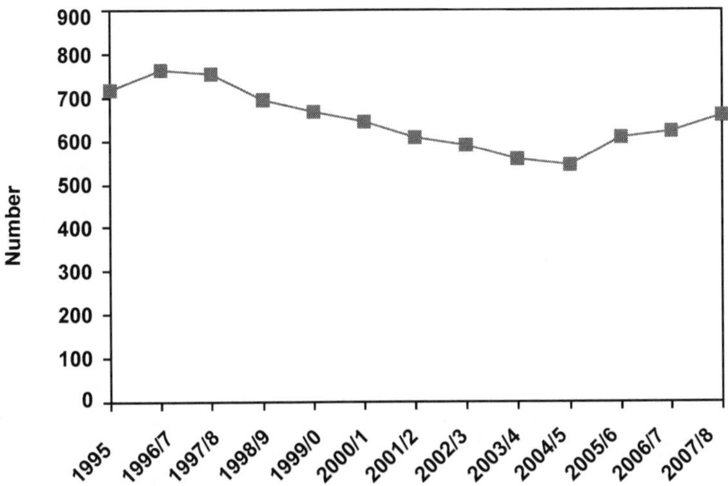

Figure 4.3 Average daily prison population of prisoners aged under 21 in Scotland
Source: Scottish Government (2008b); Scottish Executive (2004).

collection (Smith and McVie 2003). Between the ages of 12 and 17, annually administered self-completion questionnaires were used to collect data about young people's involvement in a range of offending behaviours, ranging from trivial forms of antisocial behaviour through to more serious forms of crime. Table 4.1 presents a summary of the offending behaviour reported by these young people, giving separate results for males and females.

Overall, these data show that a very large proportion of young people admitted being involved in at least one act of antisocial or offending behaviour between the ages of 12 and 17. Three-quarters of young people stated that they had been involved in some type of violence, although this mainly consisted of minor physical assaults. Behaving in an anti-social manner in public was also fairly common. Around half of young people said they had committed at least one act of theft during the six years, while just under a half said they had vandalised or set fire to someone else's property.

Around half of the young people in this study reported committing at least one serious offence[4] at some point between the age of 12 and 17, although only a quarter were persistent serious offenders (committing more than ten offences in any one year). As shown in Table 4.1, females were significantly less likely to be involved in offending than males.

Table 4.1 Self-reported offending (age 12–17)

	Males (%)	Females (%)	All (%)
Violence (assault, robbery, animal abuse)	86	63	75
Antisocial behaviour (being rowdy or unruly in public)	71	65	68
Theft (shoplifting, vehicle thefts, housebreaking)	60	49	55
Property crime (vandalism, fire-raising)	57	32	45
Serious offending (vehicle theft, joyriding, housebreaking, fire-raising, possession of a weapon, robbery and >5 assaults)	66	40	52
Persistent serious offending (more than 10 incidents in a year)	34	14	24

Source: Edinburgh Study, Sweeps 1–6.

Looking in more detail at those who committed serious offences, Figure 4.4 shows the longitudinal trend in the percentage of young people involved in any serious offending and persistent serious offending over five of the six annual sweeps of the Edinburgh Study. The trend lines show that at age 13, around a quarter of young people committed at least one serious offence and just under one in ten were persistent serious offenders. Serious offending peaked in terms of prevalence at age 14 and then declined steadily to age 17, by which time around 15 per cent were involved in some serious offending and 5 per cent were persistent serious offenders.

In order to determine whether the young people who were involved in serious offending differed from other young people, Table 4.2 compares serious offenders with other non-serious offenders and non-offenders on a range of characteristics at age 14. On almost every characteristic, serious offenders tended to be significantly different from those involved in non-serious offending and those who did not offend at age 14. Serious offenders were significantly more likely to

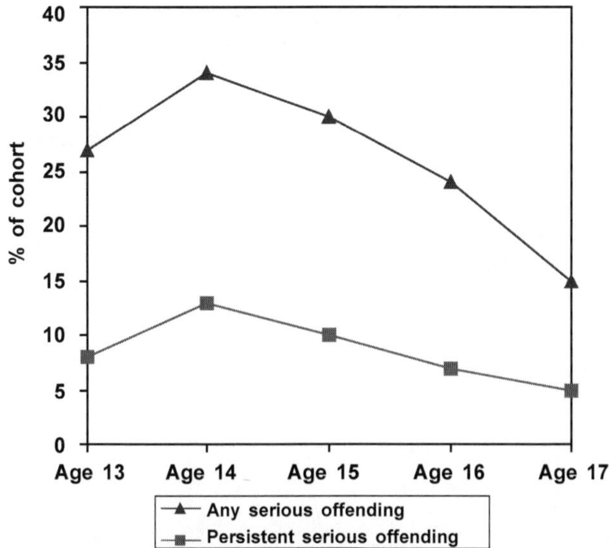

Figure 4.4 Serious offending (age 13–17)
Source: Edinburgh Study, Sweeps 2–6.

be male and to be living in conditions associated with higher social deprivation or poverty. Serious offenders were also less likely to be living with both birth parents, which is an indication of family disruption, and gave lower scores on average in response to a series of questions on parental supervision (such as parents' knowledge of where they went, who they were with and what time they would return home when going out).

Differences between the serious offenders, the non-serious offenders and the non-offenders were particularly marked in terms of their involvement in other types of 'risky' behaviour. Non-serious offenders were around three times as likely to drink alcohol regularly or to have taken drugs in the last year compared with non-offenders, whereas serious offenders were around 2–3 times more likely to have used alcohol or drugs than non-serious offenders. Serious offenders were also the most likely group to say that they would hang around the streets on most days and truant from school on a frequent basis. Around four in ten serious offenders reported that they belonged to a group they considered to be a 'gang', compared with only 22 per cent of non-serious offenders and 9 per cent of non-offenders.

In terms of their personality characteristics, serious offenders were not significantly different to other non-serious offenders in terms of their level of self-esteem (although self-esteem was higher among

Table 4.2 Comparing the characteristics of serious offenders, non-serious offenders and non-offenders at age 14

Domain	Characteristics	Non-offender (n = 1007)	Non-serious offender (n = 1729)	Serious offender (n = 1426)
Sex	% male	44	41	67
Social deprivation	% with parents in unemployment/manual work	37	41	52
	Mean neighbourhood deprivation score (0–14)	2.9	3.4	3.7
	% entitled to free school meals	15	18	26
Family dynamics	% living with both birth parents	72	67	57
	Mean score on parental supervision scale (0–9)	7.4	6.3	5.4
Risky behaviours	% who drink alcohol weekly	3	13	33
	% who took drugs in last year	3	13	44
	% who hang out most days	31	50	72
	% truanting from school >5 times in last year	1	7	23
	% belong to a 'gang'	6	17	33
Personality	Mean self esteem score (0–24)	16.0	15.2	15.2
	Mean impulsivity score (0–24)	9.2	12.9	15.0
	Mean risk taking score (0–24)	3.5	6.8	9.6
Vulnerability	% victims of violence in last year	6	18	40
	% victims of violence with a weapon in last year	1	4	23
	% who self-harmed in last year	5	10	25
	% victims of bullying at least once a week	17	18	22

those who did not offend at age 14); however, serious offenders did have significantly higher scores than other young people on a scale of impulsivity and a scale of risk-taking behaviour.

Serious offenders were also a highly vulnerable group, which is indicated on a range of indices. Four in ten serious offenders at age 14 had been a victim of violence within the last year and around a quarter had been assaulted by a weapon. One in four also reported that they had self-harmed, often by cutting themselves, and around the same proportion reported being victims of bullying behaviour on a weekly basis.

Taken together, these findings on the links between serious offending, vulnerability and social adversities provide strong support for the Kilbrandon ethos – in particular its core contention that offending behaviours are symptoms of deeper-seated needs.

The effectiveness of juvenile justice: critical issues

This final section of the chapter briefly explores critical issues relating to the effectiveness of the Scottish system of juvenile justice as it is currently implemented.

Here we again draw on findings from the Edinburgh Study to assess the promise of early intervention strategies, the impact of contacts with the system on subsequent offending and the longer-term outcomes for some young people in terms of youth-to-adult criminal justice transitions.

Early intervention

As noted above, early intervention predicated upon a risk factor paradigm forms one of the cornerstones of recent juvenile justice policy. Edinburgh Study findings, however, suggest that there could be major problems for agencies in identifying from an early age those individuals who will turn out to be serious offenders in the teenage years. Our findings show that of those involved in serious offending at age 17, only 32 per cent of them were known to the Children's Hearings system by the age of 16 and only 5 per cent were known to either social work or the Children's Hearings system by the age of 5. These data indicate that assessment of future risk based on early identification by the Children's Hearing system is not a watertight process. In fact, evidence from the Edinburgh Study generally shows that proximal influences, in particular encounters and experiences around the early teenage years, may be far more important in explaining continuity and change in offending over the mid-to-late teenage years than more distant pre-school factors (McAra and McVie 2010).

Impact of intervention

As discussed earlier in this chapter, youth justice policy in the UK over the turn of the twenty-first century was increasingly influenced by a body of 'evidence' that focused, on notions of what works (McAra 2004; Muncie and Goldson 2006). Large-scale government-sponsored evaluations focused on evaluating programme effectiveness have been commissioned in England (Hope 2005; Pitts 2003), although evaluation of youth justice interventions in Scotland has been modest in scale and ambiguous in its findings (Hill *et al.* 2005). There is, however, a growing body of international research which increasingly indicates that contact with youth justice systems generally, and more severe forms of sanctioning in particular, often does little to diminish offending, and may in fact result in enhanced risk of reoffending (Huizinga *et al.* 2003; Klein 1986; Sherman *et al.* 1998).

Recent evidence from the Edinburgh Study has contributed significantly to this debate. McAra and McVie (2005, 2007a) found that selection effects were operating at three stages of the system (police charging, referral to the Reporter and referral to a Children's Hearing) in a way that ensured that certain categories of young people – 'the usual suspects' – were propelled into a repeat cycle of referral into the Children's Hearings system, whereas other equally serious offenders escaped the attention of formal agencies altogether. The deeper young people who were identified as the usual suspects penetrated the youth justice system, the more likely it was that their pattern of desistance from involvement in serious offending was inhibited (McAra and McVie 2007a). These findings are significant because they highlight that even a system as inherently welfare-based as the Scottish Children's Hearings system, which should be better placed than most other western juvenile justice systems to reduce offending, can contribute to a process of repeated targeting and labelling. The paper concludes that the key to tackling serious and persistent offending lies in minimal intervention and maximum diversion.

Youth-to-adult transitions

There is a paucity of research tracking the longer-term outcomes for children made subject to compulsory measures of care. That which does exist indicates that 16–17 year olds in the adult criminal justice system are a particularly vulnerable group (Kennedy and McIvor 1992; Whyte 2003). Waterhouse *et al.* (1999) followed up 113 'jointly referred' children in their cohort for a period of two years. Around four-fifths of these children had a criminal conviction by the end of this period, with just under a third being sentenced to a period of custody by the courts. The majority of those with convictions were living on state benefit, were from lone parent families and had been living in local authority care at the time of their initial referral to the Hearings system. In a small proportion of cases concerns had been expressed at the initial referral about drug (19 per cent) and alcohol (28 per cent) abuse and psychiatric difficulties (11 per cent) (Waterhouse *et al.* 1999; Whyte 2003).

The findings of the Edinburgh Study are broadly supportive of previous research in the field. Youngsters in the cohort with a criminal record by age 19 were highly vulnerable: living in deprived neighbourhoods and presenting with a history of school exclusion, persistent truancy and victimisation. A high proportion of these youngsters were first known to the Children's Hearings system around age 13, but such institutional contact failed to stem their involvement in persistent serious offending (which remained high at every sweep). Importantly, children who made the transition between the hearing system and the adult criminal justice system were generally assessed by agencies as having a high volume of needs (relating to personal, family and school adversities) at the point of transition. Nevertheless, such youngsters were up-tariffed relatively quickly, with disproportionately high numbers being placed in custody by their 19th birthdays (McAra and McVie 2007b).

Concluding comments

This chapter has shown that the history of juvenile justice in Scotland is one of both stability (over the high point of welfarism from the 1970s to mid-1990s) and change (particularly in the early twenty-first century). Indeed, over 40 years since it was first published, the quotation from the Kilbrandon report (cited at the start of this chapter) remains of salience. Scottish society is still concerned to secure a more effective and discriminatory machinery for dealing with children and young people who offend, and issues relating to youth crime and justice remain politically contentious.

Importantly, existing statistical sources suggest that youth crime in Scotland is not spiralling out of control. Moreover, extant research evidence (particularly from the Edinburgh Study) is strongly supportive of Kilbrandon principles: supportive of an approach which recognises that needs and deeds are closely interrelated and which advocates diversion from formal measures wherever possible to avoid stigmatisation and criminalisation.

Taken together, this overview of youth crime and justice within Scotland would suggest that there is a need for the findings of Scottish research to feed more visibly into the policy-making process. It also suggests that the avoidance and reduction of juvenile delinquency – the core Kilbrandon aim – might best be attained through strengthening rather than transforming the welfarist infrastructure of the Children's Hearings system.

Notes

1 The Scotland Act 1998 enabled the reinstatement (after nearly 300 years) of the Scottish Parliament (elections to which were held in 1999).

2 In Scotland ASBOs for 12–15 year olds and Parenting Orders were enabled by the Anti-Social Behaviour (Scotland) Act 2004.

3 The organisation of the children's hearings system is under review. The Children's Hearings (Scotland) Bill, published in June 2009 but subsequently withdrawn, contained provisions for the creation of a new national body, the Scottish Children's Hearings Tribunal, with responsibility for all functions of the Children's Panel including recruitment, selection and training of panel members.

4 This includes theft of/from a motor vehicle, riding in a stolen vehicle, carrying an offensive weapon, housebreaking, fire-raising, robbery and six or more incidents of violence.

References

Anderson, S., Bromley, C. and Given, L. (2005) *Public Attitudes Towards Young People and Youth Crime in Scotland: Findings from the 2004 Scottish Social Attitudes Survey*. Edinburgh: Scottish Executive Education Department, http://www.scotland.gov.uk/Resource/Doc/55971/0015628.pdf.

Aries, P. (1973) *Centuries of Childhood*. Harmondsworth: Penguin.

Cavadino, M. and Dignan, J. (1997) *The Penal System: An Introduction*, 2nd edn. London: Sage.

Gelsthorpe, L. and Morris, A. (1994) 'Juvenile justice 1954–1992', in M. Maguire, R. Morgan and R. Reiner (eds), *The Oxford Handbook of Criminology*, 1st edn. Oxford: Clarendon.

Hallet, C., Murray, C., Jamieson, J. and Veitch, B. (1998) *The Evaluation of the Children's Hearings in Scotland, Volume 1 'Deciding in Children's Interests'*. Edinburgh: Scottish Office Central Research Unit.

Hill, M., Walker, M., Moodie, K., Wallace, B., Bannister, J., Khan, F., McIvor, G. and Kendrick, A. (2005) *Fast Track Children's Hearings Pilot: Final Report of the Evaluation of the Pilot*. Edinburgh, Scottish Government, http://www.scotland.gov.uk/Publications/2005/06/14103237/32402.

Hope, T. (2005) 'Pretend it works. Evidence and governance in the evaluation of the reducing burglary initiative', *Criminology and Criminal Justice*, 4 (3): 287–308.

Huizinga, D., Schumann, K., Ehret, B. and Elliot, A. (2003) *The Effects of Juvenile Justice Processing on Subsequent Delinquent and Criminal Behavior: A Cross-national Study*. Washington, DC: Final Report to the National Institute of Justice.

Kennedy, R. and McIvor, G. (1992) *Young Offenders in the Children's Hearing and Criminal Justice System: A Comparative Analysis*. Stirling: University of Stirling Social Work Research Centre.

Kilbrandon Committee (1964) *Report on Children and Young Persons*. Edinburgh: HMSO.

Klein, M. (1986) 'Labelling theory and delinquency policy – an empirical test', *Criminal Justice and Behaviour*, 13: 47–79.

McAra, L. (2002) 'The Scottish juvenile justice system: policy and practice', in J. Winterdyk (ed.), *Juvenile Justice Systems: International Perspectives*, 2nd edn. Toronto: Canadian Scholars' Press.

McAra, L. (2004) 'The cultural and institutional dynamics of transformation: youth justice in Scotland and England and Wales', *Cambrian Law Review*, 35: 23–54.

McAra, L. (2005) 'Modelling penal transformation', *Punishment and Society*, 7 (3): 277–302.

McAra, L. (2006) 'Welfare in crisis? Youth justice in Scotland', in J. Muncie and B. Goldson (eds), *Comparative Youth Justice*. London: Sage.

McAra, L. (2008) 'Crime, criminal justice and criminology in Scotland', *European Journal of Criminology*, 5 (4): 481–504.

McAra, L. and McVie, S. (2005) 'The usual suspects? Street-life, young offenders and the police', *Criminal Justice*, 5 (1): 5–36.

McAra, L. and McVie, S. (2007a) 'Youth justice? The impact of agency contact on desistance from offending', *European Journal of Criminology*, 4 (3): 315–45.

McAra, L. and McVie, S. (2007b) *Criminal Justice Transitions*, Research Digest No. 14, http://www.law.ed.ac.uk/cls/esytc/findings/digest14.pdf.

McAra, L. and McVie, S. (2010) 'Youth Crime and Justice: Key Findings from the Edinburgh Study of Youth Transitions and Crime'.

McIvor, G., Barnsdale, L., MacRae, R., Dunlop, S., Brown, A., Eley, S., Malloch, M., Murray, C., Piacentini, L., Popham, F. and Walters, R. (2006) *The Evaluation of the Airdrie and Hamilton Youth Court Pilot*, Research Findings No. 85. http://www.scotland.gov.uk/publications/2006/06/13155439/1.

McGuire, J. (ed.) (1995) *What Works: Reducing Re-offending: Guidelines from Research and Practice*. Chichester: Wiley.

Morris, A. and McIsaac, M. (1978) *Juvenile Justice? The Practice of Social Welfare*, Cambridge Studies in Criminology. Cambridge: Heinemann.

Muncie, J. and Goldson, B. (2006) 'England and Wales: the new correctionalism', in J. Muncie and B. Goldson (eds), *Comparative Youth Justice*. London: Sage.

Piacentini, L. and Walters, R. (2006) 'The politicization of youth crime in Scotland and the rise of the "Burberry Court"', *Youth Justice*, 6 (10): 43–59.

Pitts, J. (2003) 'Changing youth justice', *Youth Justice*, 3 (1): 3–18.

Radzinowicz, L. and Hood, R. (1986) *A History of English Criminal Law, Volume 5: The Emergence of Penal Policy*. London: Stevens.

Scottish Children's Reporter Administration (2008) *Annual Report 2007/08*. http://www.scra.gov.uk/cms_resources/SCRA%20Annual%20Report%20200708%20web%20version.pdf.

Scottish Executive (1999) *Safer Communities in Scotland*. Edinburgh: Scottish Executive, http://www.scotland.gov.uk/library2/doc01/scis-00.htm.

Scottish Executive (2000) *It's a Criminal Waste: Stop Youth Crime Now: The Report of the Advisory Group on Youth Crime*. Edinburgh: Scottish Executive.

Scottish Executive (2002) *Scotland's Action Programme to Reduce Youth Crime*. Edinburgh: HMSO.

Scottish Executive (2003) *Scotland's First Youth Court Opens*, Press Release. http://www.scotland.gov.uk/pages/news.

Scottish Executive (2004) *Prison Statistics Scotland, 2003*. Edinburgh: Statistical Bulletin Criminal Justice Series.

Scottish Executive (2005) *Getting it Right for Every Child: Proposals for Action*. http://www.scotland.gov.uk/Publications/2005/06/20135608/56098.

Scottish Executive (2006) *Criminal Proceedings in Scottish Courts, 2004/05*. Edinburgh: Statistical Bulletin Criminal Justice Series.

Scottish Government (2008a) *Preventing Offending by Young People: A Framework for Action*. http://www.scotland.gov.uk/Publications/2008/06/17093513/0

Scottish Government (2008b) *Prison Statistics Scotland, 2007/08*, Edinburgh: Statistical Bulletin Crime and Justice Series.

Scottish Government (2009) *Criminal Proceedings in Scottish Courts: Statistical Bulletin*. http://www.scotland.gov.uk/Publications/2009/04/27103325/0

Sherman, L. W., Gottfreson, D. C., Mackenzie, D., Ecj, J., Reuter, P. and Bushway, S. D. (1998) *Preventing Crime: What Works, What Doesn't, What's Promising*, Research Brief. Washington, DC: National Institute of Justice, US Department of Justice, Office of Justice Programmes.

Smith, D. J. and McVie, S. (2003) 'Theory and method in the Edinburgh Study of youth transitions and crime', *British Journal of Criminology*, 43 (1): 169–95.

Waterhouse, L., McGhee, J., Loucks, N., Whyte, B. and Kay, H. (1999) *The Evaluation of the Children's Hearings in Scotland, Volume 3 Children in Focus*. Edinburgh: Scottish Executive Central Research Unit.

Whyte, B. (2003) 'Young and persistent: recent developments in youth justice policy and practice in Scotland', *Youth Justice*, 3 (2): 74–85.

Chapter 5

Gender, crime and criminal justice in Scotland

Lesley McMillan

Introduction

Women and men are differentially connected to the social world and their experience of crime and victimisation is, in important respects, distinct. The focus on women's experiences 'can take us a long way towards recognising some of the effects of gender-blind thinking' (Walklate 2004: 18). This chapter addresses women as both perpetrators and victims of crime (although, as will be demonstrated, these two categorisations are not mutually exclusive) it discusses sentencing and imprisonment, the characteristics and experiences of women offenders and community sanctions for women. The relationship that young women have with crime is then considered before moving on to look at prostitution, domestic abuse and sexual victimisation and the distinct features of these in the Scottish context. It demonstrates that while there have been significant developments in Scotland over recent years there is still some way to go in terms of addressing the social conditions that lead to both women's offending and victimisation, and in delivering an appropriate and just criminal justice response.

Offending and victimisation

Offending

The most persistent 'fact' evident in academic research on crime and victimisation, self-report studies and official statistical data on reported crime (Burman 2004) is that women commit significantly less crime than men. It is nonetheless acknowledged that official statistics do not represent the 'true' level of criminal behaviour and are an artefact of the reporting and recording process, in itself mediated by other social factors. Nonetheless, an analysis of this data shows us that women commit considerably less crime than men and usually commit less serious crime, which is most often offences related to shoplifting, public order and petty assault (Barry and McIvor 2008). Despite this, women are often treated more harshly in the criminal justice system, often reaching prison not as a result of having committed a serious offence but having failed to comply with a community disposal. This 'gender gap' has been a key point of discussion in feminist criminology and gender-related research on crime with scholars seeking to explain the gender difference (see, for example, Heidensohn and Gelsthorpe 2007). Here I explore the Scottish context and the extent to which this reflects the situation elsewhere.

An analysis of Scottish data confirms that women are less likely to be convicted of criminal activity than men. In 2007/8 women constituted only 15 per cent of all convictions in Scotland and men outnumbered women for convictions in all crime and offence categories with the exception of 'other' crimes of indecency (mostly prostitution related) where women made up 63 per cent (Scottish Government 2009a). While the peak age of criminal activity for females (19) and males (18) is similar, the proportion convicted of an offence at peak offending age is not: 7 per cent of 18-year-old males in Scotland were convicted of an offence in 2007/8 compared with less than 1 per cent of the 19-year-old female population (Scottish Government 2009a).

Further evidence comes from the Scottish Crime and Justice Survey (SCJS) 2008/9 sweep which found that in the 47 per cent of crimes where details of the offender were provided, males (74 per cent) were more likely than females (11 per cent) or mixed gender groups (15 per cent) to be offenders.

Given the relatively small raw numbers of female offenders, any significant change in numbers up or down can be interpreted as a large percentage change and can often be overemphasised, particularly in the media, and interpreted as a 'rising tide' of female criminality (Batchelor 2001, cited in Burman 2004). This has led to a recent overemphasis and unwarranted 'panic' about female criminality.

Victimisation

There is an 'interactive relationship between having been a victim of crime and future offending by girls and women' (Renzetti 2006), and this, together with the interaction between disadvantage and abuse, is a recurring theme throughout this chapter.

In terms of general patterns of victimisation, men are generally more likely to be victims of crime than women. Data from the 2008/9 SCJS show that the most likely crime victim profile is young men aged 16–24 years of age (a victimisation rate of 36 per cent compared with 29 per cent for females of the same age group) (Scottish Government 2009b). The same survey also reports that men (6 per cent) are more likely to be the victims of violent crime compared with women (3 per cent), again with 16–24-year-old men being the highest risk group with 18 per cent reporting victimisation from violent crime compared with 6 per cent of females in this age group.

In Scotland men are at much greater risk of violence from strangers and acquaintances, whereas much of the violence perpetrated against women is carried out by males who are known to them, often with whom they either currently have, or have previously had, an intimate relationship. Research in England also tells us that women are most likely to be raped by men they know, with 54 per cent of rapes committed by men that women either are, or have been, intimate with, and 29 per cent by other known men (Walby and Allen 2004). As will be seen below, women also have high rates of victimisation from domestic abuse during their lifetime. In short, the risk and pattern of violent victimisation – and particularly sexually violent victimisation – is quite different for men and for women (see below).

Women offenders, sentencing and imprisonment

Women's routes into offending behaviour are often different to those of men. It is therefore questionable whether the criminal justice system, largely designed and operated by and for men, is appropriate for women offenders. Women form a mere 5 per cent of the prison population in Scotland (Scotland Prison Commission 2008). The majority are held in Scotland's only female prison, HMP and YOI Cornton Vale in the suburbs of Stirling, and are therefore at a distance from their home area, children and family. Research on women in prison paints a picture of lives characterised by marginalisation, poverty, disadvantage, unemployment, psychological distress, victimisation and abuse (Loucks 2004). While these issues also affect men (see, for example, Chapters 2 and 12, this volume), women arguably experience them to a greater degree and with a disproportionate impact, particularly in view of their relatively disempowered status in society. Given this, and the strong relationship between female offending and social class, it can be argued that welfare-based interventions attempting to address social marginalisation may more effectively meet women's needs and the risk of reoffending than punitive responses.

The influential report, *Women Offenders – A Safer Way* (1998), which followed a series of seven suicides by young women at HMP and YOI Cornton Vale between 1995 and 1997, stated that 'the backgrounds of women in prison are characterised by experiences of abuse, drug misuse, poor educational attainment, poverty, psychological distress and self-harm' (p. 13) and that 'almost all women offenders could be safely punished in the community without major risk of harm to the general population. A few are in prison because of the gravity of their offence but the majority are there because they have not complied with a community disposal' (p. 42). Despite all-party support for the recommendation from Social Work Services and the Prisons Inspectorate that 'the number of women offenders who are sent to prison could and should be reduced', the female prison population in Scotland continues to rise. The average daily prison population of women in 2007/8 was 371, showing an 87 per cent increase over the last ten years, far greater than the 20 per cent rise in the male prison population (Scottish Government 2009c). Similarly, between 1998 and 2008 the custodial remand rate for women increased by 83 per cent. As a result of this there is significant overcrowding at HMP Cornton Vale, contributing to what a recent Prison Inspectorate report described as a 'state of crisis' (HMIP 2010: para. 1.1).

Evidence suggests therefore that women are increasingly being treated as a high-tariff high-risk group despite the fact their offending is not serious in nature (Barry and McIvor 2008). This is largely a result of the increase in the numbers of women entering the system and more punitive sentencing practices in relation to women offenders (Hedderman 2004, cited in Barry and McIvor 2008). Carlen and Tombs (2006) suggest this harsher approach, even when women have committed even minor offences, is in part a result of sentencers' mistaken belief that prison can more effectively meet women's needs, that sentencers must be seen to be tough and that community disposals are often too rigorous and set women up to fail.

Characteristics and experiences of women offenders in Scotland

Loucks' (1998) research, conducted with female prisoners in Scotland, well illustrates the disadvantages faced by many of Scotland's female offenders and the impact of poor life choices and circumstances on their offending behaviour and routes into custody. She found that one-third had injected drugs at some point in their lives and slightly more than half were addicted to drugs. One-third reported being under the influence of alcohol at the time of their offence and many had alcohol-related problems, with binge-drinking being more common than regular heavy drinking or alcohol addiction. She also found a high proportion (82.2 per cent) had experienced violence and abuse with women reporting combinations of sexual, physical and emotional abuse throughout their lives, and many were currently living in abusive adult relationships. Over one-third had attempted suicide, and psychological distress, depression, hopelessness and anxiety were commonly experienced in prison (Loucks 1998). More suicide attempts were made outside than inside prison, which was not in itself the only cause of suicidal behaviour among women prisoners. The experience of prison could, however, exacerbate existing problems of general disadvantage combined with abuse and alcohol or drug withdrawal. Suicides among male prisoners is also of concern and is often given comparatively less attention by the media.

Further evidence of disadvantage experienced by female prisoners is illustrated when exploring educational background and attainment. Loucks found that over 90 per cent had left school at 16 or under. Later research by Henderson (2001) found that 61 per cent of her sample of the Scottish female prison population left school without any qualifications and that two-thirds were dependent on state benefits. Those who had been employed were more often than not in unskilled jobs, and half reported that their offence was motivated partly by financial need, suggesting that women's involvement in crime is often related to their role as carers for dependent children and responsibility to provide for others' needs. More women than men are also prosecuted for not having a TV licence, despite that fact that both men and women are equally likely to commit this offence. Women's status as primary carers and the fact they are more likely to be in the home makes them more vulnerable to criminalisation, a process more likely to affect women in lower socio-economic groups (Equal Opportunities Committee 2010).

Alternatives to prison and gender-specific interventions

There are compelling arguments for reducing the number of custodial sentences given to women, and academics have long questioned the appropriateness of prison for women and the under-use of community disposals (McIvor 2004; Rumgay 2004). As the majority of prisoners in Scotland and elsewhere are male, custodial culture and programmes prioritising security and control are dominated by the needs and experiences of men (Carlen 1983; Stern 1998). Moreover, the characteristics of female offenders indicates their vulnerability and suggests the importance of gender-specific and gender-appropriate interventions for women, addressing their underlying problems including multiple disadvantage, low self-esteem, limited educational and social capital and mental health (Sheehan *et al.* 2007).

A major problem, however, is the poor provision of community penalties for women. Research by Barry and McIvor (2008) in Lothian and Borders found that 'the lack of gender-specific services for women was seen as a major obstacle to effective engagement [with women offenders] as was the perhaps misguided assumption that women should and could benefit from the same services offered to men, such as employability or offending behaviour problems' (p. 68). It is difficult to fine women on very low incomes (see also Chapter 11, this volume) and it is also often more difficult for them to successfully complete community service orders given that they are more likely to be caring for dependent children and have other daytime commitments. Tombs' (2004a) research suggests that sentencers often think it better to send a woman to prison, even for a minor offence, than to set her up to fail with a too rigorous community sentence.

The most significant development in Scotland in terms of alternatives to prison for women offenders has been the 218 Centre in Glasgow, seen by policy-makers as an 'opportunity to substantially reduce the number of women who received custodial sentences, with particular recognition of the link between women's offending and drug misuse' (Malloch *et al.* 2008: 385). It aims to provide community-based services for women over 18 years of age involved in the criminal justice process and seen as at risk of reoffending and imprisonment, and provides multi-agency support through a day service and residential unit which includes psychological services, health care and prescribing, and emotional support. The gender-specific nature of these programmes recognises women's distinct pathways into offending and shifts the focus from punishment to rehabilitation.

An evaluation of the centre (Malloch *et al.* 2008) found that the characteristics of women referred reflected those of the female prison population, highlighting their vulnerable nature. Most had limited education, little experience of employment, many had no fixed address (44 per cent), 83 per cent suffered from depression, 45 per cent had self-harmed or attempted suicide, 97 per cent had used heroin and 52 per cent had a problem with alcohol. Seventy per cent of women were involved with the criminal justice system for offences of shoplifting. Despite some problems, the Centre has, on the whole, been a success, resulting in reduced or ceased alcohol and/or drug use, increased well-being, self-care and better mental health, and while the study was limited, anecdotal evidence suggested that it had diverted some women from custody, at least in the short term (Malloch *et al.* 2004). It was also not possible to evaluate its impact on the prison population which, argue the authors, requires a wider change in sentencing practices as prison remains at the centre of penal policy in Scotland. Moreover, any significant reduction in women's offending requires, not the psychological 'individualising' of women's problems but rather taking account of their wider social structural position and what Tombs (2004b) calls the 'material conditions' of women's offending.

Young women and crime

The distinct features of youth offending and the criminal justice response in Scotland are dealt with in Chapter 5 (this volume). This section will restrict attention to specific issues in relation to young women, gender, crime and criminal behaviour.

This significance of gender as a predictor of offending behaviour is true for young people as well as adults (Walklate 2004), although it is much less marked in adolescence (Moffitt *et al.* 2001) when minor offending rates cluster closer together. This said, we have relatively little empirical evidence about young women who offend and as a result there is a risk that young women and their needs are overlooked, and that anecdotal evidence is misinterpreted and taken to be representative of young female offenders overall (Burman and Batchelor 2009).

The longitudinal Edinburgh Study of Youth Transitions and Crime (ESYTC) conducted with a single cohort of 4,000 children aged 12–15 who began school in Edinburgh in 1988, described in Chapter 5 (this volume), found, consistent with Moffitt *et al.* (2001), that boys were much more likely to be involved in serious delinquency and serious violent offences but that there was more similarity between boys and girls for the less serious offences (Smith and McAra 2004). Between the ages of 12 and 14 delinquency rates rose more sharply for girls than boys, but at age 15 rates for girls fell away in comparison with boys, suggesting that girls pass through the turbulent period associated with offending earlier than boys (Smith and McAra 2004: 13). In terms of factors associated with gender and offending, some gender differences emerge. Socio-economic factors were more likely to be associated with girls' offending than boys', suggesting a greater influence of poverty and deprivation. Additionally, the study found that low self-esteem, having friends of the opposite sex and weak attachments to school were more significant for girls than boys (Smith and McAra 2004).

It is important to note that the ESYTC found that young people's delinquency is to some extent 'natural and normal, and will fade as young people grow into adulthood provided there is no drastic response to the offending that is seriously damaging to the teenager' (Smith and McAra 2004: 21). Given this, it is extremely important not to have an overly punitive criminal justice response to youth offending and to combat moral panics around the so-called 'rising problem' of criminal and violent behaviour among young people and the accompanying panic about 'gang activity', evident in media reports and also taken up by policy-makers and government officials (see Burman and Batchelor 2009). Discussions such as these often depict young women as disorderly, out of control, drunk and prone to violence and a key element of the 'youth problem' (Batchelor 2005).

Burman and Batchelor (2009) argue that it is important to view these concerns through the lens of the increased politicisation of youth crime that has taken place post-devolution and the move away from the penal-welfarist ethos of youth justice described in Chapter 5 (this volume). Despite this (arguably misplaced) concern about supposedly rising offending by young women there are very few programmes or interventions designed specifically for young women in Scotland (Burman 2004). The Scottish Prison Service does not allocate responsibility for young female offenders to the portfolio of any of its staff, nor does HMP YOI Cornton Vale provide any programmes specifically directed towards young female offenders (Scottish Government 2009f).

Overall there are small numbers of young female offenders. The majority of their offences are non-violent, and while data suggests some rise in girls' violent offences, most violence in Scotland is still committed by males (Burman and Batchelor 2009). It is also possible that the increase observed in young women's participation in violent crime may not be a rise in incidents overall, but an increased response in terms of reporting, recording and prosecution (Batchelor 2005). As Worrall (2004) has detailed for England and Wales, the panic surrounding so-called 'ladettes' has meant that 'troublesome young girls' are now seen as 'naughty little madams', that the extent of the problem is often over-exaggerated in media reports, and that 'violent girls' now exist as a category in penal discourse.

As in England and Wales, young women in the justice system, like their adult counterparts, have histories of abuse, abandonment, a lack of emotional and financial resources and a variety of childhood victimisations, and have often run away from home (Batchelor 2005; Burman and Batchelor 2009; Chesney-Lind and Pasko 2004). Young women are also subject to peer influence and, in situations with weak family ties and a lack of support, friendships with other peers become more important (Burman *et al.* 2003). Young women's offending is also related to the transition from youth to adulthood and the search for identity, in contrast to adult women's offending so often brought on by other life stresses and problems (McIvor 1998, cited in Burman and Batchelor 2009). It is also important not to see young women who offend solely as 'victims' and indeed, recent literature has drawn attention to the need to be cognisant of young women's agency and to recognise that some of their behaviour may represent survival strategies (Batchelor 2005). Scottish justice policy needs nonetheless to be more aware of the dangers of overlooking this small group of young women and to devote more attention to their pathways into offending, and to the interventions which they require when they do offend and enter the justice system.

The preceding review of the dimensions of inequality associated with women's gender and victimisation are exposed as being similar to those elsewhere in the UK. There follows a focus on one aspect of women's offending, prostitution, and two aspects of women's victimisation, domestic abuse and sexual violence, that allows a more specific exploration of the expression of gender issues in this jurisdiction.

Prostitution

In Scotland prostitution in terms of selling sex is not illegal, but behaviours associated with it are – for example, soliciting and keeping a brothel. Prostitution (as crimes of indecency) is one offence category where women are over-represented and where offending and victimisation overlap quite markedly. The lives of sex workers are generally characterised by risk and many women are subsequently victimised through physical assault, rape and sexual assault (Martin 2006).

It is estimated that approximately 1,400 women are involved in street prostitution in Scotland, the vast majority of whom are in Glasgow (1,000–1,200) and, research suggests, it is usually a survival behaviour brought about by a lack of resources, often linked to drug use and poverty (Scottish Executive 2004). Glasgow's Routes Out of Prostitution Social Inclusion Partnership reported that the most likely reasons for attending their intervention team were drug use, homelessness and housing issues, child abuse, mental health, trauma and sexual violence (Routes Out of Prostitution 2003). The recognition of prostitution as a survival behaviour born of limited life choices is crucial in that it does not support the idea that prostitution is a life choice or a sexual behaviour but suggests that it reflects women's marginalised position and also that prostitution is exploitative and part of the continuum of violence against women (Kelly 1988).

Arguably it is men's demand for prostitution that is the heart of the problem. However, until recently no legal action was taken against men who solicited sex from prostitutes, rather women were (and are) criminalised for their involvement. Recent legislation in Scotland has taken steps to address the problem but arguably not gone far enough. The Prostitution (Public Places) Scotland Act 2007 takes the step of criminalising the sex-buyer by making it an offence to loiter in a public place with the intention of purchasing sex from a prostitute. However, on the implementation of this reform the de facto 'tolerance zones' operating in Edinburgh and Aberdeen (but not Glasgow where the emphasis is on zero tolerance), and which may have given some women engaged in prostitution a degree of protection (albeit in the short term), were ended, thereby potentially returning the women to their previous level of risk of violence from men.

Current legislation does not go as far as feminist campaigners wanted as it fails to take steps to reduce the criminalisation of women involved in prostitution. Feminist campaigners hoped the

Scottish government would introduce legislation similar to that found in Sweden where sex-buyers, 'pimps' and those involved in human trafficking for the sex trade are criminalised, whereas women involved in prostitution are conceptualised as victims whose lives are characterised by poverty, disadvantage, poor immigration status, abuse and limited life choices. As such, they are not criminalised, and although they may be arrested, they are then directed towards social support and services aimed at helping women find routes out of prostitution. The legislation effectively enshrined in law that women are not for sale (Ekberg 2004) and reiterated the belief that prostitution is an intrinsic part of the continuum of violence against women (Kelly 1988).

Domestic abuse

Domestic abuse in Scotland, as with other countries, is a significant and widespread problem and one that is intrinsically gendered. Research tells us that serious violence within intimate relationships is not symmetrical and men are more likely to be violent towards women. We also know women's violence within intimate relationships contrasts with that of men in terms of intensity, frequency, level of injury inflicted and subsequent emotional impact (Dobash and Dobash, cited in Hoyle 2007).

In Scotland there were 53,861 incidents of domestic abuse recorded by the police in 2008/9 with an overall incidence of 1,039 per 100,000 population (Scottish Government 2009d). The gendered nature of domestic abuse is evident as incidents with a female victim and male perpetrator represented 84 per cent of all incidents recorded in 2008/9. We also know that women are at risk of repeat victimisation, as 61 per cent of victims in recorded incidents had previously experienced domestic abuse, with 44 per cent having experienced domestic abuse on four or more occasions. It should be noted that not all Scottish police forces have databases that record repeat incidents so the 'true' figure may be higher.

The prevalence of domestic abuse is notoriously difficult to measure due to its 'hidden' nature: it takes place in the private sphere of the home. It is also notoriously under-reported so figures on police reporting and recording should not be taken to represent the 'true' nature of domestic abuse prevalence. Indeed, the SCJS 2008–9 sweep found that fewer than one in five (21 per cent) of all domestic abuse incidents were reported to the police (Scottish

Government 2009g). Women do not often report assaults to the police, especially if their abuser is known to them, which is most often the case (Koss and Heslet 1992), because they fear they will not be believed and because they fear further violence from their abuser.

The SCJS found a domestic abuse incidence rate of 5 per cent of survey respondents, and a domestic abuse prevalence rate from age 16 of 18 per cent of survey respondents (Scottish Government 2009g). Arguably, Scotland has been at the forefront of developments in domestic abuse policy. It was in Scotland that the first re-education programme for perpetrators of domestic abuse was introduced (Dobash and Dobash 2000) and where the acclaimed Zero Tolerance campaign, subsequently adopted by other countries and areas, was funded and developed (Kitzinger and Hunt 1993). Significantly too, Scotland has adopted the term 'domestic abuse' as distinct from 'domestic violence'. The former recognises that domestic abuse may involve behaviours other than, and including, physical violence and can also include psychological, emotional, financial and social features and is therefore considerably broader than 'domestic violence' would suggest. Scotland's *National Strategy on Domestic Abuse* aims 'to take all practicable measures toward elimination of domestic abuse including a clear acknowledgement that responsibility for abuse lies firmly with the perpetrator' (p. 7) and also recognises that domestic abuse 'is associated with broader inequalities in society' and 'is part of a range of behaviours constituting an abuse of male power' (Scottish Executive 2000: 5).

The Protection from Abuse (Scotland) Act 2001 is one such 'practicable measure' that offers greater protection to those leaving abusive relationships in that it allows for a power of arrest to be attached to an interdict. While the Act is significant in that it recognises the greater protection victims of domestic abuse require, it has also been limited in impact due to women's lack of knowledge of the legislation, the cost of using the Act and difficulties in securing powers of arrest (Cavanagh *et al.* 2003). The evaluation of the legislation also found that powers of arrest were not always enforced by the police, and the requirement that a breach of the interdict must amount to a crime before any prosecution could result undermined its effectiveness. As such 'the effects of these limitations are being felt by those already vulnerable, victims of abuse who, in consequence, continue to find it extremely difficult to secure protection from the legal system' (Cavanagh *et al.* 2003: 87).

Another significant development in Scotland was the introduction of specialist domestic abuse courts, piloted in Glasgow from 2004, and which, following a 2007 evaluation, were expanded to cover the majority of the city's domestic abuse cases. This is a dedicated Sheriff court that allows domestic abuse cases to be fast-tracked through the justice process and offers the ASSIST programme to provide support for victims and their families and the CHANGE programme for the perpetrators of domestic abuse. An evaluation found that it did increase the effectiveness of responses to domestic abuse and led to a greater number of guilty pleas, a higher conviction rate and a lower case attrition rate in comparison with cases held in non-specialised courts (Scottish Executive 2007). This success and widespread praise from key criminal justice figures led to calls for the scheme to be expanded Scotland-wide; however, recent reports suggest this has been put on hold due to a lack of funding (Leask 2009). Arguably, while Scotland has been at the forefront of key developments in the area of domestic abuse, a commitment to deliver resources to support this is required for ongoing success.

Rape and sexual violence

Rape and sexual violence are significant social problems but as with domestic abuse, prevalence data is limited and there is currently no prevalence study in Scotland. However, the Scottish Crime and Justice Survey (SCJS) now includes a selection of questions on sexual victimisation. Research elsewhere suggests that women face a disproportionately high risk of sexual victimisation in comparison with men (Kessler *et al.* 1995). Additionally, under-reporting of rape is a significant issue. Reasons thought to influence women's decision to not report rape include not naming the incident as rape, a fear of not being believed, a fear of being blamed and a lack of confidence in the criminal justice process (Kelly and Regan 2003).

The attrition rate for rape in Scotland is an ongoing problem. An analysis of attrition data over the last three decades shows steadily increasing reporting rates, more or less consistent prosecutions and convictions, and a conviction rate that continues to decrease (Burman *et al.* 2009) and is currently 3.7 per cent of recorded rapes (Scottish Government 2009a). Between 1977 and 2006 rape reports in Scotland increased by 451 per cent, including historic offences (Burman *et al.* 2009). However, prosecutions and convictions remain alarmingly low and demonstrate that justice is not being delivered for victims of rape. Table 5.1 details the number of rapes recorded, prosecuted and convicted in Scotland in 2007–8. Fewer than one in ten of all

Table 5.1 Rape recording, prosecution and conviction figures: Scotland 2007–8

Number of recorded rapes	908
Rape prosecutions	88
Rape convictions	34
Rape prosecution rate	9.7%
Rape conviction rate	3.7%

Source: Scottish Government (2009a).

recorded rapes (which represents a significantly smaller number than the actual incidence of rape) were prosecuted and only 34 of the 908 recorded rapes resulted in a conviction.

If we contrast the outcomes of criminal cases overall with that of rape cases we find very powerful evidence that the prosecution of rape is problematic. For all crimes proceeded against in 2007/8 in Scotland, a total of 3 per cent were acquitted on a 'not guilty' verdict. However, the acquittal rate for rape and attempted rape following a 'not guilty' verdict was 30 per cent, and for indecent assault 19 per cent. Additionally, rape and sexual assault cases had the highest proportion of 'not proven' verdicts, by quite a significant margin at 24 per cent, which accounts for 45 per cent of all 'not proven' verdicts (Scottish Government 2009a).

In 2007/8, only 40 per cent (n = 48) of all rape and attempted rape cases that came to court had 'guilty' verdicts. Rape has the lowest conviction rate of all crimes by a staggering margin, with the next nearest proportion of 'guilty' verdicts being indecent assault at 67 per cent, and serious assault and attempted murder at 74 per cent of all cases proceeded against in court receiving a 'guilty' verdict (Scottish Government 2009a). In contrast, the proportion of all offences proceeded against in Scottish courts in 2007/8 that received a 'guilty' verdict was 91 per cent (Scottish Government 2009a), a figure that compares very unfavourably with the 40 per cent conviction rate for rape and attempted rape, giving further evidence that victims of serious sexual assaults are considerably less likely to receive justice than victims of other crimes.

In Scotland the legal definition of rape remains gendered and refers specifically to vaginal penetration of a female victim by the penis of a male perpetrator, although long-awaited legislation to radically overhaul rape law, including the definition, will come into force in Scotland in 2010. There have been some significant developments in terms of rape law in the last few decades. For example, rape in marriage was criminalised in Scotland in 1989 following the case of *Stallard* v. *HMA* in Stirling High Court, two years earlier than in England. This is often misreported in literature that wrongly states that rape in marriage was criminalised in Britain in 1991 (for example, Lees 1997), and fails to acknowledge that Scotland is a different legal jurisdiction. In recent decades great concern has been raised about the use of women's sexual history in rape trials and the further victimisation this produced as well as its contribution to a culture that blames women for sexual violence perpetrated against them and that in some way their previous conduct would somehow 'invite' sexual violence. The Law Reform (Miscellaneous Provisions) (Scotland) Act 1985 introduced 'shield' legislation that prevented the use of sexual history and character evidence of the complainant. It was in practice largely ineffective though because three rather loose exception clauses allowed judges to admit evidence under certain circumstances and in practice they did (Brown *et al.* 1993). This legislation was superseded by the Sexual Offences (Procedure and Evidence) (Scotland) Act 2002 that introduced stricter guidelines on sexual history evidence and also prevented the accused from cross-examining the complainant in a rape case. This latter feature was prompted by *HMA* v. *Anderson* (2000) where the accused cross-examined his 13-year-old victim for three hours causing considerable distress. An evaluation of the effectiveness of the 2002 Act in preventing the use of women's sexual history evidence found that applications to use it were frequently made, particularly where consent was a defence against the rape charge. In addition where granted, the defence often went beyond what had been initially agreed, and even when applications were refused the defence often introduced such evidence nonetheless (Burman *et al.* 2007), suggesting that the legislation, while representing a legislative 'gain', has limitations in practice.

Concerns about existing rape legislation in Scotland led to the Scottish Law Commission undertaking a review of rape legislation that resulted in a comprehensive report and recommendations for change (Scottish Law Commission 2007). These included a widening of the definition of rape to include other forms of sexual penetration, including anal, oral and penetration by use of an object, and also widened the definition of who could be a victim of rape to include men and transgendered women. It also recommended a statutory definition of 'consent' be introduced to legislation as existing legislation did not provide one and therefore left it open to interpretation. This is highlighted in the case of *Marr* v. *HM Advocate*

(1996) where the jury requested clarification from the judge about the definition of consent. The judge responded: 'The definition of consent is a common, straightforward, definition of consent. It's the common English word given its normal meaning. And that, I am afraid, is it. Consent is consent. What does consent mean? Is that the only question you have? Thank you very much.' This highlights the lack of understanding of consent on the part of juries and criminal justice personnel. The legislation that resulted from the Scottish Law Commission's report, the Sexual Offences (Scotland) Act 2009 that comes into force in 2010, has introduced a wider definition of rape and also introduces a definition of consent as 'free agreement' and provides a list of circumstances where consent cannot be freely given, for example when a victim is unconscious. This is undoubtedly a step in the right direction but it remains to be seen whether this new legislation impacts on the significant problem of rape case attrition and the alarmingly low conviction rate currently seen in Scotland. However, what is also required in Scotland is active steps to reduce the extent to which public attitudes are supportive of rape myths that place responsibility for rape and sexual assault on the part of women and not the men who perpetrate it.

Unfortunately there has been a dearth of research on rape and sexual violence in the Scottish jurisdiction in comparison to that conducted in England and Wales in recent years (for example, Harris and Grace 1999; Lea *et al.* 2003; Lees 2002; McMillan and Thomas 2009; Temkin 2003). While much of the research conducted south of the border has relevance for the criminal justice response to rape in Scotland, there are peculiarities of the Scottish justice process in relation to rape and sexual assault that are worthy of further research, in particular the policing of rape and sexual violence in Scotland as this is the stage of the criminal justice process where most case attrition occurs (Chambers and Millar 1983; Gregory and Lees 1997; Kelly *et al.* 2005; Temkin 2002). Chambers and Millar (1983) did consider the policing stage of the justice process when conducting their research almost three decades ago but no significant research has been conducted on the policing of rape in Scotland since. The research that has been conducted since has concentrated on the later stages of the criminal justice process (Brown *et al.* 1992; Burman *et al.* 2007). Some research currently being conducted will hopefully address this gap and give us a more comprehensive understanding of the problems surrounding rape reporting, recording and prosecuting in Scotland and allow steps to be taken to improve the criminal justice response.

Concluding comments

It is clear that in Scotland, as elsewhere, women's experience of crime as both offenders and victims is different to that of men. Women are less likely to commit crime than men, the crimes they do commit are less serious and their criminal behaviour is often born of limited life choices, marginalisation and socio-economic need that, while also affecting men, have a disproportionate impact on women. Similarly, women are less likely to be the victims of crime and young men remain at the greatest risk of criminal violence. However, women are the primary victims of violence and abuse in the home and within intimate relationships and are those most likely to be sexually victimised, most often by men they know. The risk for women, then, is the men they love, live with, are related to and work with.

There is an interrelationship between women's victimisation and their subsequent offending behaviour and an understanding of this is required if we are to provide an adequate criminal justice response and meet the needs of women. The evidence presented suggests that the criminal justice response when women are offenders, and when they are victims, is currently inadequate. Prison and custodial practices do not meet the needs of women, and legislation and interventions for domestic abuse and rape and sexual assault, while moving in the right direction, are woefully inadequate for addressing the gravity of the problem. The Gender Equality Duty now requires all public authorities to eliminate unlawful discrimination and harassment and to promote equality of opportunity between men and women, and this includes an obligation to assess the impact of policies and practices on both sexes. This will require the agencies of the criminal justice system to address the needs of women as both victims and offenders, and while some work is underway, significant change is still to be made (Equal Opportunities Committee 2010).

An analysis of gender, crime and criminal justice draws attention to the inadequacies of the criminal justice process for women – both as victims and as perpetrators. Dobash and Dobash (1992) explicitly draw attention to the patriarchal nature of the law and legal apparatus and the impossibility of addressing women's oppression through an institution whose procedures and language are imbued with patriarchal beliefs. It is clear that Scotland is some way away from what Carlen (1990) calls a 'women-wise penology' and also from addressing the specific needs of women when they are subject to victimisation at the hands of men.

References

Barry, M. and McIvor, G. (2008) *Chaotic Lives: A Profile of Women in the Criminal Justice System in Lothian and Borders*. Peebles: Lothian and Borders Community Justice Authority.

Batchelor, S. (2005) '"Prove me the bam!" Victimisation and agency in the lives of young women who commit violent offences', *Probation Journal*, 52 (4): 328–75.

Brown, B., Burman, M. and Jamieson, L. (1992) *Sexual History and Sexual Character Evidence in Scottish Sexual Offence Trials*. Edinburgh: Scottish Office, Central Research Unit Papers.

Brown, B., Burman, M. and Jamieson, L. (1993) *Sex Crimes on Trial*. Edinburgh: Edinburgh University Press.

Burman, M. (2004) 'Breaking the mould: patterns of female offending', in G. McIvor (ed.), *Women Who Offend*. London: Jessica Kingsley

Burman, M. and Batchelor, S. (2009) 'Between two stools: responding to young women who offend', *Youth Justice*, 9 (3): 270–85.

Burman, M., Brown, J. and Batchelor, S. (2003) '"Taking it to heart": girls and the meanings of violence', in E. Stanko (ed.), *The Meanings of Violence*. London: Routledge.

Burman, M., Lovett, L. and Kelly, L. (2009) *Different Systems, Similar Outcomes? Tracking Attrition in Reported Rape Cases: Scotland Country Report*. London: Child and Women Abuse Studies Unit.

Burman, M., Jamieson, L., Nicholson, J. and Brooks, O. (2007) *Impact of the Law of Evidence in Sexual Offence Trials: An Evaluation*. Edinburgh: Scottish Government Social Research

Carlen, P. (1983) *Women's Imprisonment: A Study in Social Control*. London: Routledge.

Carlen, P. (1990) *Alternatives to Women's Imprisonment*. Buckingham: Open University Press

Carlen, P. and Tombs, J. (2006) 'Reconfigurations of penality: the ongoing case of the women's imprisonment and reintegration industries', *Theoretical Criminology*, 10: 337–60.

Cavanagh, K., Connelly, C. and Scoular, J. (2003) *An Evaluation of the Protection from Abuse Scotland Act 2001*. Edinburgh: Scottish Executive.

Chambers, G. and Millar, A. (1983) *Investigating Sexual Assault*. Edinburgh: Scottish Office Central Research Unit.

Chesney-Lind, M. and Pasko, L.J. (2004) *The Female Offender: Girls, Women and Crime*, 2nd edn. Thousand Oaks, CA: Sage.

Dobash, R. E. and Dobash, R. P. (1992) *Women, Violence and Social Change*. London: Routledge.

Dobash, R. E. and Dobash R. P. (2000) 'The politics and policies of responding to violence against women', in J. Hanmer and K. Itzen (eds), *Home Truths about Domestic Violence*. London: Routledge.

Ekberg, G. (2004) 'The Swedish law that prohibits the purchase of sexual services: best practices for prevention of prostitution and trafficking in human beings', *Violence Against Women*, 10 (10): 1187–218.

Equal Opportunities Committee (2010) *Female Offenders in the Criminal Justice System*. Edinburgh: Scottish Parliament.

Ferraro, K. F. (1995) *Fear of Crime: Interpreting Victimization Risk*. Albany, NY: State University of New York Press.

Gregory, J. and Lees, S. (1999) *Policing Sexual Assault*. London: Routledge.

Harris, J. and Grace, S. (1999) *A Question of Evidence? Investigating and Prosecuting Rape in the 1990s*. Home Office Research Study 196. London: Home Office.

Heidensohn, F. and Gelsthorpe, L. (2007) 'Gender and crime', in M. Maguire, R. Morgan and R. Reiner (eds) *The Oxford Handbook of Criminology*. Oxford: Oxford University Press.

Henderson, S. (1997) *Hidden Findings: The Edinburgh Women's Safety Survey*. Edinburgh: City of Edinburgh Council.

Henderson, S. (2001) *Women Offenders: Effective Management and Intervention*, Scottish Prison Service Occasional Paper No. 2001. Edinburgh: Scottish Prison Service.

HM Inspectorate of Prisons (2010) *Report on HMP and YOI Cornton Vale*. Edinburgh: Scottish Executive.

Hoyle, C. (2007) 'Feminism, victimology and domestic violence', in S. Walklate (ed.), *Handbook of Victims and Victimology*. Cullompton: Willan Publishing.

Kelly, L. (1988) *Surviving Sexual Violence*. London: Polity Press.

Kelly, L. and Regan, L. (2003) *Rape: Still a Forgotten Issue*. London: Child and Women Abuse Studies Unit.

Kelly, L., Lovett, J. and Regan, L. (2005) *A Gap or a Chasm? Attrition in Reported Rape Cases*, Home Office Research Study 293. London: Home Office.

Kessler, R. C. *et al.* (1995) 'Post-traumatic stress disorder in the national co-morbidity survey', *Archives of General Psychiatry*, 52.

Kitzinger, J. and Hunt, K. (1993) *Evaluation of Edinburgh District Council's Zero Tolerance Campaign*. Edinburgh District Council Women's Committee.

Koss, M. P. and Heslet, L. (1992) 'Somatic consequences of violence against women', *Archives of Family Medicine*, 1.

Lea, S., Lanvers, U. and Shaw, S. (2003) 'Attrition in rape cases: developing a profile and identifying relevant factors', *British Journal of Criminology*, 43: 583–99.

Leask, D. (2009) 'Abuse court roll-out in jeopardy', *Scotland on Sunday*, 20 December.

Lees, S. (1997) *Ruling Passions: Sexual Violence, Reputation and the Law*. Milton Keynes: Open University Press.

Lees, S. (2002) *Carnal Knowledge: Rape on Trial*. London: Women's Press.

Loucks, N. (1998) *HMPI Cornton Vale: Research into Drugs and Alcohol, Violence and Bullying, Suicides and Self-injury and Backgrounds of Abuse*, Scottish

Prison Service Occasional Paper No. 1/98. Edinburgh: Scottish Prison Service.

Loucks, N. (2004) 'Women in prison', in G. McIvor (ed.), *Women Who Offend*. London: Jessica Kingsley.

McIvor, G. (2004) 'Service with a smile? Women and community "punishment"', in G. McIvor (ed.), *Women Who Offend*. London: Jessica Kingsley.

McMillan, L. and Thomas, M. (2009) 'Police interviews of rape victims: tensions and contradictions', in M. Horvath and J. Brown (eds), *Rape: Challenging Contemporary Thinking*. Cullompton: Willan Publishing.

Malloch, M., McIvor, G. and Loucks, G. (2008) '"Time out" for women: innovation in Scotland in a context of change', *Howard Journal*, 47 (4): 383–99.

Martin, S. E. (2006) 'Female drug offenders and the drug/crime sub-culture: gender, stigma and social control', in C. Renzetti (ed.), *Rethinking Gender, Crime and Justice*. Los Angeles: Roxbury.

Moffitt, T. E., Caspie, A., Rutter, M. and Silva, P. A. (2001) *Sex Difference in Anti-social Behaviour*. Cambridge: Cambridge University Press.

Nicholas, S., Povey, D. Walker, A. and Kershaw, C. (2005) *Crime in England and Wales 2004–5*. London: Home Office.

Renzetti, C. (ed.) (2006) *Rethinking Gender, Crime and Justice*. Los Angeles: Roxbury.

Routes Out of Prostitution (2003) *Routes Out Annual Report*. Glasgow: Routes Out of Prostitution.

Rumgay, J. (2004) 'Living with paradox: community supervision of women offenders', in G. McIvor (ed.), *Women Who Offend*. London: Jessica Kingsley.

Scottish Executive (2000) *National Strategy on Domestic Abuse*. Edinburgh: Scottish Executive.

Scottish Executive (2004) *Being Outside: Constructing a Response to Street Prostitution*. Edinburgh: Scottish Executive.

Scottish Executive (2007) *Evaluation of the Pilot Domestic Abuse Court*. Edinburgh: Scottish Executive Justice Department.

Scottish Government (2009a) *Criminal Proceedings in Scottish Courts 2007/8*. Edinburgh: Scottish Government

Scottish Government (2009b) *Scottish Crime and Justice Survey 2008/9: First Findings*. Edinburgh: Scottish Government.

Scottish Government (2009c) *Prison Statistics Scotland 2007/8*. Edinburgh: Scottish Government.

Scottish Government (2009d) *Domestic Abuse Recorded by the Police in Scotland 2008/9*. Edinburgh: Scottish Government.

Scottish Government (2009e) *Safer Lives: Changed Lives – A Shared Approach to Tackling Violence Against Women in Scotland*. Edinburgh: Scottish Government.

Scottish Government (2009f) *HM Inspectorate of Prisons: Report on Young Offenders in Adult Establishments*. Edinburgh: Scottish Government.

Scottish Government (2009g) *2008–9 Scottish Crime and Justice Survey: Partner Abuse*. Edinburgh: Scottish Government.

Scottish Law Commission (2007) *Report on Rape and Other Sexual Offences*. Edinburgh: Scottish Law Commission.

Sheehan, R., McIvor, G. and Trotter, C. (eds) (2007) *What Works with Women Offenders*. Cullompton: Willan Publishing.

Smith, D. J. and McAra, L. (2004) *Gender and Youth Offending: The Edinburgh Study of Youth Transitions and Crime*. Edinburgh: Centre for Law and Society, University of Edinburgh.

Stern, V. (1998) *A Sin Against the Future: Imprisonment in the World*. London: Penguin Books.

Temkin, J. (2002) *Rape and the Legal Process*. Oxford: Oxford University Press.

Temkin, J. (2003) 'Sexual history evidence – beware the backlash', *Criminal Law Review*, April, pp. 217–42.

Tombs, J. (2004a) *A Unique Punishment: Sentencing and the Prison Population in Scotland*. Edinburgh: Scottish Consortium on Crime and Criminal Justice.

Tombs, J. (2004b) 'From "a safer way to a better way": transformations in penal policy for women', in G. McIvor (ed.) *Women Who Offend*. London: Jessica Kingsley.

Walby, S. and Allen, J. (2004) *Domestic Violence, Sexual Assault and Stalking: Findings from the British Crime Survey*, Home Office Rsearch Study No. 276. London: Home Office Research, Development and Statistics Directorate.

Walklate, S. (2004) *Gender, Crime and Criminal Justice*. Cullompton: Willan Publishing.

Worrall, A. (2004) 'Twisted sisters, ladettes, and the new penology: the social construction of "violent girls"', in C. Adler and A. Worrall (eds), *Girls' Violence: Myths and Realities*. Albany, NY: State University of New York.

Case law

HMA v. *Anderson* (2000) – unreported case
Marr v. *HM Advocate* (1996) SCCR 696
Stallard v. *HMA* (1989) SCCR 248

Chapter 6

Race, ethnicity, crime and justice in Scotland

Hazel Croall and Liz Frondigoun

Introduction

Globally, migration has been associated with fears of 'the other', of terrorism, urban unrest and the spread of organised crime. Criminological work on race, ethnicity, crime and justice in the UK has been dominated by the largely English experience of police racism, racist violence and successive processes of criminalisation. Scotland's different history has been associated with perceptions of greater equality and tolerance. Nonetheless, this reputation contains an element of mythology (de Lima 2005) and Scotland has not been free of racist and ethnically motivated violence and the criminalisation of some immigrant groups. This chapter will explore these issues, focusing, largely for reasons of space, on race and ethnicity, while recognising their complex interrelationship with issues of sectarianism and faith. The chapter will start by briefly outlining patterns of immigration in Scotland and providing an overview of issues of race, ethnicity and crime. Racist violence and victimisation in Scotland will then be explored along with policing and responses to terrorism before discussing the distinctiveness of the Scottish experience.

Race, ethnicity and immigration: the Scottish experience

Scotland has traditionally been a country characterised by emigration, although a combination of socio-economic and geographic factors have been associated with the immigration of a variety of groups, most fleeing poverty and oppression. Some arrived in Scotland's ports en route to America; others, like the Irish, due to poverty and the proximity of Scotland. From the mid-seventeenth century Scottish merchants, including Glasgow's Tobacco Lords, made wealthy by owning and trading with the sugar and tobacco plantations of the West Indies and the eastern seaboard of America, returned home, bringing their house slaves with them. Many prominent Scottish families had slaves, some of whom were kept in very poor conditions (Edward 2008). One such was Joseph Knight, the subject of a fictionalised account (Robertson 2004), who was baptised and through a succession of court cases was successful in establishing that the law of Scotland did not recognise the state of slavery (*Knight* v. *Wedderburn* (1778)).

The Irish formed a prominent group across Scotland with regular steamships arriving in Glasgow from Belfast, some characterised by 'slave like' conditions (Kay 1980). As many as 8,000 Irish immigrants per week were estimated to have arrived in Glasgow in the 1840s during the Irish famine (Edward 2008; Kearney 1990). The Irish worked across Scotland, some in farms during the harvest and later many, reflecting the strong concentration in the West of Scotland as in Liverpool, worked as 'navvies' who played a major role in building the Glasgow underground.

A small Jewish community was located in Edinburgh from the 1780s. A century later, many Jews fleeing persecution in Russia arrived in Scotland en route to America. Some settled, arriving on the East Coast or at Greenock. Jewish street traders and tailors lived in Glasgow's Gorbals, forming the basis of a Jewish community which has now dispersed to other areas.

An early Italian immigrant was David Rizzio, a musician and courtier, who became Mary Queen of Scots' secretary and was famously murdered at the Palace of Holyrood in Mary's supper chamber in 1566. In the latter part of the nineteenth century, Italians of different origins arrived in Scotland with the population increasing to 4,500 by 1914. They became street pedlars and musicians and later hairdressers and some set up the celebrated ice cream parlours (Edward 2008).

Other groups came from Eastern Europe, with the Lanarkshire Lithuanians working in blast furnaces and mines (Kay 1980) numbering an estimated 5–6,000 by 1914. They were often described as Poles, who also migrated to Scotland, with the first Scottish Polish Society being founded in Edinburgh in the 1830s. Around 8,000 Polish people are estimated to have been living in Scotland during and after the Second World War (Edward 2008).

Immigrants also arrived from China, the earliest of whom were sailors jumping ship. Later Chinese immigrants arrived in Scotland from Hong Kong and the new territories, notably during the 1960s. As will be seen below the largest minority ethnic group in Scotland is now from the Indian subcontinent, with many, as elsewhere in Britain, having arrived to fill gaps in the labour market, particularly in transport. In Glasgow for example, the Asian community numbered around 100 in 1947, but had reached 12,000 by 1971 (Edward 2008).

The small size of Scotland's minority ethnic population makes it difficult to obtain reliable statistics, and the conflation into 'Asian', 'Black and Minority Ethnic' (BME) or 'Other Ethnic Group' in Census groupings masks its heterogeneity (de Lima 2005). The 2001 Census, the most comprehensive data set currently available, shows that minority groups constituted around 2 per cent of the total population, with Pakistanis forming the largest single group, followed by Chinese, Indian, 'Any Mixed Background' and 'Other Ethnic Group', as can be seen in Table 6.1. Fifty-eight per cent of 'Any Mixed Background', 55.4 per cent of 'Black Scottish or Other Black' and 47.4 per cent of Pakistanis were born in Scotland. Minority ethnic youths are more likely to identify themselves as having hybrid identities such as 'Black Scottish or Other Black' or 'Any Mixed Background'. Mixed ethnic populations are identified as being the fastest-growing minority, which Finney and Simpson (2009: 163) consider the 'best indicator of integration'. Sixty per cent of Scotland's minority population is found in Glasgow, Edinburgh, Aberdeen and Dundee, although there is also a significant presence of migrant workers, particularly from Poland and other Eastern European countries, in rural areas (de Lima and Wright 2009).

There is, therefore, a rich mix of ethnicities, cultures and hybrid identities (Hopkins 2007a, 2007b) – Scottish Pakistani, for example – within Scotland, which are not well reflected in official statistics. Many Asian young people report a very strong identification with Scotland as opposed to, for example, with Britain or Pakistan (de Lima 2005; Frondigoun *et al.* 2007; Hopkins 2007a, 2007b), and particularly distinctive to Scotland is the wearing by Asian young men of the kilt on ceremonial occasions such as graduations. There is also a sub-group of the Scottish Nationalist Party called Scots Asians for Independence[1] and the first MSP of Asian immigrant origin, the late Bashir Maan, was elected as an SNP list member.

While statistics are limited and comparisons with England difficult to make due to a lack of comparative research (de Lima 2005), some general points can be highlighted. The overall minority ethnic

Table 6.1 Scottish population by ethnic group, 2001

	% of total population	% of minority ethnic population
Indian	0.3	14.79
Pakistani	0.63	31.27
Bangladeshi	0.04	1.95
Chinese	0.32	16.04
Other South Asian	0.12	6.09
Caribbean	0.04	1.75
African	0.1	5.03
Black Scottish or Other Black	0.02	1.11
Any Mixed Background	0.25	12.55
Other Ethnic Group	0.19	9.41

Adapted from GROS, 2001 Census.

proportion of 2 per cent for Scotland contrasts with an equivalent figure of 9 per cent for England with a much smaller Afro-Caribbean group. de Lima (2005) points out that, as elsewhere in Britain, race and ethnicity are strongly interrelated with other socio-economic inequalities, with higher numbers of Pakistani, Bangladeshi and African groups living in overcrowded accommodation – 30 per cent compared with 12 per cent Scottish people (de Lima 2005). Minority ethnic groups are also twice as likely to be unemployed as white Scots and Indian, Pakistani and Chinese employees work longer hours. In Scotland, the most deprived tenth of the population contained 9 per cent Pakistani, 10 per cent Bangladeshi and 11 per cent white Scottish (Scottish Executive 2006).

Race, ethnicity and 'othering'

It is important to explore the terms race and ethnicity before discussing their relationship with crime. To sociologists, race is a social process as very few clear cut biological differences have been found to differentiate between purportedly 'racial' groups. Race is therefore a process of attributing assumed differences to an 'other' group, often on the basis of superiority ('us') and inferiority ('them'), and often related to the history of colonialism. Ethnicity, encompassing aspects of language, nationality, culture and religion, is assumed to be freer of 'biological baggage' (Smith 2009) than race but also involves notions of relative superiority and inferiority – rarely for example is the term ethnic 'majority' used. Racism, a highly contested term (see, for example, Smith 2009), refers to the differential treatment of people on the grounds of their assumed membership of a racial group, and a key part of racism is what is generally described as racial violence, a term which refers not only to violence on the basis of skin colour but which can include acts of violence, ranging from genocide to more routine forms of harassment, which are based on assumed membership of a racial or ethnic group.

Indeed, the term racist may, albeit controversially, be applied to crimes with white victims, although some regard it as intrinsically related to relationships of historical oppression (Iganski 2008). The three Pakistani men who killed the white schoolboy Kriss Donald in Glasgow's Pollokshields in March 2004 (BBC 2006) were convicted of a racially motivated murder, having randomly selected a white boy as a victim. In Scotland there have also been reported instances of violence against the English, sometimes referred to as Anglophobia. In one reported attack, a young English woman was badly beaten in Aberdeen when, according to the *Aberdeen Evening Express*, 'a racist thug heard her speak and beat her to the ground ... just for being English'.[2]

Race involves processes of 'othering', often linked to periods of social, economic and/or political crisis, when fear of those who are unlike us becomes heightened and the 'other' comes under the gaze of suspicion. 'Othering' is more easily applied to those with visible differences such as colour of skin and mode of dress (Iganski 2008), one example being women wearing the burkha, which combines visible difference with an appearance that may seem threatening through its perceived association with militant Islam (Minton 2009).

A key role in othering is played by the mass media which constructs generalised, stereotyped and unfavourable portrayals of migrants by the habitual juxtaposition of loaded words, such as 'bogus' with 'asylum seekers'. The media have also tended to exaggerate the so-called problem of asylum seekers. Barclay *et al.* (2003: 91) found that media reporting of asylum seekers was judgmental in nature and that 'the negative language used ... called into question the reliability of asylum claimants'. Immigrants are often portrayed as a strain on the economy and as receiving more than their fair share of welfare benefits (Ray *et al.* 2004) whereas, as happened with the Roma in Glasgow, they may receive little practical information or help (Poole and Adamson 2008) and face exploitative employment practices, accommodation charges and related social welfare issues (Canton *et al.* 2008). Negative media imaging of new immigrant populations also veils their positive impact on the economy (Ratcliffe 2004).

Othering is also associated with the processes of criminalisation described in Chapter 2 and specific racial and ethnic groups have been associated with crime. An early Scottish example was the treatment of Gypsies, the 'whole race' of whom were, in 1609, ordered to leave Scotland by a certain day and not to return under pain of death. To Hume, this 'loose and lazy race' could be distinguished by:

> the black eye and swarthy complexion – a peculiar language of gibberish ... the practice of palmistry and fortune-telling, – and the custom of living (so far as this climate will permit) in the open air, and solitary places. (Hume 1844: 474–5)

Historical continuity and the unthinking association between 'rogues' and 'travellers' can be seen in the recent headline 'Council in bid to boot rogue Travellers off Aberdeen site' (*Aberdeen Evening Express* 2009).[3]

A range of groups have been subject to othering. Highlanders who migrated South were seen as an inferior race by *The Scotsman* in 1846 (Edward 2008: 26). There were widespread concerns about the influx of the 'barely civilised' Irish (Edward 2008: 38) who were blamed for many of the evils afflicting Glasgow such as typhus. A report to the General Assembly of the Church of Scotland, entitled 'The Menace of the Irish Race to Our Scottish Nationality' expressed fears about the development of Irish ghettoes in Glasgow and Edinburgh (Edward 2008), and noted 'Wheresoever knives and razors are used, wheresoever sneak thefts and mean pilfering are easy and safe, wheresoever dirty acts of sexual baseness are committed, there you will find the Irishman in Scotland with all but a monopoly of the business'. In 2002 the Church of Scotland formally apologised for this bigotry and its involvement in fuelling sectarianism. The Italian ice cream parlours were, in the 1900s, identified as yet another of Glasgow's evils, with the police complaining that they encouraged young people to 'hang about and loaf' (Edward 2008: 84). There have been some anti-semitic incidents in Glasgow, most recently in 2006, and as will be seen below, Asian, Chinese and other groups have also complained of racism and racial violence.

Across Britain, many groups have been criminalised, and the popularly used word 'Hooligan' was said to be originally based on the Irish 'houlihan' family (Pearson 1983). In the middle of the twentieth century, black youth were widely associated with mugging (Hall *et al.* 1978), the urban unrest of the 1980s and more recently with drug-related and gun crime (Phillips and Bowling 2007; Smith 2009). Asians, for many decades widely perceived to be less likely to be involved in crime (Webster 2007), have more recently been associated with gang violence and urban unrest in the North of England, often as a reaction to far right political groups. This is part of what Hudson (2007: 159) describes as 'new criminalisations' which have also involved Eastern European immigrants, said to be associated with organised crime and new 'Mafias', along with asylum seekers, whose treatment, involving detention and 'dawn raids', implies association with criminal processes, while the detention of adults and children goes beyond what would be acceptable in relation to criminal justice. Scotland has seen a different pattern of criminalisation – with little to no criminalisation of black youth or similar patterns of racialisation. Moral panics, for example, about 'hoodies' or 'neds', and the associated criminalisation of the 'dangerous people and dangerous places' discussed in Chapters 2 and 3, draw on inequalities of class and social exclusion rather than race or ethnicity. However, there is evidence in Scotland of the new criminalisations of Asians, Eastern Europeans and asylum seekers.

Race, ethnicity crime and victimisation in Scotland

Patterns of crime and victimisation in Scotland also differ from the rest of the UK. Discussions in England and Wales focused, for many decades, on what is now seen as the rather narrowly constructed 'race and crime' debate which hinged around the extent to which a 'race factor' and racism on the part of the police and criminal justice agencies led to the disproportionate involvement of black people at all stages of the criminal justice process (Phillips and Bowling 2007). While to some this indicated institutional racism, to others, such as Lea and Young (1993), a combination of demographic factors (particularly the younger age structure and socio-economic status of minority groups), relative deprivation and police activity would in any event produce higher numbers of some minority ethnic groups in courts and prisons. Particularly contentious were the higher numbers of black people in prison, the disproportionate use of stop and search powers against black youth perceived as over-policing, and the failure of the police to recognise a racial motive in complaints of racially motivated crime. More recently there have been indications of higher rates of stop and search for Asian youth in the wake of terrorist activity.

These discussions had less relevance to Scotland, where race has been a less salient political issue (de Lima 2005; Miles 1993) and where, perhaps as importantly, the issue has been subject to little research (Ditton 1999). Race and ethnicity are not routinely counted in statistics relating to offenders, the booster samples taken by the Scottish Crime and Victimisation Survey (SCVS) have been small and there are few breakdowns in the High Level Summary of Equality Statistics (Scottish Executive 2006). The police do not regularly monitor figures for stops, searches and arrests and any apparent growth in the numbers of minority ethnic offenders can be attributed to the increasing size of the minority ethnic community (Adams 2007a). Following a small study in the 1990s Ditton (1999) comments on the overall similarity between the views of minority ethnic and white groups in relation to policing and racism, in contrast to the situation in England. Moreover, Scotland does not have such disproportionate numbers of minority ethnic groups in prison which formed the starting point for investigations of discrimination. In June 2005, for example, a total of 2.46 per cent of the Scottish prison population were described as being from ethnic minorities (in comparison to 2 per cent of the general population), in sharp contrast to the figure of 25 per cent of the population of prisons in England and Wales in the same year (Phillips and Bowling 2007). However, the most up-to-date prisons statistics for Scotland show that at 30 June 2008, 4.3 per cent (approximately) of the prison population were from minority ethnic groups, which is a considerable increase on the 2005 figures and, as will be seen below, there are issues surrounding stop and search and police activity.

Victimisation

Minority groups are subject to higher levels of crime victimisation, often as a result of socio-economic factors (Francis 2007; Phillips and Bowling 2007) in England and also in Scotland (Adams 2007a). Of considerable concern is victimisation from specifically racist violence evidenced by, for example, the use of racist language or slogans related to the victim's actual or assumed membership of a specific group. Such 'hate crime' may also be based on religion, disability, gender or any other assumed differentiation (Iganski 2008). Like all forms of violence, this can be conceptualised as forming a continuum ranging from, at one end, verbal taunts and harassment through more serious verbal and physical abuse and damage to property such as racist slogans, to, at the extreme end, serious physical violence and homicide.

Following the Stephen Lawrence case and the subsequent Macpherson Report (1999) in England and Crown Office reports following the death of Surjit Singh Chhokar in Scotland (Campbell 2001; Jandoo 2001), there have been improvements in the recording and availability of information about racial victimisation, hitherto recognised as having been under-reported as victims lacked confidence in the police to recognise any 'racist' element in offences. The more widely used definition of a racist incident is now 'victim centred' in that it is 'any incident which is perceived to be racist by the victim or any other person' (Scottish Government 2009b).

The Crime and Disorder Act 1998 created two new statutory (as opposed to common law) offences of racially aggravated behaviour and racially aggravated harassment. The total number of such incidents recorded by the police fell by 1 per cent from 2006/7 to 2007/8 (from 5,321 to 5,243), a levelling-off of reports following a steady increase since 1999 (Scottish Government 2009a). The highest rates are found in urban areas (Aberdeen, Dundee, Edinburgh and Glasgow). Most, around one-third, take place in the street, shops and dwelling houses and the most frequently recorded crime (around one half) was racially aggravated conduct, followed by breach of the peace, minor assault, fire-raising/vandalism and racially aggravated harassment. Around 50 per cent of victims were of Asian origin, the majority Pakistani. Around three-quarters of victims were male. Approximately 95 per cent of known perpetrators were of white origin, around 46 per cent were aged 20 or under, with around 23 per cent being under 16. Incidents involving 'white non-British' victims increased. Overall, these figures are difficult to interpret, with rising rates widely acknowledged to be a product of improved recording due to efforts on the part of the police and victim support agencies to encourage the reporting of incidents. Rates are lower than in England and Wales, with the highest per capita figures of 2.21 and 2.13 per 1,000 of the minority ethnic population in Glasgow and Edinburgh respectively, comparing favourably with figures of 10.64 for Asians and 9.23 for black people in London (Iganski 2008).

These figures say little about how people experience these incidents. For example, verbal harassment may seem relatively trivial, but, when repeated, can have a profound effect on a person's quality of life (Francis 2007; Phillips and Bowling 2007). Many have stressed that incivilities, verbal taunts and minor aggression are part and parcel of the everyday life of minority ethnic groups in England (Bowling

1999), findings which have been confirmed in Scotland. Respondents in Chahal and Julienne's (1999) study in Glasgow, Belfast, Cardiff and London reported that incidents were too numerous to remember, confirmed in a later study in Glasgow and Edinburgh (Frondigoun *et al.* 2007). To some young Asians, a perceived increase in incidents after 9/11 and 7/7 permeated their general feelings of safety (Frondigoun *et al.* 2007), with many being called 'Bin Laden' or told to go 'back to Afghanistan'. The location of incidents in the street, shops and routine encounters underlines their everyday nature (Iganski 2008; Webster 2003).

At the other end of the continuum, as has been noted in England and Wales, the racist element in homicides has often been underplayed. In 1989 for example, Ahmed Abuukar Sheekh and his cousin, refugees from Somalia, were stabbed and killed in Edinburgh. Evidence of the association of the perpetrators with the National Front was put aside and the murder was not recorded as racially motivated. Following protests, the police agreed that the murder should be classified as a racial incident and the Chief Constable tightened police procedures. Racism was also downplayed following the death from stabbing of Imran Khan in Shawlands in February 1998, despite a history of racial tension in a local secondary school. The perpetrators had been expelled for racial harassment and the case highlighted the emergence of racial tension between so-called gangs in Glasgow's southside.[4]

A significant case was that of Surjit Chhokar, who was stabbed to death outside his home in Overtown, Lanarkshire, on 4 November 1998. In March 1999 Ronnie Coulter was tried for his murder, but lodged a special defence naming two other men, both of whom had originally been arrested and charged. He was found not guilty of murder but of assault, and the trial judge was critical of the failure to put all in the dock. Subsequently, in November 2000, the two other men were tried but found not guilty. This led to claims of institutionalised racism in the Scottish criminal justice system, and the Lord Advocate ordered two inquiries into the case – one focusing on Crown Office decision-making (Campbell 2001) and the other on prosecution liaison with the Chhokar family (Jandoo 2001). Both were critical and found that the family's needs had not been met and recommended greater monitoring of ethnicity within the criminal justice process. This case bore some similarities to the Stephen Lawrence case in London. In this case the Metropolitan Police were widely criticised for assuming that the victim, Stephen Lawrence, and his friend had initiated the violence, an assumption which hampered the subsequent investigation and contributed to a failure to prosecute those widely assumed to have been responsible. They also failed to deal with the Lawrence family appropriately. The subsequent Macpherson Report (1999) made a series of recommendations about police procedures, including improvements in the reporting and recording of racist incidents, the investigation and prosecution of racist crime, arrangements for family liaison, the treatment of victims and witnesses and the use of stop-and-search powers. Similar recommendations were made in the Chhokar inquiry.

There is also a close interrelationship between ethnicity and gender. There is, however, little research on the specific experiences of minority ethnic women beyond the everyday racial abuse in the street or public places to which all in minority ethnic groups can be subjected (Iganski 2008). The impact of racist incidents in residential areas can, however, fall more heavily on women who are more likely to be at home and afraid to go out (Chahal and Julienne 1999), and women wearing headscarves reported feeling uncomfortable about 'looks' they had received (Frondigoun *et al.* 2007). In one incident, an Algerian woman was sexually assaulted in Glasgow and she and her baby had stones thrown at them (Adams 2007b).

Women also suffer from gendered inequalities within some minority communities and from a clash of values between British and traditional cultures. Frondigoun *et al.* (2007) report, for example, that 'women are traditionally subordinated in minority ethnic family relations, even more so where arranged marriages are the cultural norm'. This can be difficult for young Scottish-born minority ethnic girls to accept and Parekh (2008: 111) argues that for many young women this clash of cultures, or as it is understood within their own culture, 'rebellion', has led to 'intimidation and violence … [and] sometimes horrifying, cases of 'honour killing' and abduction'. The Scottish Government[5] identifies a total of 40 reported incidents of forced marriages from January to October 2008, although many are unreported. To interest groups such as Amina – the Muslim Women's Resource Centre – forced marriage amounts to a form of domestic abuse.[6]

Criminal justice and policing

As outlined above, in England the over-policing of minority ethnic communities and institutionalised racism within the police were and continue to be key issues confirmed by the Macpherson Report (1999). In Scotland, by contrast, the police were said to have good relationships with minority ethnic communities (Scottish Executive 2003), seen for example, in attendance at mosques and consultation with community elders, and issues such as stop and search have generally been perceived to be of less significance (Reid Howie 2002). Nonetheless, while issues of community policing in general have been far less extensively researched in Scotland (Donnelly 2005), a number of Scottish studies have found that young people are concerned about harassment and over-policing and that Asian young men in particular feel that they are stopped more often than white youth and report experiences of cultural insensitivity (Frondigoun *et al.* 2007; Goodall *et al.* 2003). Cars, as in England (Phillips and Bowling 2007), can be a source of contention. Young Muslim men, who do not drink and generally can afford better cars, like to gather in parks and streets or cruise around in cars which, they felt, could attract suspicion. One respondent, with a professional occupation, reported having been stopped twice in one day (Frondigoun *et al.* 2007). According to one Chinese respondent:

> Oh Chinese drive a Mercedes! He must be dodgy. Pull him over and see what that is about. (Frondigoun *et al.* 2007: 50)

Also contentious has been the policing of Asian festivals such as Eid, during which many young people celebrate on the streets and drive around in cars with horns blaring. Some young Asians have compared the responses of the police adversely to the policing of white drunkenness, whereas to the police they were responding to complaints about rowdiness from older people within the community.

The policing of racist incidents has also attracted criticism with members of minority ethnic groups reporting unsympathetic responses from the police and an unwillingness to report incidents as racist (Goodall *et al.* 2003). Some felt that there was little point in reporting racism as 'nothing will come of it', although some youths felt that the third generation were more likely to report racism than their parents.

While critical of the police, however, Asian youth in one study welcomed community policing, particularly initiatives in which police offers liaised directly with young people. Some Muslim youth also felt that racism in general and the police were 'better' in Scotland – based on their family connections in, for example, the North of England (Frondigoun *et al.* 2007).

There is far less information about the significance of race and ethnicity in other parts of the criminal justice process, although the

Chokkar Inquiry referred to above did find evidence of institutional racism on the part of the Procurators Fiscal in respect of liaison with the Chhokar family and failing to provide an interpreter (Jandoo 2001). Its recommendation that there should be an Inspectorate of Prosecution in Scotland was accepted and appropriately its first thematic report dealt with the Crown Office and Procurator Fiscal Service's response to race issues.[7] There is also little information about the proportions of minority ethnic groups who work in the different agencies. For example, the Crown Office and Procurator Fiscal Service states on its careers page that it provides 'equality of opportunity in relation to employment, career development and promotion to all, where eligible, on the basis of ability, qualifications and suitability for the work'. Similarly, the Scottish Prison Service states that it recruits in line with the Civil Service Commissioners' Code on the basis of fair and open competition and selection on merit. The SPS annual report for 2008/9 shows that approximately 2.9 per cent of their staff were from a minority ethnic group. In 2005 minority ethnic groups accounted for 1 per cent of police officers, support staff and special constables compared with 2 per cent of the Scottish labour force as a whole (Scottish Executive 2006). A study on the experiences of BME police officers, support staff and resigners in Scotland found that 76 per cent believed there to be racism within the police with 69 per cent reporting an experience of racism. While many lacked confidence in the complaints system, the majority did not perceive discrimination in career terms, but saw it as present in the occupational culture (Onifade 2002).

The impact of terrorism on policing and criminalisation

At a global level fears of terrorism have had a profound affect on policing and the criminalisation of minority ethnic groups The Irish in Britain as a whole became a suspect community amid fears of paramilitary activity (Hillyard 1993), and more recently, following 9/11, the emergence of Al Qaeda, described as a 'loose network of Islamic revolutionaries' (Martin 2010: 290), has been associated with increased suspicion of young Muslim men.

Scotland has directly suffered from two major terrorist incidents, the bombing of the Pan Am flight over Lockerbie in December 1988 and the failed attempt to bomb Glasgow Airport in June 2007. There were some indications of increased levels of racist attacks after 9/11 and in the aftermath of the bombing incident at Glasgow Airport.

Websites and discussion forums were said to have attracted racist and anti-Islamic comments, and Mohammad Sarwar, a Glasgow-based Muslim Labour MP, also claimed that threats were made towards Muslims.[8] Media reports were seen by many young Muslims as responsible for a growth of Islamophobia and for increased levels of racism. Frondigoun *et al.* (2007) found they had a 'sense of fear, of being watched and mistrusted ... (post 9/11) ... in the course of their daily lives ... [and that] ... rucksacks became a big issue ... [you get] stared at going to and from college if wearing a rucksack' (Frondigoun *et al.* 2007: 39). Also:

> Islamaphobia, it's the media that is bring it up, because it's not all Muslims, okay, just one person, maybe like use a name, but why say a Muslim extremist, and that is really annoying ...' (2007: 42)

There have also been criticisms of reported harassment of Afghans by Strathclyde Police Special Branch, particularly while travelling through Glasgow Airport,[9] along with publicised debates about harassment by the British Transport Police carrying out searches under s. 44 of the Terrorism Act 2000, claimed by the Scottish Justice Minister Kenny McAskill to be following a 'diktat from London' (BBC News 2007).

At the same time, the actions of Scottish police forces have been favourably contrasted with those of English forces, with the Metropolitan Police having praised Strathclyde Police 'for their positive race relations' (Jardine and Bellamy 2009). Mann (2008) also reports positively on the handling of the aftermath of the Glasgow Airport incident, citing consultations with the Muslim community about intelligence reports and pointing out that:

> the Muslim community didn't experience the bursting of doors, violating the sanctity of the Mosque, bundling innocent people in the police vans or using violence against any individual as had been happening in England. In other words Scotland did not share the experience of Finsbury Park and there were no headlines – 'Finsbury Park[10] comes to Glasgow'. (Mann 2008: 242)

Support for police-community relations and the handling of this incident was also expressed by some minority ethnic youths who said it was:

> exemplary ... the way they released information so it had no relation to the mosque, so people can't make the link ... was decent of them ... I think they dealt with it very, very well and they have done a lot within the community to try and build up relationships ... (Colville 2008: 28)

The policy context

While a full discussion of relevant policies in relation to racial and ethnic minorities lies beyond the scope of this chapter it is useful to outline briefly the policy context. In 2004 the then Scottish Executive set out its proposals for 'a managed scheme of immigration' to address Scotland's population decline and to fill the skills gap in *New Scots: Attracting Fresh Talent to Meet the Challenge for Growth* (Scottish Executive 2004). More recently the Scottish Government's campaign One Scotland[11] lays out 12 objectives specifically aimed at tackling issues of racism within a multicultural Scotland. It seeks to raise awareness of racism and its negative impact along with recognising the valuable contributions of other cultures. In the more specific context of policing, issues of racism form part of joint working with the government, local authorities and voluntary agencies under the Single Outcome Agreements (SOAs)[12] and community planning partnerships to address issues of ethnicity, crime, racism, health and housing.

The Association of Chief Police Officers in Scotland (ACPOS) has a diversity strategy which confers on individual forces a duty to 'engage with their communities, prevent, report, record and investigate hate crime'. As seen above, the Jandoo Report highlighted the need for a more responsive police approach, and the 2003 HMIC Report *Pride and Prejudice* (Scottish Executive 2003) viewed relationships between the police and minority ethnic groups in Scotland positively compared with England and profiled examples of good practice. It also urged Scottish constabularies to be mindful of the dynamic nature of their environment and the importance, for example, of being responsive to the needs of new immigrant populations such as refugees, asylum seekers and those from Eastern Europe. They also pointed to the need to address changes in the more established minority ethnic populations, in respect of which it was felt that young people had different perceptions, aspirations and opinions from their elders. ACPOS's statements also stress the importance of encouraging victims of hate crime to report it and of efficient monitoring of reported incidents.[13] While there is evidence to support the introduction of these monitoring systems there is, as yet, little evidence to establish their efficacy.

A large number of national, community and voluntary organisations, such as, for example, the Council of Ethnic Minority Voluntary Sector Organisations (CEMVO), the Black and Ethnic Minorities Infrastructure in Scotland (BEMIS), Edinburgh and Lothian's Racial Equality Council (ELREC), the Glasgow Anti-Racist Alliance (GARA) and the Scottish Ethnic Minority Sports Association (SEMSA) are also involved[14] in addressing issues of under-representation and institutional racism along with raising awareness of racially motivated and hate crime. These include joint activities with the police such as Asian/police cricket and BME/police football matches which help, they argue, to enhance understanding of different cultures and to reduce structural barriers in an informal setting. Further research, however, is needed to evaluate the success or otherwise of these initiatives.

Concluding comments

To what extent can the claim that Scotland is distinct be confirmed and what might account for this? On the one hand, Scotland has not seen the development of 'ghettoes' such as the banlieus in France, certain areas in Brixton and Birmingham or, more recently, in the former textile producing areas of the North of England (Webster 2003; Ray *et al.* 2004) which have been associated with racial tension and urban unrest. Policing has been less politically contentious and levels of racial violence are lower. Crimes such as mugging have not been racialised, and there is little evidence of disproportionate numbers of minority groups in police stations, courts or prisons. At the same time members of minority groups experience racism as an everyday and routine experience, do complain of police insensitivity and partiality, do not trust the police to deal fairly with complaints of racist incidents and newer migrants have been subjected to higher levels of criminalisation and public fears of competition over jobs. The continued existence of deeply rooted sectarianism also challenges Scotland's reputation for tolerance as does a System 3 survey which found, in June 2002, that one in every 25 Scots acknowledged that they had perpetrated racial abuse (GARA 2008). The report following the Chhokar case substantiated the existence of institutionalised racism and that this was one of a series of racist murders. The overall conclusion is therefore mixed.

A variety of factors might account for some divergences between Scotland and other jurisdictions, although in the absence of comprehensive comparative research it is difficult to draw any firm conclusions. Whereas in England race has been central to conceptions of nationalism, race has arguably had less political significance in Scotland whose constitutional status prior to devolution meant that nationalism was related to the English 'other' and to independence (Miles 1993). Devolution indeed led to a greater focus on issues of race and ethnicity and to more research (de Lima 2005). Issues of immigration have also been played out in the different context of Scotland's declining population, with the Fresh Talent Initiative providing a contrast to the framing of immigration policy in England around the perceived need to control numbers (de Lima and Wright 2009). Nonetheless, in periods of recession, growing levels of social exclusion may exacerbate racism and the arrival of substantial numbers of Eastern European migrants, along with generalised fears about terrorism, may have exacerbated negative feelings towards 'others'. GARA's (2008) 'state of the nation' report cites survey figures suggesting that over 25 per cent of respondents felt that the presence of ethnic minorities in Scotland made it more difficult to find a job, fears which had risen in the last five years. The new criminalisations of Asians, Eastern Europeans and asylum seekers have affected Scotland through the UK, Scottish and local press. While some aspects of policing are welcomed, there remain issues to be addressed. In this respect there may be differences between, for example, community police and others, and in particular between national UK and Scottish policies, as indicated by the example of the transport police and in respect of the detention of asylum seekers at Dungavel, determined by UK rather than Scottish-based policy. These considerations underline the need for greater recognition of the distinctiveness of Scotland in relation to these issues and to the potential of more comparative research.

Notes

1 http://www.sm[upitj/prg/yse/index.php?option=con_content&task=view&id=1&Itemd=3
2 http://news.stv.tv/.../69606-msps-debate-hate-crime-while-police-investigate-attack-on-english-woman/
3 http://www.eveningexpress.co.uk/Article.aspx/1144536
4 www.irr.org.uk/carf/feat12.html (accessed 19 September 2009)

5 http://www.scotland.gov.uk/Topics/People/Equality/violence-women/forcedmarriage
6 http://www.mwrc.org.uk/docs/documents/Forced%20Marriage%20consultationMWRC.doc
7 http://www.scotland.gov.uk/Publications/2005/03/20744/53296
8 http://news.bbc.co.uk/1/hi/scotland/glasgow_and_west/6924745.stm
9 http://www.sundayherald.com/news/heraldnews/display.var2453803.0.afghan_communities_protest_at_harassment_by_police_force_hailed_as_role_model.php
10 Reported on BBC News, Monday, 20 January 2003: 'Anti-terror police raid London mosque'. Seven men were arrested after 150 police took part in an anti-terrorism raid on Finsbury Park mosque in north London which Scotland Yard said was intelligence-led and linked to investigations into the discovery of the deadly poison ricin in a flat in nearby Wood Green earlier that month. http://news.bbc.co.uk/1/hi/england/2675223.stm
11 http://www.scotlandagainstracism.com/onescotland/22.1.6html
12 http://www.scotland.gov.uk/Topics/Government/local-government/SOA
13 http://www.scotland.gov.uk/Resource/Doc/47102/0025113.pdf
14 http://semsa.org.uk/pages/about-semsa.php

References

Adams, L. (2007a) 'Minorities twice as likely to be victims of crime', *The Herald*, 23 June. http://www.heraldscotland.com/minorities-twice-as-likely-to-be-victims-of-crime-1.861812 (accessed 18 June 2009).

Adams, L. (2007b) 'Asylum seeker and baby sexually attacked', *The Herald*, 12 April. http://www.heraldscotland.com/asylum-seeker-and-baby-sexually-attacked-1.856014.

Barclay, A., Bowes, A., Ferguson, I., Sim, D. and Valenti, M. (2003) *Asylum Seekers in Scotland*. Edinburgh: Scottish Executive. http://www.scotland.gov.uk/Resource/Doc/47032/0025606.pdf (accessed 25 November 2009).

BBC (2006) 'Trio jailed for Kriss race murder'. http://newsvote.bbc.cu.uk/mpapps/pagetools/pring/news.bbc.co.uk/1/hi/scotland/glasg (accessed 14 October 2009).

Bowling, B. (1999) *Violent Racism: Victimisation, Policing and Social Context*. Oxford: Clarendon Press.

Campbell, Sir A. (2001) *The Report of an Inquiry into Crown Decision-Making in the Case of the Murder of Surjit Singh Chhokar*. http://scottish-parliament.biz/business/committees/historic/equal/reports-01/chhokar-b-01.htm.

Canton, N., Clark, C. and Pietka, E. (2008) *Migrant Cities Research: Living Together Programme*. Glasgow. Edinburgh/London: British Council and the Institute for Public Policy Research. http://bit.ly/33vIcJ.

Census 2001. Edinburgh: General Register Office. http://www.gro-scotland.gov.uk/census/censushm/index.html.

Chahal, K. and Julienne, L. (1999) *We Can't All Be White: Racist Victimization in the UK*. York: Joseph Rowntree Foundation.

Colville, E. (2008) 'Community Engagement in Glasgow: Young Muslims' Perspectives'. Unpublished Research Student Report, Glasgow Caledonian University.

Crown Office and Procurator Fiscal Service (n.d.) *Careers*. http://www.copfs.gov.uk/Working/recruitment/careers-introduction (accessed 26 January 2010).

de Lima, P. (2005) 'An inclusive Scotland? The Scottish Executive and racial inequality', in G. Mooney and G. Scott (eds), *Exploring Social Policy in the 'New' Scotland*. Bristol: Policy Press, pp. 135–56.

de Lima, P. and Wright, S. (2009) 'Welcoming migrants? Migrant labour in rural Scotland', *Social Policy and Society*, 8: 391–404.

Ditton, J. (1999) 'Scottish ethnic minorities, crime and the police', in P. Duff and N. Hutton (eds), *Criminal Justice in Scotland*. Aldershot: Ashgate, pp. 302–18.

Donnelly, D. (2005) 'Policing the Scottish community', in D. Donnelly and K. Scott (eds), *Policing Scotland*. Cullompton: Willan Publishing.

Edward, M. (2008) *Who Belongs to Glasgow?* 2nd edn. Edinburgh: Luath Press.

Finney, N. and Simpson, L. (2009) *Sleepwalking to Segregation?* Bristol: Policy Press.

Francis, P. (2007a) '"Race", ethnicity, victims and crime', in P. Davies, P. Francis and C. Greer (eds), *Victims, Crime and Society*. London: Sage, pp. 109–41.

Friedman-Kasaba, K. (1996) *Memories of Migration: Gender, Ethnicity and Work in the Lives of Jewish and Italian Women in New York, 1870–1924*. New York: State University of New York.

Frondigoun, L., Croall, H., Hughes, B., Russell, L., Russell, R. and Scott, G. (2007) *Researching Minority Ethnic Young People in Edinburgh and the Greater Glasgow Area*. Glasgow: Glasgow Caledonian University.

Glasgow Anti-Racist Alliance (GARA) (2009) *The State of the Nation: Race and Racism in Scotland 2008*. Glasgow: GARA. http://www.gara.org.uk.

Goodall, K. with Choudri, R., Barbour, R. and Hilton, S. (2003) *The Policing of Racist Incidents in Strathclyde*. Glasgow: University of Glasgow.

Grover, C. (2008) *Crime and Inequality*. Cullompton: Willan Publishing.

Hall, S., Critcher, C., Jefferson, T., Clarke, J. and Roberts, B. (1978) *Policing the Crisis: Mugging, the State and Law and Order*. London: Macmillan.

Hillyard, P. (1993) *Suspect Community: People's Experience of the Prevention of Terrorism Acts in Britain*. London: Pluto Press.

HMIC (2003) *Pride and Prejudice: A Review of Police Race Relations in Scotland*. Edinburgh: Scottish Executive.

Home Office (2008) *Control of Immigration: Quarterly Statistical Summary, United Kingdom, October–December 2008*, 2nd edn. London: Home Office.

Hopkins, P. E. (2007a) 'Global events, national politics, local lives: young Muslim men in Scotland', *Environment and Planning A*, 39 (3): 1119–33.

Hopkins, P. E. (2007b) 'Young people, masculinities, religion and race: new social geographies', *Progress in Human Geography*, 31 (2): 163–77.

Hudson, B. (2007) 'Diversity, crime and criminal justice', in M. Maguire, R. Morgan and R. Reiner (eds), *The Oxford Handbook of Criminology*, 4th edn. Oxford: Clarendon Press, pp. 158–78.

Hume, D. (Baron) (1844) *Commentaries on the Law of Scotland Respecting Crimes*, 4th edn. Edinburgh: Bell & Bradfute, pp. 474–5.

Iganski, P. (2008) *'Hate' Crime and the City*. Bristol: Policy Press.

Jandoo, R. (2001) *Report of the Inquiry into the Liaison Arrangements following the Murder of Surjit Singh Chhokar*. Edinburgh: Crown Office.

Jardine, C. and Bellamy, K. (2009) *Race and Hate Crime Prevention in Scotland*, Briefing Paper 15. Edinburgh: Criminal Justice Social Work. http://www.cjsw.ac.uk.

Juliani, R. N. (1998) *Building Little Italy: Philadelphia's Italians before Mass Migration*. Philadelphia: Pennsylvania State University Press.

Kay, Billy (ed.) (1980) *Odyssey: Voices from Scotland's Recent Past*. Edinburgh: Polygon Books.

Kearney, R. (1990) *Migrants: The Irish at Home and Abroad*. Dublin: Wolfhound Press.

Knight v. *Wedderburn* (1778) National Archives of Scotland (CS235/K/2/2). http://www.nas.gov.uk/about/071022.asp.

Layard, R. (2006) *Happiness: Lessons from a New Science*. London: Penguin.

Lea, J. and Young, J. (1993) *What Is to Be Done About Law and Order?* 2nd edn. London: Pluto Press.

Macpherson, Sir W. (1999) *The Stephen Lawrence Inquiry. Report of an Inquiry by Sir William MacPherson of Cluny*, CM 4262-1. London: HMSO.

Mann, B. (2008) *The Thistle and the Crescent*. Argyll: Argyll Publishing.

Martin, G. (2010) *Understanding Terrorism: Challenges, Perspectives and Issues*, 3rd edn. Thousand Oaks, CA: Sage.

Miles, R. (1993) *Racism after 'Race Relations'*. London: Routledge.

Minton, A. (2009) 'Fear and distrust in 21st-century Britain', in D. Utting (ed.), *Contemporary Social Evils*. Bristol: Policy Press/Joseph Rowntree Foundation.

Onifade, D. (2002) *The Experiences of Black/Minority Ethnic Police Officers, Support Staff, Special Constables and Resigners in Scotland*. Intra Vires Consultants, Scottish Executive Central Research Unit.

Parekh, B. (2008) *A New Politics of Identity: Political Principles for an Interdependent World*. Basingstoke: Palgrave Macmillan.

Pearson, G. (1983) *Hooligan: A History of Respectable Fears*. London: Macmillan.

Phillips, C. and Bowling, B. (2007) 'Ethnicities, racism, crime and criminal justice', in M. Maguire, R. Morgan and R. Reiner (eds), *The Oxford Handbook of Criminology*, 4th edn. Oxford: Clarendon Press.

Poole, L. and Adamson, K. (2008) *Report on the Situation of the Roma Community in Govanhill, Glasgow*. Glasgow: Oxfam.

Ratcliffe, P. (2004) *Race, Ethnicity and Difference: Imagining the Inclusive Society*. Maidenhead: Open University Press.

Ray, L., Smith, D. and Wastell, L. (2004) 'Shame, rage and racist violence', *British Journal of Criminology*, 44 (3): 350–68.

Reid Howie Associates Ltd (2002) *Police Stop and Search among White and Minority Ethnic Young People in Scotland*. Edinburgh: Scottish Executive Central Research Unit.

Robertson, J. (2004) *Joseph Knight*. London: Fourth Estate.

Rolfe, H. and Metcalf, H. (2009) *Recent Migration into Scotland: The Evidence Base*. Edinburgh: Scottish Government Social Research.

Scottish Executive (2003) *Pride and Prejudice: A Review of Race Relations in Scotland*. Edinburgh: Scottish Executive (on behalf of HM Inspectorate of Constabulary). http://www.scotland.gov.uk/Resource/Doc/47102/0025113.pdf.

Scottish Executive (2004) *New Scots: Attracting Fresh Talent to Meet the Challenge for Growth*. Edinburgh: Scottish Executive. http://www.scotland.gov.uk/Resource/Doc/47210/0025759.pdf (accessed 25 November 2009).

Scottish Executive (2006) *High Level Summary of Equality Statistics: Key Trends for Scotland 2006*. http://www.scotland.cov.uk/Publications/2006/11/20102424/12 (accessed 20 June 2009).

Scottish Government (2007) *Racist Incidents Recorded by the Police in Scotland*. http://www.scotland.gov.uk/Publications/2007/03/26094831.

Scottish Government (2008) *Forced Marriage: A Civil Remedy?* http://www.scotland.gov.uk/Resource/Doc/248674/0071298.pdf.

Scottish Government (2009a) *Prison Statistics Scotland: 2008–09*, Statistical Bulletin: Crime and Justice Series. http://www.scotland.gov.uk/Publications/2009/11/27092125/9 (accessed 26 January 2010).

Scottish Government (2009b) *Racist Incidents Recorded by the Police in Scotland, 2004–5 to 2007–8*. http://www.scotland.gov.uk.

Scottish Prison Service (n.d.) *Annual Report and Accounts 2008/09*. http://www.sps.gov.uk/MultimediaGallery/efcfee50-5a5a-4f16-87bf-90b6be6534a7.pdf (accessed 26 January 2010).

Smith, D. (2009) 'Key concepts and theories about "race"', in H. S. Bhui (ed.), *Race and Criminal Justice*. London: Sage, pp. 9–29.

Webster, C. (2003) 'Race, space and fear: imagined geographies of racism: crime, violence and disorder in Northern England', *Capital and Class*, 80: 95–122.

Webster, C. (2007) *Understanding Race and Crime*. Maidenhead: McGraw-Hill/Open University Press.

Chapter 7

Corporate crime in Scotland

Jenifer Ross and Hazel Croall

Introduction

The considerable impact of corporate crime and the complex issues surrounding its control are generally absent from discussions of criminal justice. Indeed the definition and criminal status of this vast area of crime have long been debated by criminological and legal scholars (Croall 2001; Nelken 2007). Defining white-collar crime as 'crime committed by a person of respectability and high social status in the course of his occupation', Sutherland (1949: 9) sought to challenge the focus of criminology on lower-class crime and draw attention to the 'human misery' caused by illegal business activities, many of which were subject not to criminal but to regulatory law, and widely perceived as 'not really crime'. While the subjectivity of calling them crime was strongly criticised (Tappan 1947) it raised important questions about the very distinctive way in which these offences are dealt with in relation to law, prosecution and punishment.

A crucial question raised by Sutherland's work was the organisational nature of offences, leading to a broad distinction between crimes involving primarily personal profit, such as embezzlement, and those, such as breaches of health and safety legislation, directed at the profitability or survival of the corporation itself, known as corporate crime. Within organisations the division of labour creates a diffusion of responsibility which makes it difficult to pin 'blame' on a 'guilty' individual. 'I was only following orders' is a standard defence for organisational offences, from seemingly trivial breaches of safety regulations to genocide (Punch 2000). This ability to hide behind the 'corporate veil' and deny responsibility along with an absence of the immediate, personal, and confrontational elements of victimisation distinguishes corporate from so-called conventional crime and contributes to its ambiguous criminal status (Wells 2001).

These considerations reflect the ability of powerful groups to resist the full criminalisation of their activities (Carson 1979; Pearce 1976) and the term 'crimes of the powerful' is often used (Whyte 2009). This can incorporate crimes of state agencies who also break rules to support organisational goals – the police, for example, may doctor evidence in order to secure what to them is the justifiable conviction of 'guilty' persons (Punch 2009). For reasons of space, this chapter will focus on corporate crime and, as recent public attention has focused on corporate activity causing death and serious injury, much of the chapter focuses on these aspects. It will start by looking at the overall scope of corporate crime before exploring some key cases in depth and looking at how the legal system has approached its control.

Exploring corporate crime in Scotland

It is extremely difficult to quantify the impact of corporate crime in Scotland or any other jurisdiction (Croall 2008). Most offences do not appear in official crime figures or victim surveys. Many victims are unaware of any harm, and if they are, do not define it or report it as 'crime' to the appropriate regulatory agency. Prosecutions are rare and information has to be gleaned from a very different range of sources to other crimes. These include the records of enforcement agencies such as the HSE, relevant government departments and information collected by interest groups such as trade unions and victim or consumer groups. Investigative journalism provides further information and media reports, readily available on the Internet, can be used to access these sources (Croall 2009b; Tombs and Whyte 2010). Taken together, these confirm the major financial impact of corporate crime along with its high toll of deaths, injuries and illness. This section will provide a broad overview of these harms, emphasising, in line with the focus of the chapter, safety issues.

Before looking at these it is important to stress the financial impact of corporate crime. While the total cost of fraud is notoriously difficult to calculate (Levi and Burrows 2008), HM Inspectorate of Constabulary for Scotland has estimated that it costs each Scottish citizen around £330 each year, excluding tax evasion (*The Herald*,

9 February 2009). Scotland's banks were severely affected by the financial crisis of 2008/9, and in the United States some have argued that the much criticised 'bonus culture' and exorbitant rewards given to senior executives are criminogenic, as they encourage taking risks with 'other people's money' and have been associated with accounting frauds which inflate a company's profits to boost bonuses (Friedrichs 2009). Consumers are adversely affected by a wide range of activities, often described in non-criminal terms such as 'mis-selling' or 'consumer detriment' – the latter estimated to cost consumers £6.6 billion annually (Office of Fair Trading 2008). Falsely describing goods as 'low fat' or 'organic', making misleading claims about cosmetics and using misleading packaging are routinely practised means of deceiving consumers (Croall 2009a). In a form of corporate anti social behaviour, the *Evening Times* (2009) reported on the fining, by Glasgow City Council, of 245 major high-street retailers for littering.

Some criminologists have used the phrase 'corporate violence' to describe corporate activities which cause physical harm (Tombs 2007) and it has been calculated that the deaths of workers as a result of inattention to safety and work-related illnesses far exceeds that of homicide in any one year (Tombs 2000). In Scotland, HSE figures indicate that 113,000 people in 2007/8 suffered from an illness which they believe was caused or made worse by work. These also record a total of 32 fatal and 2,721 major injuries to workers in Scotland, along with 5 fatal and 1,267 non-fatal injuries to members of the public.[1] Ninety-one offences were prosecuted in 2007. Fatality rates are highest in the construction industry (Tombs and Whyte 2007) with Scottish figures being among the highest rates (*The Herald*, 21 September 2009). Figures list what are often called 'accidents' rather than 'crime' although as many as two-thirds have been estimated by the HSE to have resulted from a failure to comply with regulations (Slapper and Tombs 1999; Tombs 2000). Behind these statistics lie not only mass deaths such as those explored below, but a long list of individual deaths and injuries for which companies are convicted, such as the two Scottish coal workers crushed by a dumper truck (*The Herald*, 26 August 2008), and the electrician killed working on a fitness centre in Dundee for Mitie (*The Herald*, 15 October 2008). Two offshore energy firms were also fined a total of £1.2 million in 2008 following the death of an oil worker (Williams 2008).

Physical harms as a result of corporate activity are not restricted to the workplace, with consumers' health threatened by food poisoning caused by the neglect of food safety and hygiene regulations. One of the most serious cases of E-coli led to the deaths of 21 pensioners in Wishaw and the conviction of the butcher concerned, John Barr (Croall and Ross 2002). Consumers are also threatened by dangerous products such as imported toys and do-it-yourself products to which could be added the long-term health risks posed by the, often unregulated, thousands of chemicals and additives in foods, cosmetics and everyday household cleaning products (Croall 2009a).

Corporate crime has a differential impact on specific groups. While there are exceptions, such as the ICL Plastics case outlined below, it is very often the lowest paid and non-unionised workers who are killed or injured at work (Tombs and Whyte 2007), and women working in modern-day sweatshops or child labour used on a global scale suggest other exploited groups. The consumer 'detriment' referred to above most adversely affects low-income groups and the National Consumer Council (NCC 2003) has identified these, along with those living in a deprived area and those with 'skills difficulties', as 'vulnerable' consumers.

Controlling corporate crime in Scotland

A major distinction in relation to corporate crime is between so called 'real' crimes and business crime, much of which is dealt with not by the traditional (mainly common law) criminal law, but by regulatory criminal or administrative law, which do not carry notions of blame and criminal responsibility. Most regulatory offences do not require proof of *mens rea* which is a key element in definitions of traditional criminal offences, encompassing, depending on the crime, proof of intention or recklessness towards the conduct or harm caused. Although this can aid prosecution for a regulatory offence by removing an element that can sometimes be difficult to prove, it also removes an important element of perceived moral culpability, even where, as is often the case, elements of *mens rea* are in fact present.

Regulatory law emerged out of a long process of negotiation in which the difficulties of finding a company guilty of intending to cause harm by, for example, using dangerous work practices (Carson 1979) led to an accommodation whereby businesses agreed to strict liability, on the basis that prosecution would be selective. Enforcers developed what have come to be known as 'compliance' strategies based on a different set of aims to those associated with the police. Rather than seeing themselves as there to secure justice by publicly prosecuting those accused of being 'guilty' of a crime, regulatory enforcers seek to protect the public by attempting to secure maximum levels of compliance – using a range of weapons or tools such as education or persuasion – with prosecution being seen as an often costly last resort which may be counterproductive. This rests on the assumption that the majority of businesses are able and willing to comply, with prosecution being reserved for the minority of recalcitrant 'rogues' – a distinction which has underpinned the justification for the use of regulatory as opposed to criminal sanctions (Croall 2004). Cost-effectiveness is therefore the basis for not prosecuting offenders – unlike conventional criminals. The regulatory form of law is generally associated with fewer prosecutions, fewer convictions and lower sentences for the corporate offender.

A major problem has surrounded the legal liability of corporations. Like most comparable jurisdictions, the Scottish criminal justice system has had no problem in constructing criminal liability for regulatory offences to encompass the corporation as offender/criminal. Equally, in common with other systems which have developed on an individualistic model, it is only relatively recently that it has become accepted that a corporate body may be guilty of a traditional crime as well as regulatory crime. Most of the regulatory offences were drafted with corporate bodies in mind, and establishing responsibility is a straightforward matter. Even there, however, the precise basis of corporate responsibility is rarely explicit and can therefore be contested. Efforts to argue that the 'controlling mind' doctrine (discussed below) should apply to health and safety offences were unsuccessful (*R* v. *British Steel* [1995] IRLR 310; *R* v. *Gateway Foodmarkets Ltd* [1997] IRLR 189), but the courts were not prepared to accept that the principle of vicarious liability (whereby an employer is responsible for the actions of an employee) applied, leaving it unclear whether there was a cut off point in a company hierarchy for such liability (*R* v. *Gateway Foodmarkets Ltd*, p. 192). Legislation now specifies that an employer cannot use fault of an employee as a defence to a health and safety offence (Management of Health and Safety at Work Regulations 1999, r.21).

So far as traditional crime is concerned, the Scottish courts have essentially followed the approach of the English courts and applied the controlling mind doctrine to allocate responsibility to a corporation. The first attempt to prosecute a company (for 'shameless indecency', a crime since abolished as contrary to Article 7 of the European Convention on Human Rights (*Webster* v. *Dominick* 2003 SCCR 525)), was unsuccessful as the High Court of Justiciary held that this was not the sort of crime which a company could commit, even though the conduct complained of was selling 'top-shelf' magazines for which individual shop owners had been convicted (*Dean* v. *John Menzies (Holdings) Ltd* 1981 JC 23). In the second case, for attempted fraud, although it was held to be competent to prosecute the company (using the controlling mind approach), the prosecution was dropped as the company was wound up (*Purcell Meats (Scotland) Ltd* v. *McLeod* 1986 SCCR 672). It was not until the prosecution of Transco in 2003 for culpable homicide that the question was closely debated, legally and politically.

Corporate criminal liability has arisen sharply as a legal and political issue in a number of countries, usually as a result of workplace disasters. It is partly the scale of death that has raised the incidents in importance, but also the perception of corporate fault or neglect as a cause which was being inadequately recognised by the law. In England, Canada and Australia as well as Scotland, public and political concern over particular incidents led to official inquiry, court action perceived as only partly meeting the requirements of retribution or deterrence, and actual or proposed change in the law. In England the key incident was the sinking of the ferry *Herald of Free Enterprise* at Zeebrugge in 1987, when 188 crew and passengers died. A statutory investigation found that '[f]rom top to bottom the body corporate was infected with the disease of sloppiness' (Department of Transport 1987: para. 14). Changes to the Merchant Shipping Acts and the regulatory system were introduced as a result of the recommendations. A prosecution of certain directors and managers of the company together with the company for manslaughter resulted in the acquittal of all, including the company, which could only have been found guilty if the 'controlling minds' of the company had been guilty (*R* v. *P & O European Ferries (Dover) Ltd* (1990) 93 Cr App Rep 72). It was partly the contrast between the acquittal and the findings of the investigation that led to the Law Commission including corporate manslaughter in its review of manslaughter and proposing an offence of corporate homicide (Law Commission 1994, 1996). It took a further ten years before the enactment of a corporate manslaughter offence (below).

In Canada in 1992 an explosion in the Westray mine in Nova Scotia which killed 26 miners had a similar impact. The company was charged with a number of non-criminal administrative offences and a prosecution of two managers for manslaughter was ultimately dropped. A Royal Commission of Inquiry which sat from 1992 to 1996 uncovered 'a story of incompetence, of mismanagement, of bureaucratic bungling, of deceit, of ruthlessness, of cover-up, of apathy, of expediency, and of cynical indifference'.[2] Consequential public and political concern led to the passing of statute C-45/2003, which amended the Canadian Criminal Code to make prosecution of companies for crime dependent on establishing the *mens rea* not of the controlling minds of the company but on identification with 'senior officers', while permitting aggregation of the acts of employees and officers of a company to construct the criminal behaviour itself. Although this represents a move away from the controlling mind approach, it still requires identification with an individual officer or group of officers. It is debatable whether it will have a significant effect on the ability to prosecute corporations for corporate fault and whether it is much more than a rhetorical reaction to the disaster (Bittle and Snider 2006).

In Australia in 1998 a gas explosion at the Esso natural gas plant at Longford, Victoria which killed two workers and injured eight was a catalyst for the re-examination of safety law and corporate criminal responsibility. A Royal Commission set up to report on the explosion identified a number of failures on the part of Esso and rejected its placing of blame on individual workers (Longford Royal Commission 1999). After a four-month trial the company was found guilty of breaches of the Occupational Health and Safety Act 1985 and fined $2 million, the sentencing judge highlighting Esso's failure to accept responsibility and its 'obfuscation' in its defence (*DPP* v. *Esso* [2000] VSC 263). Changes to the regulatory system resulted. Australia had already adopted a form of corporate criminal responsibility additional to the controlling mind doctrine based on 'corporate culture' (Criminal Code Act 1995, s. 12). This had not been adopted in any of the states until, in 2002 and 2005, Australian Capital Territories (ACT) and Northern Territory introduced the new doctrine, while ACT introduced new crimes of causing death and serious injury applying to employers including the senior officers of companies (Crimes (Industrial Manslaughter) (Amendment) Act 2003 ACT).

In Scotland a series of disasters have caused legal and political concern at the failure of regulatory law to impose adequate and appropriately targeted sanctions.

Piper Alpha

In 1988 the world's worst off-shore disaster occurred in the North Sea when the Piper Alpha oil production platform operated by Occidental Petroleum was destroyed by fire after a series of explosions, killing

167 workers. Before this catastrophe, even with an apparent decline in serious incidents, the 'relentless' price in terms of death and injury in the 'race' to bring the oil ashore had been highlighted (Carson 1981: 5). Enforcement of safety law was carried out by the Petroleum Engineering Directorate, answerable to the Department of Energy. This conflict between economics and safety was not just a historical legacy of a separate pre-existing system but was the result of an explicit political decision that the off-shore oil industry should be administered differently because of the central importance of oil to the British economy (Burgoyne Report 1980: 16, quoted in Carson 1981: 210). An inquiry, chaired by Lord Cullen, was set up by the Department of Energy to report on the causes of the disaster. The Report identified many failures: in the permit to work system which led to lack of communication between shifts and use of machinery which was under maintenance, and in the emergency procedures and rescue arrangements. It criticised Occidental Petroleum for these failures and for being inadequately prepared for a major emergency (Cullen 1990). Occidental had previously been convicted of an offence in 1987 when a similar failure resulted in the death of a worker carrying out maintenance work (Miller 1991: 182).

Occidental were not prosecuted for any offence arising out of the disaster. Occidental was an international company, and the investigation of the Cullen Inquiry – and presumably of any potential prosecution – was hampered by the refusal of five of its senior managers to testify to the Inquiry. As they lived outside the UK they could not be compelled to do so (Miller 1991: 187). The Report was also critical of the Department of Energy's enforcement, both operationally and institutionally. Its inspections were superficial and it was understaffed by 50 per cent. It recommended ending the conflict between the Department's two roles by transferring responsibility to the HSE, which took place in 1991. Changes to substantive regulatory law, requiring safety cases to be approved by the HSE before work could start, were introduced in 1992. The combination of a large unaccountable international company and a poor regulatory framework had been fatal.

Transco

In December 1999 a family of four in Larkhall in Lanarkshire were killed when their house was destroyed by a gas explosion, caused by leakage from severely corroded pipes. Following privatisation and demerging the licensed public gas suppliers were Transco plc, responsible for the pipes since 1986 when the company was incorporated. In 2003 the company was indicted for the culpable homicide of the family and also for an offence under s. 3 of the Health and Safety at Work etc. Act 1974 (HSWA).[3] The maximum penalty for culpable homicide and a s. 3 offence is the same, an unlimited fine. The difference between the two therefore did not necessarily lie in the sanction which might be imposed, but in the moral implications of conviction for a common law crime compared with conviction for a regulatory crime. Not only was this the first time such an indictment had been laid against a company, but the Crown Office adopted an innovative approach to corporate criminal liability which went against the jurisprudence of the English courts by not naming a controlling mind for whose wrongdoing the company would be liable, instead alleging a collective, aggregated fault. At a preliminary hearing in 2003, Lord Carloway, the trial judge, found the indictment relevant against the company and rejected a human rights challenge against the trial being heard by a jury (Transco 1).[4] Transco were successful in their appeal against the former ruling (Transco 1), and unsuccessful in their appeal against the latter (Transco 2).[5] For two months it had looked as if the company was going to be prosecuted for culpable homicide in a ground-breaking approach to corporate liability, but with the decision of the appeal court, this did not happen. Instead Transco faced trial on the s. 3 charge, with substantially the same facts but different legal, social and moral implications.

The company from start to finish did not accept any blame other than in the technical sense that it was responsible for the pipes. It attempted to have Lord Carloway recused from presiding over the trial after he had refused to order disclosure of advice about prosecution from the HSE to the Crown Office. They argued that he could not be impartial since he had had to read that part of the report in order to decide whether it was appropriate to disclose it. This argument was rejected (Transco 3).[6] After a six-month trial, a jury found the company guilty of the s. 3 offence, for failing to replace the corroded pipes when they had known since at least 1986 of the need to replace them. Lord Carloway imposed a £15 million fine, the highest UK fine for a health and safety offence. Although s. 3 is a regulatory offence, one of the key reasons for selecting such a large fine was that throughout the trial 'the corporate mind of Transco ha[d] little or no remorse' (Carloway 2005).

ICL Plastics

In May 2004 an explosion destroyed the Grovepark Mills factory of ICL Plastics in Maryhill, Glasgow, killing nine workers and injuring 33. The explosion was caused by liquid petroleum gas (LPG) escaping from corroded pipes. ICL Plastics Ltd was a privately owned company, the holding company for a group of companies, including ICL Technical Plastics Ltd, the occupier of the destroyed factory, and five other companies including one named Stockline Plastics Limited, which for a while gave its name to the disaster. There was speculation that since this was a private company, with readily identifiable individuals as controlling minds, the Crown Office might attempt a prosecution of the company for culpable homicide based on more traditional principles than in the Transco case. However, this did not take place. Among the dead was the managing director of the company, with other managers being among those injured. This may be one reason for that decision. ICL Plastics Ltd and ICL Technical Plastics Ltd both pled guilty to offences under ss. 2, 3 and 4 of the HSWA. The corroded pipe had been laid in 1969, a yard raised over it in 1973 burying the pipe underground, and no maintenance or risk assessment carried out until the explosion. The HSE had identified a possible problem with those pipes in 1988, but a compromise was reached between the company and the HSE which did not involve excavating and inspecting the pipework (Gill Report 2009: 30). In sentencing the company Lord Brodie rejected the defence advocate's characterisation of the company failures as 'inadvertent' since they had done nothing to satisfy themselves that the pipes were sound (Brodie 2007). Both companies were fined £200,000, set at that level with a view to enabling them to keep trading.

Political and trade union dissatisfaction with the legal response eventually led to the UK and Scottish Parliaments jointly setting up a public inquiry chaired by Lord Gill, which reported in 2009 (Gill 2009). The Report found not only that the explosion was the fault of the company but also that there had been evasion and non-cooperation with the HSE, and also failure by the HSE itself. There had been a history of HSE visits during the 1980s concerning the storage of the LPG culminating in several recommendations in 1988, including the excavation and examination of the pipes. It found that the then managing director of the company deliberately misled the HSE at this time, and throughout his period as managing director from 1982 to 1998 'pursued a policy of non-cooperation with HSE on safety questions affecting the [LPG] tank installation' (Gill

2009: 86). The HSE failed to pursue the issue of the pipes with the company, eventually reaching a compromise agreement about the siting of the LPG tank, with no provision concerning the pipes. The report concluded that the HSE's actions overall were characterised by "an inadequate appreciation of the risks associated with buried LPG pipework and unventilated voids; and by a failure to properly carry out check visits" (Gill 2009: 94). Lord Brodie had sentenced the company on the basis that it apparently had 'a good safety record prior to May 2004, going back to the 1960s' (Brodie 2007). This is not borne out by the Gill Report. Before the establishment of the statutory inquiry a group, mainly of academics from Stirling and Strathclyde universities, carried out an examination of working conditions at ICL before the explosion, using action research methods, drawing on the testimony of seven ICL workers and ex-workers, and identifying inadequate safety measures and lack of consultation with workers about safety (Beck *et al.* 2007; Taylor and Connelly 2009). In a return to the concerns arising out of Piper Alpha some 20 years previously, there had been a toxic combination of company and regulatory failure.

Corporate liability

Another dichotomy in the case of corporate crime is between the responsibility of the corporation and the responsibility of the corporate officers, including directors and senior managers. In discourse about corporate crime, in particular corporate killing, the term may be used to ascribe responsibility to the corporate body on whose behalf the criminal behaviour was carried out, or to a corporate officer or senior manager at fault in either causing or failing to prevent the harm. As a legal concept it refers to the former; as a concern to the public and particularly to the victims of crime or their relatives, it is at least as likely to refer to the officers, with a campaign for 'jail sentences for employers who negligently kill' (Families Against Corporate Killing).[7] These forms of guilt are not mutually exclusive. Corporate guilt does not excuse and need not replace individual guilt, and vice versa. However, the principles of criminal liability make it difficult to hold companies responsible for traditional crime, while regulatory offences usually arise out of breach of duties placed on organisations (as employer or as in charge of an undertaking). Most such statutes include provision for a secondary offence applying to an officer of an organisation whose actions or neglect contributed to the crime, such as s. 37 of the HSWA, but prosecutions under this section are rare and in Scotland there has only been one.

The Scottish courts have adopted the English controlling mind approach. This requires an individual or group of individuals of sufficient seniority within the corporation to be identified with it to be guilty of the crime, and for that guilt to be in turn ascribed to the corporate body (Transco 1). Although for economic crime the Privy Council (essentially the same judges as sit in the Supreme Court) has indicated that it would consider as a controlling mind someone representing the company in a particular transaction and not responsible for policy generally, this is not a significant departure from the controlling mind principle since the individual concerned still had to be at the 'commanding heights' of the organisation (*Meridian Global Funds Management Ltd* v. *Securities Commission* [1995] 3 All ER 918). It has been widely commented that this doctrine is more easily applicable to the small privately owned company with one or very few directors who can be readily identified with it and are more likely to be directly involved in any operations. It is not so readily applicable to the large corporation with more directors and a diffuse organisational structure, where the controlling minds are less likely to have operational involvement (Slapper and Tombs 1999; Wells 2001). But it is in the large company that the concept is more needed. The criminal law is based on doctrine which is attuned to holding the individual to account. Regulatory law requires to be expanded, or more rigorously enforced, to reflect individual corporate failure. At the same time, some other means of attributing liability to companies than the controlling mind approach needs to be found.

This has been acknowledged in a number of jurisdictions, but often simply by lowering the level of the officers with whom the company can be identified. The Canadian 'senior officer' is someone who plays an important role in the establishment of an organisation's policies or is responsible for managing an important aspect of its activities, including a director, CEO and chief financial officer (Bill C-45, Criminal Code, s. 2). The UK Corporate Manslaughter and Corporate Homicide Act 2007 (CMCHA) ascribes liability to the fault of 'senior management', that is persons who play significant roles in decision-making or actual organisation of the whole or a substantial part of the activities of the organisation (CMCHA, s. 1(4)(c)). In Australia two concepts of corporate fault sit alongside the controlling mind doctrine: for crimes involving negligence, the concept of management or systems failure (Criminal Code Act, s. 12.4); for crimes of intention or recklessness that a 'corporate culture' authorised or permitted the commission of the offence, that is an attitude, policy, rule, course of conduct or practice existing within the organisation or the relevant part of the organisation (12.3). If Lord Carloway's view of corporate liability had been accepted by the appeal court (Transco 1), it would have resulted in a doctrine sitting somewhere between the Canadian and Australian. It would not be necessary to identify either one individual or group of individuals at controlling-mind level, and the combined actions or *mens re*a of individuals or committees at senior decision-making level would be sufficient.

Since criminal law is not a reserved matter, the Scottish Parliament has the competence to legislate on it (Scotland Act 1998 (SA), s. 29). Because of public disquiet at the failure of the Transco culpable homicide trial, an Expert Group was appointed to review the law relating to corporate liability for culpable homicide. It sat during the Transco health and safety trial and proposed the creation of an offence of corporate killing with corporate liability based on organisational failure to put policies and practices into effect to ensure health and safety, or allowing a corporate culture to be established which let the offence take place. It also proposed separate and secondary offences against individuals who caused death or serious injury (Scottish Executive 2005: 20–1).

Having received the report, the then Scottish Executive abandoned plans for Scottish legislation and acceded to the passing of CMCHA as UK legislation, which adopted the senior management test and made no new provision for individual responsibility. Company law is a reserved matter (SA, Sch. 5, C1), and while corporate liability and corporate homicide clearly touch on the law as it relates to companies, no amendments to company legislation were required for CMCHA, nor would they have been required for any legislation proposed by the Expert Group. Health and safety legislation is also reserved (SA, Sch. 5, H2) which would preclude amendment to HSWA, and could be seen as sitting uneasily with the creation of new workplace offences which did not involve traditional forms of criminal responsibility. It seems to be accepted that this whole area is a reserved matter (Ewing 2009), but it is hard to see why this should be so. There is no competency reason why the Scottish Parliament could not legislate for a fresh approach to corporate criminal liability within the Scottish criminal justice system as a whole.

Enforcement and sanctions

Fatal and serious injuries at work have historically been higher in Scotland than in other parts of Britain (Beck *et al.* 2007: 29). While the industry and occupational make-up of Scotland may be significant, problems have also been revealed with the regulatory system itself. Failures in the operation of HSE inspection were identified in both the Cullen and Gill Reports into Piper Alpha and ICL Plastics as causes of the disasters (Cullen 1990; Gill 2009). Deficiencies in the quality and frequency of inspections by local authority inspectors were also identified in a Fatal Accident Inquiry into the 21 E-coli deaths referred to above (Cox 1998). There are problems with resourcing, and in recent years investigations and inspections have declined in Scotland,[8] and across the UK, with inspections based on 'risk assessments' leading to the inspection only of those premises considered to be most dangerous, a situation which, coupled with the decline in Inspectors, amounts, argue Tombs and Whyte (2007: 17), to the collapse of enforcement.

Historically Scotland has also had lower rates of prosecution and sentences (Beck *et al.* 2007). All prosecution in Scotland is carried out by the Crown Office and 50 specialist agencies report to the prosecution service, including the HSE, SEPA and local authority Environmental Health and Trading Standards inspectors. These are all areas of technical as well as legal and evidential complexity. These problems have been acknowledged at the institutional level and as a result specialist prosecutors have been established for environmental and health and safety cases in 2004 and 2008 respectively.[9] It remains to be seen whether this will result in a higher level of and more effective prosecution.

Much of the disquiet with how corporate offenders are dealt with by the courts centres on the sanctions that are imposed. Where the offender is a corporate body rather than an individual the focus is on the fine. The fine is a blunt, and inadequate, instrument to perform all the aims of criminalisation, not least deterrence and retribution. Although the highest fine for a health and safety offence was imposed after the conviction of Transco, this nonetheless amounted to a mere 5 per cent of the company's after-tax profits and less than one per cent of its overall turnover (SGC 2010). Moreover, it is out of step with what has historically been a lower level of fine in Scotland than elsewhere in Britain (Beck *et al.* 2007). Fines are also limited by the so called 'deterrence trap' as too large a fine may have an adverse spillover effect on employees who may lose their jobs, on shareholders and on surrounding communities.

Fines in health and safety cases have been acknowledged by the courts themselves to be too low and guidelines drawn up in England, first of all by the Court of Criminal Appeal (Croall and Ross 2002) and then, but only for health and safety offences involving death, by the English Sentencing Guidelines Council (SGC). Their Guidelines relate to sentencing both for corporate manslaughter and health and safety offences involving death (SGC 2010). Scotland does not have an equivalent body. A Scottish Sentencing Commission sat briefly between 2003 and 2006 with a limited remit and at the time of writing the Scottish Government is consulting on the setting up of a Scottish Sentencing and Sentencing Guidelines Council (see Chapter 10, this volume). In Scotland, a Member's Bill, the Criminal Sentencing (Equity Fines) (Scotland) Bill is currently being considered by the Scottish Parliament. It proposes the introduction of Equity Fines which, being targeted at company shares, would avoid the deterrence trap, enable larger monetary fines and be directed at shareholders. While some argue that 'innocent' shareholders should not be penalised, others contend that shareholders take a risk by investing, can profit from offences and can influence management decisions (Croall 2005), an argument accepted in principle by the SGC (2009: para. 68). The fate of this proposal is at present uncertain.[10]

Guidance is given from time to time in individual cases by the High Court of Justiciary sitting as a court of criminal appeal. Detailed guidance was given in the case of an overly lenient sentence where an inadequately secured load had fallen off the lorry transporting it, crushing a car behind and killing the passenger and seriously injuring the driver. A fine of £3,750 was increased to £30,000. The appeal court applied the guidelines from English case law, considering aggravating and mitigating factors and accepting that the objective of a fine is to 'achieve a safe environment for the public and bring the message home to managers and shareholders' (*HM Adv* v. *Munro & Sons (Highland) Ltd* 2009 SLT 233). In determining the level of fine the court made reference to turnover and profit of the company, as a differently constituted court had done in the previous year, approving fines of £240,000 on two companies whose failures had caused the death of a worker (*LH Access Technology Ltd and Border Rail & Plant* v. *HM Adv* 2009 SCCR 280). Reference to turnover or profit was rejected by the English Sentencing Guidelines Council in spite of advice that turnover should be used from the Sentencing Advisory Panel (SAP).[11]

A percentage of turnover is the mechanism for the (much higher) administrative penalties applicable under the Competition Act. There is a history of its acceptance by the Scottish courts for sentencing corporate offenders (Croall and Ross 2002).

There is also a need for alternatives to the fine in the search for the appropriate way to impose sanctions on corporations which will provide deterrence and retribution, and there is also considerable potential in rehabilitative and restorative approaches (Croall 2005; Croall and Ross 2002; Law Reform Commission, New South Wales 2003). In some jurisdictions, companies are given probation orders, particularly appropriate for smaller businesses whose survival would be endangered by large fines. Companies could also be given appropriately designed Community Sentences which have the potential to contain a restorative element. These kinds of sanctions were proposed for offences other than those dealt with in the CMCHA (McRory 2006), although the subsequent Regulatory Enforcement and Sanctions Act 2008 only introduced them for administrative, and not criminal, proceedings. The CMCHA also provides for publicity orders but there have yet to be convictions under this Act. A small but significant change could be the introduction of Company Background Inquiry Reports as all too often the court has insufficient information about the company's previous compliance record, its financial assets and other relevant information, and any such information is often provided by the company itself. These could be compiled by appropriate court-appointed experts and the cost paid by the defendant company (Ewing 2009). A provision to this effect was accepted as an amendment to the current Criminal Justice and Licensing (Scotland) Bill on 13 April 2010.

Concluding comments

Corporate crime raises issues of equity in relation to criminal and social justice central to the themes of this book. Many forms of corporate crime have a more severe impact on already disadvantaged groups – yet, as the discussion and case studies in this chapter indicate, there remain many shortcomings in the way in which the law and criminal justice satisfies victims' demands for convicting and punishing those responsible. The long-awaited passage of the CMCHA and the promise of heavier sentences may go some way towards this: however, they remain to be tested. Moreover, these proposals only deal with the mercifully small number of cases which lead to death, leaving many other corporate harms subject to lower levels of investigation, prosecution and punishment. The McRory Report (2006) and the Regulatory Enforcement and Sanctions Act assume that the criminal law is over-used and envisage a much lower rate of prosecution. This, coupled with the regulatory degradation described by Tombs and Whyte (2009), amounts to the effective decriminalisation of many regulatory offences.

Given that this is taking place in the context of global neoliberalism and deregulatory policies across the UK and elsewhere, can there be a distinctive Scottish approach? The essentially political, rather than legal, decision to adopt the English form of legislation in the CMCHA arguably represents a missed opportunity to pass a more radical piece of legislation influenced by Canadian or Australian examples. The proposal for Equity Fines, in itself limited to only a small number of potential cases, is unlikely to proceed, although in respect of Corporate Inquiry Reports some progress may be made. The impact of the specialised prosecution arrangements remains to be seen but, as Walters argues in Chapter 8 (this volume), could be a positive step. There remains a gap in relation to sentencing and it could be argued that these matters could and should be considered by any new Sentencing Commission, providing an opportunity for an innovative Scottish approach.

Notes

1 http://www.hse.gov.uk/statistics/regions/scotland/index.htm
2 'The Westray Story', Report of the Westray Mine Public Inquiry (1997). http://www.gov.ns.ca/lwd/pubs/westray/.
3 Indictment in *HM Advocate* v. *Transco* 2003. http://www.corporateaccountability.org/dl/Cases/Transco.doc
4 *Transco plc* v. *HM Advocate* 2004 SCCR 1 (Transco 1). Lord Carloway's judgment is at pp. 9–30.
5 *Transco plc* v. *HM Advocate* 2004 SCCR 553 (Transco 2).
6 *Transco plc* v. *HM Advocate* 2005 SCCR 117 (Transco 3).
7 Families Against Corporate Killers (FACK) information leaflet. http://www.hazardscampaign.org.uk/fack/about/fackleaflet08.pdf .
8 'STUC highlights HSE cuts as injury statistics show little improvement', STUC Press Release, 29 October 2008. http://www.stuc.org.uk/news/557/stuc-highlights-hse-cuts-as-injury-statistics-show-little improvement (accessed 27 May 2010).
9 Crown Office 'Specialist Prosecutors'. http://www.copfs.gov.uk/About/roles/pf-role/specialists (accessed 30 November 2009).

10 http://www.scottish.parliament.uk/s3/bills/48-CriminalSentencing/index.htm

11 Sentencing Advisory Panel, 'Advice to the Sentencing Guidelines Council: Sentencing for Corporate Manslaughter and Health and Safety Offences Involving Death'. http://www.sentencing-guidelines.gov.uk (accessed 22 May 2010).

References

Beck, M., Cooper, C., Coulson, A., Gorman, T., Howieson, S., McCourt, J., Taylor, P., Watterson, A. and Whyte, D. (2007) *The ICL/Stockline Disaster: An Independent Report on Working Conditions Prior to the Explosion.* Stirling and Glasgow: Universities of Stirling and Strathclyde. http://www.hazards.org/icldisaster/icl_stockline_report.pdf.

Bittle, S. and Snider, L. (2006) 'From manslaughter to preventable accidents: shaping corporate criminal liability', *Law and Policy*, 28: 470–96.

Brodie, Lord (2007) Sentencing Statement, 28 August. http://www.hazards.org/icldisaster/sentencingstatement.pdf.

Burgoyne, J. H. (1980) *Offshore Safety* (The Burgoyne Report), Cmd. 7841. London: HMSO.

Carloway, Lord (2005) Sentencing Statement, 25 October. http://news.bbc.co.uk/1/shared/bsp/hi/pdfs/26_08_05_transco.pdf.

Carson, W. G. (1979) 'The conventionalisation of early factory crime', *International Journal for the Sociology of Law*, 7: 37–60.

Carson, W. G. (1981) *The Other Price of Britain's Oil.* London: Martin Robertson.

Cox, G. L. (1998) *Determination in the E-coli 0157 Fatal Accident Inquiry.* Dumfries and Galloway: Sheriffdom of South Strathclyde.

Croall, H. (2001) *Understanding White Collar Crime.* Buckingham: Open University Press.

Croall, H. (2004) 'Combating financial crime: regulatory versus crime control approaches', *Journal of Financial Crime*, 11 (1): 45.

Croall, H. (2005) 'Penalties for Corporate Homicide', Annex to Scottish Executive Expert Group on Corporate Homicide. Available on: http://www.scotland.gov.uk/Publications/2005/11/14133559/36003.

Croall, H. (2008) 'Unusual suspects', *Scottish Left Review*, 48, September/October, pp. 12–13.

Croall, H. (2009a) 'White collar crime, consumers and victimization', *Crime, Law and Social Change*, 51: 127–46.

Croall, H. (2009b) 'Community safety and economic crime', *Criminology and Criminal Justice*, 9 (2): 165–85.

Croall, H. and Ross, J. (2002) 'Sentencing the corporate offender: legal and social issues', in N. Hutton and C. Tata (eds), *Sentencing and Society.* Aldershot: Ashgate, pp. 528–47.

Cullen, Lord (1990) *The Public Inquiry into the Piper Alpha Disaster* (The Cullen Report), Cmd 1310. London: HMSO.

Dawson, D. M. and Brooks, B. J. (1999) *The Esso Longford Gas Plant Accident: Report of the Longford Royal Commission*. Government Printer for the State of Victoria.

Department of Transport (1987) *Formal Investigation into the MV Herald of Free Enterprise Report of Court No. 8074*. London: HMSO.

Evening Times (2008) '250 firms fined in blitz on littering', 3 September. http://www.eveningtimes.co.uk/250-firms-fined-in-blitz-on-littering-1.962408 (accessed 22 May 2010).

Ewing, F. (2009) Reply to debate on Criminal Justice and Licensing (Scotland) Bill 26 November, col. 26191.

Friedrichs, D. O. (2009) 'Exorbitant CEO compensation: just reward or grand theft?', *Law and Social Change*, 51: 45–72.

Gill, Lord (2009) The ICL Inquiry Report, House of Commons and Scottish Parliament, HC838 SG/2009/129.

Herald, The (2007) '200,000 Scots claim work is making them ill', 1 November.

Herald, The (2008) 'Scottish coal fined £400,000 over double death', 26 August (www.heraldscotland.com/mitie-faces-large-fine-after-death-of-electrician-1.892078).

Herald, The (2008) 'Mitie faces large fine after death of electrician', 15 October (www.heraldscotland.com/scottish-coal-fined-pound-400-000-over-double-death-1.888099).

Herald, The (2009) 'Construction death rate higher in Scotland', 21 September.

Law Commission (1994) *Involuntary Manslaughter: A Consultation Paper*, No. 135. London: HMSO.

Law Commission (1996) *Legislating the Criminal Code: Involuntary Manslaughter*, No. 237. London: HMSO.

Law Reform Commission, New South Wales (2003) *Sentencing Corporate Offenders*, Law Reform Commission of New South Wales Report 102. Available at: www.lawlink.nsw.gov.au/lrc.nsf/pages/r102.

Levi, M. and Burrows, J. (2008) 'Measuring the impact of fraud in the UK: a conceptual and empirical journey,' *British Journal of Criminology*, 48 (3): 293–318.

Macrory, R. (2006) *Regulatory Justice: Making Sanctions Effective. Final Report*. London: HMSO.

Miller, K. (1991) 'Piper Alpha and the Cullen Report', *Industrial Law Journal*, pp. 176–87.

National Consumer Council (2003) *Everyday Essentials: Meeting Basic Needs. Research into Accessing Essential Goods and Services*. London: National Consumer Council, January.

Nelken, D. (2007) 'White collar crime', in M. Maguire, R. Morgan and R. Reiner (eds), *The Oxford Handbook of Criminology*, 4th edn. Clarendon: Oxford University Press.

Office of Fair Trading (OFT) (2008) *Consumer Detriment: Assessing the Frequency and Impact of Consumer Problems with Goods and Services*. April. http://www.oft.gov.uk/news/press/2008/49-08.

Pearce, F. (1976) *Crimes of the Powerful*. London: Pluto Press.

Punch, M. (2000) 'Suite violence: why managers murder and corporations kill', *Crime, Law and Social Change*, 33 (3): 243–80.

Punch, M. (2009) 'Police corruption: deviance, accountability and reform', in *Policing*. Cullompton: Willan Publishing.

Scottish Executive (2005) *Expert Group Report on Corporate Homicide*. http://www.scotland.gov.uk/Resource/Doc/1099/0019260.pdf

Sentencing Guidelines Council (SGC) (2010) *Corporate Manslaughter and Health and Safety Offences Causing Death*. http://www.sentencing-guidelines.gov.uk/docs/guideline_on_corporate_manslaughter.pdf.

Slapper, G. and Tombs, S. (1999) *Corporate Crime*. London: Addison Wesley Longman.

Sutherland, E. (1949) *White Collar Crime*. New York: Holt, Reinhart & Winston.

Tappan, P. W. (1947) 'Who is the criminal?', *American Sociological Review*, 12 (10): 96–102.

Taylor, P. and Connelly, L. (2009) 'Before the disaster: health, safety and working conditions at a plastics factory', *Work, Employment and Society*, 23 (1): 160–8.

Tombs, S. (2000) 'Official statistics and hidden crimes: researching health and safety crimes', in V. Jupp, P. Davies and P. Francis (eds), *Doing Criminological Research*. London: Sage, pp. 64–81.

Tombs, S. (2007) 'Violence, safety crimes and criminology', *British Journal of Criminology*, 47 (4): 531–50.

Tombs, S. and Whyte, D. (2007) *Safety Crime*. Cullompton: Willan Publishing.

Tombs, S. and Whyte, D. (2010) 'Crime, harm and corporate power', in J. Muncie, D. Talbot and R. Walters (eds), *Crime: Local and Global*. Cullompton: Willan Publishing, pp. 137–72.

Wells, C. (2001) *Corporations and Criminal Responsibility*, 2nd edn. Oxford: Clarendon.

Whyte, D. (ed.) (2009) *Crimes of the Powerful: A Reader*. Maidenhead: Open University Press.

William, P. (2008) 'Offshore firms fined £1.2 million over death of oil worker', *The Herald*, 10 October.

Chapter 8

Environmental crime in Scotland

Reece Walters

Introduction

Scotland's built and natural environment is a major asset for us to enjoy in life and business. That's why we need to protect and enhance it. Clean air and water, and uncontaminated soil, support and protect our public health and wellbeing … They are the inspiration for much of Scottish art and literature. And the natural and built environment are sources of wealth and economic opportunities – especially for fishing, farming, forestry, aquaculture, renewable energy and tourism. (Scottish Government 2009)

> People [in Scotland] in the most deprived areas are far more likely to be living near to these sources of potential negative environmental impact than people in less deprived areas. (Fairburn *et al.* 2005)

The protection of the environment continues to capture international media and political headlines. A mounting body of research points to the perils facing essential natural resources such as water, soil and air from climate change by the economic activities of world trade (Brown *et al.* 2009). The dangers confronting environmental destruction are so severe that the United Nations' Intergovernmental Panel on Climate Change has referred to global warming as a 'weapon of mass destruction' (IPCC 2007).

The 4th of June 2009 was designated as 'World Environment Day', one of several events identified by the United Nations in a year demarcated for addressing the perils of climate change. To commemorate this day, Achim Steiner, the UN Environment Programme Executive Director, delivered a keynote address under the banner 'Your Planet Needs You: Unite to Combat Climate Change' (UNEP 2009a). It signalled a call to all nations to mobilise resources to conserve natural habitats and diminish environmental degradation.

This call to reduce environmental degradation and reach designated international targets has been reflected in domestic policies and practices of numerous sovereign nations, notably the expanding amount of municipal, EU and international environmental law. There are collectively more treaties, protocols, directives and statutes that address environmental issues than any other area of law, including trade, health, security, employment and education (Walters 2009a).

Along with other EU countries, Scotland has made numerous legislative and policy initiatives to meet international environment targets (see 'Greener Scotland', Scottish Government 2010). One of the stumbling blocks to achieving environmental objectives is wilful and illegal acts that result in environmental destruction. Scottish regulatory officials have been outspoken in condemning acts of environmental criminality. For example, SEPA Chairman Ken Collins has stated:

> The impact of environmental crime can be significant, in environmental, social and economic terms and Scotland's criminal justice system has an important role to play. It acts as a preventative mechanism as well as a form of punishment for wrongdoers. In this sense both prosecutors and the judiciary have a genuine and significant role to play in environmental protection. (Quoted in Scottish Government 2003)

In addition, Scotland has reportedly been a leader in tackling acts of corporate environmental crime. In 2004, the then Lord Advocate Colin Boyd QC stated:

> The pollution of rivers by raw sewage or chemical spillage and the dumping of rubbish in the heart of communities is a real threat to human health and to the environment. The specialist environmental prosecutor initiative is a partnership agreement with Sepa to actively improve the COPFS specialism in environmental law. (Quoted in Kelbie 2004)

One in three Scots perceive the environment to be the single most important global challenge; however, one in ten perceive it as a national priority, preferring to emphasise employment and industry as more crucial (Scottish Government 2008). Herein lies a significant tension. So often the creation of industry results in environmental damage and the balance between 'acceptable' or 'tolerable' environmental destruction for essential trade is often precarious and fraught with political and economic interests. The conflict between environmental protection and trade is a global issue where the priorities of the free market are emphasised. It is clear that the commercial activities of corporations and the policy priorities of states allow for a whole range of activities that cause environmental damage. While some are illegal, others are not. This chapter examines environmental or eco-crime in Scotland and explores the challenges facing regulators when trade and economic prosperity are prioritised. It seeks to identify how harm and inequality are intricately entwined with trade and the environment, and how environmental crime, involving states, corporations and the general public, has distinctive characteristics in Scotland that provide both lessons for regulation and practice.

Devolution and environmental policy in Scotland

The first decade of devolution in Scotland has witnessed an integration of environmental matters into Scottish Government policy. For some commentators, devolution provided an opportunity for campaign movements to influence environmental policy. Scandrett (2007), for example, identifies how Friends of the Earth were able to introduce and debate notions of environmental justice to coincide with the new Scottish Parliament. Devolution provided a window through which community activism came to engage with political power and shape environmental policy. As Scandrett argues:

> At a local level, Scotland had seen a number of local campaigns in environmental pollution hotspots, largely in working-class areas, many of which FoES has supported. In response to these locally based environmental problems, FoES ran a series of activities aimed at mobilizing and supporting resistance communities, building capacity and linking them into the national policy process. The issues faced by these communities were varied and included waste landfill, opencast mining, gravel quarrying, fish

> farming, incinerators, industrial pollution, road building and semiconductor factories. (2007: 3)

The intersection of activist movements such as Friends of the Earth, Greenpeace, the Association for the Protection of Rural Scotland, Glasgow Earth First and Scottish Heritage with the Scottish Green Party was able to create a platform about environmental protection that centred on social inequality. It could be argued that devolution provided the impetus for a Scottish distinctiveness with greater regard for 'the social' in issues of environmental protection and regulation (discussed further below). While bound to implement EU environmental law, Scotland maintains, to some extent, a preparedness to uphold notions of environmental justice that recognise the structural inequalities of the nation's most economically disenfranchised. Before expanding on this point further, it is necessary to wrestle with and chart the terrain within which 'environmental crime' is constructed.

Mapping the landscape: defining environmental crime

Environmental crime is a contested and constructed term. Indeed both of the terms 'environment' and 'crime' are subject to widespread debate with specific social, political and historical meanings (Muncie *et al.* 2009). For example, international law has not specifically defined what the environment is or what it is not. Instead, different UN-affiliated bodies and meetings have provided various meanings which together form customs and principles which are recognised by law. The United Nations and international conferences under the auspices of the UN and the International Court of Justice have quite deliberately avoided defining what the environment is. While terms such as 'environmental protection', 'environmental damage' and 'environmental impacts' are frequently reflected in international rhetoric and within treaties and protocols, definitions of the environment are conspicuously absent in international law. The preferred position of the international community in matters of definition is to adopt the common-sense approach in asserting that the environment is 'a term that everyone understands and no one is able to define' (Caldwell, quoted in Birnie and Boyle 2002: 4). In UK law, the environment is defined as 'all, or any, of the following media, namely the air, water and land' (Environment Protection Act 1990, s. 1).

This broad and sweeping definition of the environment is also reflected in the amorphous nature of international definitions of environmental crime. Interpol (2007) divides 'environmental crime' into 'pollution' and 'wildlife crime', comprising, respectively, the illegal disposal of waste that contaminates air, water and land, and the unlawful trade in endangered species. These two broad categories are further expanded upon by the United Nations Interregional Crime and Justice Institute (UNICRI), which focuses on 'crimes against the environment' prohibited by international law. UNICRI categorises crimes against the environment as:

- illegal trade in wildlife in contravention to the 1973 Washington Convention on International Trade in Endangered Species of Fauna and Flora (CITES);
- illegal trade in ozone-depleting substances (ODS) in contravention to the 1987 Montreal Protocol on Substances that Deplete the Ozone Layer;
- dumping and illegal transport of various kinds of hazardous waste in contravention to the 1989 Basel Convention on the Control of Transboundary Movement of Hazardous Wastes and Other Wastes and their Disposal;
- illegal, unregulated and unreported (IUU) fishing in contravention of controls imposed by various regional fisheries management organisations;
- illegal logging and trade in timber when timber is harvested, transported, bought or sold in violation of national laws.

Other environmental offences may share similar characteristics with these five accepted categories. These include:

- biopiracy and transport of controlled biological or genetically modified material;
- illegal dumping of oil and other wastes in oceans (i.e. offences under the 1973 International Convention on the Prevention of Pollution from Ships (MARPOL) and the 1972 London Convention on Dumping);
- violations of potential trade restrictions under the 1998 Rotterdam Convention on the Prior Informed Consent Procedure for Certain Hazardous Chemicals and Pesticides in International Trade;
- trade in chemicals in contravention to the 2001 Stockholm Convention on Persistent Organic Pollutants;

- fuel smuggling to avoid taxes or future controls on carbon emissions.

(Hayman and Brack 2002: 5)

Within the UK, definitions of environmental crime tend to focus on acts of antisocial behaviour. The Home Office defines 'environmental crime' as:

- fly-tipping – dumping household or commercial rubbish in private or communal areas;
- littering – deliberately dropping litter on the streets;
- graffiti – spray-painting or otherwise marking private property or communal areas like the sides of bus shelters and houses
- vandalism – damaging private property or communal facilities like telephone boxes or playground equipment.

(Home Office 2007)[1]

The House of Commons Environmental Audit has also published findings on what it refers to as 'Corporate Environmental Crime' and defined as 'any environmental crime that has been committed by a corporate body' (House of Commons 2005: 8). Interestingly, the transnational issues mentioned above are not included while issues to do with water, sewerage and landfill are. Many countries see environmental crimes as acts of civilian disorder and not acts of serious environmental degradation caused by states and international corporations.

In Scotland, an environmental crime protocol was established in 2006 between the Crown Office and Procurator Fiscal Service (COPFS) and the Scottish Environmental Protection Agency (SEPA) to create greater effectiveness in the liaison and prosecution of environmental offences (COPFS 2006). While using the terminology 'environmental crime' it fails to provide a definition. Neither agency defines what the term means, although the Corporate Strategy of SEPA does refer to 'unlicensed operators' and those causing 'unacceptable damage' (SEPA 2008). SEPA also refers to environmental crime as 'knowingly causing pollution or illegally dumping waste' (SEPA 2007). Moreover, SEPA policies and practices seek to protect land, soil and water against commercial activities in ways not defined by the Home Office. That said, it must be remembered that all environmental legislation in Scotland is bound to follow the guiding principles of EU environmental law which overwhelmingly emphasises participation and cooperation in preference to regulation and enforcement (Walters 2009b).

If definitions of environmental crime are broadened beyond state terms and include the language and policy of green activists, environmentalists and academics, we see a shifting of the lens to incorporate acts of 'harm' not always embedded in law. I argue that the term 'eco-crime' is better able to capture the essence of environmental damage and conservation beyond the government-dominated notion of 'environmental crime'. In doing so, the social and the cultural are integrated into debates about environmental harm, regulation and enforcement.

When eco-crime is contextualised within notions of harm we can observe a broadening of the gaze beyond legal terrains to include discourses on risk, rights and regulation. As a result, eco-crime extends existing definitions of environmental crime to include licensed or lawful acts of ecological degradation committed by states and corporations. For Westra (2004: 309) eco-crime is unprovoked aggression, 'committed in the pursuit of other goals and "necessities" such as economic advantage'. Westra's work broadens the definition of eco-crime to include issues of human health, global security and justice. She suggests that harmful environmental actions committed in pursuit of free trade or progress are 'attacks on the human person' that deprive civilians (particularly those who are poor and marginalised) from the social, cultural and economic benefits of their environment. As a result, such actions are 'violent' and should be viewed as akin to human rights violations. Such a view is important because it contextualises environmental harms within broader notions of social justice and exclusion (we shall return to this later).

UK environmental law and enforcement

The UK has a long history of environmental law that pre-dates the UN and the EU. For example, the earliest known form of air pollution regulation in the UK dates back to Royal Proclamations of the late thirteenth century 'that recognised the problems caused by burning sea coal' (Thornton and Beckwith 2004: 292). And there is a raft of UK legislation that attempts to safeguard the British environment from acts of degradation and harm. Examples range from the Forestry Act 1967, which creates offences for the illegal felling of trees, to the Environment Protection Act 1990, which includes a whole host of offences including air pollution, contaminating water and land, illegally disposing of waste, misuse of pesticides, and control regulating the trade in endangered species. So, while the specification of some environmental offences in the UK is the result of the UK implementing international and EU law, such offences have more nationally specific sources as well. The law aims to protect the environment and creates offences on two bases:

- strict liability (this means that a person or corporation is responsible for the damage regardless of whether or not they intended to cause the damage or create the loss);
- acts of negligence that are deemed by the court to have 'caused' environmental damage and are sufficient to confirm guilt (i.e. conduct that is below legal standards required of a reasonable person in protecting individuals and the environment against foreseeable risk of harm) (see Walters 2009b).

There are ten key agencies tasked with enforcing a range of environmental offences in the UK:

- Department for Environment, Food and Rural Affairs (Defra)
- Environment Agency (England and Wales)
- Scottish Environmental Protection Agency (SEPA)
- Northern Ireland Environmental Protection Agency (NIEPA)
- Health and Safety Executive
- Forestry Commission
- Drinking Water Inspectorate
- HM Revenue and Customs
- police
- local authorities.

Such a multiplicity of agencies creates problems of coordination. Moreover, legislation passed at the EU and UK-wide level creates standards and processes that may be inconsistent with Scottish expectations. Take, for example, the laws relating to air pollution. It is estimated that 24,000 British residents die prematurely every year because of air pollution and many thousands are hospitalised (COMEAP 2009). Put another way, life expectancy in the UK is reduced by eight months as a direct result of air pollution at an annual cost of £20 billion (Defra 2009). But who are those losing months and years off their lives a result of air pollution? Is it the affluent, the professional and middle classes, or those living in deprived and impoverished areas of Britain? A specific answer to these questions is not available: there does not exist the necessary data to comment with profile accuracy. That in itself is quite telling. Can you imagine a circumstance where 24,000 people a year in Britain died as a result of an emerging youth-related street crime? Such an annual tragedy would be met with media, political and public outrage. However, the deaths associated with commercial and 'lifestyle' pollution are rendered almost invisible in a world that prioritises trade over human health. What we do know about those who lose their lives due to air pollution? The most comprehensive research undertaken on poverty and environmental quality was conducted by Fairburn *et al.* (2005). As the opening quote to this chapter identifies, social deprivation in Scotland is linked to environmental pollution and injustice. In relation to air quality, they conclude:

> People living in the most deprived areas are more likely to experience the poorest air quality than those living in less deprived areas. This was found to be true for four (nitrogen dioxide, PM10, benzene and carbon monoxide) out of the five pollutants examined (the exception being sulphur dioxide). Exceedences of the nitrogen dioxide objective (annual mean) are strongly concentrated in the most deprived areas. (Fairburn *et al.* 2005)

The UK provides an extensive system of air pollution monitoring through its Air Quality Archive. Yet the processes of enforcing the regulations are negotiated by the authorities and the polluters. A 'partnership model' exists that is very much industry-led and relies upon compliance and corporate good practice. When corporations exceed legal air pollution emission the language of 'crime', 'offences', 'violation' or 'breach' is not used. Instead, we witness the use of the term 'exceedence' to describe unlawful levels of air pollutions. Repeated exceedence often results in warning letters and when operators face prosecution, the fines available to the courts are very low. The partnership model of air pollution control in the UK is designed to enhance and facilitate trade while protecting the environment (Walters 2009c).

Data obtained under the Freedom of Information Act revealed that during 2004–May 2009 there were 9,990 air pollution incidents brought to the attention of and investigated by the Scottish Environment Protection Agency. While the SEPA database does not provide details on outcomes for all cases (such a task requires manually searching all files) it does indicate the number of prosecutions. During the five years, three prosecutions were successfully made. A total of £15,900 in fines was ordered by the courts for 'failing to contain offensive odours' (Everitt 2009). Such a low prosecution rate contradicts recent EU law air pollution breaches across Scotland that has seen a 'fifty per cent increase since the end of 2007' (ETA 2009).

The partnership model of air pollution control in the UK is designed to enhance and facilitate trade while protecting the environment. It is argued that this model fails to capture the deleterious and dangerous effects that air pollution has on human and non-human health and as such we should begin to move beyond the rhetoric of exceedence to 'eco-crime'. As Tombs and Whyte state: 'It can be assumed with confidence that the most deadly environmental pollution is caused directly by corporations' (2009: 143). Yet, at present, corporations are seen as partners who exceed air pollution levels, rather than as eco-criminals.

Environmental crime in Scotland

As mentioned in the introduction, in 2004 the Scottish Government created special prosecutors to deal with environmental crime. The pollution of waterways, the damage to the environment and the endangerment of human health were the broad remits upon which the initiative between COPFS and SEPA was launched. In taking this position, Scotland was the first country in Europe to establish a special prosecution service devoted to environmental crime. Other countries such as Australia created a Land and Environmental Court back in 1979 (see UNEP 2009), but most countries deal with environmental 'matters' within civil jurisdictions (Bodansky *et al.* 2007; Walters 2009a). One mechanism for upholding environmental justice has been mooted via a proposed International Environment Court. In 2002, at the World Summit on Sustainable Development, 130 senior judges from around the world identified that there were sufficient domestic and international laws to protect the environment but also a growing number of 'miscreant corporations and backsliding governments' that were unwilling to self-regulate or enforce laws. The judges called for a unified international court of the environment to strengthen the existing legal framework of environmental governance and in doing so to protect the world's poor who are 'often the hardest-hit victims of environmental crimes' (quoted in James 2002). As yet, such an international court has not materialised.

Scotland does not have an environmental court nor does it have a dedicated statistical database for environmental crime. It is not possible to readily extract information about annual incidences or 'reports', nor is it possible to access a database on prosecutions. Moreover, what is and what is not environmental crime provides further statistical and analytical anomalies. In addition to environmental crime, we see the term 'wildlife crime' used in Scotland.

Unlike SEPA that deals with pollution and contamination of water, air, land, sea and soil, wildlife crime involves cruelty to animals, trade in endangered species, destruction of habitats and harm to protected species (PAW 2009). A strategy dealing with wildlife crime was established in 2003 that created a partnership between regulatory bodies such as the police, local authorities, the Scottish Executive and societies responsible for the protection of flora and fauna (Central Scotland Police 2003). Conservation charities across the UK have recently called for a review of all strategies that attempt to address wildlife crime, arguing that government initiatives are failing. From a total of 3,500 reported cases of wildlife crime across the UK in 2008, only 51 resulted in conviction (BBC News 2009). The illegal trapping and poisoning of animals in Scotland (notably birds of prey) constitutes a significant area of concern. In 2008, 179 suspected cases of poisoning were investigated by the Wildlife Incident Investigation Scheme (Taylor *et al.* 2009), yet prosecutions remain rare. The Scottish Government is currently seeking public consultation on its Wildlife and Natural Environment Bill that seeks to implement a more rigorous regulatory regime for the protection of native flora and fauna (Scotland National Rural Network 2009). This Bill follows an inquiry into the investigation and prosecution of wildlife crime in Scotland, including a review of the Environmental Crime Protocol mentioned above. The investigation concluded, *inter alia*, that:

> Overall COPFS had introduced a sound system for managing wildlife crime particularly by establishing a network of specialist wildlife prosecutors who should prosecute these cases. We found, however, that this structure was not fully implemented nationally and was not always fully understood resulting in cases at times being prosecuted by non-specialist prosecutors. (HMICS 2008)

As mentioned above, SEPA is the regulatory body in Scotland dealing with acts that pollute or contaminate water, sea, land, soil and air. The major polluters of such natural resources are commercial industries. A recent audit of 405 of Scotland's 'largest and most complex' industries revealed that almost 10 per cent failed annual SEPA pollution inspections; the worst performing sector was waste management (Walsh 2009). While SEPA adopts a firm position on enforcement of environmental legislation it also acknowledges its role in 'helping' industry meet pollution standards. In 2006–7, 54 cases of knowingly causing pollution or illegal waste dumping were referred by SEPA for prosecution. In addition, SEPA issued 141 enforcement notices 'requiring improvements in operator performance' (SEPA 2007: 3). The annual reports of the Crown Office and Procurator Fiscal Service does not provide information about the results of environmental crimes referred to SEPA for prosecution (COPFS 2008). One way of gauging the extent of successful environmental prosecution is through media reports. In 2008, SEPA provides a breakdown of all its media coverage for the year. While crime is a notoriously highly reported social phenomenon, environmental crime/offending represented only 12 per cent of all print and electronic media coverage involving SEPA. The content of the 12 per cent consisted of three prosecutions involving a waste carrier, a sewerage plant and a farm (SEPA 2008b). This further serves to underline the small number of successful prosecutions involving corporate and industrial environmental crime. One case in 2008, for example, Ondeo Industrial Solutions, that operates an effluent treatment plant in Grangemouth, released oil into the Forth River causing widespread contamination. The corporation was found guilty and fined £3,000 (SEPA 2008a). These low numbers of prosecutions and minimal fines are a concern for SEPA and, along with proposed legislation mentioned above, a conference with COPFS has been proposed to prioritise the issue (SEPA 2009).

Greening the criminological landscape

Some scholars argue that there should be a shift from a focus on acts defined solely by environmental law as 'crimes' to all acts (both legal and non-legal, international and domestic) that harm human and non-human species (Bierne and South 2007). Green criminology analyses the processes of criminalisation, that is how and why certain things come to be called criminal and others not. In doing so, it argues that understanding the social dimensions of environmental damage are essential for exploring the ways that certain harms should be criminalised. In this respect, green criminology seeks to respond to official and scientific evidence about environmental damage and species decline as well as emerging social movements with environmental concerns. Hauck (2007) suggests that as a study of crime, green criminology incorporates other social and cultural meanings of 'harm' as defined by ordinary citizens. In this respect, the advocates of green criminology argue that it challenges neoliberal government and corporate rationalities (Walters 2009b).

In this sense, green criminology has its theoretical roots embedded within the traditions of radical criminological schools of thought such as feminism, Marxism and social constructionism. (These radical criminologies emerged in the late 1960s and early 1970s in the UK and the US arguing, among other things, that crime is to be found in relations of power, oppression and selective processes of criminalisation – see Muncie 2006.)

White (2008) argues that there is no one green criminological theory but rather a series of 'perspectives' or narratives that draw on various philosophical, sociological, legal and scientific traditions. He argues that the three 'theoretical tendencies' that inform green criminology are 'environmental justice', 'ecological justice' and 'species justice' (p. 15). Environmental justice is a human-centred or anthropocentric discourse with two distinct dimensions. First, it assesses the equity of access and use of environmental resources across social and cultural divides. Who has access to the benefits and profits of natural resources and why? What factors prevent all people from equally sharing in the environment? Actions that prevent, jeopardise or compromise this right are actions that violate environmental justice. Second, it explores how people (notably poor and powerless people) are affected by natural disasters, corporate activity and state actions that damage the environment. Ecological justice focuses on the relationship or interaction between humans and the natural environment. When humans develop the environment for material needs (housing, agriculture, business, consumption) this approach insists that such actions be assessed within the context of damage or harm to other living things. This position is often referred to an 'eco-centric' understanding of human and nature interaction. Some may criticise this position because it lacks acknowledgment that the reality of harm, existence, development, progress and so on will always be defined and responded to by humans. Yet ecological justice argues that an environmentally centred perspective which upholds the importance of living creatures as well as inanimate and non-living objects (such as soil, rock, water, air) provide useful insights for guiding future economic and developmental decisions (cf.

Walters 2009a). Finally, species justice is a non-human or biocentric discourse that emphasises the importance of non-human rights. It asserts that human beings are not the only creatures with rights, nor are humans superior beings. In other words, there is no hierarchy of existence with human beings at the pinnacle. All 'living things in existence' share an equal status of importance. Beirne and South (2007) argue that to prohibit or disregard non-human creatures as not of equal standing within the natural environment denies the value and worth of those species. As White (2008: 17) identifies, an analysis from this perspective aids a critique of how rights are constructed. It allows us to question the bases from which rights are created and protected. If rights are about ensuring health and well-being while minimising pain and suffering, then humans are not the only species to experience such emotions.

From the above perspective of green criminology we see the emergence of discourses that also focus on the harmful acts of states and corporations. Throughout this chapter the definition and statistics of government have been used to describe environmental crime in Scotland. As mentioned earlier, if we broaden the lens to include acts of 'eco-crime' we observe how the harmful acts of the state come into focus. Consider the following, for example:

- The Neptune Warrior Military Exercises at Cape Wrath on the northern coast of Scotland have been ongoing for many years. Various Royal Air Force and Navy operations, along with UK defence allies from the US, take part in routine bombing and weapons testing on the North West coast of Scotland. The bombing takes place within the vicinity of the North West Highlands Geopark, one of only 32 UNESCO designated geoparks for its geological diversity (Scottish Parliament 2006).
- The Fish Trade Equal Opportunities Group estimates that £80 million of fish in Scotland are illegally caught or 'black fish'. It is estimated that 5,000 fishing industry jobs had been lost in the last decade, and the North Sea 'had been left virtually empty of stocks as a result of poor implementation of quotas'. Fishing industries have been reportedly breaking the law to keep their businesses viable. The Scottish Government and the Scottish Fisheries Protection Agency have been accused of not doing enough to curb the illegal trade (BBC 2005).
- The Faslane Nuclear Naval Base at Gareloch, only 25 miles to the west of Glasgow, costs the UK taxpayer £1 billion per year for a

facility that is widely viewed as unnecessary. Its health and safety breaches have routinely resulted in oil spills in local waterways. Moreover, the base has recorded 'a catalogue' of radioactive waste mismanagement (Edwards 2009).

- The proposed £1 billion Donald Trump golf resort in Aberdeenshire has witnessed Holyrood overruling local council decisions to support the development. While the project is deemed to create employment and attract tourism, it is also considered by some to be an environmental disaster that will decimate a unique aspect of the Scottish landscape (McLaughlin 2007).
- Dounreay nuclear power facilities have operated on the north coast of Caithness under the auspices of the UK Atomic Energy Authority and the Ministry of Defence since 1955. The Committee on Medical Aspects of Radiation in the Environment (COMARE) has reported that thousands of radioactive particles have been recklessly released into the environment with the UK Government attempting to cover up its negligence (COMARE 2005; cf Farquharson and Macaskill 2005).
- The UK Government has been accused of dumping toxic household, hazardous medical and electrical waste in Brazil and Ghana. The UK Government has ordered an inquiry into British firms 'linked to shipping 90 containers containing 1,400 tonnes of waste' (Horne 2009).

The above provides examples of how governments sanction acts or fail to take adequate steps against events that are deleterious to the environment. Irrespective of whether in the name of defence, industry, trade, energy or employment, the UK and Scottish Governments have been complicit in acts that threaten or destroy both on- and offshore environments.

Social movements and environmental justice

Given the competing priorities of trade and environmentalism, government regulation through various legal instruments is often unable, unwilling and ineffective in preventing acts that harm the environment and place humans and non-humans at risk of ill health. In 2005 the Scottish Green Party accused the former Labour-Liberal Democrat Scottish Government of prioritising industry and development at the expense of the environment and Scotland's poorest communities:

> The Executive and the First Minister in particular talk about environmental justice but then they give the go ahead for major road building schemes, landfill sites and incinerators which blight our poorest communities. Their environmental commitments were always pretty threadbare, and we can see just how disappointing the delivery has been. (Scottish Green Party 2005)

Devolution in Scotland has provided the opportunity for political parties such as the Greens to represent the voices of environmentalism. However, as mentioned earlier, social movements have emerged and provide a powerful influence on the development and operation of regulatory regimes. Michael Jacobs' historic text *The Green Economy* (1991) identified how citizen participation and social movements were central to notions of environmental justice. He critiques the ways in which polluting corporations were often co-regulators with governments in futile endeavours to prevent environmental destruction and protect the rights of poor communities. His notion of 'consumer sovereignty' promoted the value and impact of 'people power'. He argued that ordinary citizens are not mere passive beings under government management but activists capable of mobilising power through protest, peaceful conflict and consumer supremacy. As a result the power of networks of collective concern could both identify eco-harms not within the radar of government regulators and provide necessary input to policies of corporations and ministers. An example of this can be found with the eco-movements concerning the M77 road extension near Glasgow that was constructed in the 1990s. Local residents formed inner urban camps of resistance, notably the Pollok Free State Protest Camp, petitioned MPs, demonstrated with regular marches, held public rallies with speakers from across the world, and erected upturned cars (such as the well known 'carhenge') as a form of sculpture protest (James *et al.* 2004). While parts of the planned extension did go ahead, certain areas of woodland were preserved. Moreover, the action proved to be the cornerstone for promoting the power of collective citizen participation. In doing so, it placed on the political agenda and within the public consciousness debates about pollution, oil, greener living, the contradictions of government and the ways in which ordinary people and their environments are adversely affected by road development. It also provided the impetus and became the forerunner for other eco-movements in Scotland to influence government environmental policy in the early years of devolution.

Concluding comments

For many, the destruction of natural habitats and the pollution of air, water and land is a global catastrophe; for others (including some government and commercial enterprises) it is a necessary by-product of commercial profit and capital accumulation. The challenge for environmental protection and regulation is that it often competes with or is superseded by the imperatives of free trade – whereby economic prosperity and quality of human life is viewed as a paramount political and social objective.

There are environmental costs in ensuring that people have the resources and technologies to enhance their lives. Can human beings maintain high standards of living without compromising the integrity of the environment? Are the two ever compatible? Sometimes state actions purportedly designed to bring about peace and security also result in environmental damage. There are adverse environmental consequences to trade and progress and to war and peace-keeping, as well as to – dare we say deliberate – illegal acts of environmental crime.

While legal interventions seek to protect the environment, the imperatives of market economies and free trade perpetuated by powerful institutions and governments provide the impetus for the continuance of eco-crime. Moreover, crimes such as deforestation or air pollution may have environmental and social impacts that extend far beyond the offending country. These are jurisdictional matters that provide serious challenges for legal recourse. The apparent lack of existing political will to address such actions also remains a cause for serious concern.

It must be said that Scotland in many instances leads the way in providing a regulatory framework for taking environmental crime seriously. While in its early stages of development, Scottish authorities demonstrate a commitment to see damaging and destructive acts against the environment treated as 'crime' and not as mere administrative misdemeanor. That said, the Scottish regulatory regimes are influenced by EU and UK law that continues to promote trade over and above environmental protection. The implementation of environmental law and policy UK-wide remains wedded to a partnership model with the industries that pollute. As such green issues and eco-crime will continue to require ongoing criminological imagination and scholarship. This chapter has argued that eco-crime necessitates a general rethinking of the parameters and horizons of the criminological landscape. Such a rethinking requires a reflection on how humans relate to the environment and what constitutes acceptable and unacceptable exploitations of flora, fauna and natural resources. It also requires a shifting of existing rhetoric to facilitate an examination of the ways in which governments exploit the environment for military and economic reasons.

Note

1 The Scottish Executive neither accepts nor rejects the Home Office definition of environmental crime.

References

BBC (2005) 'Group's "black fish" legal threat', 24 April. http://news.bbc.co.uk/1/hi/scotland/4479363.stm (accessed 25 October 2009).

BBC News (2009) 'Wildlife crime effort criticised', 18 August. http://news.bbc.co.uk/1/hi/sci/tech/8206477.stm (accessed 22 August 2009).

Beirne, P. and South, N. (eds) (2007) *Issues in Green Criminology: Confronting Harms Against Environments, Humanity and Other Animals*. Cullompton: Willan Publishing.

Birnie, P. and Boyle, A. (2002) *International Law and the Environment*, 2nd edn. Oxford: Oxford University Press.

Bodansky, D., Brunnee, J. and Hey, E. (eds) (2007) *The Oxford Handbook of International Environmental Law*. Oxford: Oxford University Press.

Brown, W., Aradau, C. and Budds, J. (2009) *Earth in Crisis – Environmental Issues and Responses*. Milton Keynes: Open University.

Central Scotland Police (2003) *A Strategy for Dealing with Wildlife Crime in Scotland*. Stirling: Central Scotland Police. http://www.centralscotland.police.uk/homepages/wildlife_crime/docs/wildlife_strategy.pdf (accessed 26 August 2009).

COMARE (2005) *COMARE 6th Report: Radioactive Particles at Dounreay*. http://www.comare.org.uk/press_releases/comare_pr03.htm (accessed 15 August 2009).

COMEAP (2009) *Long-Term Exposure to Air Pollution*. http://www.advisorybodies.doh.gov.uk/comeap/pdfs/finallongtermeffectsmort2009report.pdf (accessed 30 June 2009).

Crown Prosecution and Procurator Fiscal Service (2006) *Protocol. Crown Prosecution and Procurator Fiscal Service and the Scottish Environment Protection Agency for Submission, Processing and Monitoring of Prosecution Reports.* http://www.copfs.gov.uk/Resource/Doc/13547/0000176.pdf (accessed 15 August 2009).

Crown Prosecution and Procurator Fiscal Service (2008) *Crown Prosecution and Procurator Fiscal Service. Annual Report and Accounts for the year ended 31 March 2008.* http://www.copfs.gov.uk/Resource/Doc/13576/0000485.pdf (accessed 21 August 2009).

Defra (2009) *Pollution Prevention and Control.* http://www.defra.gov.uk/environment/ppc/index.htm (accessed 21 July 2009).

Edwards, R. (2009) 'Faslane oil spill shows poor safety standards'. http://banthebomb.org/ne/index.php?option=com_content&task=view&id=1179&Itemid=95 (accessed 25 August 2009).

Environmental Transport Association (2009) 'Air pollution in Scotland breaks EU law', 9 February. http://www.eta.co.uk/Air-pollution-in-Scotland-breaks-EU-law/node/11742 (accessed 26 August 2009).

Everitt, C. (2009) FOI Request, FO136281, 23 June.

Fairburn, J., Walker, G., Smith, G. and Mitchell, F. (2005) *Investigating Environmental Justice in Scotland. Links between Measures on Environmental and Social Deprivation*. Scottish and Northern Ireland Forum for Environmental Research. http://www.sniffer.org.uk/Webcontrol/Secure/ClientSpecific/ResourceManagement/UploadedFiles/UE4(03)01.pdf (accessed 22 October 2009).

Farquharson, K. and Macaskill, M. (2005) 'Reckless nuclear waste on beaches', *The Times*, 6 March.

HM Inspectorate of Constabulary for Scotland (2008) *Natural Justice: A Joint Thematic Inspection of the Arrangements in Scotland for Preventing, Investigating, and Prosecuting Wildlife Crime.* http://www.scotland.gov.uk/Resource/Doc/218661/0058716.pdf (accessed 25 August 2009.

Home Office (2007) *Environmental Crime.* http://www.homeoffice.gov.uk/anti-social-behaviour/types-of-asb/environmental-crime/.

Horne, M. (2009) 'UK accused of dumping toxic waste overseas', *The Scotsman*, 19 July. http://news.scotsman.com/environment/UK-accused-of-dumping toxic.5473106.jp (accessed 22 August 2009).

Hauck, M. (2007) 'Non-compliance in small-scale fisheries: a threat to security?', in P. Beirne and N. South (eds), *Issues in Green Criminology: Confronting Harms Against Environments, Humanity and Other Animals.* Cullompton: Willan Publishing.

Hayman, G. and Brack, D. (2002) *International Environmental: The Nature and Control of Environmental Black Markets*. London: Royal Institute of International Affairs.

Interpol (2007) *Environmental Crime.* http://www.interpol.int/Public/EnvironmentalCrime/Default.asp (accessed 16 January 2008).

IPPC (2007) *Climate Change: Synthesis Report*. Intergovernmental Panel on

Climate Change. http://www.ipcc.ch/pdf/assessment-report/ar4/syr/ar4_syr.pdf (accessed 28 July 2009).

Jacobs, M. (1991) *The Green Economy: Environment, Sustainable Development and the Politics of the Future*. Concord, MA: Pluto Press.

James, P. (2002) 'International judges: environmental laws not enforced', *International Herald Tribune*, 28 August.

Jones, M., Jones, R. and Woods, M. (2004) *An Introduction to Political Geography: Space, Place and Politics*. London: Routledge.

Kelbie, P. (2004) 'Scotland launches hit squad to prosecute polluters', *The Independent*, 10 February. http://www.independent.co.uk/environment/scotland-launches-hit-squad-to-prosecute-polluters-569477.html (accessed 28 July 2009).

McLaughlin, M. (2007) '£1bn golfing resort is still "alive" after ministers call in Trump plan', *The Scotsman*, 5 December.

Muncie, J. (2006) 'Radical criminologies', in E. McLaughlin and J. Muncie (eds), *The Sage Dictionary of Criminology*, 2nd edn. London: Sage.

Muncie, J., Talbot, D. and Walters, R. (2009) *Crime: Local and Global*. Cullompton: Willan Publishing.

Partnership for Action Against Wildlife Crime (PAW) (2009) *What is Wildlife Crime?* http://www.defra.gov.uk/paw/crime/default.htm (accessed 22 August 2009).

Scandrett, E. (2007) 'Environmental justice in Scotland: policy, pedagogy and praxis', *Environmental Research Letters*, 2 (4). http://iopscience.iop.org/1748-9326/2/4/045002/fulltext.

Scotland National Rural Network (2009) *Wildlife Crime*. http://www.ruralgateway.org.uk/en/taxonomy/term/167 (accessed 26 August 2009).

Scottish Environment Protection Agency (2007) *SEPA Annual Report 2007*. Stirling: SEPA.

Scottish Environment Protection Agency (2008a) *SEPA's Provisional Corporate Strategy: Our Proposals for 2008–2011*. Stirling: SEPA.

Scottish Environment Protection Agency (2008b) Agency Board Meeting, 5 August. 39/09 http://search.sepa.org.uk/sepa?action=search&q=environmental%20crime (accessed 26 August 2009).

Scottish Environment Protection Agency (2009) Minutes of the Twentieth Meeting of the South West Region Board, 22 April 2009.

Scottish Government (2003) 'Environmental Crime Seminar'. http://www.scotland.gov.uk/News/Releases/2003/05/3523 (accessed 1 August 2009).

Scottish Government (2008) *The Scottish Environmental and Attitudes Behaviour Survey 2008*. http://www.scotland.gov.uk/Publications/2009/03/05145056/3 (accessed 21 August 2009).

Scottish Government (2009) *Environment*. http://www.scotland.gov.uk/Topics/Environment (accessed 2 August 2009).

Scottish Government (2010) *Greener Scotland*. http://www.scotland.gov.uk/About/Directorates/Greener.

Scottish Green Party (2005) 'LibDems & Labour environmental justice credentials laid to waste'. http://www.scottishgreens.org.uk/site/id/4619/title/LibDems_amp_Labour_Environmental_Justice_Credentials_Laid_To_Waste.html (accessed 24 October 2009).

Scottish Parliament (2006) Business Bulletin No. 35/2006, Thursday, 2 March. http://www.scottish.parliament.uk/business/businessBulletin/bb-06/bb-03-02f.htm (accessed 26 August 2009).

Taylor, M., Sharp, E. and Geila, A. (2009) *Pesticide Poisoning of Animals in 2008. A Report of Investigations in Scotland.* http://www.ruralgateway.org.uk/sites/default/files/Pesticide%20poisonings%20of%20animals%202008.pdf (accessed 26 August 2009).

Thornton, J. and Beckwith, S. (2004) *Environmental Law*, 2nd edn. London: Sweet & Maxwell.

Tombs, S. and Whyte, D. (2009) 'Crime, harm and corporate power', in J. Muncie, D. Talbot and R. Walters (eds), *Crime: Local and Global.* Cullompton: Willan Publishing, pp. 137–72.

United Nations Environment Programme (2009a) 'General Speech for World Environment Day 2009 Globally Hosted by Mexico, by Achim Steiner, UN Under-Secretary General and UN Environment Programme Executive Director'. http://www.unep.org/Documents.Multilingual/Default.asp?DocumentID=591&ArticleID=6205&l=en&t=long (accessed 20 August 2009).

United Nations Environment Programme (2009b) 'Australia's Specialised Environment Court'. http://www.unep.org/dec/onlinemanual/Enforcement/InstitutionalFrameworks/EstablishEffectiveCourts/Resource/tabid/1059/Default.aspx (accessed 15 August 2009).

Walsh, L. (2009) 'Scottish industries fall short of environmental targets', Environmental Data Interactive Exchange. http://www.edie.net/news/news_story.asp?id=16603 (accessed 25 August 2009).

Walters, R. (2009a) 'Eco-crime', in J. Muncie, D. Talbot and R. Walters (eds), *Crime: Local and Global.* Cullompton: Willan Publishing.

Walters, R. (2009b) 'Environmental law and environmental crime', in W. Brown, C. Aradau and J. Budds (eds), *Earth in Crisis. Environmental Issues and Responses.* Milton Keynes: Open University, pp. 321–62.

Walters, R. (2009c) *Crime is in the Air: Air Pollution Regulation and Enforcement in the UK.* London: Centre for Crime and Justice Studies, Kings College.

Westra, L. (2004) *Ecoviolence and the Law (Supranational Normative Foundations of Ecocrime).* Ardsley, NY: Transactional Publishers.

White, R. (2008) *Crimes Against Nature. Environmental Criminology and Ecological Justice.* Cullompton: Willan Publishing.

Part 3

Aspects of criminal justice process and practice

Chapter 9

Policing, surveillance and security in contemporary Scotland

Nicholas R. Fyfe

Introduction: revisiting *The Policeman in the Community*

Even a cursory glance at the many different histories of Anglo-American policing research shows that one book stands out as being of seminal importance to the development of the sociological analysis of police work: Michael Banton's 1964 monograph *The Policeman in the Community*. Leading police researchers still regard it with considerable reverence and respect. For Robert Reiner (1995) it is a 'path-breaking study ... responsible for many ideas and approaches which have been repeatedly returned to'; for Simon Holdaway (1983) it is a 'foundation stone' in the development of the sociology of the police'; and for Eugene McLaughlin (2007) it is a 'classic', pioneering sociological understanding of the life worlds of the police officer. What is perhaps less often acknowledged is that Michael Banton was, at the time the research was conducted, a social anthropologist at the University of Edinburgh and he largely based *The Policeman in the Community* on research carried out with officers from Edinburgh City Police and the Scottish Police College. Indeed, despite the book's many references to *British* policing and the comparative perspective offered by Banton's time spent in several US cities, one of the key achievements of the book was (as the Preface makes clear) being able 'to see Scottish police work in a new light' (Banton 1964: xi).

Drawing attention to Banton's account is not simply a reminder that policing research in Scotland has deep roots. Rather, many of the themes of *The Policeman in the Community* have considerable resonance with, and relevance for, issues central to the policing of contemporary Scotland. Three interrelated themes in particular will be examined in this chapter: the pluralisation of policing, the policing of crime and disorder, and police governance. Each of these themes is touched on in Banton's original analysis of the policing challenges associated with 'modern' Scotland but each is still of central importance to the policing of 'late' or 'post' modern Scotland and each raises wider questions about inequality and social justice with which this volume is concerned. With respect to pluralisation, Banton argued that the police are just one element in the maintenance of order and the regulation of deviance. Indeed, he notes that the police 'appear puny compared with the extensiveness and intricacy of other modes of regulating informal behaviour' (1964: 2). At the time such a suggestion might have seemed quite radical, even provocative, but today it is commonplace to write of the 'proliferation of "policing beyond the police"' such that 'a pluralized, fragmented and differentiated patchwork has replaced the idea of the police as the monopolistic guardians of public order' (Crawford 2003: 136). But Banton went further, and in a passage which anticipates many contemporary political and conceptual concerns with active citizenship and 'responsibilisation' (Garland 1996), he argues the need for greater public involvement in the maintenance of order:

> The police have a special responsibility for the maintenance of public order but this mode of administration has, I submit, fostered among some policemen and some lay men the idea that public order is the responsibility of the police alone ... The over-identification of the police with responsibility for the maintenance of public order distracts attention from the public's responsibility. It would be advisable to investigate, more carefully than anyone has yet done, what the barriers are to increased public participation in the maintenance of order. (Banton 1964: 263 and 268)

The first section of this chapter will trace some of the uneven contours and characteristics of the pluralisation of policing in Scotland, including this emphasis on increasing public involvement in tackling disorder. This then feeds into a second theme about different policing strategies in relation to crime and disorder, a field where, as Banton observes, the public police have a 'special responsibility' but also considerable discretion in the way they exercise their powers. In a passage which contains intriguing echoes of antisocial behaviour legislation and dispersal orders introduced into Scotland from the late 1990s, he notes that, 'In the rougher neighbourhoods [the police] will disperse groups from the street corners to prevent the conditions arising in which fights and disturbances most easily start. A larger group on the pavements at the end of a church service or in a middle-class neighbourhood will be left undisturbed' (Banton, 1964: 131). In drawing attention to police discretion, Banton not only raises important questions about social justice but also highlights the issue of different styles of policing, contrasting a focus on law enforcement and order maintenance with approaches which prioritise community engagement. It is precisely such differences that continue to concern chief police officers today and the second section of this chapter considers this in the context of contrasting approaches to the policing of crime and disorder in Scotland. The third theme concerns issues of police governance and accountability. Although Banton does not explore this in detail he does draw attention to ways in which central government in (pre-devolution) Scotland 'can exert a certain control over local forces' (p. 89) and local government has statutory responsibilities for maintaining an efficient and effective force. He then goes on to contrast this with police governance arrangements in the US where in some areas there is much stronger local political influence on policing but warns that 'stories about police practice in departments corrupted by political influence can easily be assembled' (p. 93). Intriguingly, however, it is just such a model of strong local accountability that is now viewed as attractive by many politicians in Westminster (but not, so far, in Edinburgh), with talk of 'US-style elected sheriffs or police commissioners and the handing over of control of policing to New York or Chicago style elected mayors' (McLaughlin 2007: 190). In Scotland there appears less enthusiasm for such an approach but still considerable debate about the balance of influence between central and local interests in relation to police governance. These issues provide the focus for the final section of this chapter.

Pluralisation: the development of 'pick'n'mix' policing?

The pluralisation of policing that Banton hints at in his observation that 'the police' are only one among many different agencies involved in the regulation of behaviour is now a defining feature of contemporary societies. Phrases like the 'extended policing family', 'the mixed economy of policing' and local 'security networks' (see Crawford 2003; Johnston 2000; Shearing and Stenning 1987) are increasingly used to capture the diversity of public, private and voluntary providers of policing services. These comprise the public police, municipal policing (such as community wardens), civilian or voluntary policing (including membership of the special constabulary and neighbourhood watch schemes) and commercial or private policing (including uniformed guarding of mass private property, like shopping malls and office spaces). Within Scotland, there were over 500 community wardens employed by local authorities by 2008 (Donnelly 2008a: 84) with a responsibility for providing high-visibility patrols to deter crime and antisocial behaviour as well tackling environmental issues like graffiti and vandalism (Hayton *et al.* 2007). In addition several Scottish cities have also appointed city representatives to act as a further uniformed presence within the urban realm to enhance community safety and deal with environmental incivilities such as graffiti and fly tipping (see Helms 2008). With respect to voluntary policing, there are over 100,000 households within neighbourhood watch schemes and over 1,000 special constables, the unpaid, part-time volunteers who on duty assume the powers of regular police officers and can therefore supplement front-line officers on routine patrols and at special events where there might be potential for public disorder. Moreover, in an initiative which is the first of its kind in the UK, rangers in the Loch Lomond and Trossachs National Park, have become special constables so that they have the same powers of arrest as police officers in the hope that this will help tackle antisocial behaviour (*The Scotsman* 2009). And in terms of private policing, a sector notoriously difficult to measure precisely because it includes such a wide array of different activities, Scotland, like other late-modern societies, has experienced a 'quiet revolution' (Shearing and Stenning 1987). The presence of private security is now a routine and unremarkable part of the Scottish urban experience with uniformed, private security guards patrolling shopping malls and hospitals, and closed-circuit television (CCTV) surveillance systems operated by private security firms observing people in shops and banks, on buses and trains, and at football matches and in bowling alleys. Taking just one element of private policing in one city, 'security services and equipment', Glasgow has witnessed the number of firms operating in this field grow from fewer than ten in the mid-1960s to well over 100 in 2008 (Fyfe 2010; Fyfe and Bannister 1999: 348).

This expansion in private policing has partly been driven by significant changes in the configuration of land use in cities with the expansion of mass private property, including shopping malls and out-of-town retail parks. These processes of privatisation have also extended to some suburban areas, notably in the form of gated residential communities which typically rely on private policing arrangements to meet demands for security. As McLaughlin notes, some people are opting to work, shop and live 'in an increasingly securitized, privately guarded fortified enclave or "security bubble"' (McLaughlin 2007: 117). More generally, however, such behaviour can be viewed as one response to the ways in which crime and the fear of crime are significant concerns of a wide range of social groups in late-modern societies. As Crawford observes, 'The public demand for security has become a dominant feature of contemporary life' (Crawford 2003: 139–40) and in Scotland the 2006 Crime and Victimisation Survey (Brown and Bolling 2007) reported that 93 per cent of respondents considered crime to be a problem in Scotland (only alcohol and drug abuse were considered more problematic). In addition, almost a third of respondents reported that they felt unsafe while walking alone after dark (although women were more than twice as likely as men to report that they felt unsafe) while in terms of perceptions of disorder, just under half of respondents (48 per cent) considered antisocial behaviour to be a common problem in their local area. The crime of which the greatest proportion of respondents worried about becoming a victim was vehicle vandalism with half of vehicle owners 'very' or 'fairly' worried, followed by worries about having their home broken into and being mugged or physically assaulted in the street or a public space.

While investment in community wardens and support for voluntary forms of policing such as neighbourhood watch schemes and the special constabulary are a response to these public concerns, they are also part of wider shift in what Garland (2001) calls the 'culture of control'. Specifically, there has been the progressive erosion of the neo-conservative 'myth of sovereign crime control' by which the state claims to be the chief provider of security, and the rise of a neoliberal 'responsibilisation' strategy which emphasises the obligations of individuals and communities, as well as private and public bodies, in reducing criminal opportunities and in delivering policing. Strong political support for neighbourhood watch in Scotland as elsewhere in the UK, for example, probably owes less to the efficacy of such schemes in reducing crime and more to the way they support a political agenda around active citizenship and active communities. As Garland observes, the importance of neighbourhood watch schemes 'as examples of the government's project of devolved crime control is demonstrated by the fact that political commitment to these schemes far outruns their level of success in preventing crime' (Garland 1996: 453).

The neoliberal logic which underpins the pluralisation of policing in late-modern societies has significant and far-reaching implications for the public police. At one level, this is evident in a growing 'managerialisation' (McLaughlin and Murji 2001) as the police (along with other public services) across the UK have had to respond to a central government agenda of introducing market disciplines into the public sector. The implications of this 'new public management' or NPM are evident within Scottish policing in terms of new forms of financial management, the development of a performance culture (exemplified most recently by the introduction of a Scottish Policing Performance Framework), the strengthening of a 'consumer voice' (via customer surveys) and the civilianisation of many tasks previously undertaken by police officers. The latter represents a form of market testing given that it involves deciding what activities can be more efficiently provided by civilians, allowing some regular officers to return to operational duties (Fyfe and Bannister 1999). This was something that Banton had advocated back in the 1960s. Reflecting on the need for strong senior management in police forces, just as in other public and private organisations, he felt that simply appointing officers who had risen through the ranks was unsatisfactory. 'The special character of police work', he observed, 'should not conceal the fact that problems of allocation of resources ... are administrative problems requiring abilities that are not developed by pounding a beat' (Banton 1964: 268). Banton's focus was on senior management positions where police forces now typically employ civilians to be in charge of finance, human resource issues and research and development. However, the speed and scale of civilian appointments over the last 20 years has been dramatic. In 1985, there were just over 2,000 civilian staff within the Scottish police service; by 2000–1 this had risen to 5,000 and by 2006–7 there were over 8,000 (Donnelly 2008; Fyfe and Bannister 1999).

A second issue for the public police raised by the pluralisation of policing is what McLaughlin (2007) terms 'residualisation'. Increasing involvement of the private and voluntary sector in policing raises profound issues about the uneven investment in safety and security across different social groups and locations. Private policing will, by definition, focus on protecting the interests of those who can pay rather than those in greatest need of protection. The distribution of voluntary policing is also imperfectly distributed with respect to need. Neighbourhood watch schemes are typically found in relatively affluent areas with relatively low levels of house breaking. Recruitment to the special constabulary has a similarly uneven geography. Northern

Constabulary, which covers only 6 per cent of Scotland's population and has the lowest recorded crime rate (610 crimes per 10,000 people in 2006-7), has one in five of the country's specials. Strathclyde Police force area, which contains almost half of the Scottish population and is centred on Glasgow and west central Scotland, has the highest levels of recorded crime (877 crimes per 10,000 population in 2006–7) but has less than a quarter of Scotland's specials. The introduction of community wardens also raises questions about the uneven investment in security. Although the initial allocation of funding for wardens from the Scottish Government was distributed according to levels of deprivation and population size, resulting in Orkney having four wardens while South Lanarkshire had 44, future investment may well depend on the priorities and resources of individual local authorities and not just security needs.

Against this background of pluralisation, or what Reiner (1997) nicely refers to as '"pick-n-mix" policing', some commentators have conjured up a dystopian future in which police officers patrol the front lines between a world of corporate fortresses and gated communities heavily protected by private security and an underclass concentrated in urban ghettoes. While such a scenario might have some resonance in a handful of US cities, it is of little relevance to contemporary Scotland. Nevertheless, the pluralisation of policing in Scotland still raises some profound issues of inequality and social justice with regard to the emergence of a patchwork quilt of security provision in which certain social groups and particular locations or environments become 'security rich' and others become 'security poor' based not on any objective measure of need but on the ability to pay or the levels of social capital within a community.

From 'broken windows' to 'signal crimes'? Policing crime and disorder

Against this background of an increasingly pluralised policing environment how have the public police met the challenges of tackling crime and disorder? As in other areas of Scottish criminal justice (see McAra 2009) and in crime control policy more generally in late-modern societies (Garland 2001), it is possible to detect a degree of tension between, on the one hand, approaches that are characterised by a 'sovereign strategy' of intensive, state-centred exclusionary practices, exemplified by zero-tolerance policing and the use of anti social behaviour orders, and, on the other hand, more inclusionary, prevention- and partnership-based activities, evident in community policing strategies. This section will consider these different approaches to tackling crime and disorder.

The sovereign policing approach is perhaps best illustrated by the introduction of a zero-tolerance strategy by Strathclyde Police force in the mid-1990s. Labelled Operation Spotlight this strategy drew inspiration from the policing approach developed by William Bratton, Commissioner of the New York City Police Department, who prioritised the 'quality of life offences', such as drunkenness, public urination, begging, vandalism and other antisocial behaviour. Operation Spotlight took a similar approach, using high-visibility police patrols to focus on a range of specific crimes (including vandalism, litter, drinking in public, carrying weapons, underage drinking, street robberies and truancy) and locations (such as parks, the transport network, licensed premises and sporting events). The rationale underpinning both the New York policing model and Operation Spotlight was the 'broken windows' thesis developed by Wilson and Kelling (1982). This thesis contends that merely the signs of dilapidation (such as broken windows) and disorder can initiate a downward spiral of neighbourhood decline by generating a sense of fear among residents that then leads to the breakdown of informal mechanisms of surveillance and control, resulting in rising and more serious forms of crime. In Strathclyde in the mid-1990s, the then Chief Constable, John Orr, enthusiastically embraced this 'broken windows' thinking. 'I hold the firm belief', he argued, 'that minor and serious crime are not poles apart. Indeed, I believe that minor crime is often simply the breeding ground and nursery that spawns and nurtures more serious and violent crime' (1997: 113). Orr was also particularly concerned at the evidence emerging from the Scottish Crime Surveys about high levels of fear among the public. He cited the 1996 Scottish Crime Survey which indicated that 92 per cent of the public were concerned about crime, that 52 per cent were 'worried that they or someone they lived with would be the victim of crime' and that 'violent crime and disorder were also on the increase and proving difficult to combat' (Orr 1997: 109).

As in New York, however, this zero-tolerance approach triggered a fierce debate about its effectiveness and its wider implications for social justice. Supporters of Operation Spotlight pointed to police statistics which showed that over the first three-month period of the initiative detections for crimes targeted by the police rose by 30 per cent, while car crime fell by 22 per cent, housebreaking by 13 per cent and serious crime by nearly 10 per cent (Orr 1997: 119). For Orr such results were important because they would lead to reductions in the fear of crime: 'If people now feel more confident in walking their dog at night, using the park, or travelling on public transport, ... then this is ... the true evaluation of Spotlight' (Orr 1997: 122). Critics of Operation Spotlight, however, argued that it needed to be seen as one element of a 'revanchist' or vengeful approach to urban policy in Glasgow (Atkinson 2003; Macleod 2002) in which attempts to improve the economic fortunes of the city involved the targeting of vulnerable groups like the homeless and prostitutes who were viewed as detracting from attempts to revitalise the city centre. In this respect, the policing of the homeless in Glasgow, it is claimed, stood in stark contrast with the approach taken in Edinburgh where the local 'civic culture' encouraged a more compassionate approach to the policing of begging (Fitzpatrick and Kennedy 2000).

This last point is significant because it underlines the fact that Operation Spotlight was very much a local policing response to crime and disorder. More recently, there is evidence of Scotland's police forces not only adopting approaches framed at a national level but also of moving away from the sovereign policing model and focusing more on issues of prevention and partnership. The development of reassurance policing in Scotland exemplifies this shift. In 2007 ACPOS published a *Public Reassurance Strategy*, claiming that 'Public Reassurance Policing will create the environment and the opportunity to increase the public's confidence in policing, improve people's quality of life and reduce crime and disorder in our communities' (ACPOS 2007: 3). At the heart of the strategy is a commitment to engaging with local communities so that they have a primary role in identifying local policing priorities, improving police visibility, working in partnership and adopting a problem-solving approach. The principles of this strategy have been reinforced by the commitment of the SNP Government to 1,000 new community police officers and by the 'community policing vision' articulated by the Justice Committee of the Scottish Parliament at the end of their inquiry into community policing in Scotland (Scottish Parliament 2008a).

The adoption of a reassurance approach to policing is not unique to Scotland. It was pioneered in England and Wales where a National Reassurance Policing Programme was introduced in 2003 which then developed into a national Neighbourhood Policing Programme. Underpinning the reassurance approach in both jurisdictions is a commitment to ensuring officers on patrol are visible, accessible and familiar, the co-production of solutions to crime and disorder problems with partner agencies, and the targeting of signal crimes and signal disorders which drive feelings of fear and insecurity. This last point is particularly important. As the main architect of the Signal Crimes Perspective (SCP), Martin Innes, observes, SCP provides the 'theoretical engine' for reassurance policing (Innes 2008: 23). The key proposition of SCP is that some crime and disorder incidents profoundly affect how people think, feel and act in relation to their security. There are clearly similarities here with the broken windows thesis described earlier in that both perspectives indicate that incivilities are important. But there are significant differences too. Broken windows views disorder as criminogenic whereas for SCP 'the central concern is not to unpack the trajectory of how disorder promotes crime … but rather how particular incidents give rise to a range of negative effects at both the individual and neighbourhood levels' (Innes 2008: 25). Such effects can range from feeling fearful to labelling groups as troublesome to moving away from an area.

The SCP and the notion of reassurance have important implications for policing. Increased police visibility can never deliver reassurance on its own. Rather policing needs to draw upon 'community intelligence' in order to focus on those signal crimes and signal disorders which, if addressed effectively, can communicate a sense of regained order and thus 'mediate and mitigate aspects of the insecurity of our contemporary existence' (Innes 2008: 27). In Scotland, the results of research evaluating the adoption of a reassurance approach by different police forces are yet to emerge. In England and Wales, however, a Home Office evaluation of the National Reassurance Policing Programme revealed significant positive impacts on a range of outcome measures, including criminal victimisation, perceptions of antisocial behaviour and public confidence in the police (Tuffin *et al.* 2006).

It is important to recognise, however, that the shift towards prevention and partnership characteristic of reassurance policing does not mean that sovereign policing approaches to dealing with disorder have been discarded. In this regard the approach taken to the policing of antisocial behaviour (ASB) in Scotland clearly illustrates Garland's (1996) contention that at certain times and with respect to certain offences and offenders, governments are keen to reinvoke the notion of the 'sovereign state'. Indeed, the approach taken to policing ASB via the use of Anti-Social Behaviour Orders (ASBOs) and dispersal orders by the governments in Westminster and Edinburgh has been described as 'an almost hysterical form of a sovereign attempt at crime control' (Carr and Cowan 2006: 75) in which, according to *The Economist* (5 February 2005), the relevant legislation gives the state 'new powers to deal with minor offences and other crime which are scarcely less draconian than those to deal with suspected terrorism'.

Underpinned by the same 'broken windows' thinking used to support zero-tolerance approaches (i.e. that relatively minor forms of offending can lead to more serious crimes), the ASBO was first introduced in the Crime and Disorder Act 1998 and could be applied for by local authorities. Further legislation in Westminster and Edinburgh then enhanced and extended the scope of ASBOs. The Criminal Justice (Scotland) Act 2003 extended the option of applying for an ASBO to registered social landlords and the Anti-Social Behaviour (Scotland) Act 2004 extended the use of ASBOs to 12–15-year-olds and gave the police new powers to disperse groups. The latter has proved particularly controversial. It contains echoes of the Child Safety Initiative introduced the late 1990s in the town of Hamilton in the west of Scotland where the police were given powers to take any child under 16 found out on the street after 9 p.m. back to their parents' home. Known as the Hamilton curfew, it sparked considerable debate as to whether it contributed to child safety, harmed relations between police and young people or infringed civil liberties (Scottish Executive 1999). The 2004 legislation on dispersal reworks the curfew idea and states that where a senior police officer has reasonable grounds for believing 'that any members of the public have been alarmed or distressed as a result of the presence or behaviour of groups of two or more persons in public places' and 'that antisocial behaviour is a significant, persistent and serious problem' in that area, the officer can require those people to disperse and those that don't live locally to leave the area and not return for up to 24 hours. If someone refuses to comply, they can be fined or imprisoned for a period of up to three months. When these powers were being considered both the Association of Chief Police Officers in Scotland and the Scottish Police Federation argued that 'there was a danger that all gatherings of young people would become labelled as problematic' (Crawford and Lister 2007: 7). The Federation was also concerned that these new powers would raise public expectations at a time of limited police resources. Partly as a result of these anxieties, only four dispersal orders had been implemented in the 18 months after the introduction of these powers in 2004, rising to 14 by early 2007.[1] Where orders have been introduced, however, there is strong evidence of their impact. In Aberdeen Scotland's first dispersal order was introduced in 2005 along the beach boulevard area where residents routinely complained about the noise generated by young people congregating in cars and on motorbikes and scooters. Sixty-two formal dispersals were issued and Grampian Police recorded a 53 per cent drop in reported incidents in ASB after the order was introduced. In West Lothian the whole village of Mid Calder was the subject of a dispersal order in 2005–6 after complaints to the police about groups of up to 50 non-resident youths congregating in the village on weekend evenings. The order was viewed as a deterrent to stop young people choosing to use the village as a meeting place and the police saw it as a success given that calls for service fell and there was little displacement to neighbouring villages (Crawford and Lister 2007: 14–15).

In relation to the use of ASBOs, a report for the Scottish Government in 2005 indicated that 148 ASBOs had been granted in 2003–4, which as a proportion of the population was slightly higher than for England and Wales (6.9 orders per 100,000 households compared with 6.1) (Scottish Executive 2005). Intriguingly, however, not only were the highest rates of ASBO use to be found in a wide diversity of social and geographical environments (with Dundee, Orkney, North Lanarkshire and the Scottish Borders being the top four locations in 2003–4) but these locations do not necessarily have the highest incidence of ASB. Evidence from the Scottish Household Survey shows Glasgow well above the national average for the incidence of ASB but ASBO use here was relatively low. The reasons for these variations are complex but include the speed with which local authorities and social landlords have been geared up to use ASBO powers, variations in the support of the legal profession (particularly solicitors and sheriffs) for ASBOs and commitments in some locations to using other methods to resolve ASB problems Indeed, in 2009 the SNP Government made it clear that it wants ASBOs to be used more sparingly than in the past and that, unlike the previous Labour administration, it would interpret the low use of ASBOs as a positive outcome rather than a sign of failure, indicating that offending behaviour is being dealt with effectively before enforcement action is required.

Police governance: creeping centralism or a new localism?

The pluralisation of policing and the interplay between sovereign approaches and the reassurance agenda in the tackling crime and disorder agenda all raise important questions about police governance in Scotland. In relation to pluralisation attention has typically focused on contrasting the perceived inadequate and ineffective forms of accountability associated with the private security industry and voluntary forms of policing, with claims of robust and well established governance arrangements for the public police (see Stenning 2009). Space precludes examining all aspects of this debate here so the focus will be on the arrangements for the accountability of the public police. This in itself is a field of considerable controversy. When the Scottish Parliament's Justice Committee examined the issue as part of its 2008 inquiry into the effective use of police resources it noted how it had 'received contrasting evidence about the effectiveness of the current … system in ensuring the accountability and governance of Scottish police forces' (Scottish Parliament 2008a: para. 346). On the one hand, Her Majesty's Inspector of Constabulary for Scotland (HMICS), the Accounts Commission and Auditor General all raised concerns about the weaknesses of existing arrangements (particularly with respect to the role played by police boards), while the Scottish Government, ACPOS and representatives of the police boards all claimed the system was working well.

In terms of its formal architecture, police governance in Scotland today is very similar to when Banton was writing in the 1960s. As in England and Wales, it is based on a constitutional settlement known as the tripartite structure with responsibility for policing shared among three elements: central government (via Scottish ministers), local government (via police boards) and chief constables of individual forces (of which there are currently eight but when Banton was writing there were over 40). Scottish ministers have overall responsibility for policing policy in Scotland and are answerable to the Scottish Parliament. Individual police boards (comprising elected local councillors) are responsible for setting the budget for their force, appointing senior officers and playing a role in securing best value and continuous improvement. Chief constables, although answerable to their police board and Scottish ministers, have operational independence in relation to the management and utilisation of police officers and support staff. Described as an 'explanatory and cooperative' model of police governance (Marshall 1978), the balance of the relationship between the three elements of the tripartite structure has undergone significant change over the last 15 years. The Local Government etc. (Scotland) Act 1994 replaced two-tier local government with 32 single-tier (unitary) local authorities and changed the character of police governance overnight. From six regional police boards and two joint boards, Scotland now has six joint boards and just two unitary ones. For Strathclyde Police this meant that rather than dealing with one regional council the police board now comprises representatives of 12 unitary councils. Such fragmentation of local democratic involvement in policing is compounded by the way police boards have little capacity for carrying out independent scrutiny of their force's performance and therefore typically rely on their chief constables to provide information. It is unsurprising that some observers have concluded that 'The way the tripartite system works is that the key players are central government officials and chief constables with the local police board largely providing the rubber stamp' (Scott and Wilkie 2001: 58).

This perceived weakness of police boards within the tripartite structure has been further highlighted by the introduction of Single Outcome Agreements (SOAs) between the Scottish Government and local community planning partnerships (CPPs) which set out how each will work to improve the outcomes for local people. All SOAs contain outcomes which require some commitment of police resources (in relation to reductions in the fear of crime or tackling antisocial behaviour, for example) and chief constables have a statutory duty to participate in the community planning process. However, police boards have little input into the development of SOAs nor is there evidence that police boards are being consulted on how forces should balance meeting the demands set out in SOAs with the demands for other local policing needs not directly linked to SOAs. HMICS has therefore warned that 'there is a serious gap in governance arrangements for policing at a local level' (2009: para. 7.13).

The balance between the Scottish Government and local chief constables has also shifted over the last 15 years. The Scottish Government has gradually acquired statutory powers that allow it to be more interventionist (directing chief constables to include information on specific topics in their annual reports or asking HMICS to inquire into the operation of forces). The Scottish Government also has a key role in ensuring that common services are provided where this is deemed necessary for promoting the efficiency of the police. Under the Police, Public Order and Criminal Justice (Scotland) Act 2006, for example, it established the Scottish Police Services Authority (SPSA) which is governed by a board appointed by Scottish ministers and has responsibility for the delivery of police training and education (via the Scottish Police College), forensic services, the Scottish Crime and Drug Enforcement Agency and information services. Such creeping centralism is also evident in the increasingly prominent role played by ACPOS in formulating national policing policy, such as the reassurance strategy discussed earlier. As Donnelly and Scott (2005) observe, ACPOS's 'corporate significance may compromise the independence of individual chief constables, who may find it difficult to break ranks with an agreement reached jointly by their representatives and another party, especially the government' (p. 75). This dilemma for chief constables is underlined by HMICS in its review of police governance in Scotland:

> On the one hand they [Chief Constables] are bound by the current legislative framework to give primacy to the decisions of their local authority/board, while on the other hand they naturally feel obliged to work through ACPOS for the common good of policing in Scotland. (HMICS 2009: para. 7.32)

Some attempt has been made to address the issue of the national policing agenda by the announcement in 2009 by the Cabinet Secretary for Justice of a new Scottish Policing Board which will bring together central and local government partners with the police to identify strategic priorities across Scotland and how these should be addressed. The Cabinet Secretary is confident that 'The Board will act as a single collective voice for policing in Scotland, strengthening governance and accountability at the national level'. Nevertheless, concerns remain among many observers that the three legs of Scotland's tripartite system have 'a very unbalanced look about them' (Donnelly and Scott 2005: 81) particularly with respect to the local dimensions of accountability. The current emphasis on reassurance and community policing certainly creates the possibility for enhancing direct, local forms of accountability given that the success of reassurance and community-focused policing approaches hinges on a high degree of responsiveness to community concerns and giving local people a voice in establishing policing priorities. Nevertheless, while these developments are a necessary step in redressing the balance within the tripartite structure, they still leave unanswered calls for strengthening more formal, local democratic involvement.

Concluding comments: back to the future?

A comprehensive analysis of all 'the "nooks and crannies" of contemporary policing' (McLaughlin 2007) is impossible in a single chapter so the focus here has been on attempting to capture some of the key ways in which the policing landscape in Scotland has changed since the mid-1990s. Processes of pluralisation, new approaches to tackling crime and disorder, and changes in the nature of police governance are all central to the analysis of 'the new policing' of late modern societies. Furthermore, Scotland's experience in terms of the changing dynamics of policing are clearly bound up with much broader socio-cultural, economic and political trends. The pluralisation of policing, for example, is connected to a wider neoliberal political agenda in which the state increasingly looks to encourage private and voluntary forms of service delivery alongside the public police who are themselves being shaped by market disciplines. Moreover, within a social context in which fear of crime continues to create a growing demand for policing in particular locations, the emergence of 'security rich' and 'security poor' environments is inevitable. How the public police in Scotland interact with this changing landscape will be an important topic for future research. Even with an expanding 'policing family' in which partnership between the public police and other public and private agencies is a significant feature, it is still important for the state (through the police) to assert its sovereignty. The example of zero-tolerance tactics employed in the mid-1990s in Glasgow or, more recently, the implementation of dispersal orders provide compelling evidence of this.

Making these connections between policing and this complex set of broader social and political concerns associated with the 'condition of postmodernity' (Harvey 1991) is clearly an important part of developing a critical understanding of policing in contemporary Scotland. As McLaughlin observes (2007: ix): 'Postmodernity seems determined to beat out its particular complex of volatile tensions and anxieties resultant from everything from consumerization, cultural differentiation, social fragmentation through to a global war on terror on the police anvil with a merciless vengeance'. But it was just such an approach that also characterised the work of Banton in the early 1960s as he grappled with the interplay between policing and modernity. He was particularly concerned with how 'modern life seems to stress anonymity' and that there is a 'process of sloughing off a whole range of ideas about the proper ordering of the nation's life ... and moving into a phase in which none of the new ideas is assured of more than a temporary reign' (p. 261). As he explains:

> The increasing role of technological progress moves more and more of the population out of the small communities in which people have an active sense of the communal good and are able to forward it in their own ways into larger industrial communities in which people seem to be more oriented to

> private ends and where the solitary individual can do little to influence society in which he lives. If this is the case it may well make the individual member of the public less inclined to go out of his way to help the police. (1964: ix)

At the conclusion of his study, Banton was therefore quite pessimistic, worried that the rapid social changes occurring at that time would mean that the established relationships between the police and the community could not be sustained into the future without 'a variety of readjustments on the part of the police' (p. 262). As this chapter has illustrated, however, such anxieties continue into the present and the need for policing to adapt and change in response to a rapidly changing social, political and economic environment continues. The extent to which such adaptations reflect a distinctively Scottish response to wider changes remains an open question. The nature of pluralisation, the approach taken to tackling crime and disorder and the evolution of police governance in Scotland all exhibit some important differences to developments in the rest of the UK. Scotland has not opted for having Police Community Support Officers (who provide a visible police presence but do not have full constabulary powers) as they do in England and Wales, nor has it embraced a national neighbourhood policing programme or seen the same degree of central government influence over local policing units as experienced south of the border. Yet Scotland is seeing some strengthening of a national policing agenda by, for example, the creation of a national policing board and a national policing performance framework. Such developments, in turn, raise questions about the long-term sustainability of Scotland's current structure of eight police forces. Indeed, the economic downturn combined with concerns over the challenges from serious and organised crime have prompted some chief officers in Scotland to revisit a very long-running debate, which has existed north and south of the border, about whether there should be mergers of police forces. In England and Wales the creation of so-called 'super forces' was actively encouraged by the Home Office in 2005–6 only to be swiftly abandoned with a change in Home Secretary. In Scotland, the Cabinet Secretary has made it clear that there are no plans to merge forces yet some chief officers have indicated that they think the issue should be debated. Intriguingly, such a debate is now being framed in ways which Banton would no doubt recognise from when he was writing *The Policeman in the Community*. According to the Chief Constable of Strathclyde Police, 'There is a line of thinking in policing which says if you have strong community policing it doesn't matter what the structures are above that because the public relate to local cops' (*The Herald* 2009). How the relationships between the local and the national are played out in Scottish policing will be an interesting field of study and one where, as Banton indicated more than 40 years ago, police research and scholarship have an important role to play. 'Both the police and the public would benefit', he observed, 'if there were more informed and independent opinion in the universities and among the public at large about the police and their duties' (Banton 1964: 268).

Note

1 These figures stand in stark contrast to England and Wales where dispersal orders were greeted with some enthusiasm with over 200 orders authorised in 2004 and by 2006 there were over 1,000 designated dispersal zones (Crawford and Lister 2007: 9).

References

ACPOS (2007) *Public Reassurance Strategy*. Glasgow: ACPOS.

Atkinson, R. (2003) 'Domestication by cappuccino or a revenge on urban space? Control and empowerment in the management of urban spaces', *Urban Studies*, 40: 1829–43.

Banton, M. (1964) *The Policeman in the Community*. London: Tavistock Publications.

Brown, M. and Bolling, K. (2007) *2006 Scottish Crime and Victimisation Survey: Main Finding*. Edinburgh: Scottish Government Social Research.

Carr, H. and Cowan, D. (2006) 'Labelling: constructing definition of anti-social behaviour?', in J. Flint (ed.), *Housing, Urban Governance and Anti-Social Behaviour*. Bristol: Policy Press, pp. 57–78.

Crawford, A. (2003) 'The pattern of policing in the UK: policing beyond the police', in T. Newburn (ed.), *The Handbook of Policing*. Cullompton: Willan Publishing, pp. 136–68.

Crawford, A. and Lister, S. (2007) *The Use and Impact of Dispersal Orders: Sticking Plasters and Wake-up Calls*. York: Joseph Rowntree Foundation.

Donnelly, D. (2008a) 'Community wardens in Scotland: practitioners' views', *Howard Journal*, 27 (4): 371–82.

Donnelly, D. (2008b) *Municipal Policing in Scotland*. Dundee: Dundee University Press.

Donnelly, D. and Scott, K. (2005) 'Devolution, accountability and Scottish policing', in D. Donnelly and K. Scott (eds), *Policing Scotland*. Cullompton: Willan Publishing, pp. 62–89.

Fitzpatrick, S. and Kennedy, C. (2000) *Getting By: Begging, Rough Sleeping and the Big Issue in Glasgow and Edinburgh*. Bristol: Policy Press.

Fyfe, N. (2010) 'Policing crime and disorder in Scotland', in D. Donnelly and K. Scott (eds), *Policing Scotland*, 2nd edn. Cullompton: Willan Publishing.

Fyfe, N. and Bannister J. (1999) 'Privatisation, policing and crime control: tracing the contours of the public-private divide', in P. Duff and N. Hutton (eds), *Criminal Justice in Scotland*. London: Ashgate, pp. 335–54.

Garland, D. (1996) 'The limits of the sovereign state: strategies of crime control in contemporary societies', *British Journal of Criminology*, 36: 445–71.

Garland, D. (2001) *The Culture of Control*. Oxford: Oxford University Press.

Harvey, D. (1991) *The Condition of Postmodernity*. Oxford: Basil Blackwell.

Hayton, K., Boyd, C., Campbell, M., Crawford, K., Latimer, K., Lindsay, S. and Percy, V. (2007) *National Evaluation of Scotland's Community Wardens Scheme*. Edinburgh: Scottish Executive Research.

Helms, G. (2008) *Towards Safe City Centres? Re-making the Space of an Old Industrial City*. London: Ashgate.

Her Majesty's Inspector of Constabulary for Scotland (HMICS) (2009) *Independent Review of Policing*. Edinburgh: HMICS.

Herald, The (2009) 'Police chiefs urge debate on case for single force in Scotland', 30 March.

Holdaway, S. (1983) *Inside the British Police*. Oxford: Basil Blackwell.

Innes, M. (2008) 'Towards a science of street craft: the method of reassurance policing', in M. Easton, L. Gunther Moor, B. Hogenboom, P. Ponsaers and B. van Sokkom (eds), *Reflections on Reassurance Policing in the Low Countries*. The Hague: Boom Legal Publishers, pp. 15–28.

Johnston, L. (2000) *Policing Britain: Risk, Security and Governance*. Harlow: Longman.

McAra, L. (2008) 'Crime, criminology and criminal justice in Scotland', *European Journal of Criminology*, 5 (4): 481–504.

McLaughlin, E. (2007) *The New Policing*. London: Sage.

McLaughlin, E. and Murji, K. (2001) 'Lost connections and new directions: neo-liberalism, new public managerialism and the modernization of the British police', in K. Stenson and R. Sullivan (eds), *Crime, Risk and Justice: The Politics of Crime Control in Liberal Democracies*. Cullompton: Willan Publishing.

Macleod, G. (2002) 'From urban entrepreneurialism to a "revanchist" city? On the spatial injustices of Glasgow's renaissance', *Antipode*, 34: 602–24.

Marshall, G. (1978) 'Police accountability revisited', in D. Butler and A. Halsey (eds), *Policy and Politics*. London: Macmillan.

Orr, J. (1997) 'Strathclyde's Spotlight Initiative', in N. Dennis (ed.), *Zero Tolerance: Policing a Free Society*. London: IEA, pp. 104–23.

Reiner, R. (1995) 'From the sacred to the profane: the thirty years war of the British police', *Policing and Society*, 5: 121–8.

Reiner, R. (1997) 'Policing and the police', in M. Maguire, R. Morgan and R. Reiner (eds), *The Oxford Handbook of Criminology*, 2nd edn. Oxford: Oxford University Press.

Scotsman, The (2009) 'Loch Lomond park rangers are first in Britain to get police powers', 31 March.

Scott, K. and Wilkie, R. (2001) 'Chief constables: a current "crisis" in Scottish policing?', *Scottish Affairs*, 35: 54–68.

Scottish Executive (1999) *Evaluation of the Hamilton Child Safety Initiative*. Edinburgh: Central Research Unit, Scottish Executive.

Scottish Executive (2005) *Use of Anti-Social Behaviour Orders in Scotland*. Edinburgh: Scottish Executive.

Scottish Parliament (2008a) *Report on Inquiry into Community Policing*. Edinburgh: Scottish Parliament.

Scottish Parliament (2008b) *Report on Inquiry into the Effective Use of Police Resources*. Edinburgh: Scottish Parliament.

Shearing, C. D. and Stenning, P. C. (eds) (1987) *Private Policing*. Thousand Oaks, CA: Sage.

Stenning, P. (2009) 'Governance and accountability in a plural policing environment – the story so far', *Policing: A Journal of Policy and Practice*, 3 (1): 22–33.

Tuffin, R., Morris, J. and Poole, A. (2006) *An Evaluation of the Impact of the National Reassurance Policing Programme*. London: Home Office.

Wilson, J. Q. and Kelling, G. L. (1982) 'Broken windows', *Atlantic Monthly*, March, pp. 29–38.

Chapter 10

Sentencing and penal decision-making: is Scotland losing its distinctive character?

Cyrus Tata

Introduction

It is widely argued that the practice of punishment is changing profoundly in western countries. Against a background of increasing public cynicism, fear of crime, heightened insecurity and a loss of faith in legal and political institutions, it seems that over the last two decades traditional penal values are increasingly being replaced by new ones (e.g. Franko Aaas 2005; Garland 2001). This new penal world may well cause us concern. As voters demand better value for money from the criminal justice system, there appears to be less concern with the rights of the individual and more concern with 'system efficiency'. So, increasingly, you can expect to be punished not for any offence you may or may not have actually committed, but for what predictive risk-assessment technologies calculate you may probably do. As public trust in the wisdom of judges and other professionals further declines, it seems that sentences will increasingly be decided not on the basis of an assessment of you as a person but in accordance with 'actuarial justice' using predetermined scoring systems (rather like how insurance company actuaries calculate probable risks to determine premiums). Sentencing in Scotland is said to be illustrative of these major global shifts. Is it?

This chapter examines the hypothesis that the basic values of Scottish sentencing (and associated penal decision-making) are changing. It asks if Scotland is losing its traditional identity (based on a tradition of humanistic penal values[1]), and whether sentencing and penal practices in Scotland exemplify a trend towards international convergence. In doing so, the chapter also raises issues about legal and social inequality and their inter-connection.

In order to test these questions the chapter examines the evidence in Scottish sentencing and penal decision-making of three fundamental shifts. First, from the value of protecting the individual from the power of the state to the value of 'efficiency'. We will look at changes in how defence lawyers are paid and the impact on the protection of the individual accused by the state ('due process'). Is Scotland forfeiting its traditional commitment to 'due process' in favour of a rough-and-ready speedy throughput of cases ('efficiency')? Secondly, we will investigate whether Scotland is sacrificing its traditional dedication to welfare-based penal values on the altar of 'actuarial justice' (Feeley and Simon 1994), dominated by probabilistic calculations of the risk of future offending. Thirdly, we will examine whether or not the discretion of Scotland's judiciary as to how to interpret and apply the law and thus decide cases is being diminished by the rise of technocratic instruments. However, before examining these three areas, let us briefly define what is meant by 'sentencing' and then place it in its Scottish legal and institutional context.

The ambit of sentencing

Sentencing is the decision as to how to allocate state-imposed punishment in individual cases. Judicial decisions in court are traditionally thought of as sentencing, but in fact there are a number of other processes which, in effect, decide or influence the allocation of state punishment. These include, for example, decisions by prosecutors whether and how to prosecute a case, decisions whether to offer diversionary out-of-court penalties as an alternative to prosecution through court, decisions of the accused individual whether and when to plead 'not guilty' or 'guilty' and to what, reports prepared to advise and assist judicial sentencing, as well as 'back-door' release arrangements from prison (see Chapter 11). All of these contribute to and are, in effect, a part of the sentencing process. For instance, prosecution choices as to whether and how to prosecute a person and in turn their decisions how to plead set the agenda for judicial sentencing. This chapter is written for readers relatively unfamiliar with Scottish sentencing and penal processes, therefore some of its distinctive legal features will now be briefly outlined.

Sentencing in Scotland: England and Wales, it isn't!

Although a constituent part of the UK, Scotland's legal system is separate and distinct from the rest of the UK (see Chapter 1). Scottish criminal law, justice institutions and procedures have always been separate. For instance, in contrast to England and Wales, most cases are heard not by lay magistrates but by 'sheriffs', who are lawyers by professional background. Unlike a federal system (where serious matters are dealt with at national court level and other matters are required to be dealt with by the constituent states), there is no UK-wide sentencing system. Appeals directly about criminal law and justice are heard within Scotland and (unlike the rest of the UK), not by the the UK Supreme Court. In contrast to its counterpart in England and Wales (Ashworth 2005), the Court of Criminal Appeal in Scotland has (at least to date) been relatively reluctant to issue Guideline Judgments which first-instance sentencers are obliged to follow. Neither does Scotland have the sentencing policy institutions of the kind developed in England and Wales and elsewhere (Ashworth 2005, 2008). Save for murder, there are no mandatory sentences which judges must impose. Traditionally, the Scottish senior judiciary has been highly suspicious of developing any 'policy' on sentencing, arguing that the existence of any policy would undermine the principles of judicial independence and individualised justice in which every case is said to be 'unique' and dealt with as such. Similarly, the idea of any public position on 'tariffs' or 'going rates' for different kinds of cases has largely been eschewed (Hutton 2006). In short, it makes no practical sense to talk of 'the UK sentencing system'.

The long-standing separateness of Scottish sentencing law and justice is important for three reasons. First, the point is very often overlooked or misunderstood by otherwise excellent textbooks on criminology and criminal justice which treat England and Wales as synonymous with 'the UK' (see further McAra 2008; and Chapter 1, this volume). Secondly, there are under-used opportunities for fruitful comparisons to be drawn between these two close neighbours, which are broadly similar yet also quite distinct. Thirdly, it has been quite widely argued that until devolution in 1999 Scottish criminal justice had resisted many of the globalising trends towards 'efficiency', risk management and technocratic automation. Instead, Scotland was said to have 'retained a distinctively welfare approach' (Croall 2006: 589) and to have been 'relatively immune from the populist tendencies that were rapidly infecting its southern neighbour' (Cavadino and Dignan 2006: 231; cited by Croall 2006: 590). However, it has been argued that since devolution things have changed and that Scottish criminal justice is losing its distinctiveness.

Is Scotland's distinctive sentencing identity being 'detartanised'?

In an important article, Lesley McAra (2008) has suggested that Scottish criminal justice may, as she neatly puts it, be being 'detartanised' (see also Chapters 1, 4 and 13, this volume). Rather than shoring up distinctiveness, devolution and the establishment of a Scottish Parliament, (intended to democratise matters which had previously been dealt with by a small group of officials in the Scottish Office), have led to a greater politicisation of criminal justice and a degree of convergence with global trends (Croall 2006; McAra 2008). This chapter examines this thesis in the context of sentencing. Is Scotland's sentencing practice now converging with other broader global trends towards efficiency, risk-based punishment and the loss of judicial discretion to technology? Are small countries (like Scotland) being swept along with the tide of actuarial justice?

Much of the literature which has identified large-scale changes in penal values is inspired by evidence of significant change in policy, legislation and media discourse. Yet it cannot be assumed that policies, laws and the way the media talks about criminal justice filter down from 'the top' to everyday practices (Gelsthorpe and Padfield 2003; Tata 2007b). Sometimes they do filter down as intended, sometimes only partially; sometimes they are ignored or misunderstood (whether deliberately or through ignorance), and sometimes they work out in very different ways from that intended. For that reason we will now examine policy and actual practices in three case study contexts: plea decision-making, pre-sentence reports and the use of information technology in sentencing.

From 'due process' to 'efficiency'?[2] Case study: plea decision-making

The 'due process model' of criminal justice is a short-hand term for a cluster of values and principles emphasising the need to protect each individual citizen from the abuse of state power. It is, after all, the state which prosecutes the individual and seeks to punish him/her. Inspired by the classical liberal-legal suspicion of the state, due process is preoccupied with the vulnerability of the individual when confronted by the overwhelming might of the state. In the due process model the presumption of innocence is of paramount value. This means that the burden of proof lies with the state to prove the guilt of the individual. It is not for the individual to prove his/her innocence. According to this model the decision to plead 'not guilty' or 'guilty' must be made by the individual as a matter of free and informed choice, without pressure or intimidation of any kind. The individual has to be given a fair chance of defence against the potentially crushing weight of the state system. The 'efficiency model', on the other hand, is a short-hand term for a cluster of values which stress the need for the state to get through its huge volume of cases as quickly and as efficiently as possible. The efficiency model is preoccupied with resource pressures of time and money. Cases should not take up more time than absolutely necessary. Accordingly, where people might end up pleading guilty, they should be encouraged to do so as early as possible, and it is acceptable (even sensible) to encourage 'appropriate' pleas of guilty through rewards and incentives. This model also emphasises the routine and standard character of cases.

Although a fully contested trial before a jury is the iconic image in the popular imagination of criminal justice, it is, in fact, statistically speaking a remarkably rare event. In common with other English-speaking countries, such fully contested jury trials in which prosecution and defence battle it out until the bitter end constitute less than 1 per cent of all cases prosecuted in court. Why is this? In Scotland there is no right for the defendant to choose to be tried by a jury and all such decisions are taken by prosecutors, often as a matter of discretion (Moody and Tombs 1982). Only around 3 per cent of cases prosecuted are decided ('marked') by prosecutors as jury-triable. As in other English-speaking countries, around 97 per cent of cases prosecuted through the court are marked for 'summary' (non-jury triable) procedure and less than one tenth of these cases culminate in a fully contested trial (Tata and Stephen 2006). However, it is not the case that these summary cases have little at stake or should be regarded as 'trivial' (McBarnet 1981). The summary sheriff courts now have the power to imprison for up to 12 months and nearly nine-tenths of all custodial sentences are now passed in these courts (Scottish Government 2009). In other words, summary process matters: it may not be the stuff of courtroom movies, but it has real consequences for those individuals called before it. From the perspective of public policy it is central, particularly in those cases in which a custodial sentence is a distinct possibility but by no means inevitable. Given that this chapter is looking both at policy and what is typical, we will now mainly focus on summary process at the intermediate Sheriff Court-level and the decision as to how to plead.

Although not formally a sentencing decision as such, the decision of an accused person how to plead, (guilty or not guilty or some combination of the two), is in practical terms a crucial part of the sentencing process.

Plea decision-making

Since at least the early 1990s successive governments have been interested in making the Scottish criminal justice process quicker, simpler and more cost-effective. In other words, the aim has been to shift from the values of the due process model towards the efficiency model. Chief among the aims has been to cut 'waste' from the system by speeding up court cases and encouraging people who are seen as likely to end up pleading guilty to do so as quickly as possible. This brings the choice of the individual as to how to plead to the centre-stage of policy.

It is a fundamental principle of law throughout the world that the decision as to how to plead belongs to the accused. No explicit or subtle pressure should interfere with that free choice. In this way, the role of the defence lawyer is not to interfere with that choice but to be 'instructed' by his/her client and legal advice is given only in the client's best interests. Changes to the ways lawyers are paid should not, therefore, affect how cases are handled and the overall flow of cases. However, this 'consumer sovereignty model' is rather wide of the mark. Tata and Stephen explain further:

> [T]he empirical literature on the relationship between criminal defence lawyers and their clients around the English-speaking world has consistently highlighted the relative passivity of most clients [...] Moreover, the relatively weak social, educational and economic resources of most clients in summary proceedings coupled with the immediate stress and anxiety which the criminal process brings means that clients tend to be in a particularly poor position to take firm command of their defence [...] Earlier research [suggests that] many clients tended to have

> some difficulty accurately explaining the charges against them (or indeed those amended charges to which they chose to plead guilty). Furthermore, clients tended to conflate legal culpability with moral culpability. Most clients were willing to place their trust in their defence [lawyer] and take his/her advice [...] These recent findings from Scotland provide further evidence that a simple market-style consumer-sovereignty model of client satisfaction and criminal legal services is flawed [...] Pleading decisions, therefore, may ultimately be taken by clients, but they are heavily influenced and guided by the advice they receive; and shaped by expectations and agenda setting which are mediated by their [legal] advisors. (Tata and Stephen 2006: 733)

Contrary to the portrayal in US TV dramas, extremely few summary cases in Scotland are defended by lawyers who are paid privately by their clients. Most such work is conducted by defence lawyers working in private law firms which then bill the publicly funded arm's length government body called the Scottish Legal Aid Board (SLAB). What impact does this arrangement have?

In 1999 Scotland decided to move from a system in which defence firms itemised their bills according to the time spent and the type of work carried out to a new system of 'fixed fees' in which the defence lawyer's firm was to be paid an overall fee for completing the case. The idea behind the change was to make the system more efficient by discouraging defence lawyers from undertaking 'unnecessary' work, such as 'excessive' client contact and preparation and to save the cost of trials compared with early guilty pleas. Defence lawyers were to be paid a fixed amount depending on when the case concluded. Activities like case preparation and client contact were no longer to be paid as separate items. Proponents of the new fixed-fee policy felt that defence lawyers had been exploiting the system for profit ('milking the system', as it was often alleged). It was also believed that defence lawyers had a vested interest in prolonging cases, thus making the system less efficient. The government and SLAB believed that under a system of fixed fees defence lawyers would only undertake (and thus bill for) work which was truly necessary (Tata 2007a).

Did the change to fixed payments work as intended? An independent evaluation was undertaken which investigated the impact of the change in the payment system on overall legal aid spending, lawyer firm incomes, case preparation and management, and the trajectories and outcomes of cases (Tata and Stephen 2006; Tata

2007a). Overall, the policy had very mixed results. Detailed economic analysis showed that it did not cut spending. Those specialist firms which were prepared to work more intensively by taking on more cases than they did before and spending less time per case found they could make a very significant income from the new scheme. In that sense, it was suggested by some lawyers that the new fee arrangements permitted, even encouraged, a new kind of exploitation (or 'milking'), where defence lawyers were prepared to take on more cases. Overall, case preparation levels declined as a direct result of the new fee structure and this was not offset by systematic advance disclosure to the defence of prosecution evidence. (Previously the defence had subcontracted its own investigations.) Most damagingly of all to the policy, it had the *net* effect of postponing the point at which people pled guilty – the exact opposite of what was intended. This latter finding was partly due to another consequence of the policy: a reduction in levels of lawyer–client contact. Officials believed that, generally speaking, defence lawyers spent (and billed for) too much time in communication with their clients. By introducing fixed fees, lawyer–client contact was, in effect, financially discouraged. But this also meant that lawyers tended to have less time to speak to their clients to persuade them that pleading guilty at the earliest opportunity might be in their best interests.

A closely related factor in encouraging 'appropriate' early guilty pleas is the connection with certain forms of 'plea bargaining'. Plea bargaining (or 'plea negotiation') is an informal (and controversial) practice which exists in many (but not all) countries. Plea bargaining is an umbrella-term encompassing a range of practices whereby the accused gives up his/her right to trial and pleads guilty in (explicit or implicit) exchange for some perceived benefit (see, for example, Roach Anleu 2010: 154–62). There are two main forms of plea bargaining which operate in Scotland. First, 'charge bargaining' is a practice whereby the prosecution and defence agree which charges to amend or delete in exchange for a guilty plea by the accused person to the remaining charge(s). The second form is 'implicit sentence bargaining' whereby the defence offers a guilty plea in the hope of a reduced sentence compared with the sentence which would be passed for the same charge(s) if the person was to be found guilty after a trial. In Scotland sentence bargaining is implicit: the judge does not participate in any explicit discussions about the likely sentencing outcome if the individual pleads guilty and how this may or may not differ from the likely sentencing outcome if the individual is found guilty of the same charges after trial.

In Scotland implicit sentence bargaining tends to be called 'sentence discounting'. Arguments in favour of sentence discounting centre around efficiency: that it accelerates the production of 'inevitable' guilty pleas and so frees up court time.

The most prominent argument against the idea of sentence discounting is based on due process values. The big question is whether people are 'induced' to plead guilty to charges they are not guilty of. This danger of inducement to plead guilty has traditionally weighed more strongly in Scotland than in England and Wales. For example, in the case of Strawhorn, the Scottish Court of Criminal Appeal made the point forcefully:

> In this country there is the presumption of innocence and an accused person is entitled to go to trial and leave the Crown to establish his guilt if the Crown can. It is wrong therefore that an accused person should be put in a position of realising that if he pleads guilty early enough he will receive a lower sentence than he otherwise would receive for the offence. (*Strawhorn* v. *McLeod* 1987 SCCR: 413)

This did not mean that there was a 'ban' on discounting the sentence in implicit return for a guilty plea. Rather, it meant that there was to be no policy of discounting: it would all depend on the facts, circumstances and timing of the guilty plea in the individual case. Moreover, research which analysed the sentencing outcomes of a controlled sample of otherwise similar cohorts of cases suggested that there was no major and systematic practice of sentence discounting across the board in Scotland other than in certain categories of cases (notably sexual offences) (Goriely *et al.* 2001).

However, in 2003 the Court of Criminal Appeal in Scotland took the opportunity in the case of Du Plooy (*Du Plooy* v. *HMA* 2003 SCCR: 443) to issue a rare 'Guideline' sentencing judgment. Du Plooy has retained the permissive position of Strawhorn: sentencers may discount a sentence in recognition of an early guilty plea. The crucial change was to be one of greater transparency. The sentencing judge should state openly whether a discount is applied, how much it is and his/her reasons for choosing not to apply a discount (which can be up to around one third). The rationale for this new approach was based on a desire for greater efficiency: to accelerate guilty pleas (Leverick 2004). The logic is that in the course of time defence lawyers would come to know how to advise their clients because the lawyers would be able to predict what sort of discount the client should expect for an early guilty plea and thus advise the client accordingly. However, knowledge of sentencing discount case law appears to be patchy. Moreover, some practitioners appear to believe that discounting is mandatory in all cases of an early guilty plea, while some judicial sentencers may harbour their own personal policies regarding certain categories of offences as not entitled to consideration of a discount at all (Tata 2007a). So the efficiency drive of sentence discounting can and does encounter countervailing local practices which may lead to inefficiency, such as 'unnecessary adjournments' as the result of perceived inconsistencies between judicial sentencers, known as 'sheriff shopping' (Summary Justice Review Committee 2004: 31 and 208–9).

This brief case study about plea decision-making shows that in recent years in Scotland there has been, at the level of law and policy, some discernible shift towards a more explicit emphasis on efficiency values. Readers familiar with several decades of criminal justice research from around the world will know that the heavy dependence of Scottish summary justice on guilty pleas is found in many other English-speaking adversarial jurisdictions.[3] However, in reality there are, as McBarnet (1981), famously observed, 'two tiers of justice': the iconic fully contested but rare jury trial, and the daily grind of summary justice based on relinquishment of the right to trial in return for some benefit (real or perceived). It is central both to the practical operation and to the legitimacy of the 'adversarial' criminal process that the decision as to how to plead is seen to be freely made by the accused person. However, in practice that choice is limited by a range of dynamics which work with legal aid and sentence discounting changes (for good introductions see, for example, Bottomley and Bronnit 2006: 128–42; Roach Anleu 2010: 154–62). Research from several English-speaking countries has shown that guilty pleas are also driven through a range of practices, including a professional and policy 'ideology of triviality' which regards the outcomes of summary cases as relatively inconsequential (McBarnet 1981), 'court workgroups' and the incentives to maintain inter-professional relationships (for example, Eisenstein and Jacob 1991), a pervasive culture of the presumption of guilt rather than of innocence (e.g. McConville *et al.* 1994; Mulcahay 1994; Sanders and Young 2007: 443–94), the deployment of judicial demeanour and displays of emotion (e.g. Roach Anleu and Mack 2005), the use of pre-sentence reports and associated processes to facilitate and maintain 'closed' guilty pleas (Tata 2010), and the deliberate use of adjournments by judicial officers to aid the facilitation of earlier guilty pleas (Roach Anleu and Mack 2009).

Recent changes to legal aid and sentencing discount law and policy have sought to add to these dynamics and so achieve a further 'rebalancing' in favour of efficiency values. While it seems that the summary courts in particular have long relied on a high rate of guilty pleas, what is new is that both legal aid and sentencing policy are now much more overt in seeking to encourage guilty pleas (wherever 'appropriate') and as quickly as possible. Where Scottish sentence discounting law and legal aid policy were previously features which could be drawn on to support adversarial due process values in both policy and practice, they now appear to be relatively supportive of efficiency values. Nonetheless, these law and policy changes do not appear simply to be implemented on the ground in a straightforward way, but rather mesh with existing practices which may contradict efficiency goals. Is this more explicit drive towards 'efficiency' also found in other parts of the sentencing process? For instance, are pre-sentence reports now more about risk-categorisation than about the individual person being sentenced?

From welfare to risk? Case study: pre-sentence reports

The prominent role of social work in criminal justice in Scotland is said to have been one of the key reasons for Scotland's distinctive maintenance of penal welfarism at least before devolution (McAra 2005; see also Chapter 11, this volume). Pre-Sentence Reports are intended to inform, advise and assist the sentencing process. In Scotland such reports are known as Social Enquiry Reports (SERs). They place the convicted person in a broader context so that the judicial sentencer can be aware of the person's physical and mental condition, character, attitude to the offence and offending behaviour and assess the suitability of non-custodial sentences. Reports are compiled on the basis of at least one interview with the person and sometimes on the basis of enquiries to other agencies (for instance to check facts) and home visits.

Rather than being written by members of a national probation service (as in England and Wales) or by the employees of the sentencing court (as in the USA), in Scotland reports are compiled by generically trained social workers specialising in criminal justice and employed by local authorities. This may be significant in three respects. First, the fact that criminal justice social workers (CJSWs) are generically trained professional social workers may reflect and reinforce Scotland's relative commitment to penal welfare values.

Secondly, the fact that CJSWs are not the direct employees of central government may mean that they are more able to resist the latest media-fuelled whims of government policy. Thirdly, the fact that CJSWs are not employed by the courts can bring a penal-welfare perspective to the sentencing process which is different (though potentially complementary) to law's tendency to view offending as little more than individual rational choice. This difference can be a healthy thing. Welfare values explain offending by rooting it in the person's personal and social circumstances and also in the relationships with family members. In this way, SERs can, where relevant, contextualise the individual's offending within social conditions and serious social disadvantages, thus linking social and legal conceptions of justice together. This should not be the same thing as a 'sob story', but enables the sentencer to be aware of the impact of any sentencing decision not only on the individual, but also on their nearest and dearest, including children.

Are these qualities of penal-welfarism being diminished by policy changes? Partly in an attempt to enhance the quality and consistency of report writing, National Standards for criminal justice social work were introduced from 1991 (see Chapter 11). These require a greater focus not only on the person but also their offending behaviour and risk to the public. Thus has the job of CJSWs become more one of control than of welfare – more about deeds than needs? Interestingly, a major reason for the introduction of National Standards was to try to encourage the more sparing use of custody by judicial sentencers. The thinking of successive governments has been that if sentencers are better informed about both the person before them and the potential of non-custodial sentences to reduce reoffending they would be more likely to think twice about a custodial sentence for someone who is not a danger to the public (Tata *et al.* 2008; McNeill and Whyte 2007). Thus the strategy of successive governments has been to avoid seeking to develop an explicit sentencing policy (since that would be seen as 'interference' by the judiciary), but rather to try to make both reports and non-custodial sentences more credible in the eyes of judicial sentencers. National Standards have tried to make reports 'better' by making them seem tougher and more offence/risk focused and by downplaying welfare narratives. What has been the result?

A major research study was conducted over four years to assess the ways in which reports are written and how those same reports are then interpreted and used by sheriff court judges (McNeill *et al.* 2009; Tata *et al.* 2008). The research[4] focused on summary court 'cusp' cases – those cases which are 'in the balance' between a custodial and a non-custodial sentence, which are exactly the types of cases with which the policy is particularly concerned.

Through a range of techniques the intention of what report writers attempted to convey to the judicial sentencer was elicited and then *compared with* how judges (and others) read, interpreted and used those same reports (Tata *et al.* 2008). Is government strategy of influence through advice and information working? Are report writers now concerned with risk assessment rather than welfarist values?

The research found:

- SERs are central to the sentencing process in 'cusp' cases. Given pressures on the summary courts, where a person pleads guilty and so there is no trial, reports are commonly seen by lawyers and judges as the main voice of the accused person.
- SERs are written in a form of code because report writers are expected both to provide an assessment and evaluation and yet not to be explicitly judgmental. SERs have to be 'relevant' to sentencing, but at the same time they must not appear to be 'directive'. SERs are expected to be the main policy vehicle for the promotion of non-custodial sentences and yet they cannot do so explicitly. The result is that key messages in SERs are encoded. Often this works (i.e. the sentencing judge understands the code) but equally often the message is either skipped or interpreted very differently from that intended.
- CJSWs tend to reframe welfare values through the language of 'risk' and 'public protection'. Moreover, CJSWs (and especially judicial sentencers) are unconcerned by actuarial risk assessment instruments. Even though both CJSWs and judges complained about risk assessment instruments (see also Tombs 2008), when it came to dealing with actual cases in practice both professional groups were resistant to such instruments.
- Although judicial sentencers greatly valued the presence of personal and social circumstance information so as to contextualise and humanise the person, in practice most (but not all) sentencing judges tended to skip-read that information and tended instead to focus on the end sections about the offence and the individual's 'attitude to offence and offending'. This approach to reading reports has two effects. First, it undermines the requirement that the report builds up a narrative assessment – thus, for example,

reports were sometimes criticised by sentencers because the conclusion lacked 'logic'. Secondly, it means that narratives about serious disadvantage are marginalised.

- A frequent criticism made by judicial sentencers of reports is that they are not sufficiently 'realistic' about sentencing and that this damages their credibility. However, from the perspective of CJSWs it can sometimes be very difficult to know what is 'realistically' on the sentencing agenda. Even in the same courthouse, different sentencing judges can take quite different approaches to what is 'realistic'. The problem for CJSWs is that they often do not know which judge will read the SER. In any event, there is also the issue of the ethics of altering the SER for a particular sentencer.

Thus in Scottish report-writing 'old' narratives of penal-welfare appear to mesh together with 'new' narratives of risk. Furthermore, the risk discourse appears to have limited direct impact on sentencing decision-making and the policy of trying to encourage sentencers to use custody more sparingly through the provision of 'better' quality reports is undermined by the fact that what judicial sentencers want from reports varies. Thus report 'quality', as defined by judicial sentencers, is something of a moving target (Tata *et al.* 2008). Thus, while there has been clear evidence of a shift in law and policy away from welfare and towards actuarial risk-assessment, an examination of practices in actual cases suggests a more complex and 'hybridised' picture (McNeill *et al.* 2009).

Sentencing reform and the slow death of judicial discretion? Case study: the sentencing information system

Is sentencing discretion being diminished by a move towards managerial control and the rise of technocratic instruments? Some leading commentators have argued that Scotland exemplifies an international trend in which techno-rational instruments are taking over the traditional humanistic values of judicial sentencing (Franko Aas 2005; Tombs 2008).

In her widely discussed account of sentencing and the global rise of actuarial-style justice, Katja Franko Aas identifies a marked diminution of judicial discretion. Judges are, she says, losing status and control. Where once judicial sentencers were concerned with unique individuals they are increasingly being compelled to base their judgments on actuarial logic. One of the most important forces driving this change is the rise of information technology and its logics of abstraction, remoteness and standardisation. All of this is leading, Franko Aas argues, towards a radically reduced and one-dimensional conception of justice about which we should be deeply concerned. In making this case, she frequently cites the introduction of a 'Sentencing Information System' (SIS) in Scotland as one of two main sources of evidence (the other being US federal guidelines), showing a fundamental shift not only in the discourse around sentencing policy but in sentencing practice itself. So let us briefly examine the history of the SIS (Miller 2004; Tata and Hutton 2003).

As seen above, unlike other western countries, sentencing in Scotland has, until recent years, been marked by an absence of any concerted attempts at reform and the use of the SERs outlined previously has been the main way in which successive governments have sought indirectly to influence the use of custody by judicial sentencers. There have been few attempts to introduce greater 'structure' and 'accountability' of the kind seen, for example, in England and Wales (e.g. Ashworth 2005, 2008). This might be taken to mean that Scottish sentencing and the Scottish judiciary enjoy higher levels of public confidence than comparable countries. In fact, that is not the case. As in other countries, research into public opinion and attitudes to sentencing shows similarly high levels of public cynicism about sentencing and justice. However, in Scotland as elsewhere this is at least in large part due to a lack of knowledge about normal practices (Anderson *et al.* 2002; Hutton 2005). So why has Scotland not experienced the kinds of fairly significant reforms to sentencing structures as other countries like England and Wales, the USA, Canada, South Africa, Australia? Space constraints limit us to examining just one initiative spanning the 1990s and early 2000s – a period when sentencing reforms developed apace elsewhere.

In the early 1990s, the Conservative Secretary of State for Scotland, Michael Forsyth, wanted to introduce mandatory minimum custodial sentences for certain types of cases (so-called 'three strikes' legislation). The most senior judges at that time, concerned about such a move (or similar) developments which they believed would unduly restrict judicial discretion, responded with their own initiative: a Sentencing Information System (SIS) for the High Court. The idea was to harness database technology as a way of helping judges to pursue consistency[5] in sentencing. Crucially, however, the SIS would be created by judges for judges: it was a way of helping the judiciary to regulate itself and be seen to being doing so. It was not something which would be imposed on judges by outsiders. Unlike US Federal Guidelines, the SIS was never intended to be directive, but to help to inform the judges' decision-making process. In the spectrum of methods of sentencing reform, the Scottish SIS was to be 'light touch'.

In 1993 the senior judiciary approached academics at Strathclyde University Law School for help and it was agreed to establish a feasibility study and to develop a prototype. Taking such a proactive initiative is unusual for the (Scottish) judiciary. It was prominently and favourably reported in the media, and the government, which funded the project, was content to allow the judiciary to take a lead. The SIS initiative was also often cited in response to calls to restrict judicial discretion. The SIS was partly a way of heading-off political pressure to 'do something' to restrict sentencing discretion.

Implementation of the SIS was phased-in during the 1990s and handed over to the Scottish Court Service (SCS) (which serves the courts and the judiciary) in 2003. At that time the SIS contained relatively in-depth information about 15,000 sentenced cases (including appeals) over the previous 15 years with information collected in a way agreed with the judiciary. The SIS is searchable in a way which affords the user a high degree of flexibility so that patterns of case similarity can be defined in a range of different ways (including both in aggregate terms and by examining individual cases). In other words, the SIS does not attempt to direct the judge to 'the correct' sentence, but rather offers a range of possible sentences. It was decided that, with the handover to the SCS, court clerks would take over recording of information. In the event, it became quickly apparent that the quality assurance processes recommended by the university team were not followed by the SCS and the entry of data after 2003 appears not to have been reliable. Foreseeably, the SIS appears to have been left to quietly wither away. Why?

Probably the most important reason was that immediate political pressure on the judiciary dissipated – the SIS had fulfilled a tactical role to see-off political pressure. In contrast to south of the border, in Scotland immediately after devolution, judicial sentencing discretion was not on the agenda. During that time and due to changes of personnel at the apex of the judiciary, High Court judicial enthusiasm for the SIS began to cool, and as a result progress to full implementation slowed. Although the Sheriffs Association (which represents intermediate court judges) suggested to the Scottish Parliament that it would be useful for sheriffs to have something similar (Scottish Parliament Justice 1 Committee 2003) (as did the later Review of Summary Justice 2005), it was clear that the senior judiciary of the High Court were now not so keen as their predecessors.

The key underlying issue, which was never properly resolved, was who could have access to the SIS. The university team recommended public access, proposing that if managed in the appropriate way such access need not be a threat to the judiciary but an opportunity to improve public understanding of sentencing. For example, the SIS data could produce occasional reports about the true patterns of sentencing for different kinds of cases (Tata and Hutton 2003). However, nervous about access beyond the judiciary, coupled with an awareness that it would be difficult in the long term to continue to deny access, the simplest thing (given that political pressure had dissipated) would be to hope the whole thing could quietly be forgotten. That is what largely happened during the mid-2000s. But by the end of the decade, the new minority Scottish National Party (SNP) Government managed to pass the Criminal Justice and Licensing Bill which creates a presumption against custodial sentences of three months or less, and builds on the work of the earlier judicially led Sentencing Commission by creating a Sentencing Council which would have the power to develop sentencing guidelines. Meanwhile, the Scottish Labour and the Conservative parties have gone further and committed themselves to an explicit policy of mandatory minimum sentences for certain offences (notably knife-carrying). All these proposals have been strongly opposed by representations from the judiciary. One of the arguments against such 'interference' is that there is currently a dearth of systematic sentencing information available, including about the extent of any inconsistency. Thus, it is hard to escape the sense that we may, to some extent, be witnessing a cycle of history repeating itself.

So rather than being a technocratic instrument signalling the loss of judicial status and power, the story of the Scottish SIS signifies the opposite. It shows the ability of the Scottish judiciary, at least so far, to head-off, at least temporarily, the threat of 'interference'.

Concluding comments

This chapter has sought to examine the extent to which Scottish sentencing is being swept along with the tide of broader worldwide changes, by exploring three key areas. First, there have been attempts by successive governments (both before and after devolution) to achieve greater efficiency by explicitly encouraging guilty pleas where 'appropriate', and a softening of the law and policy emphasis on the presumption of innocence. However, these attempts have met with mixed success on the ground. Secondly, we have asked whether Scottish sentencing is losing its distinctive emphasis on penal welfarism. Although headline policy has sought to achieve greater emphasis on 'risk' at the expense of 'welfare', evidence of a dramatic shift in pre-sentence reports is limited. This is not least because both CJSWs and judicial sentencers are somewhat suspicious of risk instruments and also because 'risk' is often invoked by CJSWs in defence of welfare narratives. Thirdly, the Scottish SIS does not exemplify the loss of judicial discretion and status. Far from it: the SIS was not imposed on judges but initiated and created by the senior judiciary to head-off perceived political interference, and then quietly neglected when that threat was believed to have receded.

Does this mean that Scotland is retaining its distinctiveness and not moving towards the global? In headline policy terms we can find instances of convergence (e.g. the increasing emphasis in policy on risk-assessment instruments and a new Risk Management Authority, national standards for CJSWs, the attempt to speed up guilty pleas, a renewed interest in sentencing reform). So there is evidence of some policy convergence. But evidence of actual practices on the ground is much thinner and more complex. That is not to say that policy talk does not matter (it does), but that actual practices should be expected to differ, adapt or resist official changes. As elsewhere, in-depth study of actual practices reveals that there tends to be a difference between official discourse and the reality of practice on the ground (for example, Cheliotis 2006; McNeill *et al.* 2009; Tata 2007b). So there may be some globalisation of policy discourse, but we should not then imagine any simple trickle-down effect. This is more than saying that there is a big picture of globalisation with some little local variations. To build up 'the big picture' we also have to know what is happening on the ground rather than assume that 'top-down' change is inevitable (McAra 2005; Tata 2007b).

Notes

1 In this context, 'humanistic penal values' include: treating people not as inert categories to be processed, but as unique individual human beings; humane treatment; the avoidance of unnecessary punishment; human (rather than mechanical) forms of decision-making based on both rational and emotional sensibilities; judgment based on wisdom rather than a

strict or bureaucratic adherence to rules, policies or systems for their own sake; and, most importantly, treating people with respect as whole human beings of intrinsic value rather than as a means to an end.

2 Here the concepts of 'due process' and 'efficiency' are loosely borrowed from Packer (1964) which provides a simple way of starting to think about these issues.

3 Briefly put, an 'adversarial' system is based on the idea that truth emerges through a contest between two parties each battling to put their side of the story.

4 ESRC Award No. RB000239939.

5 In this context, 'consistency' means treating similar cases similarly and dissimilar cases dissimilarly. Importantly, 'consistency' does not mean 'uniformity', i.e. treating all cases the same way regardless of their differences. Consistency is a matter of equality before the law. Simply put, the sentence should not depend on which judge you happen to get.

References

Anderson, S., Ingram, D. and Hutton, N. (2002) *Public Attitudes Towards Sentencing and Alternatives to Imprisonment*, Scottish Parliament Paper 488. Edinburgh: HMSO.

Ashworth, A. (2005) *Sentencing and Criminal Justice*. Cambridge: Cambridge University Press.

Ashworth, A. (2008) 'English sentencing guidelines in the public and political context', in A. Freiberg and K. Gelb (eds), *Penal Populism, Sentencing Councils and Sentencing Policy*. Leichhardt: Hawkins Press.

Bottomley, S. and Bronnit, S. (2006) *Law in Context*, 3rd edn. Annandale, NSW: Federation Press.

Cheliotis, L. (2006) 'How iron is the iron cage of the new penology?', *Punishment and Society*, 8 (3): 313–40.

Croall, H. (2006) 'Criminal justice in post-devolutionary Scotland', *Critical Social Policy*, 26(3): 587–607.

Eisenstein, J. and Jacob, H. (1991) *Felony Justice: An Organisational Analysis of Criminal Courts*. Boston: Little, Brown.

Feeley, M. and Simon, J. (1994) 'Actuarial justice', in D. Nelken (ed.), *The Futures of Criminology*. London: Sage.

Franko Aas, K. (2005) *Sentencing in the Age of Information*. London: Glasshouse.

Garland, D. (2001) *The Culture of Control*. Oxford: Oxford University Press.

Gelsthorpe, L. and Padfield, N. (2003) 'Introduction', in L. Gelsthorpe and N. Padfield (eds), *Exercising Discretion*. Cullompton: Willan Publishing.

Goriely, T., Duff, P., Henry, A., Knapp, M., McCrone, P. and Tata, C. (2001) *The Public Defence Solicitors Office in Edinburgh: An Independent Evaluation*. Scottish Executive Central Research Unit/TSO.

Hutton, N. (2005) 'Beyond populist punitiveness?', *Punishment and Society*, 7 (3): 243–58.

Hutton, N. (2006) 'Sentencing as a social practice', in S. Armstrong and L. McAra (eds), *Perspectives on Punishment*. Oxford: Oxford University Press, pp. 155–74

Leverick, F. (2004) 'Tensions and balances, costs and rewards: the sentence discount in Scotland', *Edinburgh Law Review*, 8 (3): 360–88.

McAra, L. (2005) 'Modelling penal transformation', *Punishment and Society*, 7 (3): 277–302.

McAra, L. (2008) 'Crime, criminology and criminal justice in Scotland', *European Journal of Criminology*, 5 (4): 481–504

McBarnet, D. (1981) *Conviction*. London: Macmillan.

McConville, M., Hodgson, J., Bridges, L. and Pavlovic, A. (1994) *Standing Accused*. Oxford: Clarendon Press.

McNeill, F. and Whyte, B. (2007) *Reducing Reoffending*. Cullompton: Willan Publishing.

McNeill, F., Burns, N., Halliday, S., Hutton, N. and Tata, C. (2009) 'Risk, responsibility, and reconfiguration', *Punishment and Society*, 11 (4): 419–42.

Miller, M. (2004) 'A map of sentencing and a compass for judges: sentencing information systems, transparency, and the next generation of reform', *Columbia Law Review*, 105 (online).

Moody, S. and Tombs, J. (1982) *Prosecution in the Public Interest*. Edinburgh: Scottish Academic Press.

Mulcahy, A. (1994) 'The justifications of "justice": legal practitioners' accounts of negotiated settlements in magistrates courts', *British Journal of Criminology*, 34 (4): 411–30.

Packer, H. (1964) 'Two models of the criminal process', *University of Pennsylvania Law Review*, 113 (1): 1–68.

Roach Anleu, S. (2010) *Law and Social Change*, 2nd edn. London: Sage.

Roach Anleu, S. and Mack, K. (2009) 'Intersections between in-court procedures and the production of guilty pleas', *Australian and New Zealand Journal of Criminology*, 42(1): 1–23.

Sanders, A. and Young, R. (2007) *Criminal Justice*. Oxford: Oxford University Press.

Scottish Government (2008) *Costs and Equalities and the Scottish Criminal Justice System*. Edinburgh: Scottish Government.

Scottish Parliament Justice 1 Committee (2003) Official Report: 18 February 2003, Meeting Number 4.

Summary Justice Review Committee (2004) *Report to Ministers*. Edinburgh: Scottish Executive.

Tata, C. (2007a) 'In the interests of commerce or clients? Legal aid, supply, demand, and ethical indeterminacy in criminal defence work', *Journal of Law and Society*, 34 (4): 489–519.

Tata, C. (2007b) 'Sentencing as craftwork', *Social and Legal Studies*, 16 (3): 425–7.

Tata, C. (2010) 'A sense of justice: the role of pre-sentence reports in the production (and disruption) of guilty pleas', *Punishment and Society*, 12 (3): in press.

Tata, C. and Hutton, N. (2003) 'Beyond the technology of quick fixes', *Federal Sentencing Reporter*, 16: 67–75.

Tata, C. and Stephen, F. (2006) '"Swings and roundabouts": do changes to the structure of legal aid make a real difference to criminal case outcomes?', *Criminal Law Review*, 46: 722–41.

Tata, C., Halliday, S., Hutton, N. and McNeill, F. (2008) 'Advising and assisting the sentencing decision process', *British Journal of Criminology*, 48: 835–55.

Tombs, J. (2008) 'Telling sentencing stories', in P. Carlen (ed.), *Imaginary Penalities*. Cullompton: Willan Publishing, pp. 84–1.

Chapter 11

Fines, community sanctions and measures in Scotland

Mary Munro and Fergus McNeill

Introduction

There is a notion, widespread in Scotland, that equates justice and punishment solely with the imprisonment of offenders. In this chapter we want to show that, despite Scotland's exceptionally high rates of custody (see Chapter 12), most offenders are dealt with in the 'community' by monetary penalties and orders administered by social workers. The current political programme to market and design community penalties as 'payback' in contrast with short prison sentences will be considered against the backdrop of developments in the governance of community justice. The chapter starts by considering monetary penalties in Scotland, fines both imposed by courts and, of increasing importance, other enforcement agencies. The remainder of the chapter reviews 'community sanctions and measures', that is a range of orders which

> maintain the offender in the community and involve some restriction of his liberty through the imposition of conditions and/or obligations, and which are implemented by bodies designated in law for that purpose. The term designates any sanction imposed by a court or a judge, and any measure taken before or instead of a decision on a sanction as well as ways of enforcing a sentence of imprisonment outside a prison establishment. (Council of Europe 1992: Appendix para. 1)

The discussion is in two parts: first, the background to and current developments in community sanctions administered by local authority criminal justice social workers; secondly, a short review of the supervision and resettlement of prisoners following release.

Integrated across the chapter is a critical questioning of the themes of the collection: first, the claim that a welfarist ethos, resistant to elements of managerialism especially in criminal justice social work practices, survives to a greater degree in Scotland than elsewhere in the UK; second, the impact and significance of inequalities in the imposition and experience of community penalties. Although there has been no study comparable to Houchin's work on prisoners (see Chapters 3 and 12) in relation to the social origins of people undergoing community sanctions, it is likely that a similar correlation with social disadvantage would be evident (Houchin 2005; McNeill and Whyte 2007).

Monetary penalties in Scotland: fairness and justice

The fine tends to be used by courts and prosecutors for less serious crimes where social work involvement or custody is not seen as appropriate, although in Scotland there is almost no legislative bar on the kind of crime for which a fine may be imposed. Nonetheless monetary penalties (both fines and a much smaller number of compensation orders) have declined markedly from a peak of over 80 per cent of court sentences imposed in Scotland in the 1980s to 59 per cent in 2008–9. Over the same period the proportion of custodial sentences has increased from around 7 per cent to 13 per cent and community supervision sentences (probation, community service and other orders) from under 3 per cent to 14 per cent (Scottish Office 1995: Scottish Government 2010a). This shift in the profile of sentencing took place as the numbers of charges dealt with by the courts fell by around a third from 1984 to the present, reflecting falls in police recorded crime, an increased use of diversionary penalties (including fines imposed by Fiscals), and the wider availability and use of community sanctions as alternatives to fines. There is also evidence of a falling away of judicial confidence in the effective enforcement and repayment of fines over this period (McInnes Committee 2004).

The proportionate decline in the use of the fine as a main penalty by courts obscures the rise of monetary penalties as a direct sanction imposed by not only criminal justice agencies such as the police and Procurators Fiscal, but also other 'civilian' bodies such as parking wardens and local authority community enforcement officers (Chapter 9; also O'Malley 2009). Introduced in 1983 as an alternative to summary prosecution for motoring offences, fixed penalty notices (FPNs or 'on-the-spot' fines) have been extended most recently by the Antisocial Behaviour Act 2004 (for nuisance offences such as breach of the peace, urinating in the street and drinking alcohol in public) and the Smoking, Health and Social Care Act (Scotland) 2005 for criminal offences relating to smoking in public places. Some idea of the significance of these orders as a commonly imposed penalty is indicated by the 34 per cent drop in referrals for the relevant offences to the Fiscal in the two years from the start of the national roll-out of police-administered FPNs in April 2007 and the increase in FPNs imposed (especially within the Strathclyde Police area) from 11,013 in 2007 to 56,854 in 2009 (Cavanagh 2009; Scottish Parliament written answer S3W-31587).

From 1988 Procurators Fiscal have been able to offer an accused a conditional offer of a 'fiscal fine' as an alternative to prosecution for any offence that might be prosecuted in the district court (then the lowest tier of criminal courts). Fiscals' discretionary powers of sentencing as diversion from the criminal process were further extended, somewhat controversially, in March 2008 as part of the radical reform of summary justice enacted by the Criminal Justice (Scotland) Act 2007. The upper limit of the fines offer rose to £300 and a new power to make a compensation order offer of up to £5,000 was introduced. There is continuing press and Parliamentary disquiet about the prospect of offenders escaping prosecution by the offer of 'slap on the wrist' fines, despite an early review which suggested that decisions had been largely 'appropriate and proportionate' (Inspectorate of Prosecutions 2009). Detailed guidance to Fiscals on the decision to impose a fine is not published. However, it seems that diversion is less likely where there seems to be an emerging pattern of repeat offending and there are doubts about ability to pay. This may result in a skew in favour of diversion for the more affluent, less persistent accused. However, a recent addition to Fiscals' diversionary options is the fiscal work order, currently being piloted in four court areas, whereby a prosecutor may impose between 10 and 50 hours unpaid work on offenders who do not appear to have the means to pay a fiscal fine (Scottish Government 2008). This is a significant deprivation of liberty and as such raises questions about the extent to which pragmatism and the search for efficiency seem to be displacing questions of justice and due process (see also Chapter 10). What can be said is that these non-court 'sentences' (for that is how they will be experienced) need to be taken into account when taking an overview of Scottish penality.

The problem of fines and inequality, that is the injustice that arises from imposing fines that do not reflect differences in ability to pay, has long been recognised (Beccaria 1764; Rusche and Kirchheimer 1939). The Enlightenment Glasgow philosopher Frances Hutcheson noted that 'the sum which is severe upon the poor may be a trifle to the wealthy' (Hutcheson 1755: 336). Again in 1912 James Devon, medical officer at Glasgow Prison, noted:

> Fines fall very unequally as a burden on those subjected to them. The amount inflicted, though small, may be out of all proportion to the offender's means; half a crown is not much, but it is a great deal to the man who has not got it ... There is not one law for the rich, and another for the poor [...] but in its effect it favours the rich at the expense of the poor, and that is not to the ultimate advantage of the community. (Devon 1912: 177)

Young (1989) found that, when deciding the amount to fine, sheriffs prioritised the importance of offence-related rather than offender-related criteria in a classical jurisprudence in which retributive punishment is the primary goal. It is important to stress that there is as yet no formal guidance on setting fines in Scotland and that there has been considerable resistance to the notion that sentencers' discretionary powers to treat each case 'on its own merits' should be compromised (Sentencing Commission 2006; Tombs 2004; and see also Chapter 10, this volume). Although an accused's means should be taken into account as far as they are known to the court,[1] Young found that sheriffs calculate the fine level in terms of offence seriousness and prior record before thinking about means, while being aware of a 'going rate' for an offence in their local area (Young 1989). There is also evidence of some lay justices using the fiscal fine maximum as a starting point for setting court fines (Munro 1999). Although it seems that most (but not all) sentencers do broadly discriminate between offenders with different incomes, they do not do so consistently or by setting fines at a level that is proportionate to actual differences in means (Munro 1999; Nicholson 1994; Scottish Sentencing Commission 2006). Consequently not only may people in poverty be over-fined, the more affluent accused may be under-fined. Moreover, there remains no systematic or verifiable collection of means information to inform fines setting when the matter is first dealt with in court (McInnes 2004; Scottish Sentencing Commission 2006).

Reforms have neglected to address the primary issue of fine setting and have focused instead on enforcement[2] and pragmatic alternatives to custody for default. For example, unit or day fines are an internationally accepted approach to setting fines that allows sentencers to disentangle judgments about offence seriousness from the ability of an offender to pay.[3] In 1990 Scotland's opportunity to be the first UK jurisdiction with a functioning unit fine system was lost when a clause in the Law Reform (Miscellaneous Provisions) Scotland Bill relating fines to an 'offender's disposable income rather than a specified sum of money'[4] was abandoned because of pressure on Westminster Parliamentary time. Supervised attendance orders (SAOs) were devised as a last-minute 'back of the envelope' civil service innovation to tackle the problem of fine default imprisonment, in order to smooth the passage of the overdue Bill[5] (McIvor and Williams 1999; Munro 1999; Scottish Sentencing Commission 2006; see also Cavadino and Dignan 2007, for an account of unit fines in England and Wales; Glover 2008, on agency and poverty).

SAOs punish by imposing a 'fine on time' requiring attendance at a place of supervision for between 10 and 60 hours (later extended to 100 hours) to take part in constructive activities with the objective of 'encouraging personal and social responsibility and self-respect' (Scottish Executive 1992). This explicitly disciplinary disposal, unique to Scotland, remains the main vehicle of judicial response to fine default. Despite an inconclusive evaluation of the early pilots (Brown 1994), SAOs were made available to all courts by the late 1990s. The evidence suggests that the introduction of mandatory SAOs instead of custody on default on sums below £500 from 2007 has been effective. The proportion of annual receptions to prison for fine default has dropped from 42 per cent in 1998/9 to just under 4 per cent in 2008/9 and the actual number of people going to prison for fine default has decreased from over 10,000 in 1997 to 1,506 in 2008/9. The average daily population of fine defaulters in prison has also declined from around 75 to 11 (Scottish Government 2009a).

SAOs were also envisaged from the outset as a potential alternative court sentence for people too poor to pay a fine. In 1995 adult summary courts in Dundee trialled the use of SAOs for 16- and

17-year-olds whom the court considered would be unable to pay (many of whom would still be in education, training or on a very low income).[6] Levy and McIvor (2001) found that sentencers became 'rapidly disillusioned' because of the limited options available on breach and the pilot was both practically and formally abandoned. In 2006–7 there were renewed trials of the SAO as a sentence at first instance for those, who on verbal inquiry as to means, were considered to be in the 'direst circumstances'. The subsequent, largely positive, evaluation noted that offenders sentenced to SAOs 'were drawn from a population likely to face income poverty, as well as issues with debt' and who had chaotic lives (Scottish Executive 2007: iii).

The Summary Justice Review Committee (McInnes 2004) recognised the importance of 'targeting fines more precisely on the basis of better information about means' (p. 240) and recommended a radical review of fine setting (p. 247) including unit fines (McInnes 2004). The subsequent report of the short lived Sentencing Commission for Scotland accepted the equitable merits of the unit fine approach but concluded that the lack of a 'suitable, cost-effective mechanism by which reliable information on all offenders' means might be obtained' precluded its introduction at that point (Scottish Sentencing Commission 2006: para. 7.26). Instead, the Commission supported the use of SAOs as a sentence where there was evidence of very low income. A further objection was that because FPNs and fiscal fines were imposed without consideration of means it was difficult to see how this would be compatible, in a 'coherent system of financial penalties', with unit fines that do (Scottish Sentencing Commission 2006: para. 7.23).

There is an important distinction in principle between money punishments, which involve the deprivation of property, and all other punishments, including community sanctions, which impact in some way on personal freedom and involve the deprivation of liberty (Devon 1912; Young 1999). It may be argued that in Scotland there is an emerging parallel system of low-end justice for people in poverty in the use of the SAO as a sentence, community sanctions and, perhaps to come, fiscal work orders as alternatives to court-imposed or diversionary fines. The effect of this patchwork pragmatism is a bifurcation of the impact and experience of punishment as between those accused who can afford to pay up and thereby maintain their autonomy and distance from the justice system and those in poverty who cannot.

Community sanctions and criminal justice social work

Historical background

Until 1963, when payment of fines by instalments was first made routine in Scotland, offenders unable to pay were subject to immediate imprisonment as the 'alternative', often for very short periods and in considerable numbers. For example, in 1904, 16,000 people were committed to prison for this reason from Glasgow courts alone. The 'wholesale resort' to the imprisonment of the Glasgow poor, both men and women, was the impetus behind the Glasgow Corporation decision in 1905 to appoint ex-police officers as probation officers to make recommendations to 'Magistrates in regard to the infliction and payment of fines, and conditional liberation' (Murray 1906: 54). This pilot scheme drew not on English experiences but on earlier probation initiatives in Massachusetts and, closer to home, in Dundee (McNeill 2005; McNeill and Whyte 2007).

The Probation of Offenders (Scotland) Act 1931 signalled both the intention to make probation available nationally and, to some extent, a paradigmatic shift from police-based supervision towards the emerging notion of 'treatment' through social casework. Perhaps because of this changing approach to practice, one of the provisions of the 1931 Act expressly prohibited the appointment of serving or former police officers as probation staff. As well as creating the first comprehensive set of local services by establishing probation committees in each local authority, the 1931 Act established a Central Probation Council to advise the Secretary of State.

Despite developing professionalisation, between 1931 and 1968 the Scottish probation services struggled to establish themselves as providers of credible alternatives to imprisonment (and other sanctions) for adult offenders, though they had greater success in establishing their work with juveniles (McNeill 2005). The Criminal Justice (Scotland) Act 1949 gave the courts new powers to make wider use of probation with adults but the reluctance to use probation as a disposal for adult offenders was an enduring problem in Scotland.

When organisational change did arrive, it was the result of the Kilbrandon Report (1964) and the Social Work (Scotland) Act 1968 which created both generic local authority social work departments and the Children's Hearings system (see Chapter 4). Aside from the development of a more explicitly welfarist ideology, there were two key pragmatic reasons why probation services were subsumed within generic social work departments at this point. Firstly, probation officers were among the best trained social workers at that time and were therefore needed in the new departments. Secondly, the low numbers of adults on probation meant that separate probation services would have been unsustainable in some areas once juveniles became the responsibility of the new social work departments. This was despite considerable expansion in the 1960s and the advent of new responsibilities for fines supervision in 1964, for the aftercare of prisoners in 1965 (following the Criminal Justice Act 1963) and for parole supervision in 1968 (see below).

Most commentators agree that the 1970s and 1980s represent a period of comparative neglect for probation in Scotland (see McIvor and Williams 1999; McNeill and Whyte 2007). Although community service emerged as a credible disposal during this time (introduced in Scotland in 1979, seven years later than in England and Wales), the numbers of probation orders declined and, much to the consternation of some sheriffs, criminal justice work became a low priority in many social work departments struggling to cope with ever-expanding child care and protection work. It was to correct this neglect and to address a penal crisis resulting from overcrowding in Scottish prisons (see Chapter 12) that the Scottish Office introduced 100 per cent ring-fenced central funding for most criminal justice social work services in 1991 so that the criminal justice social work budget did not, for the first time since the Kilbrandon reforms, have to compete with other calls on social work resources. The first National Objectives and Standards (NOS) were issued at this time (Social Work Services Group 1991a).

National Standards focused on reducing the unnecessary use of custody by promoting community disposals in general and direct alternatives to custody in particular. Restoring credibility was clearly linked to developing approaches to supervision that were perceived to be effective in reducing reoffending. Indeed, practice guidance succinctly outlined the then state of knowledge about 'what works' (Social Work Services Group 1991b), signalling a shift towards a 'responsibility model' (Paterson and Tombs 1998) which recognised that offenders should be held accountable for their choices, albeit that these choices should be understood within their social context. In most local authorities, new specialist teams and new management structures were created to drive forward the reforms and the (re-)development of practice. However, in Scotland, alongside this focus on effective practice to 'responsibilise' offenders and reduce reoffending, the welfare tradition proved durable, and was progressively recast, in policy terms, in an ongoing concern to improve the social inclusion of offenders, as well as in an enduring commitment to penal reductionism (McIvor and McNeill 2007b; McNeill and Whyte 2007). In some important respects, this enduring welfarism, expressed in the professional values and commitments of many criminal justice practitioners and buttressed by the influence of civil servants in the then Scottish Office, may have insulated Scotland against the development of the 'punishment in the community' model then developing in England and Wales (Robinson and McNeill 2004). This model recast probation and community service as proportionate punishments rather than, in the Scottish model, as alternatives to punishment (Moore and Whyte 1998).

By the late 1990s, research was beginning to suggest that although the 100 per cent funding initiative had driven up standards and, with them, the use made of probation and community service (see Figure 11.1), this had had no discernible impact on the rate of imprisonment in Scotland (Paterson and Tombs 1998). If probation had started the century as an alternative to imprisonment for fine default, the evidence suggested that, for all the investment and development, it also ended the century as an alternative to fines (see above). As Figure 11.1 shows, there are now about 20,000 orders for various forms of community sanctions made per annum, but the Scottish prison population continues to rise, seemingly inexorably (see Scottish Prisons Commission 2008, and Chapter 12, this volume). At the same time, just as in England and Wales, the emphasis in policy, reflected in revisions to the NOS (Social Work Services Group

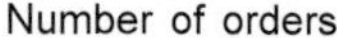

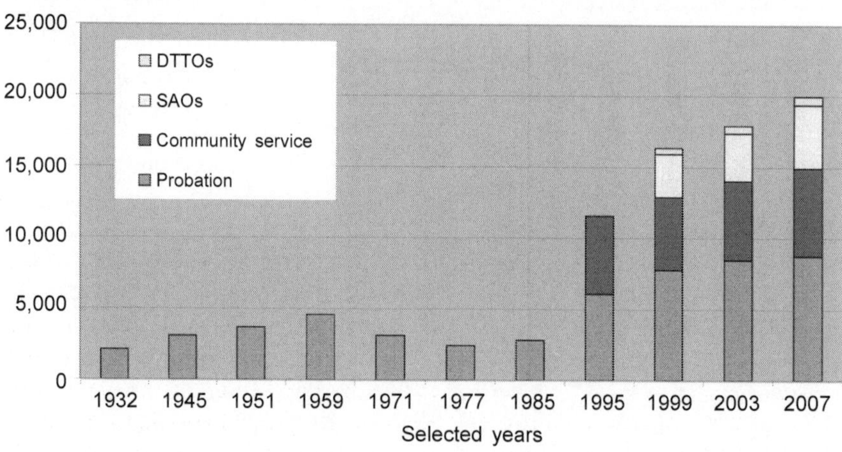

Figure 11.1 Use of community sanctions in Scotland (selected years)

1996; Scottish Executive 2000) was shifting towards risk, public protection and reducing reoffending rather than reducing the use of imprisonment. This was reflected most clearly in a Scottish Office (1998) consultation paper – *The Tough Option* – which was concerned mainly with the reorganisation of services and eventually led, in 2002, for both strategic and organisational reasons to the establishment of 11 'groupings' of local authorities (Robinson and McNeill 2004).

Attempts to develop evidence-based practice resulted in the introduction of advanced professional qualifications in criminal justice social work (1993), the Getting Best Results Initiative (in 1998 and for a few years thereafter) and, more recently, the establishment of the Criminal Justice Social Work Development Centre for Scotland and of an Effective Practice Unit in the Community Justice Division of the Scottish Government. Scotland also now has a joint prisons and community justice accreditation panel (the Scottish Accreditation Panel for Offender Programmes, established in 2006) which is intended as a kind of mechanism to 'quality assure' (in advance) structured rehabilitative programmes for offenders in both settings, although critics have raised doubts both about the merits of accreditation systems and about their operation in practice (Mair 2004; McNeill 2001).

In broad terms, many of these developments are similar to those in England and Wales. That said, the Scottish approach, thus far, has been less centralised and prescriptive, relying as it does on the cooperation of the local authorities and other stakeholders. Moreover, in terms of the way in which 'evidence-based practice' is understood, it has perhaps been more inclusive in its consideration of evidence. Thus, for example, while the insights of 'what works' and other 'treatment' studies have greatly informed developments, the emerging evidence about desistance from offending and how that process is best supported has also found a receptive audience amongst policy-makers and practitioners (McNeill *et al.* 2005; McNeill *et al.* 2009).

Criminal justice social work and community sanctions in the twenty-first century

During the 1990s and especially since devolution, there have been many new initiatives, policy statements and pieces of legislation, too many to detail here, some of which mirrored developments in England and Wales (see McIvor and McNeill 2007a). An important distinction remains the organisational arrangements. Scottish Labour Party proposals in 2003 to establish a single 'Corrections Service for Scotland' on the NOMS model were rejected on consultation. A compromise solution emerged in the creation of eight Community

Justice Authorities (CJAs) in 2006 to facilitate strategic planning across their areas and between partner agencies (Management of Offenders (Scotland) Act 2005). It should be noted that such 'management' terminology has always been somewhat dissonant with Scottish probation traditions and values, not least because it defines 'offenders' by their offending and casts them as an object to be managed rather than a human subject with whom practitioners should engage.[7]

The election of a minority Scottish National Party administration in 2007 produced yet another interesting twist in the tale of Scottish criminal justice social work. The four key documents produced since 2007 are *Reforming and Revitalising: Report of the Review of Community Penalties* (Scottish Government 2007); *Scotland's Choice: Report of the Scottish Prisons Commission* (Scottish Prisons Commission 2008); the Government response *Protecting Scotland's Communities: Fair, Fast and Flexible Justice* (Scottish Government 2008) and the Criminal Justice and Licensing Bill, currently before the Scottish Parliament. Though none of these dispenses with rehabilitation as part of the purpose of community sanctions, collectively they attest to the emergence of an increasing emphasis on reparation – on offenders paying back for their crimes – perhaps principally because this is seen as a more credible basis from which to argue for reducing a rapidly escalating prison population.

For example, the heart of the Scottish Prisons Commission's report, and the core of the choice that the Commission sets out, can be found in their first two recommendations:

> 1 To target imprisonment better and make it more effective, the Commission *recommends* that imprisonment should be reserved for people whose offences are so serious that no other form of punishment will do and for those who pose a significant threat of serious harm to the public.
> 2 To move beyond our reliance on imprisonment as a means of punishing offenders, the Commission *recommends* that paying back in the community should become the default position in dealing with less serious offenders.
>
> (Scottish Prisons Commission 2008: 3)

The Commission's remedy for Scotland's over-consumption of imprisonment centres on a range of measures that it considers necessary to enact their second recommendation and make 'paying back in the community' the 'default position' for less serious offenders. The concept of 'payback' is defined as follows:

> In essence, payback means finding constructive ways to compensate or repair harms caused by crime. It involves making good to the victim and/or the community. This might be through financial payment, unpaid work, engaging in rehabilitative work or some combination of these and other approaches. Ultimately, one of the best ways for offenders to pay back is by turning their lives around. (Scottish Prisons Commission 2008: para. 3.6)

Several ways of paying back are identified – through restorative justice practices, through financial penalties, through unpaid work, through restriction of liberty (electronically monitored curfews) and, perhaps most interestingly in this context, through 'paying back by working at change'. Working at change in turn is linked to engagement in a wide range of activities that might seem likely to address the issues underlying offending behaviour (drug and alcohol issues, money or housing problems, peer group and attitudinal issues, family difficulties, mental health problems and so on). Notably the notion of paying back by turning one's life around represents a very neat, if underdeveloped, reframing of engagement in rehabilitation as an act of reparation.

Around the time of the publication of *Scotland's Choice*, the UK Cabinet Office published a report on *Engaging Communities in Fighting Crime*, written by Louise Casey (Casey 2008). It sought solutions to perceived problems of public confidence in criminal justice in general and community penalties in particular. She proposed the rebranding (yet again) of community service, this time as 'community payback'. Yet Casey's 'payback' is quite different from the Scottish Prisons Commission's; it centres on making community service more visible and more demanding. She suggests that payback should not be something the general public would choose to do themselves (it should be painful or punishing) and that offenders doing payback should wear bibs identifying them as such (it should be shaming). In a recent paper exploring the available research evidence about public attitudes to probation in the light of Casey's recommendations, Maruna and King come to the following conclusion:

> Casey is absolutely right to utilise emotive appeals to the public in order to increase public confidence in the criminal justice system [...] However, if Casey's purpose was to increase confidence in community interventions, then she drew on the exact wrong emotions. Desires for revenge and retribution,

> anger, bitterness and moral indignation are powerful emotive forces, but they do not raise confidence in probation work – just the opposite. To do that, one would want to tap in to other, equally cherished, emotive values, such as the widely shared belief in redemption, the need for second chances, and beliefs that all people can change. (Maruna and King 2008: 347)

Looking south at these developments – and the public sensibilities to which they somehow relate – and thinking more particularly about the way that 'payback' is cast in the Scottish Prisons Commission's report, some very meaty issues for criminal justice social work and community sanctions emerge.

Social workers in Scotland have tended to consider themselves as purveyors of (usually rehabilitative) alternatives to punishment, rather than as purveyors of alternative punishments. Somehow the notion of punishing, as opposed to supporting, supervising, treating or helping, seems inimical to the ethos, values and traditions of social work. But, as Antony Duff (2001) has argued convincingly, we can and should distinguish between 'constructive punishment' and 'merely punitive punishment'. Constructive punishment can and does involve the intentional infliction of pains, but only in so far as this is an inevitable (and intended) consequence of 'bringing offenders to face up to the effects and implications of their crimes, to rehabilitate them and to secure … reparation and reconciliation' (Duff 2003: 181). This seems very close in some respects to the ideas of challenging and confronting offending which have become widely accepted in social work in recent years, partly in response to political pressures to get tough but also, more positively, in response to the legitimate concerns of crime victims that their experiences should be taken more seriously.

Duff's work also helps with a second problem, since he recognises (as social workers have done for decades) that where social injustice is implicated in the genesis of offending, the infliction of punishment (even constructive punishment) by the state is rendered morally problematic, because the state is itself complicit in the offending through having failed in its prior duties to the 'offender'. For this reason, Duff suggests that probation officers or social workers should play a pivotal role in mediating between the offender and the wider polity, holding each one to account on behalf of the other. Again, this discomfiting space is one which many social workers will recognise that they occupy and through which, with or without official or public support, they seek to promote social justice within criminal justice.

It may be therefore that Duff's work provides some of the conceptual resources with which to populate the concept of payback constructively. To the extent that the new centrality of reparation compels criminal justice social work to engage in punishing offenders, his notion of constructive punishment and his insistence on the links between social justice and criminal justice might help to buttress a Scottish social work version of payback from drifting in the punitive and probably futile direction of its namesake south of the border. We should not underestimate the challenges of holding on to the constructive potential of the concept of making good by and to offenders, and the importance of communication, dialogue and participation being part of the process. Maruna and King are surely right that 'selling' probation (or payback) to the public stands a better chance of succeeding if we pitch it in terms of our collective interest in second chances and changed lives, but we cannot underestimate the difficulties of making this pitch in conditions of insecurity – which politicians, the media and even justice professionals sometimes seek to exploit rather than to moderate.

The challenge that criminal justice social work faces therefore is not just working out how to make community payback work in practice, but also, more broadly and perhaps more fundamentally, how to engage and communicate with government, communities, offenders and victims so as to substantiate the concept, realise its potential and minimise its risks. That enterprise seems central to the ongoing project of avoiding the damage that the 'demoralising' of imprisonment does to the whole community and that the progenitors of Scottish probation recognised and sought to avoid (City of Glasgow 1955). Importantly, by 'demoralising' they meant not merely 'depressing' (as in the current usage) but rather something more literal, that is the damaging of the moral character of the prisoner with which they associated damage to the fabric of the whole community.

Risk, surveillance and resettlement of prisoners

> The truth is that most prisoners are off their heads on release. They depart the premises but few leave it. (Collins 2000: 10)

Concern with those who have been incarcerated should not end at the prison gate, even if this obligation is simply construed in terms of reducing the likelihood of reoffending. Indeed, nearly three-quarters of prisoners released from a short sentence (six months or less) in

2005–6 were reconvicted and over half (54 per cent) returned to prison on a custodial sentence within two years (Scottish Government 2009b). In the quote that opens this section, Hugh Collins, himself a former prisoner, reminds us of the psychological dislocation of imprisonment in addition to acute practical needs such as signing on, getting work, dealing with medical and addiction problems, as well as readjusting to family relationships and roles, or to social isolation, that create obstacles to desistance.

Throughcare practices and post-custodial resources, such as specialist accommodation, have been poorly developed in Scotland, except perhaps as patchy voluntary sector provision (McIvor and McNeill 2007b; McNeill and Whyte 2007; see also Chapter 12, this volume). There has been a failure to meet basic resettlement needs that would contribute to reintegration and desistance among ex-prisoners, especially the majority, those released from sentences of less than twelve months with whom there has been no statutory engagement. Nonetheless, political commitments to reduce high rates of reoffending, coupled with headline-attracting automatic early release practices that seemed to be at odds with the expectation of both courts and victims, have resulted in recent policy attention (Scottish Sentencing Commission 2005). The introduction of CJAs as an alternative to a single 'corrections agency' was discussed above. In this context, the significance of s. 1 of the Management of Offenders (Scotland) Act 2005 was that it established, for the first time, a statutory duty to cooperate on the part of prisons, local authorities and CJAs in relation to people released from prison.

In 2007, the Scottish Parliament chose to ignore advice from a range of academics and professionals in the field and passed the unworkable Custodial Sentences and Weapons Act which required that all prisoners serving more than 14 days in custody would be subject to some form of supervision on licence when released. Although justified both in terms of bringing clarity to release arrangements and ensuring the supervision of short-term prisoners, this was in practice a complex and potentially very costly initiative (Tata 2007). Following the 2007 election the SNP Government deferred implementation and asked the Prisons Commission to reconsider the question. The Commission concluded that there was 'clear evidence that release without support and, where need be, supervision leads to many offenders returning to chaotic lifestyles with no family support, home or services. It is therefore no surprise that reoffending rates are high and that many offenders end up serving a life sentence by instalments' (Scottish Prisons Commission 2007: 50). The Criminal Justice and Licensing Act

2010 replaces unimplemented parts of the 2007 legislation with a new 'short-term custody and community sentence' to apply to a period to be prescribed by the Government, (but which looks likely to be initially set at less than 12 months), comprising automatic release at the 50 per cent point, followed by a nominal licence period for the remaining 50 per cent.

This historic neglect of the short-term prisoner contrasts with developing practices of surveillance for public protection over others for potentially extended periods (see Weaver and McNeill 2010, for a more detailed account). Longer-term prisoners (serving four years or more) and life sentence prisoners may be released under various forms of licence during which they are subject to the disciplines of supervision and also the support of criminal justice social workers. The decision to release is made by the Parole Board for Scotland as is the decision to recall 'in circumstances where such action is considered necessary in the public interest' (Parole Board for Scotland 2009). Since 2004, the Board has been empowered to make release on licence conditional on electronic monitoring ('tagging') and, indeed, in the case of one sex offender has imposed such a condition for ten years (*The Herald*, 30 April 2007).

Electronic monitoring has been more frequently deployed to enforce the 'Home Detention Curfew' (HDC) since its introduction in 2006 of low-risk prisoners serving less than four years (and controversially, to longer-term prisoners from 2008). This is in effect a 'back-door' use of tagging to ease prison overcrowding, albeit that it is justified in terms of more effective offender management and the reduction in reoffending agenda. Release is an administrative decision made by the Scottish Prison Service and the offender is still counted as part of the prisoner population (363 of 7,952 Scottish prisoners in January 2010) though resident in the community and managed by a private company, Serco. HDC has been dogged by criticisms from both the judiciary, who claim that such administrative decisions undermine the sentencing powers of the court, and politicians, who consider this to be yet another example of 'soft touch Scotland' and who question what are perceived to be high levels of breach and recall. As Nellis predicted, 'the fortunes of EM [electronic monitoring] in Scotland are currently caught up not in the Orwellian spectre of overcontrol, but in a press-augmented scandal of undercontrol' (Nellis 2006).

It is, perhaps unsurprisingly, in relation to sexual and violent offenders that post-release supervision is most restrictive,[8] although the apparatus of coordination, monitoring and managing the risk posed by dangerous offenders in the community is still in a formative phase

(SWIA 2009). The key framework is, since 2007, the Multi-Agency Public Protection Arrangements (MAPPAs) organised within the CJAs and set up by the Management of Offenders Act 2005. Obliged by a statutory duty to cooperate, all relevant agencies including local authorities, voluntary organisations and, crucially, health services are jointly charged with the 'management' of such offenders (and restricted patients under mental health legislation) (Weaver 2010). The Scottish Government has been reluctant to agree to demands for the public notification of the addresses of sex offenders although it intends to roll out nationally a sex offender disclosure scheme piloted on Tayside, in which members of the public may seek information on someone who has unsupervised access to their children (Scottish Government 2010b).

Another Scottish innovation in this field is that, for those sexual and violent offenders who are assessed by the Risk Management Authority to pose the greatest risk, an Order for Lifelong Restriction (OLR) may, since 2006, be imposed by the High Court following conviction. This in effect gives the court power to impose a life sentence for offences for which a life term is not otherwise available. There are indications that this power is being used sparingly as intended. However, it remains to be seen how the currently perceived imperatives of public protection and risk management may be balanced with questions of justice as proportionality and rights.

Concluding comments

This overview of community sanctions in Scotland attempts to rebalance what is otherwise a dominant preoccupation with the prison in public discussion about criminal justice. In setting a discussion of monetary penalties and post-release work with offenders alongside criminal justice social work, something of the complexity of the resulting 'map' of justice is suggested. Although there has been an acceleration and deepening of reform to settled Scottish practices since devolution, changes to the governance of criminal justice social work in the early 1990s also emerge as key to understanding the present landscape. The story has been one of both pragmatic and 'back of the envelope' innovations peculiar to this jurisdiction (SAOs, CJAs, for example), and a local, sometimes sceptical, version of wider zeitgeist concerns with managerial and actuarial risk management and public protection objectives, moderated and sometimes in conflict with welfarist practice cultures (McNeill *et al*. 2009) This is to edge towards a view that despite inevitable external influences, such as the above, in relation to adult criminal justice, this jurisdiction has distinctive features to be understood not simply in terms of a legacy of 'welfarism' but also, for example, in terms of legal culture and political history, not by any means always progressive (see Chapter 10). However, as Armstrong and McNeill have suggested, it might be that the spirit of *Scotland's Choice*, in severing penal policy from (prison) crisis management, has opened up new ways of thinking about criminal justice (Armstrong and McNeill 2009). It remains to be seen if this opportunity for a fundamentally divergent trajectory will founder, as have other ambitions, for lack of strategic diversion of penal resources to community agencies on the one hand and institutional conservatism on the other.

The dangers of divergent punishment resulting from income inequality was considered in relation to monetary penalties, as was the intimate connection between Edwardian responses to poverty and offending and the emergence of foundation models of probation in Scotland. The continuing location of social work in criminal justice in a discomfiting space between polity and offender implicitly testifies to the persistent significance of social injustice and offending. Equally, the survival of social work in criminal justice (thus far) perhaps implicitly testifies to some level of official or at least professional recognition of the need to connect social justice and criminal justice.

Notes

1 Section 211, Criminal Procedure (Scotland) Act 1995.
2 Fine enforcement has recently (2008) become the responsibility of the Scottish Courts Service: see http://www.scotcourts.gov.uk/payyourfine/index.asp.
3 The penalty is pronounced in court by the sentencer in terms of 'units' and the value of each unit in a particular case is related to the offender's income.
4 Section 51, Law Reform (Miscellaneous Provisions) (Scotland) Bill 1990.
5 Comment made by a (then) senior Scottish Office official to Mary Munro.
6 Section 236, Criminal Procedure (Scotland) Act 1995 as amended.
7 It may be for this reason that the Community Justice Authorities were so named (as a counterweight to 'offender management') and that the reform plan currently under development within the Justice Department (in response to the Scottish Prison Commission's (2008) report) has

recently been renamed the 'Reducing Reoffending Programme' rather than the 'Offender Management Programme'.

8 Scotland does not have the indeterminate sentence of Imprisonment for Public Protection (IPP).

References

Armstrong, S. and McNeill, F. (2009) 'Choice versus crisis: how Scotland could transform the way we think about prisons and punishment', *Criminal Justice Matters*, 75 (1): 2–4.

Beccaria, C. (1764) *On Crimes and Punishments.*

Brown, L. (1994) *A Fine on Time: The Monitoring and Evaluation of the Pilot Supervised Attendance Order Schemes*. Edinburgh: The Stationery Office.

Casey, L. (2008) *Engaging Communities in Fighting Crime*. London: Cabinet Office.

Cavadino, M. and Dignan, J. (2007) *The Penal System: An Introduction*, 4th edn. London: Sage.

Cavanagh, B. (2009) *A Review of Fixed Penalty Notices (FPNs) for Antisocial Behaviour*. Scottish Government (web only).

Collins, H. (2000) *Walking Away*. Edinburgh: Rebel Inc.

Council of Europe (1992) Recommendation No. R (92) 16 of the Committee of Ministers to Member States on the European Rules on Community Sanctions and Measures.

Devon, J. (1912) *The Criminal and the Community*. London: John Lane/Bodley Head.

Duff, A. (2001) *Punishment, Communication and Community*. New York: Oxford University Press.

Duff, A. (2003) 'Probation, punishment and restorative justice: should altruism be engaged in punishment?', *Howard Journal*, 42 (1): 181–97.

City of Glasgow (1955) *Probation. A Brief Survey of Fifty Years of the Probation Service of the City of Glasgow 1905–1955.* Glasgow: City of Glasgow Probation Area Committee.

Glover, C. (2008) *Crime and Inequality*. Cullompton: Willan Publishing.

Herald, The (2007) 'Sex offender tagged for 10 years', 30 April. http://www.heraldscotland.com/sex-offender-tagged-for-10-years-1.857059.

Houchin, R. (2005) *Social Exclusion and Imprisonment in Scotland*. Available on the SPS website at http://www.sps.gov.uk.

Hutcheson, F. (1755) *A System of Moral Philosophy*. Glasgow: Foulis.

Inspectorate of Prosecution (2009) *Summary Justice Reform: Thematic Report on the Use of Fiscal Fines*. Edinburgh: Scottish Government.

Kilbrandon Report (1964) *Children and Young Persons (Scotland)*, Cmnd 2306. Edinburgh: HMSO.

Levy, L. and McIvor, G. (2001) *National Evaluation of the Operation and Impact of Supervised Attendance Orders*. Edinburgh: Scottish Executive.

McInnes Committee (2004) *The Summary Justice Review Committee: Report to Ministers*. Edinburgh: Scottish Executive.

McIvor, G. and McNeill, F. (2007a) 'Probation in Scotland: past, present and future', in L. Gelsthorpe and R. Morgan (eds), *Handbook of Probation*. Cullompton: Willan Publishing.

McIvor, G. and McNeill, F. (2007b) 'Developments in probation in Scotland', in G. McIvor and P. Raynor (eds), *Developments in Social Work with Offenders*. London: Jessica Kingsley.

McIvor, G. and Williams, B. (1999) 'Community based disposals', in P. Duff and N. Hutton (eds), *Criminal Justice in Scotland*. Aldershot: Ashgate/ Dartmouth, pp. 198–227.

McNeill, F. (2001) 'Developing effectiveness: frontline perspectives', *Social Work Education*, 20 (6): 671–87.

McNeill, F. (2005) 'Remembering probation in Scotland', *Probation Journal*, 52 (1): 23–38.

McNeill, F. and Whyte, B. (2007) *Reducing Reoffending: Social Work and Community Justice in Scotland*. Cullompton: Willan Publishing.

McNeill, F., Batchelor, S., Burnett, R. and Knox, J. (2005) *21st Century Social Work: Reducing Reoffending: Key Skills*. Edinburgh: Scottish Executive.

McNeill, F., Burns, N., Halliday, S., Hutton, N. and Tata, C. (2009) 'Risk, responsibility and reconfiguration: penal adaptation and misadaptation', *Punishment and Society*, 11 (4): 419–42.

Mair, G. (2004) 'What works: rhetoric, reality and research', *British Journal of Community Justice*, 3 (1): 5–18.

Maruna, S. and King, A. (2008) 'Selling the public on probation: beyond the bib', *Probation Journal*, 55 (4): 337–51.

Moore, G. and Whyte, W. (1998) *Social Work and Criminal Law in Scotland*. Edinburgh: Mercat Press.

Munro, M. (1999) *Setting Fines in Scottish Summary Courts*. MPhil dissertation, University of Glasgow.

Murray, J. (1906) 'Social reformation of criminals', *Journal of the Royal Philosophical Society of Glasgow*, 37: 46–58.

Nellis, M. (2006) *The Ethics and Practice of Electronically Monitoring Offenders* (seminar notes). http://www.gssw.ac.uk/pdf/electronically_monitoring_offenders.pdf.

Nellis, M. (2006) 'Electronically monitoring offenders in Scotland 1998–2006', *Scottish Journal of Criminal Justice*, 12: 74–96.

Nicholson, L. (1994) *Monetary Penalties in Scotland*. Edinburgh: HMSO.

O'Malley, P. (2009) *The Currency of Justice. Fines and Damages in Consumer Societies*. Abingdon and New York: Routledge-Cavendish.

Paterson, F. and Tombs, J. (1998) *Social Work and Criminal Justice Volume 1: The Policy Context*. Edinburgh: The Stationery Office.

Robinson, G. and McNeill, F. (2004) 'Purposes matters: examining the ends of probation', in G. Mair (ed.), *What Matters in Probation Work*. Cullompton: Willan Publishing.

Rusche, G. and Kirchheimer, O. (1939) *Punishment and Social Structure*. New York: Russell & Russell.

Scottish Executive (2000) *National Standards for Social Enquiry and Related Reports and Court Based Social Work Services*. Edinburgh: Social Work Services Group.

Scottish Executive (2006) *Reducing Reoffending: National Strategy for the Management of Offenders*. Edinburgh: Scottish Executive.

Scottish Executive (2007) *Evaluation of a Pilot to Test the Implementation of Supervised Attendance Orders as Disposals of First Instance (s. 236 SAOs)*. Edinburgh: Scottish Executive.

Scottish Government (2007) *Reforming and Revitalising: Report of the Review of Community Penalties*. Edinburgh: Scottish Government.

Scottish Government (2008) *Protecting Scotland's Communities: Fair, Fast and Flexible Justice*. Edinburgh: Scottish Government.

Scottish Government (2008) *Reducing Court Time for Low-Level Offenders*, Press Release, 5 March. http://www.scotland.gov.uk/News/Releases/2008/03/05094104.

Scottish Government (2009a) *Prison Statistics Scotland: 2008–09*. Edinburgh: Scottish Government.

Scottish Government (2009b) *Reconviction Rates in Scotland: 2005–06 and 2006–07 Offender Cohorts*. Web only.

Scottish Government (2010a) *Criminal Proceedings in Scottish Courts, 2008/09*, Statistical Bulletin. Web only.

Scottish Government (2010b) Press release: *Green Light for Disclosure Plans*, Press Release. http://www.scotland.gov.uk/News/Releases/2010/02/26150410.

Scottish Office (1995) *Criminal Proceedings in Scottish Courts, 1994*, Statistical Bulletin. Edinburgh: Scottish Office.

Scottish Office (1998) *Community Sentencing: The Tough Option: Review of Criminal Justice Social Work Services*. Edinburgh: Scottish Office Home Department.

Scottish Parliament (2010) Written Answer S3W-31587. http://www.scottish.parliament.uk/business/pqa/wa-10/wa0302.htm#11.

Scottish Prisons Commission (2008) *Scotland's Choice: Report of the Scottish Prisons Commission*. Edinburgh: Scottish Government.

Scottish Sentencing Commission (2005) *Early Release from Prison and the Supervision of Prisoners on Their Release*. http://www.scottishsentencingcommission.gov.uk/publications.asp.

Scottish Sentencing Commission (2006) *Basis on which Fines are Determined*. http://www.scottishsentencingcommission.gov.uk/publications.asp.

Social Work Services Group (1991a) *National Objectives and Standards for Social Work Services in the Criminal Justice System*. Edinburgh: Scottish Office.

Social Work Services Group (1991b) *Social Work Supervision: Towards Effective Policy and Practice: A Supplement to the National Objectives and Standards for Social Work Services in the Criminal Justice System*. Edinburgh: Scottish Office.

Social Work Services Group (1996) *Part 2 – Service Standards: Throughcare.* Edinburgh: Scottish Office.

Sunday Herald (2009) 'Crime and punishment', 9 May. http://www.heraldscotland.com/crime-and-punishment-1.826702 (accessed 9 January 2010).

SWIA/HMIC/HMIP (2009) *Multi-Agency Inspection: Assessing and Managing Offenders Who Present a High Risk of Serious Harm.* Edinburgh: Scottish Government.

Tata, C. (2007) 'The end to "dishonesty" in sentencing? The Custodial Sentences Act will be fogged by confusion'. http://cjscotland.org.uk/index.php/cjscotland/dynamic_page/?id=9 (accessed 20 January 2010).

Tombs, J. (2004) *A Unique Punishment: Sentencing and the Prison Population in Scotland.* Edinburgh: Rethinking Crime and Punishment/SCCCJ.

Weaver, B. (2010) *Multi-Agency Protection Arrangements (MAPPA) in Scotland: What Do the Numbers Tell Us?* Scottish Centre for Crime and Justice Research. http://www.sccjr.ac.uk/pubs/Multi-Agency-Protection-Arrangements-MAPPA-in-Scotland-What-do-the-numbers-tell-us/228.

Weaver, B. and McNeill, F. (forthcoming 2010) 'Public protection in Scotland: a way forward?', in M. Nash and A. Williams (eds), *The Handbook of Public Protection.* Cullompton: Willan Publishing.

Young, P. (1989) 'Punishment, money and a sense of justice', in P. Carlen and D. Cook (eds), *Paying for Crime.* Milton Keynes: Open University Press.

Chapter 12

Prisons and imprisonment in Scotland

Jacqueline Tombs and Laura Piacentini

Introduction

The incarceration rate in Scotland has increased dramatically since the 1990s and is now one of the highest in Western Europe (World Prison Brief 2009). In 2008 150 persons were imprisoned per 100,000 of the population; similar to the rate of 152 in England and Wales. These rates compare with 96 in France, 92 in Italy, 89 in Germany and 67 in Finland. While other countries, notably the USA, the Russian Federation, China and several in Eastern Europe, have far higher incarceration rates, they have very different histories and cultures. Nonetheless, even though international comparisons are not straightforward (Pease 1994) and the rate of imprisonment varies greatly between jurisdictions and over time (Cavadino and Dignan 2005; Christie 1994; Rutherford 1984), Scotland's rate relative to countries with similar social and demographic characteristics is undoubtedly high; more than double the rates in Denmark, Finland, Norway, Sweden and Switzerland. This high rate of incarceration exists despite decreasing crime rates (SCCCJ 2010) and the availability in Scotland of one of the widest ranges of 'alternative' community-based sentences anywhere in the world.

Levels of crime, however, do not explain levels of incarceration. Some countries with similar or higher crime rates than Scotland have lower rates of imprisonment, for example Sweden. Some with only slightly lower crime rates have dramatically lower prison rates, for example Finland. And some with lower crime rates, for example Spain, have higher imprisonment rates. Though taking different approaches, what the countries with the lowest imprisonment rates (of between 60 and 100 per 100,000 of the population) have in common is that they have pursued penal policies that have explicitly sought to contain or reduce imprisonment levels.[1] The Scandinavian countries in particular, with their comparatively broad commitment to egalitarianism and generous welfare support (Pratt 2008a, 2008b), have premised their penal policies on the recognition that crime is a social problem; this approach contributed to a radical reduction in the prison population in Finland during the latter part of the twentieth century (Lappi-Seppala 2007). Conversely, countries with the highest imprisonment rates have increasingly turned to criminalisation and the 'prison solution' (Mathieson 2000) in response to social ills. In these countries, which include England and Wales and Scotland, rises in prisoner numbers have been shown to relate to legislative and policy changes encouraging more use of imprisonment and the imposition of longer sentences, especially in relation to drug offenders (Hough *et al*. 2003; Tombs 2004a; Walmsley 2000).

The high use of imprisonment in Scotland today is, however, a recent phenomenon. For many years the rate of imprisonment was relatively moderate in comparison with England and Wales and other Western European jurisdictions. This changed from the early 1990s onwards. The explanation for this change is rooted in a complex interplay of factors including: the emergence of a more punitive climate of political and media opinion; some changes in patterns of offending; sentencers' perceptions that there have been changes in patterns of offending, especially those related to the seriousness of offending and dependent drug use; other changes in criminal justice practices and procedures; and legislative and policy changes that have encouraged inflationary drift in sentencing (Tombs 2004a). Given that all of these factors – and the wider social, economic and demographic conditions – contribute to explaining Scotland's expanding prison population, political choices could be made to reduce the use of imprisonment. The Scottish Prison Commission (SPC) recognises this and recommends a reduction to an average daily prison population of 5,000 (SPC 2008: 6), a rate of just under 100 per 1,000 of the general population. Different choices about the use of imprisonment have been made in the past and could be made again.

This chapter, in providing a review and critique of how incarceration features in contemporary penal policy and practices in Scotland, engages with these issues. In particular it shows how incarceration reflects wider social divisions and inequalities in Scottish society and comments on questions of penal distinctiveness.[2] In doing so, it aims to address three main questions. First, how did prisons and imprisonment emerge and develop in Scotland? Second, what are the key contemporary features of imprisonment and the prison population? Third, what are the future prospects for prisons and imprisonment in Scotland?

Historical context

This section sets the human, social and economic costs of the massive expansion in Scotland's prison population since the 1990s in historical context. It traces how prisons as 'holding places' became places where people were imprisoned as a specific form of punishment and how they subsequently came to be conceptualised as capable of delivering something more than punishment. It identifies some key policy shifts in moving from locally administered prisons to a prison system controlled by central government and highlights one of Scotland's most enlightened penal experiments, the Special Unit at Barlinnie Prison in Glasgow.

Prison as punishment

In Scotland, as in other Northern European countries, the 'prison' as a penal institution – a place where people are deprived of their liberty as punishment – emerged slowly from the sixteenth century onwards (Morgan and Liebling 2007) and developed along similar lines, albeit with its own distinctive features. In general terms imprisonment, as a specific form of punishment, grew in significance from the mid-eighteenth to the mid-nineteenth centuries. By the late eighteenth century disciplinary prisons (Foucault 1977) had begun to supplant physical punishments as an institutional 'solution' (Mathieson 2000) for dealing with the impoverished criminals who were overwhelmingly drawn from the newly industrialised working class (Rusche and Kirchheimer 1968; Melossi and Pavarini 1981). By the end of the eighteenth century the prison, where a differentiated class of criminals could be held in captivity as punishment, had been established (Ignatieff 1978). Though prisons have historically had three uses – custodial, coercive and punitive – the primary function of the modern prison, which took shape from the early nineteenth century onwards, is punitive rather than custodial-coercive (Radzinowicz and Hood 1990). Punishment became carceral rather than corporal, aimed at addressing the mind rather than the body (Foucault 1977).

Nonetheless the extent to which the prison was used as punishment varied across Europe.

While prisons existed in Scotland from the late sixteenth century onwards, they were rarely used as a direct punishment for crime until the mid-nineteenth century; typically punishments were corporal and immediate. Coyle (1991) observes that before 1597 every barony, lordship and burgh had its own 'thieves' hole' for local offenders. In 1597 a statute called 'Prison Houses suld be bigged within all Burrowes' made local burghs solely responsible for prisons which were essentially legalised cells serving local courts. Prisoners were held only for brief periods until they had paid a debt, while awaiting trial or, after trial, until sentences of execution, transportation or banishment were carried out. Over the next two centuries the prison increasingly became used as a place where people were sent as punishment though Scotland, in comparison with England and Wales, had significantly lower levels of imprisonment throughout this period (Coyle 1991: 23).

Reformative ideas

Scotland was also early in introducing the idea that the prison might be about something more than punishment. Under the influence of William Brebner, governor of the Glasgow Bridewell ('house of correction') between 1808 and 1845, ideas about reformation informed emerging prison regimes early in the nineteenth century. The Bridewell had a 'separate system' by 1826, several years before a similar system, known as the 'Philadelphia System', operated in the Eastern Penitentiary in Philadelphia, USA (Coyle 1991: 29) and almost 20 years before the 1842 opening of England's Pentonville 'model prison' where prisoners were to live separately and in silence. Brebner's system of 'separation without solitude' was quite unlike 'the screened boxes in chapel and the face masks used during exercise periods which were so common in England' (Coyle 1991: 69). Instead prisoners in Scotland received daily visits from chaplains, teachers and others. Brebner's reformative ideas also found expression in relation to prisoner re-entry; he argued that reform depended crucially on the environment to which prisoners would return and stressed the need for communication with families, education, training in work that might be available on release and arrangements to support ex-prisoners after liberation. These ideas underpinned the early emergence of a 'rudimentary form of after-care' (Coyle 1991: 29) within Scottish prisons. Aftercare was subsequently developed by the prison welfare and probation services through the nineteenth and twentieth centuries with local authority social work departments becoming solely responsible in 1972. Since 1991 central government, through 100 per cent funding to local authorities for the delivery of such services against a framework of national objectives and standards, has had overall responsibility (Paterson and Tombs 1998). The core elements of aftercare as conceptualised by Brebner underpin contemporary notions of 'throughcare' and various initiatives including the Throughcare Centre in Edinburgh Prison in 1998 (Tombs 2003) and the subsequent development of Links Centres within Scottish prisons. Such developments are indicative of the inherently welfarist penal sensibility pioneered by Brebner in connecting prisons with the community. As we shall see, however, they are marginal both to the prison system itself and to the lives of the vast majority of prisoners given the grossly disadvantaged circumstances from which they have arrived in prison and to which they will return.

Shifts in control

The use of imprisonment grew from the early nineteenth century onwards; by the middle of that century there were 84 penal establishments in Scotland. This growth was paralleled by concern among penal reformers in Scotland and in England and Wales about appalling prison conditions and about the need for reformative regimes. The Prisons Act of 1835 gave the Secretary of State power to appoint individuals to inspect every place where prisoners were confined. The first Inspector for Scotland, Frederic Hill, argued that the principles of prison discipline advocated by reformers could only be realised by adopting a country-wide uniform system of prison management. This argument was crucial to the development of the prison system with the 1839 'Act to Improve Prisons and Prison Discipline in Scotland' beginning the process of bringing local prisons under central government control. The Prisons (Scotland) Act 1877 consolidated this control through the establishment of the Prison Commission for Scotland which lasted until 1928. From 1929 central government has been solely responsible for the prison system, though there have been some recent calls from penal reformers for at least part of the system to be locally controlled (SCCCJ 2007).

In relation to levels of imprisonment, the Elgin Committee Report of 1900 made a prescient observation in emphasising that the main problem for the prison system at that time was an increasing prisoner population due to large numbers of short-termers sentenced for trivial offences. Historically Scottish courts have maintained this record, a point made repeatedly in the annual reports of the Prisoner Commissioners (Coyle 1991) and in many subsequent official reports up to and including the 2008 report of the Scottish Prisons Commission which found that 83 per cent of all prison sentences in 2005–6 were for six months or less and that more than a third of these were for troubling nuisance behaviour (SPC 2008: 13). Nonetheless, throughout most of the twentieth century until the early 1990s the rate of imprisonment in Scotland was comparatively moderate. As with prisons in other jurisdictions, at various times and in different Scottish prisons, education and welfare services emerged as did initiatives in relation to the needs of specific groups of prisoners, most notably young prisoners and women prisoners.[3] Though such developments benefit individual prisoners, it must be remembered that imprisonment deprives people of their liberty and that the prison's primary imperative is to maintain security and control in containing prisoners against their wills. In this context, one of Scotland's most enlightened penal experiments, the Special Unit at Barlinnie Prison in Glasgow, merits special attention.

A penal experiment

The Special Unit opened in 1973 in the former female block at Barlinnie Prison in Glasgow to deal with a group of prisoners, mostly long-sentence lifers, perceived as having nothing to lose by violence against staff and who could not be managed within the prison system by using available repressive measures (Nellis 2010). Several of these prisoners had spent prolonged periods in solitary confinement in the infamous 'cages' in Inverness Prison where extreme conflict resulted in the prisoners facing charges of attempting to murder six prison officers. Based on recommendations made by a government working party set up in 1971, the Barlinnie Special Unit was conceived. The paradoxical and radical penal idea was that by giving these prisoners more freedom and responsibility they would become more manageable. Throughout its existence all admissions to the unit were voluntary and prisoners could return to the mainstream prison system if they wanted. The original prison officers were also volunteers. The unit was small – ten prisoner places – and the staff/prisoner ratio high to create a therapist/patient relationship between staff and prisoners. The ethos was of a therapeutic community with the weekly community meeting between the prisoners and the staff viewed as central to relationships and the running of the unit. Within the secure perimeter around the unit – a 'prison within a prison' – prisoners had relative freedom of movement and visits were virtually unrestricted. At the beginning there were no ideas of turning 'dangerous men' into creative artists, sculptors and community leaders as some of the ex-inmates were to become: the aim was simply to contain them. The Special Unit certainly succeeded with that limited objective. Moreover, for some of the prisoners the experience was transformative. Some of the ex-prisoners became highly successful on the outside, most notably Jimmy Boyle who, for a time described as 'Scotland's most dangerous man', became a successful sculptor, writer and community leader (Smith 1984).[4] Although some of the prisoners were unable to adapt and returned to mainstream prisons, most stayed and there was very little violence (Cooke 1989, 1997). The Special Unit closed in 1996 as a consequence of emerging prison policies during the 1990s, though arguably its demise can also be explained at least in part by its success; in challenging established ideas about the 'purpose of punishment', the unit exposed the contradictions and limits of the penal system itself (Nellis 2010).

Contemporary features

The Special Unit was phased out around the same time that something different was happening in relation to imprisonment in Scotland. Since the early 1990s there has been a significant, progressive and continuing rise in the level of the prison population. The rising prison population, together with concerns about overcrowding and the poor condition of the prison estate, led to a series of official consultations, first in 2002 by the recently devolved government on the future of the prison estate (Scottish Executive 2002a) up to the 2008 report of the Scottish Prisons Commission (SPC 2008). Based on trends in prisoner numbers all of these consultations projected further increases. The latest statistical projections indicate a prison population figure of 9,600 by 2018–19 with a further 370 on Home Detention Curfew, making a total of 9,970 (Scottish Government 2010). This section critically reviews the relentless rise in the prison population since the early 1990s and the implications this has had for the prison system and for the prisoners.

Imprisonment since the 1990s

In 1993 the average daily prison population in Scotland was 5,637. By 2002 it had reached 6,404 and by 2008 it rose further to 7,835, a rate of 150 prisoners per 100,000 of the national population. At the time of writing the total prison population is 8,074 (http://www.sps.gov.uk-library-key facts). Overall, the increased custody rates are not generally for those convicted of serious crimes. Figure 12.1 provides an illustration of the relative increase or decrease, indexed to 1980, of the level of crime, the number of convictions, the numbers of persons incarcerated and the ratio between convictions and custodial disposals. Since 1980 recorded crime rose by 50 per cent until 1992 and then began to decrease; in the last two years it decreased by 10 per cent and is now at its lowest level since 1980. The numbers of persons convicted by the courts have fallen by nearly 50 per cent since 1980. However, of those convicted the numbers sent to custody

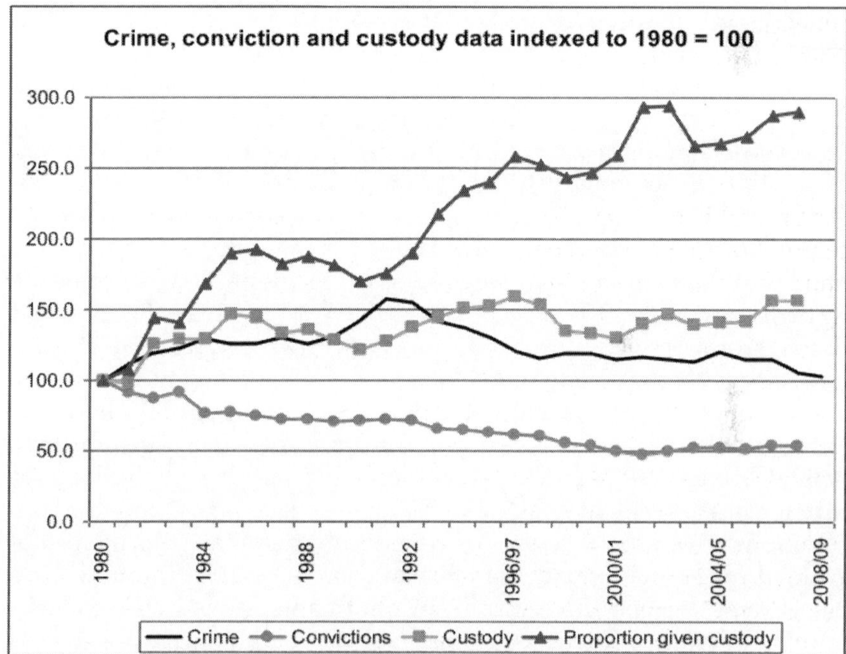

Figure 12.1 Crime, convictions, custody and ratio of convictions to custodial disposals
Source: SCCCJ (2010) based on official statistics for Recorded Crime, Criminal Proceedings in Scottish Courts and Prison Statistics.

have increased by over 50 per cent. Whereas in 1980 10,641 (4.3 per cent) of the 246,263 of those where a charge was proved were sent to custody, in 2007–8 16,686 (12.5 per cent) of the 133,076 were imprisoned – an increase of nearly 290 per cent in the proportion imprisoned. Coupled with the lengthening of prison sentences the prison population continues to rise at the same time as the level of crime continues to fall (SCCCJ 2010).

Overall, though the increase in the prison population is primarily due to the growth in the directly sentenced population, the numbers of remand prisoners and those recalled from licence/supervision have increased more rapidly than the sentenced population. The average daily population of remand prisoners has grown by 72 per cent over the past ten years (from 976 to 1,678) while the number of recalls has risen five-fold, from 100 to 599, over the same period with an even greater increase in the number of young people recalled (Scottish Government 2009). In relation to remand, the Scottish Prisons Commission noted that 'more people went to prison in 2006/2007 to await a trial or sentence (23,181) than to be punished (20,403)' (SPC 2008: 13). In spite of the presumption of innocence for those held on remand, living conditions for these prisoners are among the worst found in the prison system (Scottish Executive 2000). Most remarkable, however, is the dramatic and continuing increase in the female prison population. Over the last ten years the numbers of women in prison almost doubled – an increase of 97 per cent compared with 29 per cent for men. This is despite government commitments to reduce the number of women in prison beginning in 1998 with the government's response (Scottish Office 1998) to a joint report by the Prisons and Social Work Services Inspectors (Social Work Services and Prisons Inspectorates for Scotland 1998). The report's origins lay in a public outcry following the seventh suicide in 30 months in the mid-1990s at Scotland's only women's prison, Cornton Vale. The death of these young women (all were under 30 years old) provoked the longest-running fatal accident inquiry in Scottish legal history and the first comprehensive official review of community disposals and the use of custody for female offenders in Scotland (Carlen 2001; Tombs 2004b). Since then further government commitments to reduce women's imprisonment have been made (Scottish Executive 2002b), there has been all-party support for reduction and penal reform groups have called for action in relation to this 'unmet commitment' (SCCCJ 2006: 1; see also Chapter 5, this volume). These then are the broad parameters of the ever increasing prison population – from around 5,000 in the early 1990s to over 8,000, that is from an imprisonment rate of less than 100 to a rate of 155 per 100,000 of the general population.

The prison system

The prison system, which is legally required to accommodate ever increasing numbers of prisoners, has also undergone major managerial changes since the early 1990s. The Scottish Prison Service (SPS), established in 1993 as an executive agency of the Scottish Government, runs Scotland's prisons and operates within the wider context of the Parole Board (which reviews prisoners' sentences), the Chief Inspector of Prisons Office (which inspects standards and prison conditions) and the Scottish Prisons Complaints Commission (which investigates prisoner complaints against the SPS). During 2008–9 there were 13 publicly managed prisons and two privately managed prisons (Kilmarnock and Addiewell). In keeping with other penal systems, it is mostly adult men who are incarcerated – 95 per cent of the prison population. One prison houses women prisoners and two house young prisoners. The net cost of the SPS for 2008–9 was over £331 million, an increase of 13 per cent from 2007–8 (SPS 2009). The figure for the average annual cost of a prison place in 2007–8 was £36,000 (SCCCJ 2010). In short, prison is extremely expensive, with a high administrative turnover to process prisoners, two-thirds of whom return.

There are three points of particular note regarding Scotland's penal estate. First, with the exception of Peterhead, Scotland's prisons, in common with prisons in small penal jurisdictions more generally, contain mixed levels of category of prisoner, from remand to long-term, young adult to sex offenders, within one establishment. Studies increasingly show that mixing prisoners is unimaginative in terms of rehabilitation and that it overstretches staff. Mixing low with high-risk prisoners minimises realistic attempts at improving protection both for society and for vulnerable prisoners (HM Chief Inspector of Prisons 2009; Wahidin 2009). Second, Scotland's penal geography is largely 'even' relative to the proportion of people living in the areas where prisons are sited, with a high concentration of prisons over a small land mass. The location of most of the establishments in and around the Glasgow and Edinburgh areas where the national population is concentrated reflects patterns of prison building in most western countries (Piacentini *et al.* 2010). Third, with the opening of Scotland's two privately managed prisons, at Kilmarnock in 1999 (operated by Serco) and at Addiewell in 2008 (operated by Kalyx), roughly 20 per cent of Scotland's prisoners can be held in private prisons. This figure is not only higher than the percentage in England and Wales but the highest of any country in the world. There are no private prisons as such in mainland Europe, and in Canada and New Zealand private prisons have been taken back into the public sector. The introduction of private prisons to Scotland was and remains highly controversial.[5] The main arguments made against them include: that the state should be responsible for the justice system and running prisons for profit is wrong in principle; to the extent that private prisons produce savings (if they do) they are achieved through providing lower staffing levels; and private prisons have brought no clear benefits while presenting real risks of commercial pressures driving penal policy (SCCCJ 2006).

A further controversial debate at present concerns the desirability of introducing community prisons (SCCCJ 2007). This desire resonates with some of Scotland's earlier penal ideas about bringing communities into prisons in relation to prisoner re-entry (Brebner) and therapeutic models (the Special Unit) and reminds us that prisons were once the sole responsibility of local authorities. Community prisons, it is argued, would ensure that community services and local employers have representation inside prisons and would help families struggling to maintain contact with prisoners, a particular problem for women and young people in prison. Moreover, given that Scotland is a comparatively small penal jurisdiction in terms of total prisoner numbers, the development of small community prisons would permit more potentially rehabilitative interaction between prisoners and staff as well as with families and the communities to which prisoners will return. At present, however, when imprisonment rates continue to increase rapidly and prisons are clogged up with those imprisoned for low-level offences or on remand, overcrowding detracts from the ability of staff to undertake rehabilitative work with the small number of prisoners convicted of very serious crimes (Piacentini 2005; SPS 2010).

The prisoners

In common with other jurisdictions, the vast majority of prisoners in Scotland, whether male or female (see Chapter 5), are more economically deprived, marginalised, unskilled, educationally disadvantaged and have a lower life expectancy compared with the general population (see Chapters 2 and 4). Over 65 per cent of

Scotland's prisoners have the numeracy skills and 80 per cent the literacy skills of an 11-year-old. Unemployment is 13 times higher for prisoners on admission compared with the general population and around 70 per cent have histories of mental health and/or drug problems. Prisoners are 13 times more likely to have been in care, 15 times more likely to be HIV positive and 2.5 times more likely to have a family member convicted of a criminal offence (SPS 2008). In short, Scotland, like other countries, imprisons the sick, the poor and the marginalised even though the overwhelming number of those in prison are not there for serious offences but for low-level offences, with several previous appearances before the courts and breaches for community penalties (Carlen and Tombs 2006; Tombs and Jagger 2006).

In terms of social and economic geography, rates of incarceration vary enormously over the country (see Chapter 2). Overall rates are dramatically higher in communities with multiple forms of disadvantage:

> Just as it is a fact of life if you are born in the most deprived parts of the country that there is a greatly increased probability that you will remain poor and that you will have poor health and will die young, so it is an analogous fact that you have an increased probability of spending time in prison. (Houchin 2005: 17)

Houchin found that half of the prison population on the night of 30 June 2003 came from home addresses in only 155 of the 1,222 local government wards in Scotland. Though the overall imprisonment rate at the time was 130 per 100,000 of the general population and 237 per 100,000 males (the comparable rate for women was 10 per 100,000), for men from the 27 most deprived wards the rate was 953 per 100,000, with about one in nine young men from the most deprived communities experiencing imprisonment before the age of 23. Prisoners, Houchin argues, come from decayed communities where cultural norms have been created and carried over generations so that exclusion and falling away from mainstream values such as education, employment and stable functioning relationships is the norm (Houchin 2005).

In the context of this severe deprivation, the SPS statement of its 'Vision' has two main objectives. The first is 'reducing re-offending' where 'we will be recognised as a leader in offender management services for prisoners, that help reduce re-offending and offer value for money for the taxpayer' and the second is 'protecting the public' where 'we will maintain secure custody and good order; and we will care for offenders with humanity and provide them with appropriate opportunities' (SPS 2009: 5). This statement, with its references to security, reducing reoffending and humanity, is backed by an increasingly complex set of interrelated Scottish Government, criminal justice agencies and prison service 'objectives', 'offender outcomes', 'mission statements', 'key performance indicators' (KPIs), 'risk assessment protocols' and the like, all of which, in common with England and Wales, signify some of the major managerial shifts that occurred throughout the 1990s (see Chapters 10 and 11). Against this background, and the ever increasing prison population, the SPS continues to make rehabilitation – now reconfigured as reducing reoffending – one of its two main aims. Beginning with the 1990 publication of *Opportunity and Responsibility* (SPS 1990), followed a decade later by *Intervention and Integration* (SPS 2000), reduction of reoffending came to encapsulate integration into society (Tombs 2003). In Scottish prisons today the language of rehabilitation includes notions of inclusion, change, assistance, correction, redemption, enhancing physical and mental health and 'basic care' (HM Chief Inspector of Prisons 2009). In collaboration with Community Justice Authorities and using various risk assessment technologies in 'offender care management', the SPS is now charged with delivering national 'offender outcomes', all of which underline the extent of deprivation among the prison population while revealing, in terms of the SPS's second aim of 'protecting the public', just how few of those held in prison society needs to be protected from.

At the same time Scotland's 'offender outcomes', such as employability, housing and literacy, are consistent with the complex needs repeatedly identified as crucial to address for ex-prisoners 'going straight' on release from confinement (Maruna 2001), in the process of desistance from crime (McNeill 2003) and in developing national strategies for resettlement (Haines 1990; see also Chapter 11, this volume). However, given recent warnings from the SPS about the dangers posed by the prison population going beyond the Assessed Operating Limit, both for the health and safety of staff and prisoners and for breaches of the European Convention on Human Rights (the Convention) (SPS 2009), it is difficult to imagine how prisons can contribute significantly to positive 'offender outcomes', far less ameliorate the further deprivations necessarily experienced by those held in captivity; deprivations which are subsequently carried back into communities already burdened by high levels of disadvantage and social insecurity and where the extra capacities required of communities for successful resettlement in terms of tolerance, acceptance and inclusion are a tall order.

Human rights

Since the enactment of the Scotland Act 1998, which incorporated the Convention into Scots law, Scotland's prison conditions have been found to be seriously in breach of human rights. Successive reports of the Committee for the Prevention of Torture criticised lack of in-cell sanitation and the consequent practice of 'slopping out' (Murphy and Whitty 2007) but these practices persisted until the Napier judgments (*Napier* v. *Scottish Ministers* 2005 SC 229). These judgments found that the conditions experienced by Robert Napier while on remand in Barlinnie Prison in 2001, where he had spent long periods sharing a cell in which he had to 'slop out', breached the Convention and damages were awarded. Approximately 2,200 other prisoners then submitted similar court claims for damages. Many of these cases were suspended pending the outcome of *Somerville and others* (2007). Subsequent to this judgment Scottish Ministers agreed to settle outstanding court cases (1,250 court cases were settled by 31 March 2009) and, at the same time, required that the SPS establish an administrative scheme to deal with claims from prisoners and former prisoners who had not yet raised court actions. Here the aim was to provide a means of settling claims without the need for legal advice or proceedings in order to minimise the cost to the public of meeting Scottish Ministers' liabilities. By 31 March 2009 around 8,250 claims had been received, over 5,800 claims had been repudiated and approximately 2,240 claims had been settled. The practice of 'slopping out' no longer exists with all prisoners in Scotland now having access to toilet facilities (SPS 2009).

Human rights violations in prisons, in any jurisdiction, raise continuing questions about the decision to imprison, the experience of confinement and preparation for re-entry. The cases discussed above, in exposing the SPS to human rights challenges, have acted as instruments of reform across Scotland's prisons. More generally, however, human rights challenges demonstrate that while prisons are rule-bound institutions they are also places where the rule of law can be deficient, where the prison in effect operates as a lawless agency (Piacentini 2008). Arguably Scotland is better placed than many other jurisdictions to develop a good track record in human rights:

its jurisdiction is small and underpinning the political context is the fundamental question about the kind of penal system Scotland aspires to have. Given the Scottish Prisons Commission's recommendation in favour of prison reduction, there is considerable scope to develop a debate on linking human rights to cultural sensibilities, while recognising that the politicisation of debates on punishment cannot be separated from discussions about penal ideals (Piacentini 2004, 2008).

Concluding comments

The growth in Scotland's prison population in common with other countries that have opted for the 'prison solution' generally reflects global penal transformations and broad social and cultural changes (Garland 2001), the emergence of the prison industrial complex (Davis 2003), the use of the prison in managing poverty and marginality (Beckett and Sasson 2004; Wacquant 2009), changing public attitudes to crime and punishment (Roberts and Hough 2002) and culturally specific changes in penal policies and their impact on sentencing practices (Tonry and Frase 2001). Among the specific factors contributing to the rise in Scotland's prison population (while crime levels fall), many of which it shares in common with England and Wales, are increased use of immediate custody and remands by the courts, increases in average sentence lengths, stricter enforcement and use of prison in response to breach of community penalties and stiffer legislation and increases in recalls for prisoners released on licence/under supervision. Given this, the key question must be whether Scotland can draw on its historical traditions and cultural ideals to reverse the present trends. The current nationalist-led Scottish Government, in establishing the Scottish Prisons Commission to examine the growth in the prison population, explicitly sought to break with penal policy 'south of the border' in favour of pursuing Scandinavian models (Armstrong and McNeill 2009) which, as noted earlier, have produced much lower rates of incarceration. Somewhat paradoxically, however, the latest Criminal Justice (Scotland) Bill still commits the present government to the extant policies of other political parties to build additional prison places. What then are the prospects that Scotland will implement the Scottish Prison Commission's decarceration ambition to reduce the prison population to its level in the early 1990s of around 5,000, just less than 100 per 100,000 of the general population?

Setting a prison reduction target is, in and of itself, certainly a beginning. But it is only a beginning (Tombs 2006). The Scottish Prison Commission's Report, in common with many other official and quasi-official reports about the 'proper' use of imprisonment, reaches conclusions and makes recommendations in several areas, three of which are especially important to reimagining what and who prisons are for. First, it recommends that prison should be used only for those 'people whose offences are so serious that no other form of punishment will do and for those who pose a threat of serious harm to the public' (SPC 2008: 3). Second, it recommends that community-based penalties, reconfigured as 'community payback', should be used for those who do not have to be in prison (see Chapter 11), notably for those currently given short prison sentences. Third, it recommends 'a more restricted and rational use of imprisonment' which would enable the SPS 'to get better at regulating prisons and prisoners, at using accommodation resources intelligently to incentivise prisoners to come off and stay off drugs … and at providing and prioritising rehabilitation' (SPC 2008: 5).

Whether and how such a reconfiguration will be achieved remains to be seen. Though notions of rehabilitation in prisons have been around for centuries, from the missionary zeal of John Howard and his 'furnishing felons with tools' speech in *The State of the Prisons* (1777: 24) to the correctional claims of the current US penal system that pathways from offending into the military 'makes men out of boys' and acts as a desistance process (Bouffard and Laub 2004), the high reimprisonment rates for ex-prisoners (around two-thirds of whom return within two years of release) is testament to the prison's failure not only in preventing reoffending but also in preventing further social harm. The prison's failure to protect the public and reduce reoffending, together with the growth in prison populations internationally, has informed much of the prison abolitionist movement, which asks the question: if prison is counter-productive to reducing social harm to society, the victim and the offender, can imprisonment ever be justified?[6] Regardless of how that question is answered, what can be said now is that the prison remains a peculiar institution in which to imagine that rehabilitation can occur. The prison's primary function of keeping people in confinement against their will necessarily subverts the realisation of rehabilitative or therapeutic objectives (Carlen and Tombs 2006). Given the circumstances of Scotland's prisoners, and the communities from which they are drawn and to which they will return, any real prison reduction policy will require to both recognise and act on our knowledge that prisons cannot provide a solution to social ills and that criminal justice cannot redress the problems created by social injustice. The Scottish Prisons Commission's conclusion recognises this, arguing that, in order to limit the use of imprisonment 'we first need up-front investment in better services in and for Scotland's communities' (SPC 2008: 6). This conclusion also resonates with contemporary discussions in the UK about the possibility of using the principles of justice reinvestment (Allen and Stern 2007) to transfer resources currently invested in criminal justice to investment in redressing the problems created by social injustice. That, to use the title of the Scottish Prison Commission's Report, is now 'Scotland's Choice'.

Notes

1 See Roche (2007) on France, Webster and Doob (2007) on Canada, Lappi-Seppala (2007) and Pratt (2008a, 2008b) on Scandinavia and Tonry (2004) on Germany.
2 See Van Zyl Smit and Snacken (2009) in relation to debates about the Europeanisation of penal policy.
3 For a detailed review of the development of services within prisons throughout this period see Coyle (1991).
4 For his own inspiring accounts see Boyle (1977, 1984).
5 See Prison Privatisation Report International at http://www.psiru.org/justice.
6 See Mathieson (1974, 1986), Christie (1981) and Sim (1994) for debates on the prison as a 'social problem'.

References

Allen, R. and Stern, V. (2007) *Justice Reinvestment: A New Approach to Crime and Justice*. London: International Centre for Prison Studies.

Armstrong, S. and McNeil, F. (2009) 'Choice versus crisis: how Scotland could transform thinking about prisons and punishment', *Criminal Justice Matters*, 75: 2–4.

Beckett, K. and Sasson, T. (2004) *The Politics of Injustice*. London: Sage.

Bouffard, L. A. and Laub, L. H. (2004) 'Jail or the army: does military service facilitate desistance from crime?', in S. Maruna and R. Immarigeon (eds), *After Crime and Punishment: Pathways to Offender Reintegration*. Cullompton: Willan Publishing.

Boyle, J. (1977) *A Sense of Freedom*. Edinburgh: Canongate.

Boyle, J. (1984) *The Pains of Confinement*. Edinburgh: Canongate.

Carlen, P. (2001) 'Death and the triumph of governance? Lessons from the Scottish women's prison', *Punishment and Society*, 3/4: 459–71.

Carlen, P. and Tombs, J. (2006) 'Reconfigurations of penality: the ongoing case of the women's imprisonment and reintegration industries', *Theoretical Criminology*, 10 (3): 337–60.

Cavadino, M. and Dignan, J. (2005) *Penal Systems: A Comparative Approach*. London: Sage.

Christie, N. (1981) *Limits to Pain*. London: Martin Robertson.

Christie, N. (1994) *Crime Control as Industry: Towards Gulags, Western Style*. London: Routledge.

Cooke, D. (1989) 'Containing violent prisoners: an analysis of the Barlinnie Special Unit', *British Journal of Criminology*, 29: 129–43.

Cooke, D. (1997) 'The Barlinnie Special Unit: the rise and fall of a therapeutic experiment', in E. Cullen, L. Jones and R. Woodward (eds), *Therapeutic Communities for Offenders*. Chichester: Wiley.

Coyle, A. (1991) *Inside: Rethinking Scotland's Prisons*. Edinburgh: Scottish Child.

Davis, A. (2003) *Are Prisons Obsolete?* New York: Seven Stories Press.

Foucault, M. (1977) *Discipline and Punish: The Birth of the Prison*. London: Allen Lane.

Garland, D. (2001) *The Culture of Control: Crime and Social Order in Contemporary Society*. New York: Oxford University Press.

Haines, K. (1990) *After-care Services for Released Prisoners: A Review of the Literature*. London: Home Office.

HM Chief Inspector of Prisons (2009) *Report for England and Wales, 2008–9*. London: The Stationery Office.

Houchin, R. (2005) *Social Exclusion and Imprisonment in Scotland: A Report*. Edinburgh: Scottish Executive.

Hough, M., Millie, A. and Jacobson, J. (2003) *The Decision to Imprison: Sentencing and the Prison Population*. London: Prison Reform Trust.

Howard, J., Forsythe, W. J., Gurney, J. J., Fry, E., Maybrick, F. E., Neild, J., Clay, W. L. and Griffiths, A. ([1777] 2000 edn) *The State of the Prisons in Britain 1775–1905*. London: Routledge.

Ignatieff, M. (1978) *A Just Measure of Pain*. London: Macmillan.

Lappi-Seppala, T. (2007) 'Penal policy in Scandinavia', in M. Tonry (ed.), *Crime, Punishment and Politics in Comparative Perspective*. Chicago: University of Chicago Press.

McNeill, F. (2003) 'Desistance-focused probation practice', in W. H. Chui and M. Nellis (eds), *Moving Probation Forward: Evidence, Arguments and Practice*. Harlow: Pearson Longman.

Maruna, S. (2001) *Making Good: How Ex-Convicts Reform and Rebuild Their Lives*. Washington, DC: American Psychological Association Books.

Mathieson, T. (1974) *The Politics of Abolition*. London: Martin Robertson.

Mathieson, T. (1986) 'The politics of abolition', *Contemporary Crisis*, 10: 81–94.

Mathieson, T. (2000) *Prison on Trial*. Winchester: Waterside Press.

Melossi, D. and Pavarini, M. (1981) *The Prison and the Factory: The Origins of the Penitentiary*. Basingstoke: Macmillan.

Morgan, R. and Leibling, A. (2007) 'Imprisonment: an expanding scene', in M. Maguire, R. Morgan and R. Reiner (eds), *The Oxford Handbook of Criminology*. Oxford: Oxford University Press.

Murphy, T. and Whitty, N. (2007) 'Risk and human rights in UK prison governance', *British Journal of Criminology*, 46 (5): 798–816.

Nellis, M. (2010) 'Creative Arts and the Cultural Politics of Penal Reform: The Early Years of the Barlinnie Special Unit, 1973–1981'. Unpublished manuscript.

Paterson, F. and Tombs, J. (1998) *Social Work and Criminal Justice: The Impact of Policy*. Edinburgh: The Stationery Office.

Pease, K. (1994) 'Cross-national imprisonment rates: limitations of method and possible conclusions', in R. D. King and M. Maguire (eds), *Prisons in Context*. Oxford: Clarendon Press.

Piacentini, L. (2004) *Surviving Russian Prisons: Punishment, Politics and Economy in Transition*. Cullompton: Willan Publishing.

Piacentini, L. (2005) *Prisons and Rehabilitation in Scotland*. Edinburgh: Scottish Parliament.

Piacentini, L. (2008) 'Burden or benefit? Paradoxes of penal transition in Russia', in K. McEvoy and L. McGregor (eds), *Transitional Justice from Below: Grassroots Activism and the Struggle for Change*. Oxford: Hart.

Piacentini, L., Pallot, J. and Moran, D. (2010) 'Welcome to Malaya Rodina (Little Homeland): gender and penal order in a Russian prison', *Journal of Socio-Legal Studies*, 18 (4): 523–42.

Pratt, J. (2008a) 'Scandinavian exceptionalism in an era of penal excess: Part I – The nature and roots of Scandinavian exceptionalism', *British Journal of Criminology*, 48 (2): 119–37.

Pratt, J. (2008b) 'Scandinavian exceptionalism in an era of penal excess: Part II – Does Scandinavian exceptionalism have a future?', *British Journal of Criminology*, 48 (3): 275–92.

Radzinowicz, L. and Hood, R. (1990) *The Emergence of Penal Policy in Victorian and Edwardian England*. Oxford: Clarendon Press.

Roberts, J. and Hough, M. (2002) *Changing Attitudes to Punishment: Public Opinion, Crime and Justice*. Cullompton: Willan Publishing.

Roche, S. (2007) 'Criminal justice policy in France: illusions of severity', in M. Tonry (ed.), *Crime, Punishment and Politics in Comparative Perspective*. Chicago: University of Chicago Press.

Rusche, G. and Kirchheimer, O. (1968) *Punishment and Social Structure*. New York: Columbia University Press.

Rutherford, A. (1984) *Prisons and the Process of Justice*. Oxford: Oxford University Press.

Scottish Consortium on Crime and Criminal Justice (SCCCJ) (2006) *Women in Prison in Scotland: An Unmet Commitment*. Edinburgh: SCCCJ.

Scottish Consortium on Crime and Criminal Justice (SCCCJ) (2007) *The Cost of Unnecessary Imprisonment*. Edinburgh: SCCCJ.

Scottish Consortium on Crime and Criminal Justice (SCCCJ) (2010) *Crime and Justice in Scotland 2009*. Edinburgh: SCCCJ.

Scottish Executive (2000) *Punishment First: Verdict Later: A Review of Conditions for Remand Prisoners in Scotland at the end of the 20th Century*, HM Chief Inspector of Prisons Thematic Report. Edinburgh: Scottish Executive.

Scottish Executive (2002a) *Prisons' Estates Review*. Edinburgh: Scottish Executive.

Scottish Executive (2002b) *A Better Way*. Edinburgh: The Stationery Office.

Scottish Government (2009) *Prison Statistics Scotland: 2008–09*, Statistical Bulletin, Crime and Justice Series. Edinburgh: Scottish Government.

Scottish Government (2010) *Scottish Prison Population Projections: 2009–2010 to 2018–2019*, Statistical Release, Crime and Justice Series. Edinburgh: Scottish Government.

Scottish Office (1998) *A Safer Way: The Government's Response*. Edinburgh: The Scottish Office.

Scottish Prison Service (SPS) (1990) *Opportunity and Responsibility: Developing New Approaches to the Management of the Long-Term Prison System in Scotland*. Edinburgh: Scottish Prison Service.

Scottish Prison Service (SPS) (2000) *Intervention and Integration*. Edinburgh: Scottish Prison Service.

Scottish Prison Service (SPS) (2009) *Annual Reports and Accounts 2008–09*, SG/2009/130. Edinburgh: Scottish Government.

Scottish Prison Service (SPS) *2010 Prisoner Survey 2009: 12th Survey Bulletin*. Edinburgh: Scottish Prison Service.

Scottish Prisons Commission (SPC) (2008) *Scotland's Choice: Report of the Scottish Prisons Commission*. Edinburgh: Scottish Government.

Sim, J. (1994) 'The abolitionist approach: a British perspective', in A. Duff, S. Marshall, R. Dobash and R. Dobash (eds), *Penal Theory and Practice: Tradition and Innovation in Criminal Justice*. Manchester: Manchester University Press.

Smith, R. (1984) 'Grendon, the Barlinnie Special Unit, and the Wormwood Scrubs Annexe: experiments in penology', *British Medical Journal*, 288 (1): 472–5.

Social Work Services and Prisons Inspectorates for Scotland (1998) *Women Offenders – A Safer Way*. Edinburgh: The Stationery Office.

Tombs, J. (2003) *The Chance for Change: A Study of the Throughcare Centre Edinburgh Prison*, Occasional Paper Series No. 4. Edinburgh: Scottish Prison Service.

Tombs, J. (2004a) *A Unique Punishment: Sentencing and the Prison Population in Scotland*. Edinburgh: Scottish Consortium on Crime and Criminal Justice.

Tombs, J. (2004b) 'From "A Safer to a Better Way": transformations in penal policy for women', in G. McIvor (ed.), *Women Who Offend*. London: Jessica Kingsley.

Tombs, J. (2005) *Reducing the Prison Population: Penal Policy and Social Choices*. Edinburgh: Scottish Consortium on Crime and Criminal Justice.

Tombs, J. (2006) 'Towards decarceration', in C. Fox, G. Gall and J. Scott (eds), *Whose Justice? The Law and the Left*. Edinburgh: Scottish Left Review Press.

Tombs, J. and Jagger, E. (2006) 'Denying responsibility: sentencers' accounts of their decisions to imprison', *British Journal of Criminology*, 46 (5): 803–21.

Tonry, M. (2004) 'Why aren't German penal policies harsher and imprisonment rates higher?', *German Law Journal*, 5 (10).

Tonry, M. and Frase, R. (2001) *Sentencing and Sanctions in Western Countries*. Oxford: Oxford University Press.

Van Zyl Smit, D. and Snacken, S. (2009) *Principles of European Prison Law and Policy: Penology and Human Rights*. Oxford: Oxford University Press.

Wacquant, L. (2009) *Punishing the Poor: The New Government of Social Insecurity*. Durham, NC: Duke University Press.

Wahidin, A. (2009) 'Prisons in context', in A. Hucklesby and A. Wahidin (eds), *Criminal Justice*. Oxford: Oxford University Press.

Walmsley, R. (2000) *Prison Population Size: Problems and Solutions*. Paper presented at a Council of Europe Seminar.

Webster, C. M. and Doob, A. (2007) 'Punitive trends and stable imprisonment rates in Canada', in M. Tonry (ed.), *Crime, Punishment and Politics in Comparative Perspective*. Chicago: University of Chicago Press.

World Prison Brief (2009) http://www.kcl.ac.uk/depsta/law/research/icps/worldbrief/ (accessed 3 February 2010).

Part 4

Looking ahead

Chapter 13

Criminal justice in Scotland: overview and prospects

Mary Munro, Gerry Mooney and Hazel Croall

Introduction

> Perhaps one ought actually to be a Scotchman to conceive how ardently, under all distinctions of rank and situation, they feel their mutual connexion with each other as natives of the same country. There are, I believe, more associations common to the inhabitants of rude and wild, than of a well cultivated and fertile country; their ancestors have more seldom changed their place of residence; their mutual recollections of remarkable objects is more accurate; the high and the low are more interested in each other's welfare; the feelings of kindred and relationship are more widely extended, and in a word, the bonds of patriotic affection, always honourable even when a little too exclusively strained, have more influence on men's feelings and actions. (From Walter Scott, *The Heart of Midlothian* (1818: 393), Penguin Classics edition, 1994)

> Fuck the facts, these trivial things, they petty jealousies become part of the mythology in a place like Leith, a place fill ay nosey cunts who willnae mind their ain business. A place ay white trash in a trash country fill ay dispossessed white trash. (From Irvine Welsh, *Trainspotting* (1993: 190), Vintage Classics edition, 2004)

Scottish criminal justice was exposed to international scrutiny in an unprecedented fashion on 20 August 2009 when the Justice

Secretary announced his decision to release the man convicted of the Lockerbie bombing in 1988, Abdelbaset Ali Mohmed Al-Megrahi, on compassionate grounds, commenting that 'in Scotland, we are a people who pride ourselves on our humanity' as a 'defining characteristic of Scotland and the Scottish people' (MacAskill 2009). As he defended this decision in the face of the outrage of many in the Scottish Parliament and elsewhere he would have done so with the Parliamentary Mace and its inscription 'Wisdom – Justice – Compassion – Integrity' in view. If the political estate lays claim to these virtues on behalf of a dissenting nation to what extent may it be said that Scottish criminal justice embodies and practises them?

First though we return to the question of mythologies. One such is the idea that a particular pedigree of libertarian and 'democratic' sentiment in Scotland may be traced from the Declaration of Arbroath in 1320, then in Buchanan's 1579 secular fulminations against tyranny, through to the remarkable Scottish contribution to Enlightenment philosophy in the eighteenth century and, through twists and turns, culminating in the singing of Burns's *A Man's a Man* at the opening of the Scottish Parliament in 1998 (Reid 2006). Of course there is an obverse history that would foreground the intolerant state theocracy of Calvinism and Presbyterianism, the bloody civil wars and rebellion, the persistence of feudalism, the clearances, the pitiless industrialisation and widening social inequality, perhaps culminating in the A & E departments of major Scottish hospitals in the emergency treatment of another casualty of a drunken stabbing. However, our business here is not history, nor do we profess to have any expertise in that discipline. What is of relevance to this review is the traction of myth, especially benign myth, to Scotland's particularist view of itself, especially, as is implied in the Scott extract above, as a more rational, benevolent and equal society than that of the greater power south of the border (see Mooney and Poole 2004).

Historical criminology both of the history of the past and a detailed critical 'history of the present' is undeveloped in Scotland. This matters first because rich accounts of pivotal events such as the creation of the children's hearings system and the closure of the Barlinnie Special Unit, penetrating down to the possibly crucial role of key individuals and networks as well as wider contexts, call out for research before key protagonists with accurate memories are lost. This matters secondly because we are persuaded by Lacey's point that contemporary penal differences between relatively similar societies should be understood in terms of historical differences, and that because of these, globalisation and the communication revolution of recent years, will not necessarily or inevitably result in convergent penal policies (Lacey 2008). In thinking about Scotland, as Farmer has pointed out, the preservation of the separate legal jurisdiction at the Act of Union in 1707 has meant that the practices and institutions of law have in important ways come to represent and carry the burden of Scottish culture, identity and privilege (Farmer 1997; Michie 1997). This insight helps account for a persistent and sometimes explicit claim to an intrinsic superiority, both morally and technically, for Scottish justice. So we find that the eighteenth-century legal scholar Baron Hume defends the Scots' criminal common law against the codification he observes in England, 'a country, where, owing to the much greater number of dissolute and profligate people, and to the greater progress of every refinement, and every sort of corruption, crimes are both far more frequent, and far more various in their nature, than among ourselves' (Hume 1844 edn, p. 4). Furthermore, he observes 'our custom of punishment is eminently gentle' compared with the excessive resort to the death penalty in England (Hume 1844 edn). Writing in his *Practice of the Criminal Law in Scotland* (1833) Archibald Alison made a similar point, that Scottish practice achieved a more humane and enlightened procedure than the 'laws of some other states' (quoted in Michie 1997). However, he did so as a landed Tory who vigorously suppressed political dissent. The schizoid space between the benevolent sentiment and the perhaps harsh or malevolent actuality is one that in various forms we find recurring both in Scottish literature (for example, Stevenson's *Jekyll and Hyde* or Hogg's *Confessions of a Justified Sinner*) and the shade and the light, the complexity that is Scottish justice.

It is against this background and tradition that the first of our themes, the claim that Scottish criminal justice is distinctive in both UK and wider international contexts, may be considered. For example, McNeill and Whyte begin their account of criminal justice social work in Scotland by suggesting that in this respect at least Scotland 'stands out as a penal anachronism' in comparison with other English-speaking jurisdictions (2007). In an influential and eloquent series of papers McAra has argued that 'penal welfarism', which she defines as activity that is rehabilitative, reintegrative and 'predicated on the existence of a broader political commitment to the advancement of social justice', persisted in Scotland in the face of a 'punitive turn' in other Anglo-American jurisdictions (McAra 2005, 2007, 2008). Her claims are grounded in evidence of the survival of continuing therapeutic and rehabilitative practices of prisons, social work and the children's hearings system despite exposure to the same economic, political and social insecurities and changes that have been related to punitivism elsewhere. The explanation she offers is that welfarist values have a particular 'cultural anchorage' in Scotland related to a distinctively progressive civil society committed to a strongly social democratic tradition (see Garland 2006, on cultural analysis and understanding punishment). This has insulated it from the negative effects of both political change in London and the complex shifts in some other Anglo-American jurisdictions described in the 'culture of control' and 'new penology' theses to explain contemporary changes in justice practices (Feeley and Simon 1992, 1994; Garland 2001). It is the smallness of this 'wee jurisdiction' which enables a few individuals in the civil service, justice professions and institutions, the liberal elite, to communicate in essentially self-reflexive systems and that this, she argues, contributes to a greater degree of coherence, stability and conservatism in the face of change (McAra 2008). In relation to sentencing too, Tombs has argued that there has been a Scottish tradition of shorter sentences than in England and Wales that contributed to slower rates of increase in the prison population during the period of escalation. This, she suggests, can be attributed to the effect of political distance from Westminster at least prior to devolution and the protective effect this had from populist calls to be tough on crime (Millie *et al.* 2007).

To what extent then is this distinctiveness hypothesis validated by the accounts in the book? The clearest exposition comes, not unexpectedly, from McAra and McVie's discussion of youth and child justice (see Chapter 4). Nonetheless their historical account of the embodiment of welfarist values in the children's hearings reforms of the late 1960s throws up interesting contradictory speculation as to why, for example, this culture was prepared to tolerate an extremely low age of criminal responsibility on the one hand, and the abrupt propulsion of 16-year-olds (other than those already under supervision) into the adult criminal system on the other, especially at a period when criminal justice social work was not protected from competing priorities in generic departments. The striking paucity of research into the functioning and evidence base of the hearings system for decades after its establishment may speak to the confidence, faith and shared values of powerful and connected individuals, a concern to protect the hearings from Thatcherist scrutiny, but also it might be that the distinctiveness of the hearings system had itself become a signifier of Scottish identity and therefore not to be tampered with (Chapter 1; also Johnstone and Burman 2009).

Similarly Munro and McNeill's discussion of community sanctions (Chapter 11) reiterates the crucial practice and institutional legacy of the Kilbrandon reforms that resulted in the absorption and, for some decades, disappearance of Scottish social work with offenders as a distinct enterprise. The widespread view that criminal justice social work was properly located as a function of local government, connecting to the provision of services for all citizens, contributed to the resistance to a single corrections agency proposed in 2003, and has both in terms of professional and institutional values contributed to the persistence of and continuation of welfarist practices. Tata's observation in Chapter 10 of practices in the preparation of social enquiry reports that amount to a hybridisation of 'old' penal welfare and 'new' narratives of risk is also relevant here. However, Munro and McNeill (Chapter 11) also argue that an account of Scottish penality should pay attention to the fine as punishment, and in so doing suggest two further difficulties in relation to 'welfarism' as a commitment to social justice. The first of these is the persistent indifference to the question of setting monetary penalties systematically according to means. The second is the promotion of 'welfarist' supervised attendance orders as an alternative to the fine resulting in a degree of intervention and intrusion in people's lives simply on the grounds that they are poor.

The Barlinnie Special Unit (1973–93) was the site of an extraordinarily creative (in all senses), but perhaps accidentally, therapeutic project in the management of the most challenging of prisoners (Chapter 12). However, the important point is that it was and remains exceptional, was not replicated and was eventually abandoned. It is important to be cautious in extrapolating from this exceptionalism, or indeed official rhetoric of penal aims, to a reading of the Scottish prison service as being distinctively therapeutic or rehabilitative in practice. So we learn that it was not until it became possible to seek redress through human rights litigation following devolution for the degrading conditions experienced by prisoners that action was taken to end practices such as 'slopping out' and, as Tombs and Piacentini point out, gross overcrowding hardly contributes to positive 'offender outcomes'. There is also evidence that the penal welfarist impulse has been limited in relation to the throughcare and resettlement of prisoners. The pioneering achievements of Brebner in the early nineteenth century were also exceptional for the time and remained so until relatively recently: precedents may be set but are not necessarily followed as common practice. Paradoxically it may be argued that it is that discourses of public protection, and more recently the concern to reduce reoffending, rather than welfarism as such, that have resulted in financial and institutional investment in resettlement and reintegration.

Policing in Scotland has been and is distinct in that, with some exceptions, the British Transport Police for example, the administration and governance of the territorial forces have developed separately from those in the rest of the UK. In this context, it is perhaps more difficult to argue for the existence of any specific values or practices or culture that characterise policing here rather than elsewhere. Indeed Fyfe's account in Chapter 9 underlines the challenges, responses and practices that Scottish policing has in common with elsewhere in terms of the pluralisation of policing, the management of disorder including experiments with zero tolerance, and tensions in relation to governance and local or central control. Although there are differences between developments here and the rest of the UK, this seems to be a consequence of the diversity of structures rather than any intrinsic distinctiveness of values or approach.

Tata's discussion of sentencing in Scotland (Chapter 10) also establishes the distinctiveness of the Scottish criminal legal process, the power and independence of the judiciary and especially the weight given to discretionary decision-making at the point of sentencing. Procedures and penal decisions are justified in terms of law and expediency and are limited in their capacity to exercise social justice.

Challenging welfarist myths?

In thinking about distinctiveness, we would suggest that it is possible to be somewhat more sceptical than McAra about the alignment and characterisation of Scotland's penal institutions in terms of 'welfarism', mutualism and social justice: an alignment that connects penal habits with particular kinds of social and political values and is tinged, perhaps, with the benign romanticism of Scott in the prefacing quotation. A change of lens to incorporate a wider evidential base for analysis, as here, suggests that a focus on welfarism as a defining characteristic of pre-devolution Scottish justice risks a de-emphasis on other continuities of punitivism and exclusion, implying some kind of binary divide between 'welfare' on the one hand, and 'punitivism' on the other. The argument that Scottish welfare is now less distinctive – and arguably more punitive or less welfarist than in the past as we will consider below – carries an assumption about the nature, spread and extent of that past welfarism. A perhaps more sceptical account also serves to open up richer research questions for a 'history of the present', one that admits the possibility of other mechanisms of difference such as, for instance, a conservatism of neglect and complacency rather than progressive liberal values. Avoiding a somewhat uncritical and romanticised view of a mythical golden age is absolutely crucial if we are to understand the shape and future direction of Scottish criminal justice as it unfolds today. For example, one suggestive indicator is that in 1998, at the cusp of devolution, the imprisonment rate per 100,000 population in Scotland was 120, a rate that has a greater similarity to that of England and Wales at 125 than, say, Denmark (another small jurisdiction) at 65 (Walmsley 1999).

Furthermore, a central weakness of the distinctiveness thesis is the claim that Scotland was protected from the worst aspects of Thatcherism, which may be true at a symbolic level but for the majority of people in Scotland certainly not at a material level. In this respect McAra is not alone and her arguments here closely relate to those other accounts (McCrone 2001; Paterson 1994; Paterson *et al.* 2004) which suggest Scotland's professional and middle classes were committed to a form of welfare nationalism which 'guarded' state welfare provision (see also Law 2005; Law and Mooney 2010; McEwen 2002, 2006). This welfarism stretched to criminal justice and in particular to youth justice and in this respect penal welfarism is regarded as part and parcel of a wider welfarist ethos that was regarded as both reflecting and underpinning 'Scottish' values and attitudes. The broader discussion of inequalities, exclusion, crime and victimisation in Chapter 2, and of marginality, perceptions of urban disorder and 'problem populations' in Chapter 3, suggest that there have been systemic and long- standing social, cultural and political failures that are seriously at odds with this view.

The second theme developed in the book connects to the second limb of McAra's argument, namely that the central paradox in Scottish criminal justice is that there has been a process of 'detartanisation' that may be traced to shifts in penality shortly before devolution but which became more marked thereafter resulting in a condition she describes as 'welfarism in crisis' (McAra 2007). 'Detartanisation' stands for a process of policy convergence in which the formerly distinctive adherence to welfarist penal values gives way to a 'complex mix of competing, and somewhat competing rationales' that are associated with the late adoption and adaptation of values associated with actuarial and managerial approaches to justice

(McAra 2007). Devolution itself is seen as the key variable insofar as the viability of the welfarist position relied on a political identity that defined itself as 'not-England', and therefore consequent reforms in political governance undermined that position allowing 'more visceral, penal discourses to leech in' (McAra 1998b; and also Chapter 4, this volume). The result was an exposure of Scottish justice to a 'populist punitivism' from which it had been insulated hitherto, associated with a proliferation of new administrative arrangements ('hyper-institutionalisation') on the one hand and a weakening of consensual, elitist welfarist influences on the other.

McAra and McVie detail such processes of 'detartanisation' in their discussion of youth justice in Chapter 4. Similarly Munro and McNeill's discussion in Chapter 11 of community sanctions and criminal justice social work allude to numerous developments that mirror those of England and Wales with the crucial difference in governance referred to above. The effect of shifts in penality in relation to imprisonment are exposed in Chapter 12, in which Tombs and Piacentini lay stress on the dramatic increases in the incarcerated population since the 1990s and the complex drivers of increases in custody despite a concomitant proliferation of 'alternative' sentences. These include judicial responses to what are perceived to be changes in the profile of cases coming before the courts in terms of seriousness, as well as the significance of changes in the political milieu and an 'inflationary drift' in sentencing. The rise in the prison population is in part attributable to more and longer sentences, but also to increases in the remand population (see also Armstrong 2009), licence recalls and breaches of community orders. In the case of the last we might read some evidence of a shift away from welfarism in the direction of control and public protection on the part of statutory agencies. Thus, as a snapshot to illustrate the point, the moment represented by official acceptance in 1998 of proposals to reduce significantly the female prisoner population following suicides in HMP Cornton Vale may be contrasted with the dramatic and disproportionate rise in the imprisonment of adult and young women that actually took place over the following decade. This speaks to the weakness of 'welfarist' intentions in the face of the force of such dynamics (Chapter 5; see also Chapter 12; Barry and McIvor 2010). Furthermore, the remarkable recent history of monetary penalties, their severance from traditional judicial oversight and relocation within police and prosecution bureaucratic processes, is also suggestive of the new normalisation of social control rather than welfarist values within the Scottish justice system (Chapter 11). Similar claims may be made in relation to the 'policing' of antisocial behaviour and the criminalisation of social policy (see Chapters 3 and 9) and the politicisation of youth crime, especially under the New Labour dominated administrations of the first two post-devolution sessions of Parliament (Chapters 2 and 4).

In the context of the processes of criminal law and sentencing, Tata observes a shift away during the post-devolution period from due process (more purist justice) values in criminal procedure towards practices that give greater weight to efficiency and economy (Chapter 10). In a detailed investigation of these trends in relation to the key areas of legal aid and plea negotiation, the preparation and use of social inquiry reports and then technological innovation in informing sentencing, he finds that changes are by no means as clearly defined in day-to-day operation on the ground as their expression in rhetoric and managerial expectations might suggest. He therefore draws an important distinction between the globalisation of policy discourse and local practices and cultures that serve to modify them (see also in particular McNeill *et al.* 2009, on this 'governmentality gap' in the analysis of penal change).

Together these accounts suggest that there is evidence in support of the idea of convergence as suggested by McAra. We would depart from her analysis to the extent that it perhaps implies that punitive discourses were somehow essentially alien and external to Scotland, and admitted only because of a more permeable, weakened jurisdictional boundary following devolution, and that this is seen to be problematic. What was exceptional, we suggest, was that the political governance of Scottish criminal justice prior to devolution was restrained, constrained and limited by the 'democratic deficit' of the union settlement which allowed for the anachronistic dominance of values associated with liberal elitism, albeit that these were inclined in important respects towards penal moderation. In this reading, reforms were inhibited by the lack of opportunity pre-devolution afforded by limited Westminster time and interest in subjecting justice issues to debate, innovation and democratic scrutiny. New democratic structures following devolution including new and expanded opportunities for media engagement allowed space for the articulation of local punitive values that have much in common with those in England and Wales (Hutton 2005). Indeed, to return to the admittedly crude comparator provided by international imprisonment rates, it is noted that Scotland currently shares with its southern neighbour the dubious distinction of being 'top of the league' in comparison with most other jurisdictions in Europe (Scottish Government 2009).

Intriguingly there are also hints of new trajectories of distinctiveness since the formation of the SNP Government in 2007. In Chapter 4, McAra and McVie point to a retreat from populist rhetoric in relation to youth justice and a less 'confrontational' relationship with professional bodies. It is difficult to disentangle the politics of minority rule from genuine ideological differences, but it was noteworthy that in vexed areas of adult penal policy, imprisonment and antisocial behaviour, inquiries were set up to advise on ways forward (Scottish Government 2009; Scottish Prisons Commission 2008). The pace of change slowed: there was no rush to legislate, issues were kicked into touch. The resulting explicit policy shift away from penal escalation to moderation, from punitivism as imprisonment to an emphasis on reparative payback (Chapters 4 and 12) mark a change from the instincts of previous administrations and again opens up a space, possibly fragile, between Scottish justice and that of the other UK jurisdictions (see also below).

The third of our book-wide themes is inequality. A further departure from McAra's analysis relates to the underplaying, or indeed ignoring, of economic and social inequality as critical dimensions in relation to the explication of social justice values and Scottish distinctiveness. In our reading, class and other social divisions are important issues to which we need to be alert. These have formed central themes in chapters addressing aspects of social inequality such as class, the 'othering' of urban populations, age, gender, race and ethnicity, and by extension, the focus on the problematic of corporate and white-collar and environmental crime (Chapters 7 and 8). There is a neglect, or at least a misunderstanding, of issues of class in shaping social and in particular criminal justice policy. In turn this connects with issues of power – of questions of the relationship between welfarism and control – and the historic management of 'problem populations' (see Johnstone and Mooney 2007; Mooney 2008; and see Chapter 3, this volume) within Scottish society. Taking as central concerns the issues of inequalities and power and their relationship with crimes and criminal justice at a number of different levels (see Cook 2006; Newman and Yeates 2008), questions of social justice and injustice have featured strongly in our account as they relate to contemporary Scottish society.

In Chapter 2 we make the point that understanding how processes of criminalisation connect with inequalities matters in thinking about crime and criminal justice. The strong and enduring association between structural inequalities, class, poverty and deprivation, youth gang traditions and crime, victimisation and processes of enforcement in Scotland are outlined. Similar themes are picked up and expanded in the focus on urbanism and political and media discourses in relation to 'problem' populations in Chapter 3). The thrust of that analysis connects to the bleak negativism of Renton's voice in the quotation from *Trainspotting* above rather than to the benign sentimentalism of Scott.

McMillan (Chapter 5) explores the theme of inequality in relation to gender, drawing out distinctions between men and women both in terms of offending and victimisation, and especially how women are marginalised and discriminated against in a still essentially patriarchal criminal justice system. This discussion stresses the continuities and persistence of gender inequalities but with the hope that the working through of the new Gender Equality Duty on public authorities will serve as a catalyst for change. Croall and Frondigoun (Chapter 6) establish that the history of immigration and emigration in Scotland has resulted in a distinctive local pattern of responses to race and ethnicity that connect falsely to (yet another recurring) myth of greater and long-standing tolerance of non-sectarian differences. Again devolution is seen to mark a significant shift in discourses of nationalistic identity that were formerly defined in relation to the 'not-England', syndrome, leading to a new awareness and scrutiny of racial issues in Scotland, especially in the context of the challenges posed by terrorism and economic change. As a corrective to narratives that emphasise a concordance between disadvantage and offending, Ross and Croall (Chapter 7) offer an account of current issues in relation to corporate crime in Scotland. Questions of enforcement and sanctions, and the use of regulatory rather than criminal law, are developed especially in relation to corporate homicide. There is arguably space in law for a distinctively Scottish approach but as yet the form that this might take is unclear.

Walter's review of environmental crime (Chapter 8) clearly connects victimisation with social deprivation and notes that post-devolution politics have allowed for the representation of Green politics in Parliament. Although Scotland can be seen to have been a leader in taking environmental crime seriously, as crime rather than an administrative breach, the regulatory regime sits within UK and EU structures that promote trade rather than environmental protection, and different Scottish Governments have also pursued a strategy that privileges economic growth over environmental concerns.

Concluding comments and prospects for the future

A compilation of relatively brief essays such as offered in this collection can easily be criticised for its omissions – in our case, for example, sectarianism perhaps, or alcohol, drugs and offending, or an expanded discussion of prisoner resettlement, restorative justice, community safety or a consideration of the victim in Scottish criminal justice. We were also very much aware of having to gloss over what some may legitimately consider as essential detail. There may also be a thwarted expectation that the book would serve somehow as a parallel text with which to illuminate detailed differences between this jurisdiction and that of England and Wales (see Muir 2010). We consciously avoided this approach in any systematic way (although inevitably comparisons are drawn) because of the importance of promoting the study of criminal justice in Scotland in its own terms, albeit by stressing themes that have resonance and relevance in other places. As McAra has put it 'Scotland may be a small-scale jurisdiction but, in terms of criminological and penological theory, it has a big story to tell' (2008a).

So what might be said about the future course of criminal justice in Scotland? In capturing the moment covered by the period in which the book was prepared, we are left with a cliffhanger, as the Scottish Parliament is poised to pass or reject major changes in criminal justice policy. Even if the Criminal Justice and Licensing Bill's more progressive measures, by which we mean those tending towards penal moderation, do not survive, it is reasonable to expect the Reducing Reoffending agenda (the Scottish Government non-legislative response to the Prisons Commission) to become a platform for reframing the recent prioritisation of public protection and risk. It might be that this is a more than semantic retreat from 'offender management' – a term which has not, thankfully, become fixed institutionally following the quiet shelving of the high-level National Advisory Board on Offender Management in late 2009. There are indications that criminal justice social workers are finding it difficult to reconcile public protection and reoffending reduction objectives, especially in working with violent offenders (SWIA 2010). Yet the logic that legitimises welfarist practices in terms of public protection, a hybridisation of welfare and risk, does suggest that thinking of these as inevitably opposed is unhelpful (McIvor and McNeill 2007).

Hutton (2006) has deployed Bourdieu's concept of 'habitus' to label that bundle of influences, routines and professional assumptions that amount to the 'common sense' of discretionary and intuitive sentencing in a particular legal culture and stresses the degree to which sentencing must be understood as a social practice. Tombs argues that sheriffs' awareness of political mood and public opinion constrains sentencing because of the desirability of preserving public confidence; it is therefore to a shift in political discourse, she argues, that we must look to secure change in sentencing practice in the direction of greater or lesser punitiveness (Tombs 2004). It remains to be seen if that shift will take place in any durable way.

On the question of guidelines and sentencing, it might be that cherished and energetically defended judicial values of unfettered discretion will continue to resist anything other than the fudged and judicially dominated Scottish Sentencing Council established by the Criminal Justice and Licensing Act 2010. It was striking and somewhat curious how, in its passage through Parliament, politicians of all parties acted to reaffirm and consolidate judicial powers in relation to the Sentencing Council, rather than challenge them, in order to address 'the tension between the principle of the separation of powers and the influence of sentencing guidelines on judicial discretion' (Justice Committee, 2 March 2010, col. 2,712). Paradoxically this was done at the same time as attempts to give statutory force to a presumption against short custodial sentences[1] and, from opposition parties, to impose mandatory and lengthy prison sentences for knife possession. It is difficult to foresee how this peculiarly Scottish approach to consistency and transparency in sentencing will impact on punitiveness or otherwise, especially in the context of proposed restrictions on sentencing and the abandonment of a statutory definition of the purposes of sentencing in favour of a common-law understanding because 'purposes and principles of sentencing have been well established over the centuries and there is little or no need to put them in statute' (Justice Committee, 2 March 2010, col. 2,695). There is, however, another and interesting complication that may result from the newly discovered jurisdiction of the UK Supreme Court over Scottish criminal law (O'Neill 2010; see for a detailed analysis of possible models for a final appellate jurisdiction, Walker 2010). At this juncture it is impossible to predict the effect of this, if any, in provoking change to Scottish sentencing traditions and culture.[2] What can be said is that what seemed to be clear-cut boundaries between the criminal jurisdictions no longer appear to be as well defined, and that this may set in train profound institutional and penal changes – or may not!

It may also not be assumed that the fledgling agencies of Scottish actuarial practice such as the Risk Management Authority (2004), the

Scottish Accreditation Panel for Offender Programmes (2006) and MAPPAs (2007), are insulated from local traditions of scepticism, agency independence (as a justification for weak cooperation) and confusion as to roles in practice on the ground (SWIA/HMIC/HMIP 2009; Weaver and McNeill 2010). Key figures in these new agencies tend to be drawn from a small pool of the liberal elite, whose grounded beliefs in the primary importance of, for example, proportionality in sentencing may mean that actuarial values of public protection will not necessarily be overridden (McAra 2005).

The SNP Government has differed from its predecessors in the explicit turn, at least rhetorically, towards Scandinavian states, especially Finland, for models in education and health as well as penal matters. However, there are other global and transnational processes at work which cannot be grasped by a focus on narrow policy transfer alone. Devolution has reignited questions and issues of 'borders', both between the different parts of the UK – but also between the UK, other European countries and elsewhere. It has challenged the political boundaries and coherence of the United Kingdom, and Europeanisation and globalisation have brought processes of debordering or rebordering. This throws up questions of boundaries, belonging and identity – and of citizenship (Greer 2009; Wincott 2006). The critical intervention of the Justice Secretary in opposition to s. 44 of the Terrorism Act 2000 searches by the British Transport Police and divergences in relation to the treatment of refugees are examples of the tension here (Chapter 6). Proposals by Westminster politicians to repeal the Human Rights Act and replace it with a 'bill of rights' harking back to the Magna Carta would be both alien historically and constitutionally unsound and would have important repercussions in all the devolved jurisdictions, not least Scotland (Justice 2010).

The incorporation of the Human Rights Act 1998 and thereby the European Convention on Human Rights into the devolution legislation has been important not only in terms of consequent 'Strasbourg proofing' reforms in Scottish legal process but also in enabling litigation in relation to prison conditions and practices (Chapter 12). Also, despite the UK's opt-out from the EU Lisbon Treaty, it may be that Scottish criminal justice, like the other jurisdictions in the UK, will not be insulated from changes instigated at this level, and not just in relation to environmental crime (Chapter 8; Vaughan and Kilcommins 2010).

One of the first steps taken by the SNP government in 2007 was to negotiate a 'Concordat' with local authorities in which, in exchange for greater financial autonomy and various other modifications to the existing relationship between central and local government, each area was obliged to contract through the submission of a 'single outcome agreement' to meet overarching governmental objectives in relation to the delivery of public services. In the case of crime this was to contribute to a 'safer and stronger Scotland' so that 'we live our lives safe from crime, disorder and danger' (Scottish Government 2010). The effect of these in relation to justice was that, in theory at least, substantial responsibility for devising, funding and implementing policy shifted from the centre to local partnerships. It is beyond the scope of this chapter to comment on the significance of this change in governance except to note it as an important area of future interest and research.

Finally, it is difficult to predict the future shape and direction of criminal justice policy in Scotland with any degree of certainty.[3] However, while we have here and elsewhere in this book sought to go beyond some of the all-pervasive myths that characterise Scottish society and its interpretation and understanding, such myths have concrete effects. Claims to Scottish distinctiveness and assorted other 'Scottish' values are likely to be key elements in the Scottish Parliament elections in 2011: 'wisdom, justice, compassion, integrity' may not yet be defining characteristics of Scottish life, let alone criminal justice, but remain worthy values to which to aspire.

Notes

1 This was defined as six months in the original Bill but was then cut to three months shortly before the Stage 3 debate in June 2010, in order to secure the support of the Liberal Democrats.

2 As the book was going to press major emergency changes in arrest procedures relating to the right of access by an accused to legal advice have been implemented or are under negotiation, in anticipation of a critical Supreme Court ruling in Cadder v HMA (2010).

3 The UK Conservative–Liberal Democrat coalition government of May 2010 seems at the time of writing to be more pragmatic and libertarian than Labour, forced not least by financial constraints to review current approaches to criminal justice and social welfare.

References

Armstrong, S. (2009) 'Fixing Scotland's remand problem', in C. Lightowler and D. Hare (eds), *Prisons and Sentencing Reform: Developing Policy in Scotland*. Scottish Centre for Crime and Justice Research and Scottish Policy Innovation Forum. Web only: http://www.sccjr.ac.uk/pubs/Prisons-and-Sentencing-Reform/161 (accessed 27 March 2010).

Barry, M. and McIvor, G. (2010) 'Professional decision-making and women offenders: containing the chaos?', *Probation Journal*, 57 (1): 27–41.

Cook, D. (2006) *Criminal and Social Justice*. London: Sage.

Farmer, L. (1997) *Criminal Law, Tradition and Legal Order*. Cambridge: Cambridge University Press.

Feeley, M. and Simon, J. (1992) 'The New Penology: notes on the emerging strategy of corrections and its implications', *Criminology*, 30 (4): 449–74.

Feeley, M. and Simon, J. (1994) '"Actuarial justice": the emerging new criminal law', in D. Nelken (ed.), *The Futures of Criminology*. London. Sage.

Garland, D. (2001) *The Culture of Control: Crime and Social Order in Contemporary Society*. Oxford: Oxford University Press.

Garland, D. (2006) 'Concepts of culture in the sociology of punishment', *Theoretical Criminology*, 10: 419.

Greer, S. L. (ed.) (2009) *Devolution and Social Citizenship in the UK*. Bristol: Policy Press.

Hume, D. (1844 edn) *Commentaries on the Law of Scotland Respecting Crimes*. Edinburgh: Bell & Bradfute.

Hutton, N. (2005) 'Beyond populist punitiveness?,' *Punishment and Society*, 7 (3): 243–58.

Hutton, N. (2006) 'Sentencing as a social practice', in S. Armstrong and L. McAra (eds), *Perspectives on Punishment: The Contours of Control*. Oxford: Oxford University Press.

Johnstone, C. and Mooney, G. (2007) '"Problem" people, "problem" spaces? New Labour and council estates', in R. Atkinson and G. Helms (eds), *Securing an Urban Renaissance: Crime, Community and British Urban Policy*. Bristol: Policy Press, pp. 125–39.

Johnstone, J. and Burman, M. (eds) (2009) *Youth Justice*. Dunedin: Academic Press.

Justice (2010) *Devolution and Human Rights*, February. Justice. http://www.justice.org.uk.

Justice Committee of the Scottish Parliament (2010) Official Report of Proceedings – Criminal Justice and Licensing (Scotland) Bill (Stage 2), 16 March. Web only: http://www.scottish.parliament.uk/s3/committees/justice/or-10/ju10-1002.htm#Col2726.

Lacey, N. (2008) *The Prisoner's Dilemma: Political Economy and Punishment in Contemporary Democracies*, The Hamlyn Lectures 2007. Cambridge: Cambridge University Press.

Law, A. (2005) 'Welfare nationalism: social justice and/or entrepreneurial Scotland?', in G. Mooney and G. Scott (eds), *Exploring Social Policy in the 'New' Scotland*. Bristol: Policy Press, pp. 53–83.

Law, A. and Mooney, G. (2010) 'Financialisation and proletarianisation: changing landscapes of neoliberal Scotland', in N. Davidson, P. McCafferty and D. Miller (eds), *Neoliberal Scotland*. Newcastle: Cambridge Scholars Publishing, pp. 137–59.

McAra, L. (1999) 'The politics of penality: an overview of the development of penal policy in Scotland', in P. Duff and N. Hutton (eds), *Criminal Justice in Scotland*. Dartmouth: Ashgate, pp. 355–80.

McAra, L. (2005) 'Modelling penal transformation', *Punishment and Society*, 7 (3): 277–302.

McAra, L. (2007) 'Welfarism in crisis: crime, control and penal practice in post-devolution Scotland', in M. Keating (ed.), *Scottish Social Democracy: Progressive Ideas for Public Policy*. Brussels: PIE/Peter Lang.

McAra, L. (2008a) 'Crime, criminology and criminal justice in Scotland', *European Journal of Criminology*, 5: 481.

McAra, L. (2008b) *Global Politics and Local Culture: Crime Control and Penal Practice in a Small Nation*. Online publication at: http://www.cjscotland.org.uk/pdfs/McAraESC08.pdf.

MacAskill, K. (2009) 'Decisions on the applications for prisoner transfer and compassionate release in relation to Abdelbaset Ali Mohmed Al-Megrahi'. Web page: http://www.scotland.gov.uk/News/This-Week/Speeches/Safer-and-stronger/lockerbiedecision (accessed 27 March 2010).

McCrone, D. (2001) *Understanding Scotland: The Sociology of a Nation*, 2nd edn. London: Routledge.

McEwen, N. (2002) 'State welfare nationalism: the territorial impact of welfare state development in Scotland', *Regional and Federal Studies*, 12: 66–90.

McEwen, N. (2006) *Nationalism and the State: Welfare and Identity in Scotland and Quebec*. Brussels: PIE/Peter Lang.

McIvor, G. and McNeill, F. (2007) 'Developments in Probation in Scotland', in G. McIvor and P. Raynor (eds), *Developments in Social Work with Offenders*. London: Jessica Kingsley.

McNeill, F. and Whyte, B. (2007) *Reducing Reoffending: Social Work and Community Justice in Scotland*. Cullompton: Willan Publishing.

McNeill, F. *et al.* (2009) 'Risk, responsibility and reconfiguration: penal adaptation and misadaptation', *Punishment and Society*, 11 (4): 419.

Michie, M. (1997) *An Enlightenment Tory in Victorian Scotland: Career of Sir Archibald Alison*. Edinburgh: Tuckwell Press.

Millie, A., Tombs, J. and Hough, M. (2007) 'Borderline sentencing: a comparison of sentencers' decision-making in England and Wales, and Scotland', *Criminology and Criminal Justice*, 7 (3): 243–67.

Mooney, G. (2008) '"Problem" populations, "problem" places', in J. Newman and N. Yeates (eds), *Social Justice: Welfare Crime and Society*. Maidenhead: Open University Press, pp. 97–128.

Mooney, G. and Poole, L. (2004) '"A land of milk and honey": social policy in Scotland after devolution', *Critical Social Policy*, 24 (4): 458–83.

Muir, R. (2010) 'Crime and justice after devolution', in G. Lodge and K. Schmuecker (eds), *Devolution and Practice 2010*. London: IPPR, pp. 166–88.

Newman, J. and Yeates, N. (eds) (2008) *Social Justice: Welfare, Crime and Society*. Maidenhead: Open University Press.

O'Neill, A. (2010) 'End o' anither auld sang?' *Law Society of Scotland Journal Online*. Available at: http://www.journalonline.co.uk/Magazine/55-3/1007717.aspx.

Paterson, L. (1994) *The Autonomy of Modern Scotland*. Edinburgh: Edinburgh University Press.

Paterson, L., Bechhofer, F. and McCrone, D. (2004) *Living in Scotland: Social and Economic Change since 1980*. Edinburgh: Edinburgh University Press.

Reid, G. (2006) 'Foreword', in G. Buchanan (1579) *A Dialogue on the Laws of Kingship among the Scots*, eds M. S. Smith and R. A. Mason. Saltire Society.

Scottish Government (2009) *Review of National Antisocial Behaviour Strategy*. Web page: http://www.antisocialbehaviourscotland.co.uk/asb/3143.201.445.html (accessed 26 March 2010).

Scottish Government (2010) *A Safer and Stronger Scotland*. Web page: http://www.scotland.gov.uk/About/scotPerforms/objectives/safeAndStronger (accessed 26 March 2010).

Scottish Prisons Commission (2008) *Scotland's Choice – Report of the Scottish Prisons Commission*. Edinburgh: Scottish Government.

SWIA (2010) *Improving Social Work in Scotland: A Report on SWIA's Performance Inspection Programme 2005–09*. Edinburgh: Scottish Government.

SWIA/HMIC/HMIP (2009) *Multi-Agency Inspection: Assessing and Managing Offenders who Present a High Risk of Serious Harm*. Edinburgh: Scottish Government.

Tombs, J. (2004) *A Unique Punishment: Sentencing and the Prison Population in Scotland*. Edinburgh: Scottish Consortium and Crime and Criminal Justice.

Vaughan, B. and Kilcommins, S. (2010) 'The governance of crime and the negotiation of justice', *Criminology and Criminal Justice*, 10: 59.

Walker, N. (2010) *Final Appellate Jurisdiction in the Scottish Legal System*. Scottish Government. Web only: http://www.scotland.gov.uk/Publications/2010/01/19154813/0.

Walmsley, R. (1999) *World Prison Population List*, 1st edn, Research Findings No. 88. London: Home Office.

Weaver, B. and McNeill, F. (2010) 'Public protection in Scotland: a way forward?', in M. Nash and A. Williams (eds), *The Handbook of Public Protection*. Cullompton: Willan Publishing.

Wincott, D. (2006) 'Social policy and social citizenship: Britain's welfare states', *Publius: The Journal of Federalism*, 36 (1): 169–88.

Index

Added to a page number 'f' denotes a figure 't' denotes a table and 'n' a note.

218 Centre 95–6
Aberdeen 46t, 99, 113, 115, 119, 185–6
abuse 94
  see also domestic abuse
accidents 134
Accounts Commission 187
Act to Improve Prisons and Prison Discipline in Scotland (1839) 242
Act of Union (1707) 7, 263
Action Plan to Reduce Youth Crime 71, 72
active citizenship 176
actuarial justice 73, 195, 196, 208, 274
advanced marginality 52
adversarial systems 204, 213n
Afghans, harassment of 124
after-care 241–2
agency 98
air pollution 158, 159–61, 168
Air Quality Initiative 160
Al Qaeda 123
Al-Megrahi, Abdelbaset Ali Mohmed 262
alcohol 23, 25, 44–5, 81, 94
Alison, Archibald 263
Amina – the Muslim Women's Resource Centre 121
Anglophobia 115
anti-semitism 116
antisocial behaviour 44, 186
  corporate 134
  discourses 49
  environmental crime 157
  policy 56
  as a social housing issue 54, 55
  socialisation of 11–12
  tackling 48, 49–50, 58–9, 178, 184, 188
  young people 79, 80t
Antisocial Behaviour Act (Scotland) Act (2004) 10, 57–8, 185, 218
Antisocial Behaviour Orders (ASBOs) 55, 57–8, 181, 184, 185, 186
Antisocial Behaviour Team (Dundee) 45
anxiety 94
appeals 197
'arc of prosperity' countries 13
Asians 113, 117, 120, 122, 126, 127
assault 24, 70, 99
  see also sexual violence/assault
Assessed Operating Limit 250
ASSIST programme 102
Association of Chief Police Officers in Scotland (ACPOS) 125, 183, 185, 188–9
Association for the Protection of Rural Scotland 155
asylum seekers 115, 117, 125, 127
at-risk children 73, 75
Auditor General 187
Australia 137, 138, 143, 161
Avonspark Street 49

Baby P 30, 54
Bangladeshis 114
banks, associated with fraud 134
Banton, Michael 175–6, 190–1, 192
Barlinnie Special Unit 243–4, 265
Barr, John 31, 135

best interests 71
binge-drinking 94
Black and Ethnic Minorities Infrastructure in Scotland (BEMIS) 126
black immigration 112
black youth 116–17
blame 22, 30, 132–3, 140
bonus culture 32, 134
'booze and blade' culture 23, 27, 35
borders, issue of 274
Borstals 68
boundaries 274
Boyd, Colin 153
Boyle, Jimmy 244
boys, and delinquency 97
Bratton, William 182
Breakthrough Glasgow 53
Brebner, William 241, 265
Bridewell 241
British Crime Survey 7
British Transport Police 124, 266, 274
Brodie, Lord 141, 142
Broken Britain 30
broken society, portrayal of Glasgow as 52–3
'broken windows' thesis 58, 182, 184, 185
Brown, Gordon 55
bullying, and offending 83
burden of proof 199
bureaucratic infrastructure 71–2
burglary 26

Cabinet Secretary for Justice 189, 191, 261–2, 274
Canada 137–8, 143
Canadian Criminal Code 138
Carloway, Lord 140, 144
'Cashback for Communities' programme 58
CCTV 49, 50, 55, 178
Census (2001) 113
Central Probation Council 222
centralism 188
Centre for Social Justice report (2008) 30, 53
CHANGE programme 102
charge bargaining 202
Chhokar, Surjit Singh 119, 120, 123
Chicago mobsters 29
Chicago School of Sociology 48
chief constables 187, 188–9
Chief Inspector of Prisons Office 247
child guidance clinics 69
Child Safety Initiative 185
child welfare 68–9
Children Act (1908) 68
Children Act (1948) 69
Children (Scotland) Act (1995) 71, 75–6
Children and Young Persons Act (1969) 70
Children and Young Persons (Scotland) Act (1932) 68
Children and Young Persons (Scotland) Act (1937) 68
Children's Hearings 9, 69, 74, 75–6, 83, 85, 86n
Children's Hearings (Scotland) Bill (2009) 86n
children's homes 68
Children's Panels 75
Children's Reporters 74–5, 77
children's services 73
Chinese immigrants 113
Church of Scotland 116
cities 22, 23, 43–4, 48, 50–1
  see also urban crime/disorder
citizen participation 167–8
citizenship 72, 274
city centre representatives (CCRs) 51
city centres 44, 51
civic culture 9, 67, 69, 70, 73, 183
civic surveys 47
civil orders 72
civil society 7, 10, 264
civilianisation of policing 180
class
  differences/inequalities 11, 23
  and female offending 93
  see also dangerous classes; middle class; working class
climate change 153
common law 263
common police services 188
community activism 154–5
community intelligence 184
Community Justice Authorities (CJAs) 225–6, 230, 232, 233n, 250
community planning partnerships (CPPs) 125, 188
community policing 122, 183, 189, 191
community prisons 248
Community Reparation Orders 58
community safety 44, 48, 72
Community Safety Partnerships 72
community sanctions 95, 216–33, 253, 265, 268
  corporate 147
  criminal justice social work 225–9
  historical background 222–5
  monetary penalties 216, 217–21, 268–9
    see also fines
  use (1932–2007) 224f

community wardens 51, 178, 179, 181
Company Background Inquiry Reports 147, 148
comparative criminal justice texts 6
compensation orders 217
'compliance' strategies 31–2, 135–6
Concordat 275
conditionality of welfare 11, 52
consent 105
conservation charities 162
conservation projects 47
Conservative-Liberal Democrat coalition 275
Conservatives 10, 70
consistency 213n
construction industry 134
constructive punishment 228, 229
consumer detriment 134, 135
consumer sovereignty model 200–1
consumer vulnerability 135
consumerism 33, 57
contested jury trials 199, 204
control 270
'controlling mind' doctrine 136, 138, 140, 143, 144
convictions 35–6
  gender and 91
  for rape 102–3
  ratio to custodial disposals 245f
  young offenders 77, 78f, 85
Cornton Vale 92, 93, 97, 246, 268
corporate crime 132–49
  controlling 135–42
  criminal and social justice 147–8
  enforcement and sanctions 145–7
  environmental 31, 157
  impact of 133–5
  victims 133
corporate culture 144
corporate guilt 141, 142, 143
corporate killing 144
corporate liability 135, 136, 137, 140, 142–5
corporate manslaughter 137
Corporate Manslaughter and Corporate Homicide (CMCHA) Act (2007) 143, 144, 147, 148
corporate polluters 163, 167
corporate responsibility 68, 135, 136, 138, 142
Corporate Strategy (SEPA) 157
corporate violence 134
Corrections Service for Scotland 225
corruption 44
Coulter, Ronnie 120
Council of Ethnic Minority Voluntary Sector Organisations (CEMVO) 126
council housing 49–50, 54–9
Court of Criminal Appeal (Scottish) 146, 197, 203
crime
  designing out of 49
  income inequality 23–7
  levels 238
  literature/fiction 3, 4, 28, 29, 43
  media portrayal 4, 22, 57
  public fascination with 4
  social inequality 21–3, 32–3, 36
  socialisation of 11–12
  socio-economic factors 27–32, 34, 97
  statistics 24, 91
  urban *see* urban crime/disorder
  see also fear of crime; offending
crime consciousness 50
crime control 6, 181
crime and disorder, policing 181–6
Crime and Disorder Act (1998) 119, 185
crime prevention 72
Crimes (Industrial Manslaughter) (Amendment) Act (Australia, 2003) 138
criminal careers 29
criminal justice
  dominance of working class in 21
  and ethnicity 122–3
  female offenders 91, 92
  national standards 71, 206
  over-representation of disadvantaged groups 4
  patriarchal nature 106–7
  public confidence 183, 209, 227
  regulation of public space 51
  Scotland
    criminology and neglect of 6
    detartanisation 8–10
    distinctiveness 7, 197, 198, 212, 263–72
    and inequalities 34–6
    international scrutiny 261–2
    myths and misunderstandings about 5–8
    policy convergence 6, 10, 71–3
    prospects for the future 272–5
    structure 12–13
    welfarism 9, 10, 11, 223–4, 233, 266–72
    see also youth justice
  statistics 7
  and welfarism 49
Criminal Justice Act (1963) 223
Criminal Justice Bill (2010) 147
Criminal Justice and Licensing Bill (2009) 74, 211, 226, 272

Criminal Justice and Political Cultures: National and International Dimensions of Crime Control 6
Criminal Justice in Scotland 8
Criminal Justice (Scotland) Act (1949) 222
Criminal Justice (Scotland) Act (2003) 185
Criminal Justice (Scotland) Act (2007) 218
Criminal Justice (Scotland) Bill 252
criminal justice social work 76, 206, 225, 225–9, 268
Criminal Justice Social Work Development Centre 5, 225
criminal justice social workers 205–6, 207, 212, 228, 272
criminal law 144, 148
Criminal Sentencing (Equity Fines) Bill 146
criminalisation 9, 49, 86
  ability of powerful groups to resist 133
  environmental harm 163–6
  impact of terrorism on 123–5
  imprisonment rates 239
  and inequality 12, 36, 271
  race, ethnicity and 111, 116, 117, 127
  rape in marriage 104
  of social policy 11–12
  of women 94, 99–100
  see also decriminalisation
criminality 23, 44, 47, 56
criminological gaze 12–13
criminology 4, 5, 6, 12, 22, 45, 111, 132, 163–6, 262–3
Crown Office and Procurator Fiscal Service (COPFS) 123, 157, 161, 162, 163
Cullen Inquiry 139, 145
culpability 201
culpable homicide 137, 140, 141, 144
cultural influences, gang violence 29
cultural tolerance, middle class crimes 32
culture of control 179
culture of vindictiveness 33
curfews 59, 185, 231, 244
Curran, Margaret 57, 58
cusp cases, summary justice 206–7
custodial sentences 206, 217, 231
Custodial Sentences and Weapons Act (2007) 230

dangerous classes 69
dangerous products 135
dangerous urban areas 45–6
data zones (SIMD) 25, 26, 37n
day fines 220
Dead Wood 43
Dean v. John Menzies (Holdings) Ltd (1981 JC 23) 137
deaths
  E-coli 135, 145
  pollution-related 159
  work-related 134, 137, 146
decriminalisation 148
defence lawyers 200–2
deforestation 168
delinquency 97
demonisation 30
dependency cultures 53, 56, 59
depression 94
deprivation *see* multiple deprivation; neighbourhood deprivation; social deprivation; urban deprivation
deprived areas 26, 27, 44–5, 135, 152, 160, 249
desistance 230
detartanisation 8–10, 71–3, 198, 267–8
deterrence 68, 147, 178
deterrence trap 146
devolution 127, 268, 271, 274
  confusion about criminal justice 7
  and environmentalism 154–5, 167
  inequalities 10–11
  policy convergence 71
  policy transfer 13
  social policy 8–9
Devon, James 219
disadvantaged groups 4, 36, 49–50, 94, 147
disadvantaged neighbourhoods 44
discretion *see* judicial discretion; police, discretion; sentencer discretion
dispersal orders 184, 185–6, 192n
diversion, fiscal 218–19
diversity strategy (ACPOS) 125
domestic abuse 100–2, 121
domestic abuse courts 102
Donald, Kriss 115
Donald Trump golf course 166
Dounreay nuclear power facilities 166
DPP v. Esso [2000] VSC (263) 138
drug misuse 81, 94
drug offences 24
Du Plooy v. HMA (2003 SCCR 443) 203
due process 196, 198–9, 203, 213n
dumping, of waste 153, 157, 163, 166
Duncan Smith, Ian 30
Dundee 4, 22, 23, 45, 46t, 52, 54, 55, 56, 59, 113, 119, 220–1
Dungavel 127

E-coli fatalities 135, 145
early intervention, youth justice 73–4, 83–4
Eastern European immigrants 112, 117, 125, 127
eco-centric 164
eco-crime 158, 165–6, 168, 169
ecological justice 164
economic crime 143
economic recession 25, 32, 134, 191
economics, safety and 139
Edinburgh 22, 46t, 47, 99, 112, 113, 116, 119, 120, 183, 247
Edinburgh and Lothian's Racial Equality Council (ELREC) 126
Edinburgh Study of Youth Transitions and Crime (ESYTC) 67, 78–9, 83–4, 85, 96–7
Effective Practice Unit 225
efficiency 197, 199, 203, 204, 205, 213n
electronic monitoring 58, 231
Elgin Committee Report (1900) 242–3
employment 26, 51, 94
enforcement agencies 31–2, 159
Engaging Communities in Fighting Crime 227
Engels, Frederick 47
England and Wales
  dispersal orders 192n
  imprisonment rate 238
  percentage of ethnic prison population 118
  racist incidents 120
  reassurance policing 183, 184
  rise in crime (1989–92) 25
  super forces 191
  victimisation 26
  youth justice 70, 71
Environment Protection Act (1990) 155, 158–9
Environmental Audit (House of Commons) 157
environmental costs, high standards of living 168
environmental crime 31, 152–69
  defining 155–8
  green criminology 163–6
  impact of 153
  Scotland 161–3, 168–9
Environmental Crime Protocol 162
environmental destruction/degradation 152, 153, 154, 155, 158, 159, 167, 168
Environmental Health and Trading Standards inspectors 31, 145
environmental justice 154, 164, 166–8
environmental law 153, 155, 157–8, 158–61, 169
environmental policy 154–5, 169
environmental protection 152, 155, 168, 271
equality 111
equality of opportunity 123
equity 147
Equity Fines 146, 148
Esso gas explosion 138
ethnic minorities
  criminal justice and policing 121–3
  joint activities with police 126
  policy context 125–6
ethnic population 113–14
ethnicity
  crime and victimisation 118–21
  and immigration 111–13
  and othering 114–17
Europe, imprisonment rates 238
European Convention on Human Rights 136, 250, 274
Europeanisation 12, 274
evidence-based practice 72, 84, 225
exceedence, rhetoric of 160, 161
exclusion *see* school exclusion; self-exclusion; social exclusion
Expert Group, corporate liability 144
extended policing family 50, 177

false description, of goods 134
family characteristics/dynamics 26, 30, 82t
Family Intervention Projects (FIPs) 55, 56
family stability, market society 33
farmers, involvement in fraud 31
Faslane Nuclear Naval Base 165–6
Fast Track hearings 57
fear of crime 4, 11, 46, 48, 50, 179, 183, 188, 190, 195
fear of the other 50, 111
female offenders
  alternatives to prison 95–6
  educational attainment/background 94
  as high-tariff, high-risk group 93
  likelihood of conviction 91
  prison population 92, 93, 246
  sentencing and imprisonment 92–4
  young 96–8
female offending 91, 106
The Ferris Conspiracy 28
fictional crime 4, 28, 29, 43
financial crisis (2008/9) 25, 32, 134, 191
financial impact, corporate crime 133–4
fine default 220, 222
fines
  corporate crime 138, 140, 141, 145–7, 148

enforcement, Scotland 233n
environmental crime 161, 163
see also equity fines; fiscal fines; monetary penalties
fiscal fines 35, 218, 221
fiscal work order 218–19
fishing industries 165
fixed fee policy 201–2
fixed penalty notices (FPNs) 218, 221
food poisoning 134–5
forced marriages 121
Forestry Act (1967) 158
fraud 30–1, 32, 133–4, 137
'free agreement', consent as 105
Freedom of Information Act 160
Fresh Talent Initiative 127
Friends of the Earth 154, 155

gang culture 23, 29, 44
gang violence 27–30, 57, 117
Gangs of Dundee 23
gated communities 178–9, 181
Geddes, Patrick 47–8
gender
ethnicity and racist abuse 121
and inequality 271
and offending 80t, 82t, 90–1
and victimisation 91–2, 106
see also men; women
Gender Equality Duty 106, 271
gender-specific interventions 95–6
gentifrication 47, 48–9
Getting Best Results Initiative 225
Getting it Right for Every Child: Proposals for Action 73
ghettoes 54, 116, 126, 181
Gill Report 141, 145
girls, and delinquency 97
Glasgow 22, 23, 49, 51, 52, 247
218 Centre 95–6
alcohol retail and deprived areas 44–5
anti-road protest 167
antisocial behaviour 186
Bridewell 241
city centre representatives 51
domestic abuse courts 102
gang violence 27–30
Good Neighbour Charter 55
homicide rate 28
immigrants 112, 113, 116
labelling as dangerous and brutal 45
Operation Blade 57
'othering' in media reporting 4
policing of the homeless 183
private security 178
probation initiative, fine default 222
racist incidents 119, 120, 121
Routes Out of Prostitution Social Inclusion Partnership 99
SIMD data zones 25
urban deprivation and imprisonment 46
zero tolerance 190
Glasgow Airport bomb incident (2007) 123, 124
Glasgow Anti-Racist Alliance (GARA) 126, 127
Glasgow Earth First 155
Glasgow East 35, 43, 52–4
A Glasgow Gang Observed 28
Glasgow's Guantanamo 53
global warming 152
globalisation 9, 12, 212, 262, 274
Godfather movies 29
Good Neighbour Charter 55
Goths 50
Grampian Police 186
green criminology 163–6
The Green Economy 167
Greenock 52, 112
Greenpeace 155
guilt
environmental damage 159
see also corporate guilt; presumption of guilt
guilty pleas 202, 203, 204, 205, 211–12
'guilty' verdicts, rape/assault 103
gypsies 116

habitus 273
Hamilton curfew 185
Hamish McBeth 4
harassment 119–20, 122, 124
'hard men' 28
'hard working' majority 55
harm
corporate crime 134–5
environmental crime 158, 163–6
hate crime 118–19, 125
Health and Safety at Work (HSWA) Act (1974) 140, 144
Health and Safety Executive (HSE) 31, 134, 139, 140, 141, 142, 145
health and safety offences 31, 132, 134–5, 136, 140, 145, 146
Health and Social Services and Social Security Adjudications Act (1983) 71
Her Majesty's Inspector of Constabulary for Scotland 187, 188, 189
Herald of Free Enterprise 137
high visibility policing 50, 178, 182
Highlanders 116
Hill, Frederic 242

HMA v. Munro & Sons (Highland) Ltd (2009 SLT 233) 146
HMA v. Anderson (2000) 104
Home Detention Curfew (HDC) 231, 244
Home Office 7, 157, 191
homeless 33, 36, 50, 183
homicide 28, 70
  see also culpable homicide; racially motivated murder
'hooligan' 116
hopelessness 94
Howard, John 253
human rights 158, 251–2, 265
Human Rights Act (1998) 274
human trafficking 100
humanistic penal values 208, 212n
Hume, Baron 263
Hutcheson, Frances 219

ice cream wars 29
ICL Plastics 135, 141–2, 145
ICL Technical Plastics Ltd 141
identity 98, 271, 274
ideology of triviality 204
ill-health/illnesses 53, 134
immigration 111–13, 125, 127
implicitness, sentence bargaining 202
imprisonment 35–6, 230
  and deprivation 46, 249
  fine default 220, 222
  as punishment 240–1
  rates 4, 33, 238, 239, 249
  since the 1990s 245–7
  SPC recommendations 226
  young offenders 68, 77, 79f
  see also prisons
income inequality 11, 23–7, 233
individualised justice 197
industrial capitalism 69
industrial schools 68
inequalities 10–11, 12
  and criminal justice 34–6, 270, 271
  and fines 219–20
  pluralisation of policing 181
  see also income inequality; social inequality
information technology 209
injury/injuries 27, 134, 135, 145
Innes, Martin 184
innocence, presumption of 199, 203, 246
insecurity 11, 27, 51, 195, 251
institutional racism 117, 120, 123, 126
intention 143
inter-generational gang membership 29
Intergovernmental Panel on Climate Change (UN) 152
internal-exotic other, council schemes as 54–9
International Court of Justice (UN) 155
International Environment Court 161
international law (environment) 155
Interregional Crime and Justice Institute (UN) 156–7
Intervention and Integration 250
Inverclyde 25, 35, 46, 46t
Inverness Prison 243
Irish, as suspect community 123
Irish immigrants 112, 116
Islamophobia 124
Italian immigrants 112, 116
It's a Criminal Waste: Stop Youth Crime Now 71

Jack, Ian 7
Jamieson, Cathy 58, 72
Jandoo report 120, 125
Jewish immigrants 112
job seekers allowance 26
joint police boards 187
joint working 73, 125
judicial discretion 196, 198, 208–11
judicial independence 197
jury trials 199, 204
just deserts 73
Justice Committee 187
justice reinvestment 254

key performance indicators 71
Khan, Imran 120
Kilbrandon Report (1964) 67, 69, 70, 71, 72, 83, 86, 222, 265
knife violence/culture 28, 29, 57
Knight, Joseph 112

Labour *see* New Labour
labour market training programmes 51
Labour/Liberal Democratic coalition 57, 73
ladettes 98
Land and Environmental Court (Australia) 161
Larkhill gas explosion 139–40
late modern societies 179, 180, 181, 190
Law Reform (Miscellaneous Provisions) (Scotland) Act (1985) 104
Law Reform (Miscellaneous Provisions) (Scotland) Bill 220
Lawrence *see* Stephen Lawrence case
lawyer-client relationships/contact 200–1, 202
legal aid 205
legal system 7, 197

LH Access Technology Ltd and Border Rail & Plant v. HMA (2009 SCCR 280) 146
life expectancy, air pollution 159–60
life sentences 232
living conditions, remand prisoners 246
Local Government (Scotland) Act (1994) 187
long-term prisoners 231
low-end justice 221
low-income groups, consumer vulnerability 135
low-level crime, civil orders 72
lower-class crimes 22, 32, 35, 36, 47, 132
lower-class defendants 35–6

Maan, Bashir 113
MacAskill, Kenny 23
McConnell, Jack 58
Macpherson Report (1999) 119, 121
McRory Report (2006) 148
Management of Offenders (Scotland) Act (2005) 230, 232
managerialism 10, 71, 180
mandatory minimum sentences 209, 211
marginalised localities 52
marginalised populations 49–50
market society/economies 33, 168
Marr v. HMA (1996) 105
marriage, rape in 104
masculinity 29, 57
material differences, and crime 26
Matthews, Shannon 30, 54
media 4, 21, 22, 30, 45, 57, 78, 98, 115, 124
mediation 228
men
  demand for prostitution 99
  risk of violence 92
The Menace of the Irish Race to Our Scottish Nationality 116
mens rea 135, 138
Meridian Global Funds Management Ltd v. Securities Commission [1995] 3 All ER (918) 143
Metropolitan Police 120, 124
Mid Calder 186
middle class
  colonisation, working-class areas 48–9
  crimes 30–2
migration/migrants 111, 115
  see also immigration
minimum wage 26
mis-selling 134
mixed category prisons 247
monetary penalties 216, 217–21, 268–9
  see also fines
moral geography 59, 60
moral panics 78, 97, 98, 117
motivational theory 25
mugging 126
Muir, Brandon 54
Multi-Agency Public Protection Arrangements (MAPPAs) 231–2, 274
multi-agency youth teams 72
multiple deprivation 46, 52
Muslims 122, 124

Napier v. Scottish Ministers (2005 SC 229) 251
National Front 120
National Objectives and Standards (NOS) 223
national policing, policy/agenda 188, 191
National Reassurance Policing Programme 183, 184
national standards 71, 206
National Strategy to Address Domestic Abuse 101
nationalistic identity 271
ned culture 56–9
neglect 137
negligence 143, 159
neighbourhood deprivation, perceptions of local areas 27
Neighbourhood Policing Programme 183
neighbourhood watch 179, 180
neoliberalism 9, 10, 11, 33, 47, 49, 50, 52, 148, 179, 180, 190
Neptune Warrior Military Exercises 165
new criminalisations 117
New Labour 9, 10, 32, 33, 48, 55, 57
new public management 180
New Scots: Attracting Fresh Talent to Meet the Challenge for Growth 125
New Urbanism 56
NHS fraud 30–1
No Mean City 28, 29
non-custodial sentences 206
non-serious offenders 81, 82t
'not proven' verdicts, rape 103

Occidental Petroleum 138, 139
Occupational Health and Safety Act (Australia, 1985) 138
offender management 249
offender outcomes 250
offenders
  popular representation of 21
  socio-economic status 34
  see also female offenders; sex offenders; violent offenders; young offenders

offending
  gender and 90–1
  see also crime
oil pollution 163
Ondeo Industrial Solutions 163
One Scotland campaign 125
Operation Blade 57
Operation Spotlight 6, 182–3
Opportunity and Responsibility 250
opportunity theory 25
Order for Lifelong Restriction (ORL) 232
organised crime 111, 117
Orr, John 182–3
other/othering 4, 50, 54–9, 60, 114–17, 127, 270
over-policing 35, 121, 122
overcrowding, in prisons 93, 223, 231, 244, 248
Oxford Handbook of Criminology 6, 12

Pakistanis 113, 114, 115, 119
Parenting Orders 56, 58
Parliamentary Report (1842) 47
Parole Board for Scotland 231, 247
partnership 160, 161, 162, 169, 182, 183, 184, 275
Partnership Agreement 57
pathologisation 56, 59–60
patriarchy 106–7
payback 216, 226–7, 229, 253
peer influence 98
penal experiment 243–4, 265
penal geography 247
penal policies 239
penal values 195
penal welfarism 70, 97, 196, 205, 206, 212, 242, 263–4, 267
Pentonville 241
performance culture 180
persistent serious offending 80t
persistent young offenders 34, 76
personality, and offending 82t
Peterhead 247
Philadelphia System 241
philanthropy 68–9
'pick-n-mix' policing 177–81
pimps 100
Piper Alpha 138–9, 145
plea decision-making 200–5
pluralisation of policing 176, 177–81, 186, 190, 266
poisoning, of wildlife 162
police 34–5
  crime 133
  discretion 177
  governance 177, 186–9
  mergers 191
  statistics 24
police boards 187–8
Police Community Support Officers 51, 191
police data capture 32
police liaison schemes 69
Police, Public Order and Criminal Justice (Scotland) Act (2006) 188
police-administered FPNs 218
police-community relations 124–5, 126, 191
The Policeman in the Community 175–7, 191
policies
  criminal justice 72, 84, 98, 201–2
  race and ethnic 125–6
  see also environmental policy; penal policies; punitive policy; social policy; urban policy
policing 35, 56
  crime and disorder 181–6
  distinctiveness 266
  ethnic minorities 121–3
  impact of terrorism on 123–5
  national policy/agenda 188, 191
  pluralisation of 176, 177–81, 186, 190, 266
  Scottish cities 50–1
  through social housing 49
  see also community policing; over-policing; reassurance policing
'policing beyond the police' 176
Policing Scotland 8
policy convergence 6, 10, 71–3
policy transfer 6, 13
policy-making 12, 56
Polish immigrants 112
Pollok Free State Protest Camp 167
polluters, corporate 163, 167
pollution 153, 156, 158, 159–61, 162–3, 168
'poor blaming' 22, 30
popular culture 22, 56
popular punitivism 9, 268
post-custodial resources 230
post-release supervision 230, 231–2
postmodernity 190
poverty 11, 23, 27, 36, 47, 53, 54, 58, 81, 160, 219, 221
powerful, crimes of the 133
Practice of the Criminal Law in Scotland 263
pre-sentence reports 204, 205
  see also Social Enquiry Reports
presumption of guilt 204
presumption of innocence 199, 203, 246

Preventing Offending by Young People: A Framework for Action 73
prevention 73–4, 183, 184
Pride and Prejudice 125
prison abolitionist movement 253
prison industrial complex 252
prison inspectors 242
prison population
  ethnic 118
  female 92, 93, 246
  rise in 244, 245, 246–7, 252, 268
  statistical projections 244
  young offenders 77, 79f
prison reduction target 253–4
prison system 242, 247–8
prisoners 34, 46t, 231, 248–51
prisons
  historical context 240, 241
  human rights violations 251–2
  overcrowding 93, 223, 231, 244, 248
  reformative ideas 241–2
  shift in control of 242–3
  see also imprisonment; *individual prisons*
Prisons Act (1835) 242
Prisons (Scotland) Act (1877) 242
Prisons and Social Work Services Inspectors Report (1998) 246
private prisons 247–8
private security 178–9, 180, 181, 186
privatisation 10, 47, 49
pro-social behaviour 50
probation committees 222
Probation of Offenders (Scotland) Act (1931) 222
probation officers 223, 228
probation orders 147, 223
probation services 222–3
problem behaviours 49, 55
problem places 43, 47, 56
problem populations 48, 49, 52, 54, 59, 185, 270, 271
problem-solving approach 183
problematic working-class youth cultures 56–9
Procurators Fiscal 35, 76, 218
professional qualifications, CJSW 225
property crime 11, 25, 26, 80t
proportionality 224
prosecution 35, 196
  of children 70, 74
  corporate crime 135, 136–7, 138, 139, 145, 148
  environmental crime 161, 162, 163
  of rape 103
prostitution 99–100
Prostitution (Public Places) Scotland Act (2007) 99
Protecting Scotland's Communities: Fair, Fast and Flexible Justice 226
Protection from Abuse (Scotland) Act (2001) 101
proximal influences, youth crime 83–4
psychological distress 94
public confidence, criminal justice 183, 209, 227
public cynicism 209
public interest discourse 71
public protection 71, 72, 76, 207, 231–2, 250, 265, 272, 274
Public Reassurance Strategy (ACPOS) 183
public safety, city centres 51
public space, privatisation of 49
punishment
  changing nature of 195
  constructive 228, 229
  prison as 240–1
  Scottish 263
  youth justice 68, 72
  see also imprisonment; sanctions; sentencing
punitive policy 10, 48
punitive welfarism 52, 266
punitivism 33, 48
  see also popular punitivism; social punitivism
Purcell Meats (Scotland) Ltd v. McLeod (1986 SCCR 672) 137

quality of life 119, 183
'quality of life' offences 182

R v. British Steel [1995] IRLR (310) 136
R v. Gateway Foodmarkets Ltd [1997] IRLR (189) 136
R v. P & O European Ferries (Dover) Ltd (1990 CR App Rep 72) 137
race
  crime and victimisation 117–18
  ethnicity and immigration 111–13
  less political significance, Scotland 127
  and othering 114–17
racially aggravated behaviour 119
racially aggravated harassment 119–20
racially motivated murder 115, 120–1
racism 114–15, 124, 125
racist 115
racist incidents 119, 122
radical criminologies 164
Ragged Schools 68
rape 70, 92, 99, 102–6
rape law 103–4

rape trials 104
reassurance policing 183–4, 186, 189
recidivism 36
recklessness 144
reconciliation 228
reconvictions 230
recorded crime 4, 45, 181, 245
Reducing Reoffending Programme 233n, 272
referrals, to Children's Reporters 77, 84
reformatories 68
Reforming and Revitalising: Report of the Review of Community Penalties 226
Regulatory Enforcement and Sanctions Act (2008) 147, 148
regulatory law 135–6, 143
rehabilitation 228, 247, 250, 253
reintegration 230, 266
release decisions 231
remand prisoners 246
remand rate, for women 93
Renfrewshire 46t
reoffending, reducing 206, 223, 230, 249–50, 266, 272
reparation 226, 227, 228, 229
repeat victimisation 26
resettlement 230, 250, 266
residualisation 180–1
respect 29, 220
responsibilisation 11, 73, 176, 179, 223
restorative justice 72, 147, 227
retributiveness 73, 147, 219, 227–8
revanchism, urban policy 59, 183
risk assessment 73, 207
risk categorisation 205
risk management 72, 197, 212, 231–2
Risk Management Authority 212, 232, 274
risky behaviours, offending 82t
Routes Out of Prostitution Social Inclusion Partnership 99

Safer Communities in Scotland 71
safety
  conflict between economics and 139
  see also community safety; health and safety; public safety
sanctions
  corporate crime 145–7
  see also community sanctions
Sarwar, Mohammad 124
Scandinavia, penal policies 239
scars 29
schemies 59
school exclusion 85
school psychological services 69
Scotch and Wry 4
Scotland Act (1998) 86n, 144, 251
Scotland's Action Programme to Reduce Youth Crime 71, 72
Scotland's Choice: Report of the Scottish Prisons Commission 226, 227, 233
Scotland's People Annual Report 24
Scots Asians for Independence 113
Scottish Accreditation Panel for Offender Programmes 225, 274
Scottish Centre for Crime and Justice Research (SCCJR) 5
Scottish Children's Reporter Administration (SCRA) 76
Scottish Consortium for Crime and Criminal Justice (SCCCJ) 24
Scottish Court Service (SCS) 210
Scottish courts 76
Scottish Crime and Justice Surveys (SCJS) 24, 91, 100–1, 102
Scottish Crime Surveys 182
Scottish Crime and Victimisation Surveys (SCVS) 23, 118, 179
Scottish Environmental Protection Agency (SEPA) 24, 145, 153, 157, 160–1, 162, 163
Scottish Ethnic Minority Sports Association (SEMSA) 126
Scottish Executive 162, 167
Scottish Fisheries Protection Agency 165
Scottish Government 146, 161, 162, 165, 181, 188, 232, 252
Scottish Green Party 155, 166–7
Scottish Heritage 155
Scottish Household Survey 27, 186
Scottish Index of Multiple Deprivation (SIMD) 24, 25, 26, 37n
Scottish Institute for Policing Research (SIPR) 5
Scottish Law Commission 104
Scottish Legal Aid Board (SLAB) 201
Scottish Liberal Democrats 57
Scottish Ministers 187
Scottish National Party (SNP) 13, 24, 58, 73, 74, 113, 183, 186, 211, 226, 230, 274, 275
Scottish Parliament 144, 187, 230, 262, 272
Scottish Police College 188
Scottish Police Federation 185
Scottish Police Services Authority (SPSA) 188
Scottish Policing Board 189
Scottish Policing Performance Framework 180

Scottish Polish Society 112
Scottish Prison Service (SPS) 76, 123, 231, 247, 250
Scottish Prisons Commission (SPC) 226, 230, 239, 242, 243, 244, 246, 252, 253, 254
Scottish Prisons Complaints Commission (SPCC) 247
sectarianism 116, 126
secure accommodation 71
securitization, urban space 49
security
  uneven investment in 181
  see also insecurity; private security
security rich/security poor 181, 190
self-esteem 81–3, 97
self-exclusion 54
self-harm 83
self-reported offending, young people 80f
senior management
  corporate liability 143
  police 180
A Sense of Freedom 28
sentence discounting (bargaining) 202, 203–4, 205
sentencer discretion 219
sentencing 195, 196–8
  change in practice 273
  detartanisation 198
  judicial discretion 208–11
  public opinion 209
  social inequality 35–6
Sentencing Commission (Scottish) 146, 221
Sentencing Council (Scottish) 211, 273
Sentencing Guidelines Council (SGC) 146
Sentencing Information System (SIS) 209–10
Sentencing and Sentencing Guidelines Council (Scottish) 146
'separation without solitude' 241
serious offenders 80–3, 84
serious offending 79, 80t, 83
sex offenders 231, 232
sexual history, use in rape trials 104
Sexual Offences (Procedure and Evidence) (Scotland) Act (2002) 104
Sexual Offences (Scotland) Act (2009) 105
sexual violence/assault 99, 102–6, 121
shameless indecency 136–7
Sheekh, Ahmed Abuukar 120
sheriff courts 102, 199
sheriff shopping 204
sheriffs 197, 210, 219
Sherifs Association 210
Shettleston Man 53–4
'shield' legislation 104
shoplifting 91, 96
short-term prisoners 231
Signal Crimes Perspective (SCP) 184
Single Outcome Agreements (SOAs) 125, 188, 275
slopping out 251
Smoking, Health and Social Care Act (Scotland) (2005) 218
Social Attitudes Survey (Scottish) 78
social democratic tradition 10, 264
social deprivation
  consumer vulnerability 135
  crime and 22, 23, 24, 27, 81, 82t, 271
  environmental pollution and injustice 160
  prison population 249
social engineering, mixed-tenancy 48–9
Social Enquiry Reports (SERs) 205–8, 209, 269
social exclusion 32–3, 72, 127
social housing 49–50, 53, 54–9
social inclusion 58, 72, 224
social inequality 21–3, 32–3, 36, 155
social injustice 254
social justice 147–8, 177, 181, 228, 229, 266, 270
social landlords 49, 55
social movements, and environmental justice 166–7
social policy 8–9, 11–12, 48
social problems 11, 26, 53
social punitivism 50
social welfare 11, 49, 52, 53
social work *see* criminal justice social work
Social Work and Community Justice in Scotland 8
Social Work (Scotland) Act (1968) 69, 222
socio-economic factors, and crime 27–32, 34, 97
socio-spatial dynamics, criminology and neglect of 45
socio-spatial pathologisation 56
Somerville and others v Scottish Ministers sc 140 2008 sc (HL) 45, 251
sovereign policing model 179, 182, 183, 184–5
spatial concentration, disadvantaged groups 49–50
spatial polarisation 11
special constables 178, 179, 180–1
species justice 165
Stallard v. HMA (1989) 104
state agencies, crime 133, 165–6
'state of the nation' report (GARA) 127

The State of the Prisons 253
Steiner, Achim 153
Stephen Lawrence case 119, 120–1
stereotyping 115
stigmatisation 9, 33, 60, 86
Stockline Plastics Ltd 141
stop and search 117
Strathclyde Police 6, 57, 124, 181, 182, 187, 191
Strathclyde University Law School 210
Strawhorm v. McLeod (1987 SCCR 413) 203
Street Gangs of Dundee 23
street prostitution 99
strict liability 135, 159
structural inequalities 271
structural theorists 22
Student Handbook of Criminal Justice and Criminology 6
suicides 37n, 93, 94, 246
summary cases 35, 199–200, 201, 204, 206–7
summary courts 205, 220–1
Summary Justice Review Committee 221
super forces 191
supervised attendance orders (SAOs) 220–1
supervision, post-release 230, 231–2
supervision requirement, youth justice 76
surveillance *see* CCTV
survival strategies, female 98, 99
suspect subjects 35, 49, 50–1, 59, 60, 84, 123
Sutherland's Law 4
System 3 survey 126

Taggart 4
tagging 58, 231
tartan noir 4
tax evasion 30, 32, 44
technology 190–1, 197, 209
television 4, 22, 57
territorialism 28, 57
terrorism 123–5
Terrorism Act (2000) 124, 274
Thatcherism 267
theft 80t, 86n
therapeutic community 243–4
Thomson, Arthur 29
three strikes legislation 209
throughcare 230, 242
tolerance 111, 126
tolerance zones 99
The Tough Option 225
town planning 44
Trainspotting 4, 23, 261
Transco 137, 139–40, 144
transitions, youth-to-adult 84–5, 98
transnationalism 12, 13
travellers 116
tripartite structure, Scottish constitution 187, 188, 189
'true crime' genre 4, 43
turnover, and level of fine 146–7

under-reporting 100, 102
underclass 22, 30, 33, 53–4, 181
unemployed 36, 51
unemployment 24, 25–6, 29, 49, 53, 58, 249
unit fines 220
unitary police boards 187
United Nations 152–3, 155, 156
urban crime/disorder
  cities and assumptions/narratives of 23, 43, 44, 45, 48
  definitions of 49
  and deprivation 46
  and ethnicity 116–17
  spatial binary of rural lawfulness and 44
urban deprivation 46, 53–4
urban ecology 44, 47–50, 60
urban elites 44, 60
urban ghettoes 181
urban pathology 59–60
urban policy 48, 49, 50, 183
urban regeneration 44, 47, 51, 52, 54, 58
urban spaces 45–6, 48, 49, 50–1, 52, 55, 57
urban suspects 49
urbanisation 69
usual suspects 35, 84

vandalism 24, 44, 157, 178, 179
vehicle vandalism 179
verbal harassment 119–20
vicarious liability 136
victimisation
  corporate crime 133
  of ethnic minorities 118–21
  and exclusion 33
  gender 91–2, 106
  and inequality 24, 26–7, 271
  middle class crimes 31
  race, crime and 117–18
  sexual 102
vindictiveness, culture of 33
violent crime 24, 25, 26, 30, 79, 80t, 92, 97, 98, 111
  see also assault; corporate violence; gang violence

violent offenders 231, 232
vocabulary, gang culture 29
voluntary policing 178, 179, 180, 187
vulnerability, and offending 82t

Wales *see* England and Wales
waste, dumping 153, 157, 163, 166
wealth, inequitable distribution 11
weapon searches 57
Webster v. Dominick (2003 SCCR 525) 136
welfare dependency 53, 56, 94
welfare ghettoes 54
welfare reform 52
welfarism
  criminal justice 9, 10, 11, 49, 223–4, 233, 266–72
  youth justice 69–70, 73, 75, 76, 267
  see also child welfare; penal welfarism; social welfare
West Dumbartonshire 46t
Westray mine explosion 137–8
'what works' 72, 84, 223, 225
white-collar crime 132
Why Kids Kill 57
wildlife crime 156, 162
Wildlife Incident Investigation Scheme 162
Wildlife and Natural Environment Bill 162
The Wire 22
women
  criminalisation 94, 99–100
  domestic abuse 100–2, 121
  ethnicity and racial abuse 121
  male violence 92
  prostitution 99–100
  rape and sexual violence 102–6
  see also female offenders; female offending
Women Offenders – A Safer Way 93
Women Who Offend 8
work-related deaths 134, 137, 145, 146
work-related illnesses 134
workfare schemes, punitive 51, 52
working-class
  areas, gentrification of 48–9
  dominance in criminal justice 21
  problematic youth cultures 56–9
  risky lifestyles 60
  see also lower-class crimes; lower-class defendants
worklessness 30, 53, 54
workplace injuries 134, 135, 145
World Environment Day 152
World Summit on Sustainable Development (2002) 161

young offender institutions, early 68
young offenders
  Fast Track hearings 57
  female 96–8
  imprisonment 68
  knife crime 28
  persistent 34, 76
  serious/non-serious 80–3, 84
  socio-economic status 34
young people
  labelling as problematic 185
  over-policing and harassment of 35, 122
  pathologisation 59
  targeting of suspect 50
  transitions 84–5, 98
  see also black youth; Muslim youth
youth court scheme 57, 72, 76
youth courts 68
youth crime 11
  extent and pattern of 76–83, 86
  perceptions of 78
  politicisation of 97
youth cults 50
youth cultures 56–9
youth gangs 57, 81
youth justice 67–86
  bureaucratic infrastructure 71–2
  detartanisation 10
  effectiveness 83–5
  history and development of 68–74
  policy 72, 84, 98
  structure and operation 74–6
  welfarism 9, 69–70, 73, 75, 76, 267
Youth Justice 76
youth unemployment 25–6

zero tolerance 30–1, 51, 99, 101, 181, 182–3, 190
zones in transition 48